Urban and Regional Policies for Metropolitan Livability

Cities and Contemporary Society

Series Editors: Richard D. Bingham and Larry C. Ledebur,
Cleveland State University

Sponsored by the
Maxine Goodman Levin College of Urban Affairs
Cleveland State University

This new series focuses on key topics and emerging trends in urban policy. Each volume is specially prepared for academic use, as well as for specialists in the field.

SUBURBAN SPRAWL
Private Decisions and Public Policy
Wim Wiewel and Joseph J. Persky, Editors

THE INFRASTRUCTURE OF PLAY
Building the Tourist City
Dennis R. Judd, Editor

THE ADAPTED CITY
Institutional Dynamics and Structural Change
H. George Frederickson, Gary A. Johnson, and Curtis H. Wood

CREDIT TO THE COMMUNITY
Community Reinvestment and Fair Lending Policy
in the United States
Dan Immergluck

PARTNERSHIPS FOR SMART GROWTH
University-Community Collaboration for Better Public Places
Wim Wiewel and Gerrit-Jan Knaap, Editors

REVITALIZING THE CITY
Strategies to Contain Sprawl and Revive the Core
*Fritz W. Wagner, Timothy E. Joder, Anthony J. Mumphrey, Jr.,
Krishna M. Akundi, and Alan F.J. Artibise*

THE UNIVERSITY AS URBAN DEVELOPER
Case Studies and Analysis
David C. Perry and Wim Wiewel, Editors

PEOPLE AND THE COMPETITIVE ADVANTAGE OF PLACE
Building a Workforce for the 21st Century
Shari Garmise

CITIES IN THE TECHNOLOGY ECONOMY
Darrene L. Hackler

CITIES IN A TIME OF TERROR
Space, Territory, and Local Resilience
H.V. Savitch

URBAN AND REGIONAL POLICIES FOR METROPOLITAN LIVABILITY
David K. Hamilton and Patricia S. Atkins, Editors

Urban and Regional Policies for Metropolitan Livability

David K. Hamilton and Patricia S. Atkins

editors

CITIES AND
CONTEMPORARY
SOCIETY

M.E.Sharpe
Armonk, New York
London, England

Library of Congress Cataloging-in-Publication Data

Urban and regional policies for metropolitan livability / David K. Hamilton and Patricia S.
Atkins, editors.
    p. cm.—(Cities and contemporary society)
  Includes bibliographical references and index.
  ISBN 978-0-7656-1768-2 (cloth : alk. paper)—ISBN 978-0-7656-1769-9 (pbk. : alk. paper)
  1. Metropolitan areas—United States. 2. Regional planning—United States.
3. Urban policy—United States. I. Hamilton, David K. II. Atkins, Patricia S.

HT334.U5U65 2008
307.760973--dc22   2007028050

Printed in the United States of America

The paper used in this publication meets the minimum requirements of
American National Standard for Information Sciences
Permanence of Paper for Printed Library Materials,
ANSI Z 39.48-1984.

∞

BM (c)   10   9   8   7   6   5   4   3   2   1
BM (p)   10   9   8   7   6   5   4   3   2   1

Contents

List of Tables and Figures

Tables

Figures

Preface

Regional level governance is becoming more necessary as public policy and service delivery problems spread farther across more local government boundaries. Most Americans no longer live at the municipal level. Our lives intersect with large chunks of our own metropolitan area territory, and our individual daily quality of life depends upon the activities others are simultaneously pursuing elsewhere in our metropolitan area. Every time a fender bender creates gridlock at rush hour on the beltway, many are agonizingly reminded of this. This reality makes regions the catchment area for addressing and resolving local governance problems. It seems that we are entering a regional age.

In the 1960s and 1970s, policymakers and government leaders focused on cities, and much of it was grim, reflecting the real municipal crises many cities passed through. Municipal policy and government problems were unending, including disastrous financial outcomes and harrowing societal confrontations. Discontent typified the public psyche of the 1960s and 1970s. In response to the urban problems, urban studies programs in universities were started and research proliferated. Scholars published books and periodical articles on urban policy issues for use in the classroom and to inform an interested public about the urban condition and its attendant problems. One classic is the 1967 *The Metropolitan Enigma: Inquiries into the Nature and Dimensions of America's "Urban Crisis,"* edited by James Q. Wilson. Other examples include Shank and Conant's 1975 *Urban Perspectives: Politics and Policies,* Lineberry and Sharkansky's 1971 *Urban Politics and Public Policy,* Schmandt and Bloomberg's (editors) 1969 *The Quality of Urban Life,* and Stone, Whelan, and Murin's 1979 *Urban Policy and Politics in a Bureaucratic Age.* A host of other books of this genre were published during this time. They covered urban problems such as race, crime, health, housing, education, poverty, transportation, community development, and neighborhood government. These books were indicative of the period when the major local governance policy concerns were urban problems in big cities.

During this period with the major focus on the plight of cities, there was a reform movement to restructure government in urban areas through consolidations and metropolitan government. Substantial research was done and articles and books published on the advantages and disadvantages of the government fragmentation in metropolitan areas. A countermovement encouraged and supported abundant numbers of small local governments in an urban area. This research resulted in a spirited debate over the advantages and problems of government fragmentation in urban areas, a debate that generated a lot of heat but resulted in little change in government structure. Most metropolitan areas stayed highly fragmented.

As society moves farther into the twenty-first century, we are focusing increased attention not on the urban city, but on a geographically larger metropolitan area and on urban problems that have migrated to become regionwide problems. The focus of the discussion of urban problems in the 1960s and 1970s was chiefly on the central city and its policy issues, such as the economic and population decline of the central city, urban renewal, public transportation, education, redevelopment, and so on. Many of these issues still haunt the central cities, but the discussion has migrated to the entire metropolitan area. Terms that illustrate the regional sweep of today's metropolitan problems such as: "edge cities and exurbia," "urban periphery suburbs," and "predawn commuters" were not in the lexicon of the 1960s and 1970s. Whereas the central city was the major focus of inquiry and policy prescriptions in the 1960s and1970s, the region is the focus in the twenty-first century.

An increasing amount of research is being published dealing with these policy issues. Citizens and businesses have created regional civic organizations and regional business committees concerned with regional issues, and they are focusing public attention on the region. Many have started to produce periodic reports on the state of the region with an emphasis on policy issues. At universities across the country, political science, urban economics, urban studies, and public administration programs are adding courses or course segments on regional issues.

The numerous reports, articles, and monographs on regional governance provide current scholarship on aspects of specific regional issues, but they usually are too short or too focused to provide a good understanding of the specific issue and its public policy implications. The few books that cover a number of regional policy issues are often highly selective and uneven in their coverage of regional policy issues, or they are entirely devoted to case studies of specific regions. Some books on regional issues focus at length on specific topics, such as Cervero's 1989 *America's Suburban Centers: The Land Use–Transportation Link;* Wassmer and Anderson's 2000 *Bidding for Business: The Efficacy of Local Economic Development Incentives in a Met-*

ropolitan Area; Ernst's 2003 *Chesapeake Bay Blues: Science, Politics, and the Struggle to Save the Bay,* and Calthorpe and Fulton's 2001 *The Regional City: Planning for the End of Sprawl.* Katz's 2000 edited book *Reflections on Regionalism* provides a national perspective but only on land use, private sector involvement in regional governance, and race issues. There are a number of good case study books, such as *Sprawl City: Race, Politics, and Planning in Atlanta* by Bullard (editor), *Democracy in Suburbia* (case study of a Houston suburb) by Oliver, and Savitch and Vogel's (editors) 1996 *Regional Politics: America in a Post-City Age* (chapter case studies).

While substantial research and publication of books and scholarly articles are being done, we lack a concise rendering of various regional policy issues that could be used in upper division and graduate college courses as well as for busy practitioners and an interested public. The idea for this book germinated from a college-level course on governing metropolitan areas. One focus of the course was to introduce students to regional policy issues in such a way that they could gain an overall understanding of the complexity of regional policy issues without requiring them to do major research in each substantive policy area.

A book was not readily available that provided a concise introduction into the major substantive policy areas without reading a major monograph on each policy issue or highly selective and specific journal articles that covered only selected aspects of the policies. We therefore felt that this book was needed. We also felt that an edited book bringing together chapters by scholars who are knowledgeable in their respective policy areas would be the most appropriate approach.

We realize that the policy issues presented and discussed in this edited book are not mutually exclusive of each other. The policy issues do not exist in isolation from other regional governance issues. Therefore, there is some overlap among chapters. We have tried to integrate this as much as possible, and the context of the overlap is through the lens of the major subject area of each chapter. Thus the chapters tend to complement and reinforce each other.

One theme that ties the chapters together is the impact on the quality of life of the various governance issues covered in the book. Quality of life is based on personal values, and its definition varies from person to person and group to group. People may disagree on the exact definition of the term, but certain public policy areas are generally accepted as impacting for good or ill our quality of life. Public action or inaction has a major impact on quality of life. Before we entered the regional age, local governments were the main focus of quality-of-life issues. Now that we are in a more interconnected and mobile environment, local governments by themselves are increasingly less able to have major impacts on quality-of-life issues. A regional approach is required to address quality-of-life issues that impact us in our homes, our employment, our schools, our security, our highways, and elsewhere. In our interconnected society, what one community does or does not do will have an impact on people in other communities. If we do not try to bring quality of life—what people value—to all residents in the region, it will have negative consequences and diminish the quality of life for all.

In addition to quality of life, other issues or questions that are variously addressed in each chapter are as follows:

1. What kinds of regional approaches are being taken by metropolitan regions across the country to address the policy?
2. Does any particular approach seem to be catching on, have particular salience, or stand out as a candidate for replication in other regions? Conversely, are there approaches that represent organizational strategies that are likely failures?
3. How do these strategies potentially connect across regional policy issues (and which policy areas might they be) such that they may shed light on broader governance/organizational design patterns that are emerging at the regional level? Are we indeed heading toward regional governance as loosely structured?
4. Are the regional institutions or interrelationships that have been developed within the particular policy arena fundamentally different than they were just a few years ago? If so, what dynamics are creating those changes and what are the implications within the policy area for regional governance?

This book, then, serves a number of purposes:

- It reinforces the movement of the discussion on urban governance and urban policy issues to a regional level.
- It is a valuable addition to courses on regional governance and policy because it provides a concise overview of the major policy issues confronting metropolitan areas.
- For practitioners and an interested public, this book provides a concise, readable introduction, background and current thinking, and recommendations on the major problems vexing regions.

The editors wish to thank their spouses Caroline Hamilton and Eric Siegel for their patience and support during the many hours spent on this project and Todd Hamilton for his help in doing last-minute editing and formatting of the manuscript.

Urban and Regional Policies for Metropolitan Livability

1

DAVID Y. MILLER

Exploring the Structure of Regional Governance in the United States

New ideas invariably present a challenge in finding the right words to describe them. For instance, take the changes that are occurring in the governance of urban areas. We know it is changing and, for lack of agreement on the meaning of those changes, we grab labels like "metropolitan regionalism." Regionalism is a poor choice of words, and I confess to having fallen into the trap of using the term inappropriately on occasion. I begin with it here so as to lay to rest its usage.

A dictionary definition of "ism" states it to mean a movement, doctrine, or system of belief. If we say we want to study the "city," such an investigation does not presume or advocate a particular structure or role for the city. Nor do we call its study "cityism" or "municipalism." We understand the "city" to be an important institution around which most modern societies are built. As academics, it is our explicit responsibility to study the city.

Part of our dilemma and confusion is that there exist two very different definitions of the term "city." In a sociological sense, the dictionary defines a "city" as "an urban area where a large number of people live and work." It is the second definition that causes the problem—that is, the city in a politico-legal sense. This second definition defines a "city" in the United States as "an incorporated urban center that has self-government, boundaries, and legal rights established by state charter."

In a sociological sense, the terms "city" and "metropolitan region" are interchangeable in that they accurately reflect today's urbanized America. In a politico-legal sense, the terms are not interchangeable. Today's metropolitan region has few of the characteristics of the city. For purposes of this chapter, I want to substitute the term "metropolitan region" for the term "city" when used in a sociological context. My reasons are several. First, the metropolitan region has replaced the city as the unit in which the majority of people live and business is conducted. Second, it allows us to better frame the discussion of the structured relationship between the institutions of government and governing. By that, I mean that there exists a vertical relationship in terms of the governing context created by the state and a horizontal dimension in terms of the relationship between the institutions of government and governing within a metropolitan region.

As such, the politico-legal definition of the "metropolitan region" might well be "the institutional relationships between institutions of governing in the area." Brenner (2002, 17) captures this perspective by calling the movement from city to metropolitan region the "new politics of scale." Jonas and Ward (2002, 378) raise the important question "at what spatial scale is territorial governance crystallizing?" As such, I want to advance the study of the metropolitan region, not regionalism.

In order to study the region we also need to draw a distinction between government and governance. Broad societal changes over the past half-century have had pronounced effects on both how we think about our world and how we operate in that world. As those changes relate to our public sphere, we are moving from a paradigm centered on government to one centered on governing or governance. Governing is the act of public decision making and of implementation on behalf of the collective and is no longer the exclusive domain of governments. Indeed, governments at all levels, nonprofit organizations, and the private sector now work together in new partnerships and relationships that blur sectoral lines. Private businesses, under contract to governments, deliver a wide variety of government programs. Conversely, governments often manage more private sector firms than public sector employees. Nonprofit organizations, often representing organizations of governments, are partnering with governments, private firms, and other nonprofits to deliver services. Private foundations in many metropolitan regions, utilizing revenues generated from the private sector, are working to finance public, private, and nonprofit organizations in addressing important regional public problems. Although not all would agree (Norris 2001), the study of the metropolitan region, therefore, seeks to understand the governance of a region, recognizing that governments are important building blocks of its structure. From this perspective, each metropolitan region has a structure, and metropolitan regions, collectively, could be said to have different structures.

Our research into a better understanding of the structure of governance in a metropolitan region is, at best, emerging. That said, the discussion of what ought to be an appropriate structure of governance is not new. Battle lines have been laid out for over 100 years, and skirmishes have moved the line back and forth between notions of many governments to a region and few governments to a region (McGinnis 1999; National Research Council 1999).

Figure 1.1   **The Three Dimensions of the Structure of Regional Governance**

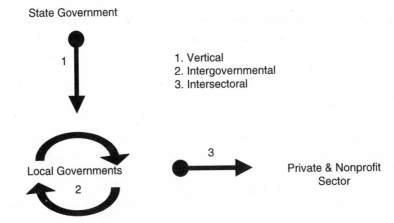

Source: Figure created by author.

Conceptually, today's discussion of how we manage a region is no different from yesterday's discussion of how we manage a city, a discussion that also had a shifting battle line.

The Three Structural Dimensions of Regional Governance

I would like to move beyond the study of the metropolitan region as a narrow debate about regionalism versus metropolitan regions or about how many governments a region ought to have. In so doing, I would like to move from prescription to description. The structure of governance in a metropolitan region has three primary dimensions as I have graphically presented in Figure 1.1. The first is a vertical dimension. It involves the fundamental relationship between the state government and the constituent local governments within its jurisdiction. A second dimension is horizontal and involves the fundamental relationships between the local governments within a metropolitan area. As such, it is an intergovernmental dimension. The third is also horizontal but involves the fundamental relationships between important constituent groups within a metropolitan area, such as civic groups and institutions, private businesses acting in the public domain, and mobilized citizens acting in a wide variety of capacities. As such, it is an intersectoral dimension. Taken together, these three dimensions play out differently in each metropolitan region, resulting in a wide variety of metropolitan governance structures throughout the United States.

After defining the three dimensions, I present a review of the emerging work that is being done on the study of the metropolitan region. I do that in three parts. The first explores a representative sample of research on the nature of the structure of governance. The second identifies an underlying tension that exists in our fundamental beliefs about the nature of local government, and the third suggests some strategies that might be employed based on managing that underlying tension.

The Vertical Dimension

Local governments are creatures of their respective state legislatures. Justice Dillon established for the courts in 1868 what is now clearly settled law that local governments are "mere tenants at will of their respective state legislatures" and could be eliminated by the legislature with a "stroke of the pen" (*City of Clinton v. The Cedar Rapids and Missouri River Railroad Company* 1868). As such, it is the state that establishes the purpose and nature of local government within its boundaries. And because it is each state making decisions about the purpose and nature of the local governments within its boundaries, the American system could be said to have fifty different vertical approaches. We are a federal system at the national-state level, but a wide variety of unitary systems at the state-local level. In some systems, the state grants relatively broad discretionary authority to local governments. In others, the state keeps local governments on relatively short leashes. In the same sense that a city charter defines the structure of governance for the city, the general grant of authority from the state to local governments defines the vertical structure of governance for the region. Conceptualizing the notion of a vertical dimension to the structure of regional governance has proved helpful in assessing, among other issues, its role in local economic development (Hamilton, Miller, and Paytas 2004).

Another way to capture this dimension is to consider the discretionary authority vested with local governments in a particular state. Zimmerman (1983) has operationalized discretionary authority based on four criteria. Those criteria are:

- Degree to which a local government can raise revenues necessary to support the functions it has decided to undertake (finance);
- Ability of a local government to choose activities or functions it wishes to undertake (function);
- Ability of a local government to regulate and determine the makeup and responsibilities of its workforce (personnel); and
- Degree to which a local government can define its own organizational structure (structure).

Table 1.1

Change in Average Metropolitan Power Diffusion Index by Region, 1997–2002

All	N	1997	2002	Percentage of change
Northeast	45	6.88	6.96	1.2
Midwest	91	5.22	5.85	12.1
South	143	3.53	3.73	5.7
West	79	3.87	4.58	18.3
Total	358	4.46	4.85	8.7

The Intergovernmental Dimension

The second dimension is horizontal and intergovernmental. By that, I mean the nature and pattern of relationships that exist within a metropolitan area *between* the local governments in the metropolitan area. It represents the distribution of power and authority between the three primary types of local governments: county governments, municipal governments, and special districts. Within the regions of the United States, a broad pattern of strong municipal government in the Northeast, higher utilization of county government in the South, and the powerful role of special districts in the West has been documented (Miller 2002; Stephens and Wikstrom 1999).

The Metropolitan Power Diffusion Index (MPDI) was developed as a way to quantify this intergovernmental dimension in a metropolitan area. A more thorough discussion of the mathematics of the index is presented elsewhere (Miller 2002). Using U.S. Census of Governments' expenditure data from all local governments in 358 metropolitan areas, an estimate of the distribution of authority between local governments is derived. As a mathematical exercise, the resulting number is simply that—a number. If there were only one local government in a metropolitan area doing 100 percent of all governmental activity, the number would be 1. If there were many governments, each doing a piece of any particular governmental activity, the number would approach infinity. As a result, the lower the number the less diffuse a metropolitan region is and the higher the number the more diffuse a metropolitan region.

The index is particularly helpful in identifying regional variations in the United States and the changing nature of the institutional relationships between governments in a metropolitan area. For the United States, the horizontal relationship between governments in our metropolitan regions is becoming more diffuse. Between 1997 and 2002, the number grew by 8.7 percent—from 4.46 to 4.85 (see Table 1.1). Because the index measures the

Table 1.2

Rate of Change in Metropolitan Power Diffusion Index by Region, 1997–2002

Change in MPDI	N	Northeast	Midwest	South	West
Over 20%	106	1	25	41	39
10 to 20%	68	9	30	18	11
0 to 10%	76	12	20	30	14
(0 to 5%)	33	11	9	9	4
(Over 5%)	75	12	7	45	11
Total	358	45	91	143	79

distribution between governments, it is relatively neutral on the issue of overall growth in government spending. The growth in the MPDI captures diffusion independent of whether all the governments in a particular region spent more. Also, the number of local governments in the United States did not grow by that amount during the period.

The index deals with the question of how government money was spent. Greater growth in activity was occurring by governments whose prior activity was more modest. It suggests that smaller municipalities may be assuming more responsibility than before. Special districts may have been called upon to do more things than they were doing before. In other words, more players are doing the business of government.

A second observation is that there are different patterns of relationships within the United States. In the Northeast, the metropolitan regions are generally more diffuse. In the South, the metropolitan regions are less diffuse. Further, the Midwest looks more like the Northeast and the West looks more like the South. Perhaps more important, the rate of change varies greatly within the United States. The already diffuse Northeast changed relatively little between 1997 and 2002. However, the Midwest and West were rapidly diffusing.

The MPDI for the South requires further analysis. We would expect, given the general trend of decentralization that is reflected throughout the literature, that the South would see highly diffusing scores. Table 1.2 breaks down each part of the United States by the change in the MPDI between 1997 and 2002. Of the 75 regions in the United States that had a diffusion score that decreased by more than 5 percent, over half (45) were in the South. Conversely, of the 106 regions in the United States that had diffusion scores that increased by more than 20 percent, close to 40 percent were from the South. In the South, there are metropolitan regions that have been able to remain relatively less diffuse, while, at the same time, there are metropolitan regions that are some of the most rapidly diffusing in the United States. Perhaps more broadly stated, over 80 percent of the most rapidly diffusing metropolitan regions are in the South and West, the least diffused parts of the United States.

The Intersectoral Dimension

A third dimension is also horizontal but involves the nature and pattern of relationships that exist within a metropolitan area between the local governments and the nonprofit (civic) sector and the private sector. As is the case with the other dimensions, there exist widely diverse relationships throughout the United States between the local governments and the civic community. Particularly as related to economic development activities, some regions have created strong and vibrant partnerships, engaging in a form of civic regionalism. Patterns that could exist include: little connection between the sectors, relatively inactive civic sectors, strong civic sectors leading a partnership, and strong civic sectors playing a support role to governments (Hamilton 1998; Wallis 1996).

This dimension has much to do with the globalization of the world economy. Michael Porter (1998, 78) has coined the term "clusters" to describe how businesses will prosper in the future. Unlike prior economic periods where businesses simply moved to areas of low production cost, businesses must now seek out areas where there exist a critical mass of businesses in a particular field that enjoy competitive success through the geographic concentration of interconnected companies and institutions. Clusters like Silicon Valley and Hollywood are Porter's classic examples of clusters that exist and are supported by "local things" that further support the existing cluster, the monopoly that cluster has in the world order, and the ability of that cluster to expand and support the local economy.

Henton, Melville, and Walesh (1997) have identified four features of clusters, or "regional habitats," that make them valuable to businesses. The first is easy access to specialized workforces. Obviously, given high concentrations of jobs in a particular field, it is easier for businesses to obtain the workforce necessary to undertake its functions. Second, clustering enhances the research and commercialization capacity for the businesses in the cluster. Third, clustering creates important innovation networks that allow the local businesses to retain a competitive advantage over other companies. Finally, clustering creates "a unique business infrastructure" that supports the companies in ways that create a working relationship between the institutions within a region and the agglomeration of businesses in that region.

Cataloging Approaches to Regional Governance

Utilizing the framework of these three dimensions provides a useful heuristic approach to assess research that is currently under way to study the metropolitan region. In this section, I explore a number of the efforts that have been undertaken to catalog the various strategies employed within the framework of my structural definition of regional governance. In presenting the following characterizations of regional governance, I do not want to imply that the list of authors is exhaustive but rather it is representative of the scholarly work that is being done on the study of regional governance. I will demonstrate that many of the studies are focused on a particular structural dimension while others cut across two or three of the structural dimensions. These representative works are summarized in Table 1.3.

Cataloging Based on Numbers of Governments

Like a number of studies, Savitch and Vogel (2000, 162–65) focused almost exclusively on the intergovernmental dimension and conceptualized regional governance strategies on a loose continuum that runs from relatively centralized to highly decentralized. On the centralized end are regions labeled "consolidationist." Represented by regions like Jacksonville, Indianapolis, and Nashville, these regions are highlighted by a relatively small number of independent local governments with authority concentrated in a small number of large public institutions. Although there are exceptions, most of the regions in this category have had this structure imposed from outside, usually through state intercession.

Although still centralized, but less so, are regions that are "multitiered." Sometimes referred to as two-tiered or federal regions, the approach is for local governments to do local activities and for regional governments to do regional activities. This idea has popular appeal in that it is patterned after the structure of the United States system of federal and state spheres of influence.

Whereas the multitiered approach creates separate spheres of activity, a more decentralized approach exists in regions where existing larger units of government are encouraged to deliver public services through interlocal agreements. Spheres of activity are replaced by spheres of efficient service delivery. These "linked function" regions focus on the belief that economies of scale are generated by larger service units while more individualized local choice options are afforded the consumers of public services. The Lakewood Plan is often cited as an example where local governments can contract with the county government for the bundle of services desired by the constituents of that particular local government. As practiced, county governments in such

Table 1.3

Typology of Regional Approaches by Researcher

Researcher	Vertical	Horizontal	
		Intergovernmental	Intersectoral
Savitch and Vogel (1996)		Consolidationist	
		Multitiered Linked functions Complex networks	
Hitchings (1998)		Ad hoc Advisory Supervisory Authoritative	
Miller (2002)		Coordinating Administrative Fiscal Structural	
Savitch and Vogel (1996)		Single-tiered	
		Mutual adjustment Avoidance/conflict	Mutual adjustment
Foster (1997)	Mandates/ prohibitions		Civic
Bollens (1997)	Regional special districts	Regional special districts	Public–private alliances
	Federal mandates Consistency with state	Councils of governments	
Frug (1980, 2002)		Consolidation	
		Ad hoc Two-tiered	

states as California have become service providers and many of the munici-palities within a particular county have become purchasers of services, either from the public or private sector.

At the most decentralized end of the continuum are regions that have large numbers of independent local governments working in both cooperative and competitive relationships. These "complex network" regions are believed to maximize citizen control and the delivery of services preferred by those citizens.

Local governments act like civil entities engaged in the act of governing and also like stores in a shopping mall, each offering a bundle of goods and services to consumers who desire and are willing to pay for those goods and services.

Cataloging Based on Coordination Approaches

Whereas Savitch and Vogel catalog the intergovernmental dimension based loosely on the number of governments in the region, Hitchings (1998), focusing on the intergovernmental dimension, catalogs metropolitan regions on the way local governments coordinate planning and economic development activities between each other and with the region as a whole. Employing a continuum that ranges from all power resting at the local level to considerable regional oversight, Hitchings identifies four broad approaches that are taken by metropolitan regions.

At the localized end are "ad hoc" regions. In ad hoc regions, local governments voluntarily work together on specific land-use issues but do not have a written plan that coordinates physical development at the regional level. Although such a region may have a council of governments, that council is primarily a forum for discussion. It is asserted that most metropolitan regions in the United States fit into this category.

A less localized approach is with regions classified as "advisory." These regions look much like ad hoc regions except that they do have a regional plan. Implementation of that plan is based on the willingness of local governments to voluntarily adhere to the plan. The third category of region is "supervisory," wherein a regional body is delegated the responsibility of administering a regional plan. The actual implementation of the plan is done at the local level, and the regional body oversees compliance and reports progress. Hitchings asserts that metropolitan regions like San Diego and Denver are representative of this type of region.

At the other end of the continuum are "authoritative" regions. These regions have both a plan and a regional body. This body has a statutory authority to develop the regional plan and then to require changes or force compliance with that plan on the part of local governments. Examples of this type of region are the Twin Cities Metropolitan Council of Minneapolis and St. Paul in Minnesota, and the Metropolitan Services District, now Metro, in Portland, Oregon. Few regions fall into the supervisory or authoritative categories. Indeed, they have been called "unique" (Stephens and Wikstrom 1999, 101).

Cataloging Based on Interaction

Rather than a catalog based on a continuum, Miller (2002), as related to the intergovernmental dimension, identified four forms of regionalism based on the primary ways governments can interact: coordinate planning and development activities, cooperate in service delivery, share fiscal resources, and realign jurisdictional boundaries. The first form is coordinating regionalism and deals with the integrated planning of the region as a whole and the consistency of local municipal strategic plans with the strategic plan of the region. It captures the same set of issues implicit within the Hitchings categories.

The second category is administrative regionalism. It comes in two primary forms—the functional transfer of services from municipal governments to either special districts or to county governments, and the day-to-day negotiations between all types of local governments that lead to a myriad of cooperation agreements at an operational level between those governments.

Utilization of special districts represents one of the most significant trends in metropolitan organization over the last half of the twentieth century. Over 13,000 special districts were created in the United States between 1967 and 2002, and the percentage of regional special districts between 1977 and 2002 increased by nearly one-third (U.S. Census Bureau 1977, 1997, 2002). In 1977, approximately 25 percent of all special districts had jurisdictional boundaries that were either coterminous with one or more counties or had a service area that was larger than a single county. By 1997, the proportion of these "regional" special districts had risen to 34 percent of all special districts. In 2002, regional special districts were 23 percent of all special districts in the United States and they comprised 36 percent of the special districts that responded to the Census survey (U.S. Census Bureau 2002, xiii, 15).

Whether this trend serves or thwarts regional goals or is a good or bad trend is a controversial issue and will be discussed later in this chapter. The relative ease of special district formation as administrative regionalism makes intuitive sense at several levels. First, initially, special districts are usually created through a long negotiation process of the existing local government actors. As such, this strengthens their legitimacy. In this manner, they are viewed by participants as practical solutions to areawide problems or to mandates imposed by federal, state, or judicial actions. As they are created, they are embedded with the traditions, norms, and values of the local institutions that brought them into existence. Second, legally, the various types of special districts are creatures or extensions of the existing local governments. Rather than an externally imposed solution that threatens existing geopolitical boundaries, these special districts are a mere convenience that reinforces those existing boundaries while purporting to allow for a more efficient and effective delivery of a particular service within the constraints imposed by the existing governance structure.

Generally, the term "urban county" is used to capture not so much the geographic location of the county, but that the county government plays a significant role in addressing urban issues within the metropolitan area. Historically, county governments have often been viewed as passive. When those county governments take on new responsibilities, particularly those that cut across a number of municipalities, they begin to resemble more active municipal governments. In the process of such a transition, those urban counties serve to further the regionalizing of metropolitan America. Although the growth of the urban county as a form of regionalism is not evident in all parts of the country, its emergence has had a significant impact where it is occurring.

Interlocal agreements are the most common form of administrative regionalism. This is represented in the myriad of cooperative service arrangements between two or more local governments. These agreements are built on the notion of governments as autonomous units in a metropolitan area negotiating agreements that are perceived to be in the enlightened self-interest of each player. Although we see evidence of this form of regionalism on a daily basis, it is usually between "have" governments, seldom between "have" and "have-not" governments. As a result, these cooperative relationships seldom serve a redistributive function.

The third form is fiscal regionalism. This form represents a set of cooperative strategies that recognizes the governmental structure of the existing configuration of local governments but creates metropolitan regional funding mechanisms for a wide variety of public purposes. As such, this is a relatively recent innovation in metropolitan cooperation. There are three broad types of fiscal regionalism: cultural asset districts, tax and revenue sharing programs, and peaceful coexistence plans.

The fourth form is structural regionalism. Structural regionalism involves boundary change. It takes the existing structure of local government in a region and significantly alters the rules of the game. Whereas the first three forms of regionalism generally retain the existing structure, this form attacks those boundaries. There are three types of structural regionalism: annexation, city/county consolidation, and mergers/consolidations. Annexation occurs generally when a part of the territory of one government is transferred to another government. This could involve transactions between two municipalities or between a county responsible for unincorporated territory within its boundaries and a municipality. City/county consolidations occur (albeit infrequently) when separate city and county governments are merged into a single government. Mergers and consolidations occur when two or more municipalities join together with either one of the governments assuming responsibility for the new territory or with the creation of an entirely new municipality comprising the merged or consolidated communities.

Frug's Approach

Frug (2002) catalogs three broad approaches to the intergovernmental dimension. Unlike the researchers identified earlier who present the approaches mostly objectively, Frug's assessment is critical and attempts to demonstrate that each approach is fundamentally flawed. The first approximates the earlier discussion of structural regionalism as presented by Savitch and Vogel (1996) and Miller (2002). It focuses on actions that change the borders of local governments (city/county consolidation, mergers, and annexations). Although Frug conceptually thinks such strategies are appropriate, his analysis, like many others, points to the infrequent utilization of this approach—so infrequent, he suggests, that it does not really represent a viable option.

The second approach is referred to as ad hoc solutions. This refers to a broad set of strategies, including the formation of special-purpose districts and the use of voluntary agreements between local governments. Such approaches, however, are also deficient in that they reinforce and exacerbate the current fragmentation of local governments. In addition, particularly as they relate to special districts, ad hoc solutions are limited to a narrow set of relatively technical services. In this regard, Frug joins a long list of critics of these approaches (Bollens 1997; Brenner 2002).

Frug's third approach is the federal or two-tiered system, also a part of Savitch and Vogel's and Miller's categories. To Frug, the two-tier model has assumed that there is a set of activities that are local and subject to the decision-making process of the locality and a set of activities that are regional and therefore subject to the decision-making processes of the region. The idea of this model has held the attraction of reformers for over a century. After all, it has made intuitive sense in that the relationship between what is local and what is regional is roughly analogous to the relationship between the states and the federal government. But Frug's critique is especially relevant when the experience of the past 100 years to create such systems has been, at best, limited. Frug (2002, 1179) states:

> the effort to create a functional division of power is based on the idea that there is a noncontroversial way to divide governmental functions between those that serve a parochial conception of self interest and those that serve the greater good. Such a neutral basis for the allocation of power is not simply illusory. The search for it has frustrated the effort to achieve regional goals. By holding out hope that it is possible to allow localities to advance a privatized notion of self interest without imposing negative consequences on outsiders, the two-tier model strengthens a narrow conception of self interest at the expense of regionalism.

Other Approaches

The authors cited to date have focused on the intergovernmental dimension of regional governments. Other efforts have attempted to incorporate two or more of the structural dimensions of regional governance. Savitch and Vogel (1996) developed a continuum of metropolitan regions that range from highly centralized and government centric to highly decentralized and less government centric. As such, their catalog is based on the dimensions of intergovernmental and intersectoral. The intergovernmental component ranges from single-tiered metropolitan government (Jacksonville) to mutual adjustment through interlocal agreements (Washington, D.C.) to outright avoidance and conflict (New York, Los Angeles, and St. Louis). The intersectoral dimension is captured in a form of mutual adjustment that is based on public–private partnerships (Pittsburgh, Charlotte).

Foster (1997), in the process of identifying the factors that may determine the extent to which the actors will engage in regional decision making, uses the concept of impulses. These impulses (vertical dimension and intersectoral dimension) can serve to either encourage or discourage regional decision-making actions, and they exist in a hierarchy. The most important ones are legal mandates or prohibitions (vertical). Very high on the list is the extent of support from the civic sector, particularly when it is linked to the desire to compete effectively against other regions for economic development (intersectoral).

Bollens (1997) catalogs a framework of regional governance that incorporates and sometimes integrates all three dimensions. One of the frameworks is built around the growing use of functionally specific regional agencies to undertake narrowly defined activities spread across all or part of the region. The growth of these agencies can be initiated in response to state laws or deferral mandates (vertical) or through the voluntary participation of local governments (intergovernmental).

Another framework is built around the emergence of regional councils of government. As voluntary associations of local governments (intergovernmental dimension), they are multipurpose but limited in independence and statutory power. Another framework captures the intersectoral dimension in the form of public–private alliances or regional civic alliances in that coalitions of public, private, and nonprofit actors and agencies come together out of mutual interest to form a consensus, develop a regional vision, and plan a strategy for action. A final framework arises from state oversight and regulation (vertical) wherein the state requires consistency or conformity to growth or economic development planning.

Unresolved Tension as a Common Theme

Frug's critique of our existing strategies toward structuring regional governance suggests that our underlying logic of thinking about the structure of the metropolitan region lacks a foundational principle. Indeed, a cursory review of the catalog of various structural dimensions of regional governance just presented demonstrates that almost any approach taken has legitimacy and any one approach can be claimed to be as good as any other.

This is not a new insight. MacKenzie (1961, 1) states, "There is no theory of local government. There is no normative general theory from which we can reduce what local government ought to be; there is no positive general theory on which we can derive testable hypotheses." Benjamin (1980, 73–74) asserts, "The absence of theory must be identified as the major problem in the study of local government. Without theory, contradictory conclusions and policy recommendations may be reached, sometimes from the same data." Walker (1986, 86) comments that "perhaps the greatest weakness of local government today is the absence of a theory that describes and interrelates the operational, political, and jurisdictional roles of local governments."

I think it is possible to reach that conclusion. It is possible to reach that conclusion because we have failed to understand or deal with the basic tension that truly prevents us from developing a foundational principle. We have two unresolved and mutually exclusive foundational principles that need to be first acknowledged and then addressed in a set of policies that manage the tension and conflict between those two competing principles before we can develop theory.

Earlier, I discussed the dependent vertical relationship of local governments and their respective state legislatures. Justice Dillon's words, "do away with local governments with the stroke of a pen," suggest that organizing a metropolitan area should be a relatively easy technical and administrative decision. After all, local governments are "mere tenants at will of their respective state legislatures (Foundation Principle 1)."

Unfortunately, it is not that simple. Justice Dillon is a lot more intelligent than I first made him out to be (Dillon 1911). In the ruling, the judge concluded his broad grant of authority by saying he could not "ever imagine so great a wrong and so great a folly (Foundation Principle 2)." Interesting words in that the courts were saying to the legislature you can, but then again you should not. Dillon was defining an important distinction, the unresolved and necessary tension between the legal nature of our local governments and their sociopolitical nature.

From a legal and administrative perspective, local governments cannot be sovereign (Frug 1980). They need to be, institutionally, subdivisions of the state, much in the same sense that authority needs some form of finality to it. Someone or some institution has to be able to make the final decision. But from a sociopolitical perspective, our local governments are seen as one of the important ways in which a citizen's constitutional right to freedom of association is advanced and protected. The "wrong" and "folly" occur when the state exercises its power to take those associational rights casually. The citizen often guards that right to associate more strongly than their willingness to participate in the affairs of the association. The importance of preserving this associational right is why threats to eliminating local governments often "touch the nerve endings of the public" (Thomas and Marando 1981, 51).

It is not my intention to resolve the tension. In the end, it probably needs to remain unresolved. But to be unresolved does not mean to be unaddressed. Rather, our approaches to the metropolitan region should be based on acknowledging the tension. Solutions should be built around balancing the two perspectives Justice Dillon so eloquently articulated so many years ago. At present, it is clear that few, if any, metropolitan areas have been able to craft such solutions.

Taking Dillon's perspective, how might we begin to craft regional strategies? Dillon left unanswered the defining question of just what the relationship between the local governments and regional institutions is. Those institutions cannot be simple extensions of constituent local governments. Conversely, they cannot be created in spite of local government. Rather, they must be explicitly designed for the purpose of creating institutions that are simultaneously local and regional.

To be a simple extension of local governments means that local governments can do anything collectively that they can do individually. Because such actions are voluntary, it means the agenda is restricted to only a few sets of activities that can generate unanimity of action. Further, they can and will act collectively only when it is in their individual private interests. In his critique of the two-tiered model, Frug argues that such a model creates a functional division of power based on the idea that governmental functions can be divided between those that serve a parochial conception of self-interest and those that serve the greater good. However, such a model merely enables localities to advance a privatized notion of self-interest. Bollens's (1997) study of special district formation in southern California concludes that representation on regional policy boards by local government officials does not create regional politicians and constituencies but allows local governments to operate in a regional forum to protect and enhance local interest even at the expense of regional goals. The notion of two-tiered government also presumes that the tension between the local and regional can be solved through separation.

Rather than address the relationship between local and regional, the strategy is to divorce them and create separate domains.

Conversely, creating regional institutions that are either divorced from local governments or created in spite of local government institutions is an equally flawed approach. Such strategies often create excessive distance between the regional organization and the constituent local governments. For instance, even the highly touted regional approaches in Minnesota and Portland are created externally and separate from their local governments. In Minnesota, the council is appointed by the governor, and in Portland, the executive is directly elected.

Structuring the Region by Addressing the Underlying Tensions

Our dilemma now is that, all too often, we devise regional strategies that either allow local interests to override regional interests, even in a cooperative regional forum, or separate local interests and regional interests, thereby creating institutions that lack local influence on regional interests. Building regional governance based on explicitly balancing the needs of the region with the associational roots of our local governments suggests a number of approaches that should be considered. Let me suggest three: one structural, one fiscal, and one planning.

The structural idea comes from Frug (2002), and that is to use the two-tiered model, not to divide power into separate spheres, but to turn regional decision making into a form of interlocal decision making. As did Frug, consider the establishment of the European Union (EU) as a governmental reorganization process not totally unlike that which a metropolitan region in the United States might go through. The sovereignty and autonomy of each nation in Europe is greater than that of our local governments. Indeed, language difference, currency incompatibility, and centuries of wars and occupations would suggest that the EU never should have been formed based on the ability of governments in the United States to form such an equivalent organization. But the EU was formed and now stands as an example and lesson that regional decision making can be, as Frug suggests, turned into a form of local decision making that balances the tension between local and regional.

This is not to suggest that we turn our metropolitan regions into mini-EUs. Rather, it is to suggest that processes were used as the EU was being crafted that worked to create a balance between local and regional. At its foundation was the understanding that the EU would be built with the authority to act regionally while retaining the authority of each constituent country. Such a perspective suggests a new way for the actors to frame the discussion on the role of regional institutions that neither trivializes the role of local governments nor patronizes the role of regional governance institutions.

From a fiscal perspective, no institutional reform balances local and regional within a single program more so than tax-base sharing. Tax-base sharing is a simple idea—take a regional resource of revenue, such as the property tax or sales tax, and distribute the proceeds to constituent local governments on objective criteria that reflect the needs of the region, taken as a whole. Its benefit is more effective and equitable impact on economic development and growth. To the degree that the fragmentation of government services and decision making in an urban area prevents any rational approach to the distribution of the gains and benefits from development and growth policies, tax-base sharing helps to mitigate the adverse effects of that fragmentation.

The largest and perhaps best-known tax-base sharing plan is in the Twin Cities of Minneapolis and St. Paul in Minnesota. Although the formula is very complex, the principle is fairly simple in that 40 percent of a municipality's growth in commercial and industrial real estate valuation is diverted from the municipality's direct control to a "pool" shared by all municipalities in the region. A uniform millage is applied to this "pooled" value, and the proceeds are distributed back to the municipalities on a need-based formula. The amount a government contributes to the pool has little relation to what it will receive in distributions—a participating government may receive much less than it contributes to the pool, and conversely, it may receive substantially more than it contributes. In this fashion, tax-base sharing serves a redistributive function.

How does tax-base sharing balance the local and the regional? First, it allows local governments to share in the growth of the area without taking away any resources that local governments currently enjoy. By taking a percentage of future or new revenues, local governments are not giving up resources that they are currently receiving. Second, tax-base sharing creates more rational urban development by minimizing the fiscal impact of private sector locational decisions. Third, it creates an incentive system that encourages all parts of the region to work for the growth of the whole. Fourth, and perhaps most important, it develops regional strategies that employ the existing structure of local governments and local decision making. By supporting the existing structure of local government and financing the needs of the region, the tension between local and regional government is balanced.

The third idea is that of new ways to harmonize regional and local plans. Control of land use represents one of the near monopoly powers of local governments. Inherent in our notion of associational rights of a local government is its ability to define and shape the purpose and nature of the community it wants to be. As such, in many states, local governments have a broad grant of authority to comprehensively plan for their community and to exercise their police powers, through zoning laws, to implement that plan. Those land-control rights of local government can be tempered by the legislatures and courts such that individual civil rights are protected. However, the rights of local governments to plan their communities within those civil rights protections has, primarily, allowed those local governments to define their local communities independent of the impact those decisions will have on the region when taken as a whole. From this perspective, local governments are exercising their private associational rights.

However, these localized decisions need to be harmonized with the interests of the region within which each localized planning process occurs in order to balance the needs of the region with the associational roots of local governments. The idea is not to replace local planning with regional planning, but to create a process by which the important community responsibility to articulate a vision of that community is tempered by the needs of the region of which that community is a part. Requiring consistency of local planning or identifying inconsistency of local plans with regional goals strikes a balance between the good that is derived from local engagement in the community and the broader context of the needs of the region.

Concluding Thoughts

The metropolitan region is slowly emerging as the conceptual and organizing framework around which future governance will occur. There are three important governing dimensions to the metropolitan region. The first is vertical and relates to the relationship between the state government and the local governments, in general, within the metropolitan region. The second is intergovernmental and relates to how those local governments within a particular metropolitan region relate to one another. The third is intersectoral and relates to how the local governments in a metropolitan area relate to other sectors (particularly the civic and private sectors).

Regions today are in pursuit of strategies that deal effectively with the relationships implied within the dimensional framework I have just laid out. Unfortunately, most of the strategies being considered fail to effectively address or balance the tension between two diametrically opposed foundational principles of local governance in the United States. One foundational principle is centrist in that local governments are mere products of state government. As such, they exist as conveniences that the state may or may not use in any exercise of its authority. The second foundational principle is that local governments are extensions of the individuals that constitute a local government as a way those individuals can practice their constitutional rights to associate.

Generally, our strategies have been to play a zero-sum game wherein one of these two foundational principles emerges as victorious. I have proposed an alternate way to structure the question. Both foundational principles have value and are instrumental in the way that the American system of governance operates. A more appropriate strategy is to recognize the legitimacy of both principles and create institutional structures that acknowledge the joint legitimacy of competing notions.

References

Benjamin, L. 1980. *The Limits of Politics: Collective Goods and Political Change in Post-Industrial Societies.* Chicago: University of Chicago Press.

Bollens, S.A. 1997. "Fragments of Regionalism: The Limits of Southern California Governance." *Journal of Urban Affairs* 19, no. 1: 105–22.

Brenner, N. 2002. "Decoding the Newest 'Metropolitan Regionalism' in the USA: A Critical Overview." *Cities* 19, no. 1: 3–21.

City of Clinton v. The Cedar Rapids and Missouri River Railroad Company. 1868. 24Iowa 455.

Dillon, J.F. 1911. *Commentaries on the Law of Municipal Corporations.* Boston: Little, Brown.

Foster, K.A. 1997. "Regional Impulses." *Journal of Urban Affairs* 19, no. 4: 375–403.

Frug, G.E. 1980. "The City as a Legal Concept." *Harvard Law Review* 93, no. 6: 1059–1154.

———. 2002. "Beyond Regional Government." *Harvard Law Review* 115, no. 7: 1763.

Hamilton, D. 1998. "Organizing Government Structure and Governance Functions in Metropolitan Areas in Response to Growth and Change: A Critical Overview." *Journal of Urban Affairs* 22, no. 1: 65–84.

Hamilton, D.; D.Y. Miller; and J. Paytas. 2004. "Exploring the Horizontal and Vertical Dimensions of Government of Metropolitan Regions." *Urban Affairs Review* 40, no. 2: 147–82.

Henton, D.; J. Melville; and K. Walesh. 1997. *Grassroots Leaders for a New Economy: How Civic Entrepreneurs Are Building Prosperous Communities.* San Francisco: Jossey-Bass.

Hitchings, Benjamin G. 1998. "A Typology of Regional Growth Management Systems." *Regionalist* 3, nos. 1 and 2: 1–14.

Jonas, A.E.G., and K. Ward. 2002. "A World of Regionalisms? Towards a U.S.–UK Urban and Regional Policy Framework Comparison." *Journal of Urban Affairs* 24, no. 4: 377–401.

MacKenzie, W.J. 1961. *Theories of Local Government.* London: London School of Economics and Political Science.

McGinnis, Michael D. 1999. "Polycentricity and Local Public Economics: Readings from the Workshop." In *Political Theory and Policy Analysis,* ed. Michael D. McGinnis, 1–30. Ann Arbor: University of Michigan Press.

Miller, David Y. 2002. *The Regional Governing of Metropolitan America.* Boulder: Westview Press.

National Research Council. 1999. *Governance and Opportunity in Metropolitan America.* Washington, DC: National Academy Press.

Norris, D.F. 2001. "Whither Metropolitan Governance?" *Urban Affairs Review* 36, no. 4: 532–50.

Porter, M.E. 1998. "Clusters and the New Economics of Competition." *Harvard Business Review* (November–December): 77–90.

Savitch, H.V., and R.K. Vogel. 1996. "Louisville and Antagonistic Cooperation." In *Regional Politics: America in a Post City Age,* ed. Savitch and Vogel, 130–57. New York: Sage.

———. 2000. "Paths to New Regionalism" *State and Local Government Review* 32, no. 3: 159–68.

Stephens, G. Ross, and N. Wikstrom. 1999. *Metropolitan Government and Governments: Theoretical Perspectives, Empirical Analysis, and the Future.* New York: Oxford University Press.

Thomas, R.D., and V.L. Marando. 1981. "Local Government Reform and Territorial Democracy." *Publius: The Journal of Federalism* 11: 49–63.

U.S. Census Bureau. 1977. *1977 Census of Governments, Volume 1, Number 1, Government Organization.* Washington, DC: Government Printing Office.

———. 1997. *1997 Census of Governments, Volume 1, Number 1, Government Organization.* Washington, DC: Government Printing Office.

———. 2002. *2002 Census of Governments, Volume 1, Number 1, Government Organization,* GC02(1)-1. Washington, DC: Government Printing Office.

Walker, D.B. 1986. "Intergovernmental Relations and the Well-Governed City." *National Civic Review* 75, no. 2: 65–87.

Wallis, A.D. 1996. "Regions in Action: Crafting Regional Governance Under the Challenge of Global Competitiveness." *National Civic Review* 85, no. 2: 15–24.

Zimmerman, J. 1983. *State-Local Relations: A Partnership Approach.* New York: Praeger.

2

NELSON WIKSTROM

Central City Policy Issues in a Regional Context

During the second half of the twentieth century, urbanists identified a variety of socioeconomic and infrastructure problems with central cities in the United States. As Oliver Williams noted in his work *Suburban Differences and Metropolitan Policies,* published almost a half-century ago, some of these are of a lifestyle nature, involving race relations, crime, poverty, health, and education. In addition to these widely acknowledged social problems, other central city challenges involve infrastructure, including water and sewer systems, roads and highways, mass transportation, and parks and recreational areas (Williams 1965). It has been argued that these central city problems serve in varying degrees to undermine the quality of life enjoyed by others in the metropolitan area, not solely central city residents.

The thesis of this chapter is that the majority of citizens residing in metropolitan areas are basically satisfied with the quality of life they enjoy, although they may grumble about inconveniences in their daily routine. They are provided the public services they need in an environment they like. We therefore need to be much more careful and precise in describing the segment of citizens who are most affected by dissatisfaction with their quality of living. We need to acknowledge that there is a small segment of the population marginalized by race and income that falls far short of enjoying an acceptable standard of living or a reasonable quality of life. This chapter also gives attention to those factors and developments that have served to regionalize quality-of-life shortcomings in a regional policy framework. Finally, the chapter concludes with some policy suggestions concerning how we can ensure an acceptable quality of life for *all* of our citizens residing in the metropolis.

Prudence and good sense require us to avoid polemics in discussing the severity of metropolitan quality-of-life shortcomings and to resist the tendency of describing the urban problems underlying this malaise as collectively constituting an "urban crisis," such as was advanced by Mitchell

Gordon in his work *Sick Cities* (1963) and many of his contemporaries in the late 1950s, 1960s, and early 1970s (Eldredge 1967; Faltermayer 1968; Whyte 1958; Glazer 1970; Tretten 1970). Peter Dreier, John Mollenkopf, and Todd Swanstrom in their insightful work *Place Matters: Metropolitics for the Twenty-first Century* have noted: "Because so much attention has been given to the concentrations of poverty in cities, many Americans may believe that cities are basket cases—like sick people with so few resources that they only serve to burden society. Nothing could be further from the truth. In fact, cities are economic dynamos that provide extraordinary benefits to society as a whole" (2004, 31).

Echoing the same sort of sentiment, Paul S. Grogan and Tony Proscio advance in their work *Comeback Cities*: "The American inner city is rebounding —not just here and there, not just cosmetically, but fundamentally. It is the result of a fragile but palpable change in both the economics and politics of poor neighborhoods" (2000, 1). This is not to ignore that the severity of core city problems depends upon the "rock that you are standing upon" and varies from community to community, neighborhood to neighborhood, and, indeed, from block to block.

Responding to the urban crisis scholarly mayhem of the 1960s, Edward C. Banfield noted in his introduction to *The Unheavenly City: The Nature and the Future of Our Urban Crisis:* "That we face an urban crisis of utmost seriousness has in recent years come to be part of the conventional wisdom. We are told on all sides that the cities are uninhabitable, that they must be torn down and rebuilt or new ones must be built from the ground up, and that something drastic must be done—and soon—or else" (1968, 3). Banfield wisely advanced that: "a problem exists only as we should want something different from what we do want or as by better management we could get a larger total of what we want" (5). He noted further:

> Most of the "problems" that are generally supposed to constitute "the urban crisis" could not conceivably lead to disaster. They are—some of them—important in the sense that a bad cold is important, but they are not serious in the sense that a cancer is serious. They have to do with comfort, convenience, amenity, and business advantage, all of which are important, but they do not affect the essential welfare of individuals or what may be called the good health of the society. (6)

Since the scholarly debates of a half-century ago concerning the severity of our urban problems, the United States has evolved into a more decidedly metropolitan society. Currently, more than 243 million Americans reside in 361 metropolitan areas. For analytical purposes, our metropolitan areas may be divided into central, or core, cities; inner, or first, suburbs; and outer suburbs.

Increasingly, the socioeconomic problems identified with our central cities in the 1960s have taken on a much more regional character, especially with regard to our inner suburbs.

The Regionalization of Core City Problems

There are a number of basic reasons and developments that account for why quality-of-life shortcomings long associated with our core cities have in the past half century taken on an increasingly metropolitan or regional dimension.

Natural Expression

First, some of these shortcomings derive from problems that, due to their ubiquitous nature, have simply followed their natural tendencies toward regional expression. These problems include air and water pollution, which do not respect our arbitrary and artificial municipal boundaries (Gonzalez 2005).

In addition, due to the nature of the market and capital expenditures involved, regional challenges of a "system-maintenance" variety involving the construction and maintenance of roads and highways, and sewer and water systems, along with mass transportation, lend themselves to a regional approach. Such service delivery operations, taking advantage of economies of scale, along with attendant lower unit costs, are usually most efficiently provided for on a regional or metropolitan basis. For instance, mass transportation in our metropolitan areas is largely provided by a regional body, such as the Massachusetts Bay Transit Authority (MBTA—Boston), Southeastern Pennsylvania Transit Authority (SEPTA—Philadelphia), Chicago Transit Authority (CTA—Chicago), and the Bay Area Rapid Transit System (BART—San Francisco)

First or Inner-ring Suburbs

Second, as a result of what the University of Chicago sociologists advanced in the 1920s as the "concentric zone theory" of urban development, or what Banfield described later in the 1960s as "the logic of metropolitan growth," core city problems have become increasingly associated with the wider metropolitan region, particularly with regard to the "first" or "pioneering" at-risk suburbs. These communities were established around cities during the turn of the twentieth century and the following few decades. The Depression followed by World War II disrupted this process, and its pent-up force was unbottled when the war came to a close (Banfield 1968, 23–44). This outward development has been stimulated by population growth, the implementation of new transportation technologies, and the relocation of middle-income households. As a consequence, metropolitan areas displayed geographical, demographic, and economic "spread" (or more negatively described as "sprawl").

Increasingly, concentrated pockets of the poor and elderly, of unemployment, of blight, of outmoded substandard housing and derelict commercial buildings, and of crime are found in many of the neighborhoods of our inner-ring suburbs, constituting linear extensions of our central city ghettos. An estimate by the U.S. Department of Housing and Urban Development stated that as many of 30 percent of the suburbs could be in decline (U.S. Congress, Office of Technology Assessment 1995). As noted by Dreier, Mollenkopf, and Swanstrom: "The problems associated with the growing spatial concentration of poverty also beset many inner-ring suburbs. One study of 554 suburbs found an increase in poverty in about half, along with a decrease in real family income in about a third during the 1980s" (2004, 29). They also reported that many inner-ring suburbs now have higher crime rates than their central cities and they often have less ability to manage the problem, citing in particular the St. Louis metropolitan region (96–97).

Myron Orfield in his well-received work *American Metropolitics: The New Suburban Reality* has developed a typology of suburbs based on their tax capacity and expenditure needs. He identified some suburbs as "at-risk communities," confronted with high social needs, but low, and often declining tax bases (2002). In an earlier work, he advanced that any first suburbs have problems providing basic services, since they lack downtown commercial properties that generate tax revenue. For example, he noted that fifty-nine Chicago suburban municipalities had a lower tax base per household than did Chicago, which was itself considerably below the national average (Orfield 1997, 162). As Drier, Mollenkopf, and Swanson noted: "Declining suburbs are depressing localities that lack the public spaces, universities, cultural institutions, nightlife, and downtowns that make central cities exciting places" (2004, 50). Banfield prophesized this development decades ago: "In the future, then, the process of housing turnover is likely to give more and better housing bargains to the not well-off, encouraging them to move ever farther outward and thus eventually emptying the central city and bring 'blight' to suburbs that were new a decade or two ago" (1968, 36).

A recently released Brookings Institution report indicated that first suburbs contain nearly one-fifth of the population of the United States.[1] Specifically, 18.6 percent of the nation's population—52,391,412 people—reside in first suburbs, compared to 12.9 percent in core cities and 14.3 percent in newer suburbs. The population of first suburbs is highly diversified. As noted by the report, from 1980 to 2000 first suburbs outpaced the nation in their increasing share of African-American, Hispanic, and Asian residents, while experiencing a decreasing share of white residents. Racial and ethnic minorities dwelling in inner suburbs constitute about one-third of the population. The varied population of first suburbs is further augmented by the fact that 17 percent of America's foreign-born reside in these localities, comparable to 24 percent in core cities, but far from the 9 percent in newer suburbs (Puentes and Warren 2006, 21). The varied population characteristics and housing values of core cities, first suburbs, and newer suburbs are found in Table 2.1.

Largely as a result of these demographic changes, first suburbs are confronted with an array of socioeconomic challenges. The problem and resolution of poverty is high on the agenda of these communities since the rate of poverty increased significantly in first suburbs during the period 1980–2000. It is of concern that, while the number of high-poverty neighborhoods was decreasing throughout the nation during this period, the number of high-poverty neighborhoods increased drastically in first suburbs. Three-quarters of these communities witnessed an increase in the number of their census tracts with at least a 20 percent rate of poverty (Puentes and Warren 2006, 8).

First suburbs are inordinately confronted with ensuring sufficient employment opportunities and an adequate range of education, health, and other social services to our present-day immigrants, largely drawn from Mexico and other nations in Central America, and Asia. They are also obligated for providing adequate housing and social services for many elderly individuals, a disproportionate number of whom reside in these communities.

Paradoxically, due to soaring housing costs and rising taxes, first suburbs are struggling to ensure that the well-off continue to reside in their communities. A recent survey typifies what the statistics reveal. It found that a majority—56 percent of Long Islanders, many of whom reside in first suburbs, stated that they have entertained the possibility of moving away from their community within the next five years because of rising property taxes and their ability to sell their homes at a substantial profit, and relocate in a less expensive area (Lambert 2005). In addition to these varied socioeconomic challenges, many first suburbs, due to their incorporation immediately following World War II, are confronted with an array of public infrastructure needs. These public needs include repairing or constructing new sewer and water lines, water treatment plants, highways and roads, and "putting in place" and operating more adequate systems of mass transportation.

A prominent example of a first suburb is Nassau County, which is situated adjacent to New York City. Nassau County, which has been well known for its high quality of life, contains extensive parklands and beaches, quality neighborhoods, a large number of well-educated citizens with high income levels, along with a highly developed transportation network for commuting

Table 2.1

Select Statistics for Core Cities, First Suburbs, Newer Suburbs, and the United States

	Population	Percent Minority Population	Percent Foreign Born	Percent Population age 65 and Over	Percent Population under age 15	Average Housing Value	Median Household Income
Core Cities	36,300,693	61.1	23.8	11.1	21.3	$186,946	$36,349
First Suburbs	52,391,412	33.4	17.1	12.5	21.5	$206,728	$52,885
Newer Suburbs	40,357,944	21.0	9.6	11.7	21.8	$173,011	$52,177
United States	281,421,906	30.9	11.1	12.4	21.4	$151,910	$41,994

Source: Puentes and Warren (2006, 21).

to New York City. Its home values are among the highest in the nation. On the other hand, the population of the county, similar to most other first suburbs, has remained stagnant since the 1960s. Racially, the nonwhite proportion of the population has grown nearly 15 percent since 1970; the proportion of foreign-born has more than doubled, and the elderly population has risen nearly 400 percent since 1950. Amid the wealth of the county are growing pockets of poverty of poorer and elderly residents, many of whom are dependent upon public transportation, need less expensive housing, and require a variety of expensive social services. Reflective of these demographic changes, Thomas Suozzi, the county executive, stated:

> We have stopped growing. America's first suburb has reached middle age. We now have little open space left to grow, and we want to preserve what we have left. Meanwhile, traffic worsens, and under current zoning laws we can't redevelop those places that could sustain more density. With no new construction or new business, with rising expenses and a flat tax base, local government will be forced to raise property taxes even further or dramatically cut existing services. To continue on that course would be catastrophe for Nassau. It would mean not simply no new business, but a loss of business and a shrinking tax base to pay higher and higher taxes. (Katz and Puentes 2006, A44)

Adding to the challenges confronting public officials in first suburbs is that they are caught in a "policy blind spot" and their needs have often gone unnoticed by federal and state policymakers. As noted in the Brookings report:

> Unfortunately, the interests of first suburbs appear underrepresented at the federal and state level. First suburbs often remain absent from larger coalitions that represent the broad interests of municipalities or, if they are represented, they are lumped in with larger "suburban" interests. This general lack of appreciation of the differences between inner and outer suburbs fails to recognize their diversity, their variable assets, and the different challenges they face. The special concerns of small, first suburban jurisdictions rarely receive a fair hearing from state legislators and agencies. (Puentes and Warren 2006, 2)

Sprawl

Third, the immense and continuing geographical expansion of our metropolitan areas has also served to regionalize infrastructure problems, particularly in regard to issues involving growth management, land use, and housing. "Sprawl" may be described as a land development or land use pattern that spreads single-family residential units over a former large, often pastoral-like, area, on the fringes of the metropolitan region. A classic example of sprawl land use is the construction of large, expensive, single family homes on a minimum lot size of three or more acres.

According to antisprawl partisans, sprawl promotes economic and racial residential segregation, environmental degradation, the decline of "open space," the separation of residential and commercial land uses, the absence of multiuse clustered development or town centers, the lack of affordable housing, excessive reliance on the automobile, and transportation congestion (Downs 1994; Freilich 1999). As noted by one study, metropolitan areas marked by the greatest amount of sprawl have significantly higher per household transportation costs. This study found that metropolitan areas with the highest amount of sprawl have average annual per household transportation expenditures that are approximately $1,300 higher than in those metropolitan areas with the least sprawl. The study noted that the latter metropolitan areas have average annual transportation expenditures per household that are nearly 19 percent below that of the metropolitan areas with the most sprawl (Cox 2003).

A particularly scathing and polemical attack on sprawl by Joel S. Hirschhorn (2005) argues that excessive dependence on the automobile that is indicative of sprawl results in an unhealthy lifestyle for many Americans. The National Research Council's study on the costs of sprawl (Burchell 2000), while acknowledging that sprawl does satisfy the preferences of households for low-density living and more consumer lifestyle choices, and that it is often difficult to systematically measure many of the costs and benefits of sprawl, concluded: "there appears to be more costs than benefits" to sprawl and the additional consumption of resources necessitated by sprawl is "basically unnecessary to achieve a high quality of life" (21).

In reaction to the costs of sprawl, antisprawl partisans have advocated the tenets of the New Urbanism, or "smart growth" development, characterized by high-density multiuse development and urban growth boundaries. Invariably, they hail the Portland, Oregon, metropolitan area for its successful containment of sprawl, through the establishment of an urban growth boundary and the substantial construction of mixed-use high-density commercial and residential development. Critics, though, observe that the metro area's sprawl has expanded into adjacent Vancouver, Washington, which lacks any growth boundary.

There is a good deal of agreement among scholars that sprawl negatively impacts our core cities. John Kain (1968) argued that sprawl serves to make for "concentrations of poverty" in core cities simply because it produces a "spatial mismatch" between disadvantaged core city dwellers seeking employment and the growth of new jobs in suburbia. Lacking a viable and reliable means of transportation, these new jobs, in many instances, are beyond the reach of unemployed core city residents. In turn, concentrations of poverty in the core city, and their association with crime and other forms of social disorganization, serve to stimulate (the so-called push effect) the movement of the job-seeking middle- and upper-class individuals out of core cities, resulting in increasing economic and residential separation between income classes in the metropolis (Jargowsky 2002, 51). Bier and Post (2003) stated that, although concentrated poverty does not directly create sprawl, it pushes families out of older (core) communities and increases demand for new suburban housing—which developers meet, largely because of government policies, in a sprawled-out manner.

In addition, sprawl and the resultant new infrastructure make available large tracts of suburban land attractive for commercial and industrial development, which, however, often results in a business disadvantage for core cities and their inability to attract new investment. It is generally acknowledged that core cities, due to ever-increasing sprawl, are particularly vulnerable to disinvestment, which has resulted in the departure of many commercial entities from their downtown business districts. As an example of core city disinvestment, Williamson, Imbroscio, and Alperowitz (2002, 10) reported that there were nearly 4,000 abandoned shopping centers in the core cities of the United States in 2002. David Rusk (1993, 75–76) has noted that when the per capita income of city residents falls below 70 percent of its suburban counterparts, the region, in most instances, reaches a "point of no return" where core city and suburban economic disparities become so severe that the city, in a broad sense, no longer is a place to invest or create jobs. Core cities experiencing a declining population and disinvestment are confronted with increasing social problems and dwindling fiscal resources.

Finally, sprawl has served to exacerbate the fiscal problems of many of our core cities. With the flight of a large portion of affluent citizens to the rapidly expanding suburbs, metropolitan economic decentralization, and the development of "edge cities" (Garreau 1991), core cities, due to what has been labeled the "iron cage of municipal finance," have often found it difficult to adequately fund their operating budgets. Reflective of the more advantaged fiscal situation of most, but not all suburbs, a study of the nation's 331 metropolitan areas found that per capita income increased by about $1,000 more for suburbanites than for core city dwellers in the 1990s (Dreier, Mollenkopf, and Swanstrom 2004, 47).

Over the past several decades significant federal and state reductions of financial aid to localities have further increased their fiscal woes. In a well-known study conducted in the late 1980s, Ladd and Yinger found that in most core cities there existed a significant gap between their ability to raise revenue and the fiscal resources they needed to provide average-quality basic services to the public. This finding led Ladd and Yinger to conclude that the typical

American city has "poor fiscal health" (1989, 9). Pagano and Hoene (2006) reported from a 2005 survey that although the fiscal condition of cities had somewhat improved this was due to the fact that cities were making greater use of various fees and charges to balance their operating budgets.

Seemingly in paradox, other scholars, while acknowledging that sprawl does result in some inconveniences and higher transportation costs per household, have argued that sprawl is simply the latest manifestation of the onward march of urbanization and that it serves, through the market, to enhance the overall quality of the lives of many of our metropolitan citizens (Gordon and Richardson 2000; 2001). For instance, Robert Bruegmann (2005) argues that sprawl, on balance, has proved to be beneficial for most urban dwellers, providing them with much cleaner, greener, and safer neighborhoods in which to dwell, and more affluence, privacy, mobility, and choice.

Wendell Cox (2003) noted that while per household transportation costs are higher in more sprawling metropolitan areas, workers residing in these areas spent annually, on average, 30 percent less time commuting to and from work than their counterparts residing in the least sprawling areas. In addition, he reported that home ownership is much greater in more sprawling metropolitan areas (70 percent), than in the more compact metropolitan areas (57 percent). Further, he noted that households in the more sprawling metropolitan areas, benefiting from the lower prices offered by larger grocery stores and "big box" retailers, spend less money on food than their counterparts dwelling in more compact metropolitan areas.

Concluding his findings, Cox advanced "All of this is to suggest that, despite its failings, the less dense American metropolitan areas have a higher quality of life. Yes, transportation expenditures may be lower in the more compact areas. However, less time is spent traveling to work, home ownership is greater and there is more living space per capita in the more sprawling metropolitan areas. Each of these factors may fairly be considered indicative of a higher quality of life" (2).

Household Preferences

We should underscore that citizens who purchase a residence in the outer suburbs are not whimsical or fools and are fully cognizant that they will be subject to a number of shortcomings, including higher transportation costs and daily routine inconveniences. In this regard, William Alonso (1981, 63–67) a noted sociologist, has acknowledged that better-off families are willing to accept long commutes to get cheaper land and larger houses in the suburbs. In his classic paper "A Pure Theory of Local Expenditures," Charles Tiebout emphasized, "The consumer voter may be viewed as picking that community which best satisfies his preference pattern for public goods . . . the greater the number of communities and the greater variance among them, the closer the consumer will come to fully realizing his preference position" (1956, 418).

Federal Policies and Programs

Federal governmental policies, commencing with the dawn of the twentieth century, have had the collective effect of spurring the growth of metropolitan regions to the detriment of core cities. For instance, the implementation of the federal income tax in 1914 allowing taxpayers to deduct home mortgage interest costs from their federal tax liability encouraged citizens to depart from core cities and purchase larger homes in the ever-expanding suburbs. Following the close of World War II, the Federal Housing Administration (FHA), the successor to the Home Owners' Loan Corporation, and the Veterans Administration (VA) enacted generous mortgage policies, which facilitated the movement of the middle class out of the city. In later years, the transition of the middle class out of core cities was further stimulated by the quasi-public, quasi-private entities known as Fannie Mae and Freddie Mac, which were heavily involved in the secondary mortgage market.

Middle-class abandonment of core cities was also the result of the enactment by Congress in 1949 of Title I of the Housing Act, providing an abundance of funding for core city urban renewal programs, and the passage of the National Interstate and Defense Highways Act of 1956, resulting in the construction of the national interstate highway system. Finally, the Clean Water Act of 1972 advanced billons of dollars to suburban jurisdictions for the construction of new sewage treatment plants and major sewer lines, facilitating the development of large, often campus-like, commercial and residential sites.

Federal policies and programs enacted by the administration of President Lyndon B. Johnson attempted to reverse past policies that resulted in deconcentration and central city neglect with policies that required consideration of urban problems and the policy responses to these problems in a structured regional framework. In this regard, the Johnson administration significantly increased the amount of federal funding for Section 701(g) of the Housing and Urban Development Act of 1965 that provided federal funding to regional councils for the preparation of regional plans and programs. Section 204 of the Demonstration Cities and Metropolitan Development Act of 1966 further stimulated the establishment of regional councils by requiring that all local applications for federal funding involving forty grant and loan programs be reviewed and commented upon by a regional council. This regional review requirement was considerably enhanced by the passage of the Intergovernmental Cooperation Act of 1968. Acting on the basis of this legislation, the Nixon administration issued Circular A-95, expanding the review function of regional councils to include over 150 federally assisted programs (Wikstrom 1977).

The overall goal of the Johnson administration to require that the local governments of metropolitan areas respond to and develop policy responses to urban problems in a regional framework was seriously derailed by President Ronald Reagan's administration and Congress in the 1980s. During this era, the federal government drastically reduced "701" funds for regional councils. Even more critically, the Reagan administration terminated the A-95 review process in favor a new approach, encouraging the states to develop their own regional review process. However, these setbacks for metropolitan regionalism were later incrementally reversed by several developments at the federal level. These developments included the passage of legislation in the 1990s that, once again, emphasized the importance of collaboration among the officials of a metropolitan area, regional planning, and the role of regional councils in the intergovernmental management system. This legislation included the Intermodal Surface Transportation Efficiency Act of 1991 and the Clean Air Act (CAA) Amendments enacted by Congress in 1990.

In order for communities and regions to secure federal highway funding, a metropolitan planning organization (MPO) must be established in each area to be responsible for the development of a comprehensive and balanced regional transportation plan. In many metropolitan areas, this responsibility has been assigned to a regional council. The CAA Amendments require that metropolitan areas develop and implement satisfactory regional air quality standards or risk losing federal funds for transportation projects (Wikstrom 2006).

With the federal government in the past several decades becoming increasingly disenchanted with core city public housing, it has adopted a metropolitan-wide strategy for housing the less advantaged through its funding of Section 8 housing vouchers and other housing programs. Unfortunately, in the past several years the Bush administration has severely decreased federal funding for Community Development Block Grant funding (CDBG), which, according to a recently completed survey of city officials, has negatively impacted the ability to provide affordable housing for the disadvantaged (Brennan and Hoene 2006). Further, President Bush urged in 2006 that the CDBG program be phased out and replaced by a new funding stream for federal community and economic development programs to be housed in the Department of Commerce (National Association of Counties 2006).

Involvement of States and Nongovernmental Organizations

The states have also been active, in varying degrees, in advancing the cause of metropolitan regionalism. Most states allow localities to engage in intergovernmental cooperation and permit them to provide services on a joint basis. The states of Minnesota, Indiana, and Oregon have been especially vigorous in promoting regional approaches. For example, in 1967 the Minnesota state legislature established the Twin Cities Metropolitan Council for the Minneapolis-St. Paul metropolitan area, with broad policy review powers. Subsequently, this body was given the additional responsibilities of administering an innovative revenue sharing program for the localities of the region, and, much later on, providing mass transportation and sewerage services.

In a more drastic step, in 1970, Indiana, without popular referendum approval, established a city-county consolidated government for the Indianapolis-Marion County area, popularly referred to as UNIGOV. Oregon played a crucial role in the varied political developments that led to voters' approval in 1978 of the establishment of the Metropolitan Services District (now Metro). Metro has a governing body directly elected by the voters, and has been repeatedly praised, as noted previously, for its smart growth policies (Rusk 1999, 158–61).

Regional councils, which in many instances have evolved from councils of governments, have been established in virtually every metropolitan area in the United States, as well as in many rural areas. Although many scholars of urban affairs have routinely discounted the value of regional councils, they have won a limited amount of praise from state and local officials for serving as a forum for the discussion of regional issues and for better acquainting local officials with each other (thereby gaining a measure of metropolitan social capital). Regional councils have been applauded for educating local officials and the citizenry about the nature of area-wide infrastructure and social problems and the desirability of approaching these problems on a coordinated regional basis. These organizations have also been acknowledged for their comprehensive regional planning and specific functional planning efforts; the latter most often involving community and housing development, economic development and growth, environment, and highways and mass transportation (Wikstrom 2002).

Finally, in addition to the above governmental and quasi-governmental entities, there are a variety of other organizations around the nation that have enjoyed some measure of success in promoting the need to respond to urban issues in a regional framework. Such organizations include broad-based ecumenical religious groups. Rusk provides a nice accounting of the Northwest Indiana Federation of Interfaith Organizations, consisting of a range of religious groups in northwestern Indiana, which he has credited with promoting a regional perspective in regard to the use of governmental facilities, urban sprawl, and land use (1999, 277–90).

Business groups, most particularly regional chambers of commerce and various public–private economic growth partnerships have played a major role in promoting regionalism, especially, more recently, by emphasizing in their agenda that the local governments in the metropolitan area must coordinate their economic growth efforts, since metropolitan regions throughout the world are vigorously competing with each other for new economic and business investment. As George A. Gonzalez (2005) has reported, regional economic elites have been in the forefront in supporting clean air policies, since they believe that such policies contribute to the creation of a positive investment climate and promote economic growth.

Urban institutions of higher education, by conducting research on various policy issues and holding seminars for community leaders, have played a significant role in the regionalism movement. One of the most comprehensive and coordinated of these university-based projects is the Ohio Urban University Program, linking the local research efforts of the major state universities in Cleveland, Columbus, Cincinnati, Akron, Dayton, Toledo, and Youngstown (Rusk 1999, 299–306).

Metropolitan Citizens and the Quality of Life

Quality of life may be regarded as a composite "output" produced by the governments and the private entities of a metropolitan area, utilizing private and public infrastructure and employees as capital and labor inputs. The public capital goods, or public infrastructure, that serve as inputs in this productive process include roads and bridges for transportation, mass transit systems, water and sewer systems, police cars and jails for public safety, and school buildings and books for education. Public labor includes bus drivers, firefighters, teachers, and police officers, who are employed directly by the government or under contract with a profit or nonprofit private vendor. Private entities that have a direct bearing on the quality of life of a metropolitan area involve commercial facilities, including factories, office facilities, shopping malls and free-standing stores, and their employees. In addition, the quality of life of a metropolitan area is a function of its overall environment, climate, and typology.

Elements of a good quality of life include a high level of public safety and justice, clean air and water, the availability of greenery and open park and play space, excellent public and private schools, a strong and diversified economy, abundant and well-paying employment opportunities, a reasonable mix of good and affordable housing, good ethnic and race relations, responsive and effective health care facilities, plentiful and affordable recreational and cultural opportunities, a pedestrian-lively and visually pleasing streetscape in town and city centers, well-stocked and -staffed public libraries, a comprehensive and effective system of mass transportation, a congestion-free public highway system, and a moderate level of state and local taxation. Additional factors promoting a good quality of life in the metropolis include the perception among the citizenry of a strong sense of political efficacy, and community and neighborhood identification.

Unlike in the past, when the metropolitan regions of a national polity largely competed internally with each other for new business investment and economic growth, the present global economy demands that metropolitan areas compete economically with their relevant counterparts throughout the world. Metropolitan regions that enjoy an overall positive and productive image along with a high quality of life will be more successful in attracting new investment and economic growth than their ill-situated peers (Gonzalez 2005).

Metropolitan Citizens: Perceptions of Quality of Life

Notwithstanding the extensive and repeated amount of attention that the mass media devote to the various socioeconomic problems of the metropolis, especially that of core city violence and crime (Drier, Mollenkopf, and Swanstrom 2004, 33), some surveys show that many metropolitan citizens view their quality of life in a positive fashion. Indeed, it could be argued that citizens who dwell in the most "exclusive areas" of our core cities, because of their close proximity to a range of commercial, cultural, and service facilities, enjoy the highest quality of life. Such citizens, for example, include those who reside in the environs of Beacon Hill in Boston, Upper East Side Manhattan in New York City, Society Hill in Philadelphia, Georgetown in Washington, DC, and along Lakeshore Drive in Chicago. Relative to this is the fact that in recent years we have witnessed a significant movement of affluent middle-class individuals, largely white, from the suburbs to the core cities, in such places as Atlanta and Washington, DC (Banks 2006). In regard to Milwaukee, an editorial in the *Milwaukee Journal Sentinel* noted: "Young urban professionals and older empty nesters are moving into Milwaukee, fueling a housing boom downtown and nearby. They value the amenities of the city: among them, the excitement that the downtown generates just by acting as a crossroads for different cultures; the closeness to art museums, playhouses, nightclubs; the almost priceless craftsmanship of many older homes; the ability to walk to restaurants and shops" (2004, 14).

A survey conducted in 2003 in the greater Richmond, Virginia area (Martin 2003) found that 78 percent of those interviewed concurred that the metropolitan area offered a positive quality of life, 72 percent agreed that the metropolitan area offered a wide variety of technical and economic opportunities, and 88 percent acknowledged that the metropolitan area provides a wide variety of recreational, artistic, and cultural opportunities.

Table 2.2

Survey of Perceptions on Quality of Life in Philadelphia Compared with National Perceptions (%)

	Inside Philadelphia	Philadelphia suburbs	National core cities	National suburbs
Excellent	13	37	19	35
Very good	23	34	31	35
Good	31	21	25	24
Total positive	67	92	75	94
Total negative or no response	33	08	25	06

Source: Pew Research Center for the People & the Press (1997).

In a parallel set of results, a telephone survey by the Pew Foundation in the Philadelphia metropolitan region in 1996, involving a representative sample of 2,517 adults with a sampling error of plus or minus 2 percentage points, reported that the majority of respondents believe that their neighborhood enjoyed a high quality of life and was a "good place to reside." Table 2.2 shows that the majority of the respondents had a positive perception about their quality of life regardless of where they lived. Although over 90 percent of suburban residents nationally and in the greater Philadelphia area indicated satisfaction with their quality of life, the figures in Philadelphia and national core cities were a respectable 67 and 75 percent, respectively.

The Quinnipiac College Polling Institute conducted a telephone survey in 1996, on behalf of the Regional Planning Association of New York City, involving 1,500 individuals with a sampling error of 2.5 percent to determine how the citizens of the New York City region perceived the quality of their life. It found that 76 percent of the respondents were either "very satisfied" (25) or "somewhat satisfied" (51) with the quality of their life. Table 2.3 shows the results of this survey. These responses document that the majority of the citizens dwelling in the New York City metropolitan region had a positive evaluation of the overall quality of their life, although it should be noted that the survey found that only 28 percent of those citizens earning less than $25,000 per year were very satisfied with the quality of their lives, while, interestingly, a somewhat lower percentage—26 percent—of those earning annually between $25,000 and $50,000 reported being very satisfied with the quality of their lives (Quinnipiac College Polling Institute 1996, 2, 9).

In the same study, the Quinnipiac College Polling Institute surveyed a sample of 400 residents of the metropolitan areas of Atlanta, Seattle, Dallas,

Table 2.3

Survey of Perceptions Regarding Quality of Life in New York Metropolitan Area (%)

	Total metro area	Inner urban counties	Outer suburbs
Very satisfied	25	24	40
Somewhat satisfied	51	51	47
Total satisfied	76	75	87
Total dissatisfied or no response	24	25	13

Source: Quinnipiac College Polling Institute (1996).

and Los Angeles to ascertain how they perceived the quality of their lives. Similar to the findings in the New York metropolitan region, the majority of the citizens in three of these metropolitan regions view the quality of their lives in a positive fashion. Table 2.4 shows the results of this survey. Specifically, 63 percent of the citizens of Atlanta, 74 percent of the citizens in Seattle, and 61 percent of the respondents in Dallas had a positive perception regarding their quality of life. Only 40 percent of the citizens of the Los Angeles metropolitan area had a positive perception about the quality of their life (Quinnipiac College Polling Institute 1996, 44).

Areas of Concentrated Economic and Racial Poverty

The above aggregate city survey data somewhat mask the fact that a number of metropolitan citizens, largely, although not exclusively, dwelling in core cities or first suburbs reside in "poverty neighborhoods" in what social scientists describe as "concentrations of poverty." To a considerable degree, these citizens are the victims of a "spatial mismatch." As the economy and the core city's geography have changed, inner-city residents have experienced declines in employment as more jobs have moved to suburbs. Concentrations of poverty have been variously defined by social scientists as those neighborhoods where 20, 30, or 40 percent of the citizens are living below the poverty line; for instance, in 2000 it was estimated that 12 percent of the poor resided in poverty neighborhoods where 40 percent of the residents were defined as poor (Dreier, Mollenkopf, and Swanstrom 2004, 28; Wilson 1987). Such areas are marked by a high rate of crime and the use of illegal drugs, abandoned houses and lots, poorly performing schools, a paucity of large grocery and drug stores, vacant businesses, abandoned cars and trucks, an oversupply of

Table 2.4

Survey of Atlanta, Seattle, Dallas, and Los Angeles on Perceptions Regarding Quality of Life (%)

	Atlanta metro area	Seattle metro area	Dallas metro area	Los Angeles metro area
Excellent	15	21	13	7
Good	48	53	48	33
Total both	63	74	61	40
Total negative or no response	37	26	39	60

Source: Quinnipiac College Polling Institute (1996).

liquor stores, a lack of banking facilities, and idle men and women "marking time" on street corners.[2]

Poverty is discussed in Chapter 8 of this book. Briefly, the central city is plagued by areas of concentrated poverty that create or exacerbate a wide range of problems. A basic problem is the lack of an adequate supply of economic opportunity structures and networks, and resultant low per capita incomes. In regard to this, Pressman and Wildavsky (1973) wrote in their study in Oakland, California, during the 1960s, that blacks were in a comparative disadvantage in the job market because:

> For the poor, unskilled minority member trying to find employment after his previous manufacturing job has been relocated to the suburbs, the situation is markedly different (than his white suburban counterpart). His informal connection with the manufacturing job market has been atrophied, for his friends and neighbors are in no better position than he. Even if he finds a job, he may not be able to commute daily, for he is either too poor to own a reliable car or the public transport system does not serve the new plant. When he turns to the expanding manufacturing job market near at hand, he finds his skills are no longer in demand, his poor educational background ill fits him to learn new skills, and he faces anew the problem of overcoming racial discrimination. (1973, 151)

Fourteen years later, William Julius Wilson in *The Truly Disadvantaged: The Inner City, the Underclass, and Public Policy* also took note of the fact that the exclusion of poor blacks, especially males, from the informal job system renders it more difficult for them to obtain employment:

... in a neighborhood with a paucity of regularly employed families with the overwhelming majority of families having spells of long-term jobless-ness, people experience a social isolation that excludes them from the job network system that permeates other neighborhoods and that is so important in learning about or being recommended for jobs that become available in various parts of the city. And as the prospects for employment diminish, other alternatives such as welfare and the underground economy are not only increasingly relied on, they come to be seen as a way of life. (1987, 57)

Wilson reiterated this theme in his subsequent volume *When Work Dis-appears: The World of the New Urban Poor*: "If you live in a neighborhood with a high unemployment rate, your social network will be less valuable in helping you find a job, regardless of how skilled, honest, or hardworking you are" (1996, 135). Black males continue to lag behind in terms of economic advancement, as is documented in *Black Males Left Behind* (Mincy 2006).

Individuals residing in concentrated poverty areas lack adequate access to health care, live in a harmful physical environment, and have a high level of emotional stress, which harms family structures. In addition, these areas have a paucity of business establishments (groceries, banks and pharmacies, for example), resulting in higher consumer and borrowing costs. Public ser-vices in the form of good schools, bus routes, or libraries are lacking. These neighborhoods have higher levels of crime of all kinds. These neighborhoods leave residents thinking they are forgotten, their voices unheard by those in a position to restore some quality of life to their neighborhood. Excluded from the political system, individuals dwelling in areas of concentrated poverty see that they lack political efficacy.

Saving Our Core Cities

While there is some evidence that some of our core cities, particularly Atlanta, Boston, Cleveland, New York, and Washington, DC, are staging an economic comeback, many of our core cities continue to be beset by serious economic, fiscal, and social problems. It is rather imperative, for a number of important reasons, that we "go about the business" of ensuring and enhancing the vital-ity of our core cities.

First is our recognition that the central city serves to identify a metropoli-tan area, constituting a larger set of mental associations, as noted by Kevin Lynch almost a half-century ago (1960). In this regard, the central city, the "flagship" of its region, serves as a larger, or regional, community image, or symbol, and provides a nomenclature for outsiders. Indicative of this, when citizens—whether residing in the core city or suburbia—venture far beyond their region, they invariably inform those with whom they meet and interact that their home locale is in part of a central region, such as Boston, Chicago, or San Francisco. Given all of this, it is neither difficult to understand nor surprising that citizens are mindful of and care about the overall appearance, health, and image of their central cities. A viable and healthy central city and larger metropolis are able to attract more investment and business activity; conversely, a metropolitan area anchored by a declining central city is less able to generate new investment. Image and appearances count.[3]

Second, another reason for ensuring the vitality of our core cities arises from their importance as centers of business activity and commerce. Indeed, a number of scholars have found that the state of the economic vitality of the central city is strongly related to the overall economic health of the region. For instance, H.V. Savitch and his colleagues reported that, on the basis of their investigation in 1987 of the regional economy of fifty-nine metropolitan areas, there was a strong economic interdependent relationship between central cities and suburbs. Savitch and his colleagues noted that suburbs surrounding healthy cities tend to be healthier than those that surround sick cities (1993).

Suburban firms significantly rely upon the rich supply of corporate services, such as banking, law, and accounting, located in city centers. They also identify with the central city for amenities like sports, culture, and recreation. In this regard, Alex Schwartz found in a survey of 5,000 large firms that central city firms provided 92 percent of the professional services contracted for in the region. He concluded: "Suburbia does not yet comprise an economically autonomous 'outer city' or 'edge city' (1993, 302). In addition, Dreier, Mollenkopf, and Swanstrom also noted:

> Urban density enhances economic efficiency and innovation. What economists call "agglomeration economies" are still important in the global economy. The density of employment in cities reduces costs of transportation and increases each business's access to skilled and specialized labor. The geographical clustering of industries in certain cities further enhances productivity. In many industries, understanding ambiguous information is the key to innovation. It cannot be communicated in an e-mail message or even a phone call; it requires the kind of face-to-face interaction that cities are good at fostering. The cultural production of these cities has been just as important as their economic role. (2004, 32)

Jane Jacobs (1969) in her seminal work *The Economy of Cities* also notes the central and innovative role that core cities play in the economic development of metropolitan regions, due to the exchange of ideas across diverse firms situated in concentrated geographical areas. These diverse firms are heavily populated by members of the "creative class," who generate new ideas, production processes, and strategies (Florida 2002). Finally, ensuring and enhancing the overall and economic vitality of our core cities will create employment opportunities for city residents residing in "pockets of poverty" who seek work, want to remain in their present place of residence, and need to use public transit for their commute.

Strategies for Assuring a Satisfactory Quality of Life for All Citizens

The following fourfold strategy is recommended to ensure that *all* of the citizens of the metropolis including inner-city residents have access to, and are the beneficiaries of, a satisfactory quality of life.

1. Core city political leaders must exercise strong, imaginative, and resourceful leadership on behalf of policies designed to stimulate job growth, the construction of affordable housing, and revenue enhancement.
2. States and cities must promote a working political alliance and encourage greater intergovernmental cooperation between core cities and first, or inner, suburbs.
3. The federal government must strengthen and more adequately fund housing mobility programs that enable residents living in inner-city concentrated poverty to relocate to neighborhoods of their choice.
4. Metropolitan areas—working with citizen and civic groups, the regional council, and the area's jurisdictions—must cooperatively adopt fair and affordable housing policies designed to ensure that all residents have decent housing where they desire to live.

The first, and foremost, element of this fourfold strategy, especially given the rise of the dominant national, indeed international, research and development economy and the declining importance of manufacturing in most core cities, is for local public and private policymakers to strategically adopt specific urban development technology policies. These policies are designed to ensure that their community is fully partaking in the global technology economy, resulting in a continuing healthy local economy and job growth. For a community to fully participate in the global technology economy, it must develop the requisite information and telecommunications technology infrastructure and networks.

Darrene Hackler maintains: "How policies influence factors such as the availability of skilled technical labor, managerial occupations, and access to capital (venture capital funds), while serving to create an entrepreneurial environment that includes both external and internal information sharing, can ultimately decide the success of a location and its economic prosperity" (2006, 10).

As part of the innovative leadership recommended under this first point, city policymakers must become more proactive in developing and implementing policies increasing the amount of affordable housing available to their citizens. For instance, Raymond J. Burby argues that city officials should adopt a more flexible approach in the implementation and enforcement of building codes, which, he contends, would result in more housing units. He states: "Strict enforcement does, in fact, hinder the ability of central cities to capture a larger share of the market for new single-family-detached and multifamily housing within metropolitan areas . . . central cities that have embraced a strict approach to enforcement will need to completely rethink their enforcement strategies if they want to be more successful in competing with suburban areas for new housing construction" (2005, 143).

Additional affordable housing units can be realized by the more intensive reuse and development of temporary, obsolete, abandoned, or derelict sites (TOADS) and the cleaning-up and reuse of contaminated "brownfield" sites. With regard to the former, Elise Bright reports that Cleveland and St. Louis, for example, have established an organizationally distinct land revitalization authority to quicken the pace at which TOADS are rehabilitated and added to the existing housing supply (2005, 31). As a result of their investigation of the cleaning-up and reuse of "brownfields" in Pittsburgh, Sabina E. Deitrick and Stephen C. Farber (2005) underscore that the successful conversion of "brownfields" into sites for the construction of new commercial enterprises and affordable housing necessitates resolving a myriad array of liability issues and the building of a community consensus involving meaningful and broad-based public participation.

Finally, city policy leaders, although they have increasingly over the past several decades diversified and enlarged the "streams" of city governmental revenues through the imposition of a myriad array of service fees and charges, should devote more serious attention to seeking "payment in lieu of taxes" (PILOTs) from community nonprofit organizations, such as charitable and educational institutions. Although only a relatively few large cities, including Baltimore, Boston, Detroit, Indianapolis, Minneapolis, Philadelphia, and Pittsburgh, are currently the recipients of such payments (Leland 2005, 212), PILOTs may be readily justified on the basis that nonprofit organizations are the beneficiaries of many city services, especially fire and police. The additional funds received by cities through PILOTs, although relatively small, could be utilized to help provide citizens with public services and a higher quality of life.

As to the second point of the strategy and given the similarity of their declining economic structure and changing demographic makeup, first suburbs and core cities confront many of the same serious fiscal-threatening socioeconomic challenges. As Banfield reported: "If what really matters is the essential welfare of individuals and the good health of the society as opposed to comfort, convenience, amenity, and business advantage, then what we have is not an 'urban problem' but an 'inner-central-city-and-larger-older-suburban' one" (1968, 12). We need to encourage these jurisdictions to form a working political alliance, which could constitute a significant political force in the national and state political arenas. After all, core cities and first suburbs, in the aggregate, contain about one-third of the nation's population, and in eight states—Connecticut, Maryland, Massachusetts, New Jersey, Rhode Island, California, Arizona, and New York—core city and first suburb dwellers constitute a majority (Puentes and Warren 2006, 8).

Such political coalitions, already well advanced in the Cleveland and Los Angeles regions (Katz and Puentes 2006), could replicate the successful efforts of Representative Myron Orfield, who played a crucial role in the 1990s in developing a core cities–inner suburban political coalition in Minnesota's legislature (Orfield 2002). Largely as a result of Orfield's leadership efforts, the Minnesota legislature commenced a study on the economic health and status of poverty in the cities of Minneapolis and St. Paul, and the inner suburbs; revised the nature of sewer and wastewater financing in the region; strengthened the area's well-known tax-base sharing program; and instituted a stronger and more effective fair-housing program for the metropolitan area. In addition, Orfield's efforts led to the Twin Cities Metropolitan Council, a region-wide body established in 1967, assuming the responsibility for the provision of mass transit services and wastewater treatment operations (Rusk 1999, 223–48).

The development of core city–inner suburban political coalitions would serve to strengthen their political visibility and position in state legislatures and in Congress, and would reduce the "policy blind spot" of inner suburbs in these bodies. Such coalitions would serve to ensure greater levels of funding for their region from the federal and state government; promote local mutually beneficial intergovernmental cooperation; increase the service role of county government; encourage local governments to develop strategies to jointly alleviate adjacent residential and commercial blight; stimulate cooperative efforts to promote economic development (mitigating destructive economic "bidding wars" between these localities) and the growth of jobs, compensated at a higher level than minimum wage; provide more housing opportunities for racial minorities and the poor; develop regional tax-sharing programs; and mobilize, empower, and incorporate Asian, African-American, Latino, and other minorities into the political process. The rise of strong core city–inner suburban political coalitions would give them the ability to push for greater resources provided by higher levels of government to these jurisdictions to deal with their myriad problems.

The third point in the strategy revolves around mobility programs. Research findings indicate that a productive strategy for ensuring a better quality of life for the inner-city poor, often mired in concentrations of poverty, is to substantially expand the use of "housing choice" or "mobility programs," further facilitating larger numbers of the disadvantaged to reside in the more desirable sections of the metropolitan area. Anthony Downs argued more than three decades ago in his work *Opening Up the Suburbs* (1973) that public policymakers need to do a much better job of ensuring suburban housing opportunities for minorities. The beneficiaries of this strategy would gain from more opportunity structures for self-development and economic advancement. Regional affordable housing policy is further discussed in Chapter 6 of this book.

Evidence gathered from the federally funded Moving to Opportunity (MTO) program documents that a change in place, along with a change in the contextual effects of the neighborhood, is beneficial for the poor. The MTO program commenced in 1993 when Congress allocated $70 million for 1,400 housing vouchers to assist poor families to move from concentrated poverty areas (defined as having a poverty rate of 40 percent or more) to areas of low poverty (defined as areas with 10 percent or less poverty). Cities involved in the program included Los Angeles, New York, Chicago, and Boston. An evaluation of the MPO demonstration program found that, among other benefits, the movement of poor individuals from a high-poverty to a low-poverty neighborhood had important mental health benefits for adults and resulted in significantly lower rates of obesity. In addition, teenage girls had lower rates of psychological distress and engaged in fewer risky behaviors (Orr et al. 2003).

Given the recent U.S. District Court ruling of *Thompson v. U.S. Department of Housing and Urban Development* (HUD) handed down in 2005, it may well be that the federal courts will adopt a more aggressive posture requiring HUD and municipal officials to implement region-wide policies designed to racially desegregate housing in our metropolitan areas. After reviewing the history of de jure and de facto racially segregated housing in Baltimore over the years, the court largely absolving Baltimore officials from blame. It charged, however, that HUD, in clear violation of the Fair Housing Act, failed to actively promote regional housing opportunities for the Baltimore region's low-income families living in federally-assisted housing. The latter requires HUD to administer housing programs in a manner designed to ensure individuals the right to pursue housing opportunities free from discrimination. The court ordered HUD and local officials in the metropolitan area to develop and implement a strategy ensuring that minorities would be able to pursue housing opportunities throughout the region (*Thompson, et al. v. HUD* 2005).

Finally, to improve the quality of life for all, we should encourage regional councils, which should be provided with greater amounts of federal and state fiscal assistance, and local governments, to develop and implement programs that ensure decent and affordable housing for all residents, but especially the poor and racial minorities, to overcome past exclusionary housing policies (Danielson 1976). To promote mobility of the poor, the Metropolitan Washington Council of Governments developed and implemented in 1972 a fair-share housing program for the greater Washington, DC, region. In 2001, it established the goal of having the region add 67,000 affordable housing units to its housing inventory. Communities in the region, including Alexandria and Loudoun County, Virginia, and Prince George and Montgomery County in Maryland, have adopted complementary fair-share housing policies (Metropolitan Washington Council of Governments 2001; Wikstrom 2002).

Summary and Conclusion

Some survey evidence suggests that the majority of the residents of the metropolis are basically satisfied with their quality of life. However, the problems and challenges long identified with central cities have become increasingly identified with the first suburbs in the metropolitan region. Among these problems, concentrations of poverty and the consequences flowing from these conditions are the most serious, since they constitute a substantial and real threat to individual well-being. Leaving empirical observations and considerations aside, we have a societal moral obligation to develop and implement federal, state, regional, and local public policies, facilitating the ability of individuals residing in concentrations of poverty to achieve a better quality of life. Poverty deconcentration can be achieved by population movement to other areas of the metropolitan region, to a better—and more equal—chance of enjoying a productive quality of life. Another means to achieve quality of life in neighborhoods of concentrated poverty is through improvement in place.[4] This means a massive commitment by municipal, state, and federal governments to bring back forgotten neighborhoods to a quality-of-life standard that once was there, that reflects the middle-class standard for quality of life, and that the market economy recognizes through housing value appreciation and exchange.

Notes

This chapter is a rather extensively revised version of a paper that I presented at the Annual Meeting of the Urban Affairs Association, Montreal, Canada, April 19–22,

2006. I wish to thank Patricia Atkins and David Hamilton for reviewing the paper and providing me with a number of incisive comments.

1. The most exhaustive collection of data relating to "first suburbs" is contained in Robert Puentes and David Warren, *One-Fifth of America: A Comprehensive Guide to America's First Suburbs. Data Report* (Washington, DC: Brookings Institution, 2006). The data contained in this publication, a product of the Brookings Institution Metropolitan Policy Program, relate to the following ten indicators—population, race and ethnicity, immigration, age, household type and size, housing, education, income and poverty, employment, and commuting.

2. A fuller picture includes those who are contributing to their neighborhood's quality of life: the man who runs an illegal grocery store in his home so that his neighbors have access to the basics; the young boys who go to school every day; the concerned parent or grandparent who will not let the children play outside because it is too dangerous.

3. Although suburbanites may well name their hometown city when they are traveling and are asked where they are from, it is difficult to know whether that is evidence that they are mindful of and care about the overall appearance, health, and image of the core city.

4. "Improvement in place" is potentially an option. Not everyone who lives in concentrated poverty wants to leave the city for the suburbs. The issue is not the city versus the suburbs, for suburbs have poverty as well. If neighborhoods of concentrated poverty were to be transformed to the standards of desirable city neighborhoods, city officials might see fewer households desiring to leave. The enormous cost of such a transformation prohibits its implementation on a widespread basis. A policy that focuses on exporting poor families to the suburbs causes three very significant problems for cities. First, it further depopulates the city of families that could be net contributors to the city's vitality (especially if it is taking the remaining homeowners). Second, it causes neighborhoods that are already partially abandoned to become more hopeless places for those who remain behind, neighborhoods that then become more burdensome to city taxpayers.

References

Alonso, William. 1981. "A Theory of the Urban Land Market." In *Urban Change and Conflict: An Interdisciplinary Reader,* ed. Andrew Blowers, 63–67. London: Harper and Row.

Banfield, Edward C. 1968. *The Unheavenly City: The Nature and the Future of Our Urban Crisis.* Boston: Little, Brown.

Banks, Manley Elliott. 2006. "Liberal and Neo-Conservative Black Urban Regimes in Washington, DC and Atlanta, Georgia, 1985 to 2000." *Journal of Race & Policy* 2 (Spring/Summer): 38–52.

Bier, Tom, and Charlie Post. 2003. *Vacating the City: An Analysis of New Homes vs. Household Growth.* Washington, DC: Brookings Institution Press.

Brennan, Christiana, and Christopher Hoene. 2006. *The State of America's Cities, 2006: The Annual Opinion Survey of Municipal Officials.* Washington, DC: National League of Cities.

Bright, Elise. 2005. "Is There a Need to Contain Growth?" In *Revitalizing the City: Strategies to Contain Sprawl and Revive the Core,* ed. Fritz W. Wagner et al., 25–40. Armonk, NY: M.E. Sharpe.

Bruegmann, Robert. 2005. *Sprawl: A Compact History.* Chicago: University of Chicago Press.

Burby, Raymond J. 2005. "Impacts of Building Code Enforcement on the Housing Industry." In *Revitalizing the City: Strategies to Contain Sprawl and Revive the Core,* ed. Fritz W. Wagner et al., 141–59. Armonk, NY: M.E. Sharpe.

Burchell, Robert W., ed. 2000. *Costs of Sprawl—2000.* Washington, DC: National Academy Press.

Cox, Wendell. 2003. *Debunking Friday the 13th: Myths of Urban Sprawl.* Chicago: Heartland Institute.

Danielson, Michael N. 1976. *The Politics of Exclusion.* New York: Columbia University Press.

Deitrick, Sabina E., and Stephen C. Farber. 2005. "Citizen Reaction to Brownfields Redevelopment." In *Revitalizing the City: Strategies to Contain Sprawl and Revive the Core,* eds. Fritz W. Wagner et al., 160–200. Armonk, NY: M.E. Sharpe.

Downs, Anthony. 1973. *Opening Up the Suburbs.* New Haven: Yale University Press.

———. 1994. *New Visions for Metropolitan America.* Washington, DC: Brookings Institution, and Cambridge, MA: Lincoln Institute of Land Policy.

Dreier, Peter; John Mollenkopf; and Todd Swanstrom. 2004. *Place Matters: Metropolitics for the Twenty-first Century.* 2d ed. Lawrence: University Press of Kansas.

Eldredge, H. Wentworth, ed. 1967. *Taming Megalopolis: What Is and What Could Be.* Garden City, NY: Anchor Books.

Faltermayer, Edmund K. 1968. *Redoing America.* New York: Harper & Row.

Florida, Richard. 2002. *The Rise of the Creative Class and How It's Transforming Work, Leisure, Community, and Everyday Life.* New York: Basic Books.

Freilich, Robert. 1999. *From Sprawl to Smart Growth: Successful Legal, Planning, and Environmental Systems.* Chicago: American Bar Association.

Garreau, Joel. 1991. *Edge City: Life on the New Frontier.* New York: Doubleday.

Glazer, Nathan, ed. 1970. *Cities in Trouble.* Chicago: Quadrangle Books.

Gonzalez, George A. 2005. *The Politics of Air Pollution: Urban Growth, Ecological Modernization and Symbolic Inclusion.* Albany: State University of New York Press.

Gordon, Mitchell. 1963. *Sick Cities.* Baltimore: Penguin Books.

Gordon, Peter, and Harry Richardson. 2000. "Defending Suburban Sprawl." *Public Interest* 139: (Spring): 65–73.

———. 2001. "The Sprawl Debate: Let Markets Plan." *Publius: The Journal of Federalism* 31 (Summer): 131–49.

Grogan, Paul S., and Tony Proscio. 2000. *Comeback Cities.* Boulder: Westview Press.

Hackler, Darrene L. 2006. *Cities in the Technology Economy.* Armonk, NY: M.E. Sharpe.

Hirschhorn, Joel S. 2005. *Sprawl Kills: How Blandburgs Steal Your Time, Health, and Money.* New York: Sterling and Ross.

Jacobs, Jane. 1969. *The Economy of Cities.* New York: Random House.

Jargowsky, Paul. 2002. "Sprawl, Concentration of Poverty, and Urban Inequality," In *Urban Sprawl: Causes and Consequences,* ed. Gregory D. Squires, 39–71. Washington, DC: Urban Institute.

Kain, John F. 1968. "Housing Segregation, Negro Employment, and Metropolitan Decentralization." *Quarterly Journal of Economics* 82, no. 2 (May): 175–97.

Katz, Bruce, and Robert Puentes. 2006. "Affluent, but Needy. As They Grow and Change, the Nation's First Suburbs, Nassau County Included, Show Signs of Stress Ahead." *Newsday,* February 12, A44.

Ladd, Helen, and John Yinger. 1989. *America's Ailing Cities: Fiscal Health and the Design of Urban Policy.* Baltimore: John Hopkins University Press.

Lambert, Bruce. 2005. "More Long Islanders Looking to Move Out, a Survey Finds." *New York Times,* December 1: A31.

―――. 2006. "Nation's Older Suburbs Struggling with New Challenges, Report Says." *New York Times,* February 16: A30.

Leland, Pamela. 2005. "Payments-in-Lieu-of-Taxes: A Revenue-Generating Strategy for Central Cities." In *Revitalizing the City: Strategies to Contain Sprawl and Revive the Core,* ed. Fritz W. Wagner et al., 201–25. Armonk, NY: M.E. Sharpe.

Lynch, Kevin. 1960. *The Image of the City.* Cambridge: MIT Press and Harvard University Press.

Martin, John. 2003. "There's No Place Like Home: Richmonders Can Be Thankful for Quality of Life." *Richmond Times-Dispatch,* November 26: A-12.

Metropolitan Washington Council of Governments. 2001. *Finding a Way Home: Building Communities with Affordable Housing.* Washington, DC.

Milwaukee Journal Sentinel 2004. Editorial, "The City-Suburban Gap." *Milwaukee Journal Sentinel,* June 23: 14.

Mincy, Ronald B., ed. 2006. *Black Males Left Behind.* Washington, DC: Brookings Institution.

National Association of Counties. 2006. *Community Development Block Grant Program and Home Investment Partnership Program.* Washington, DC.

Orfield, Myron. 1997. *Metropolitics: A Regional Agenda for Community and Stability.* Washington, DC: Brookings Institution Press.

―――. 2002. *American Metropolitics: The New Suburban Reality.* Washington, DC: Brookings Institution.

Orr, Larry; Judith Feins; Robin Jacob; and Erik Beecroft. 2003. *Moving to Opportunity for Fair Housing Demonstration: Program Interim Impacts Evaluation.* Prepared for the U.S. Department of Housing and Urban Development, Office of Policy Development and Research. Washington, DC: Abt Associates, National Bureau of Economic Research, and The Urban Institute.

Pagano, Michael A., and Chris Hoene. 2006. *City Fiscal Conditions in 2005.* Washington, DC: National League of Cities.

Pew Research Center for the People & the Press. 1997. *Trust and Citizen Engagement in Metropolitan Philadelphia: A Case Study,* April. Washington, DC: Pew Research Center for the People & the Press.

Pressman, Jeffrey, and Aaron Wildavsky. 1973. *Implementation.* Berkeley: University of California Press.

Puentes, Robert, and David Warren. 2006. *One-Fifth of America: a Comprehensive Guide to America's First Suburbs. Data Report.* Washington, DC: Brookings Institution.

Quinnipiac College Polling Institute. 1996. *The Quality of Life Poll: What It Says, What It Means.* Hamden, CT: Quinnipiac College Polling Institute.

Rusk, David. 1993. *Cities without Suburbs.* Washington, DC: Woodrow Wilson Press.

―――. 1999. *Inside Game/Outside Game: Winning Strategies for Saving Urban America.* Washington, DC: Brookings Institution Press.

Savitch, H.V.; David Collins; Daniel Sanders; and John P. Markham. 1993. "Ties that Bind: Central Cities, Suburbs, and the New Metropolitan Region." *Economic Development Quarterly* 7, no. 4 (November): 341–58.

Schwartz, Alex. 1993. "Subservient Suburbia: The Reliance of Large Suburban Companies on Central City Firms for Financial and Professional Services." *Journal of the American Planning Association* 59 (June): 288–302.

Thompson, et al. v. U.S. Department of Housing and Urban Development and Housing Authority of Baltimore City. 2005. 220 F.3d 241, 244.

Tiebout, Charles M. 1956. "A Pure Theory of Local Expenditures." *Journal of Political Economy* 64, no. 5 (October): 416–24.

Tretten, Rudie. 1970. *Cities in Trouble.* Englewood, Cliffs, NJ: Prentice Hall.

U.S. Congress, Office of Technology Assessment. 1995. *The Technological Reshaping of Metropolitan America,* OTA-ETI-643. Washington, DC: Government Printing Office.

Whyte, Willliam H., ed. 1958. *The Exploding Metropolis.* Garden City, NY: Doubleday.

Wikstrom, Nelson. 1977. *Councils of Governments: A Study of Political Incrementalism.* Chicago: Nelson-Hall.

———. 2002. "The City in the Regional Mosaic." In *The Future of Local Government Administration,* ed. H. George Frederickson and John Nalbandian, 21–30. Washington, DC: International City/County Management Association.

———. 2006. "Councils of Governments." In *Federalism in America: An Encyclopedia,* ed. Joseph R. Marbach, Ellis Katz, and Troy E. Smith. Vol. I, 130–135. Westport, CT: Greenwood Press.

Williams, Oliver P. 1965. *Suburban Differences and Metropolitan Policies.* Philadelphia: University of Pennsylvania Press.

Williamson, Thad; David Imbroscio; and Gar Alperowitz. 2002. *Making Place for Community: Local Democracy in a Global Era.* New York: Routledge.

Wilson, William Julius. 1987. *The Truly Disadvantaged: The Inner City, the Underclass, and Public Policy.* Chicago: University of Chicago Press.

———. 1996. *When Work Disappears: The World of the New Urban Poor.* New York: Knopf.

3

PATRICIA S. ATKINS

Metropolitan Forms, Fiscal Efficiency, and Other Bottom Lines

Fiscal inequity among metropolitan local governments is a fact in America. Local taxation rates vary from community to community; likewise local governments provide different mixes of services and amenities to their residents. A recent fiscal study of the Miami metropolitan area showed one well-off municipality in the region had a revenue-raising capacity that was 7,195 percent of the region's average, and, another municipality had a capacity that was only 50 percent of the region's average (Curran 2005). This wealthy enclave with thirty-three individuals averaged a per capita personal income of $141,545, which was $73,537 higher than the next highest per capita income community.

Though local governments in the United States are fiscally constrained by their states, local governments do have enough autonomous revenue-raising authority and boundary control such that fiscal disparity is inevitable, absent equalization intervention by higher governments. In fact, it is desirable to have diversity, because there is great variability in what people want in their living arrangements and services.

A family or individual who becomes a householder in a jurisdiction buys into its tax/goods package and an anticipated standard of living, where the tax/goods package of the jurisdiction is reflective of personal preferences. Metropolitan fiscal disparity is the obvious result of a metropolitan area's jurisdictions placing different tax burdens upon residents and providing different public goods provision. Such fiscal disparity can be exacerbated, though, through other reinforcing policies such as exclusionary zoning or restrictions on transit service.

Does fiscal disparity among metropolitan area local governments represent a difficulty or an asset? The tolerable margin of diversity, fiscal or otherwise, among local governments within a metropolitan area is a political and societal decision. The answer depends both upon the tolerance of an individual for disparity, a normative opinion, and upon the severity of the fiscal disparities among governments within a metropolitan area, a qualitative measurement. There are some features for humane living that everyone can accept: air that is healthful to breathe, potable water, adequate food, and choices in selecting secure, comfortable, and affordable shelter. Beyond those basics, some might include a decent education, employment with a livable wage, and convenient mobility.

Though there are techniques to determine just how fiscally unequal one city's situation is from the next in metropolitan areas, such exercises, because of their complexity, are rarely undertaken. To date, there have only been four studies of intrametropolitan fiscal disparity in the United States (Bell et al. 2004; Bell et al. 2005; Orfield 2002; Rafuse and Marks 1991). Other than these four, all other existing local fiscal disparity studies build metropolitan tax computations on statewide average tax rates rather than on metropolitan-wide average tax rates, creating measures of disparity between entire metropolitan areas within the state versus measures of fiscal disparity among local governments within an individual metropolitan area (Green and Reschovsky 1994; Sjoquist 1996).

This chapter seeks to accomplish several purposes:

- Describe fiscal disparity in tax burden and services delivery, what political economists call tax/goods packages, among local governments in metropolitan areas,
- Describe local government organizational forms in metropolitan areas and their effects upon services delivery outcomes,
- Relate local government organizational forms and services delivery in metropolitan areas to a set of values, including social equity, fiscal efficiency, and environmental responsibility, and
- Assess metropolitan polity choices in redressing deficiencies in social equity, fiscal efficiency, or environmental responsibility among local government services delivery outcomes.

Fiscal Capacity and Disparity

Fiscal disparity is the difference in fiscal capacity that exists between any two or more local governments in a metropolitan area. Fiscal capacity compares a jurisdiction's ability to raise revenue against the expenditure burdens placed upon it (Ladd 2005, 144). Local governments with a fiscal capacity index of less than 100 have below-average fiscal ability compared with the average of the local governments in their own metropolitan area and those with a fiscal capacity index greater than 100 have above-average ability.

Political economists posit that, in theory, fiscal disparity among local governments within a metropolitan area arises because household sorting into the many local governments with their differences in tax/goods packages reflects freely chosen preferences by households based upon their ability to pay. Discussions about policy responses to extremes in fiscal disparity that emerge as a result of this sorting process go directly to the most heated metropolitan political economy ideology war of the twentieth century: should the market or the polity take care of the sorting of households into their preferred tax/goods preferences and of the delivery of humane living? It has been so divisive, because as Robert L. Bish remarks, "One of the most difficult problems for local governance is to determine institutional arrangements and boundaries for local goods and services that are preferred by citizens in different geographical areas or that possess different production characteristics" (Bish 2006–7, 34).

For a good part of the twentieth century, the debate surrounding this problem fell into two schools of thought. It continues today, but a third viewpoint has emerged in the discussion. One view is polycentrism, positing that there are many local governments in a metropolitan area, that each local government in a metropolitan area has a differing tax/goods package, and that residents choose to live in the local government with the tax/goods package that most matches their personal preferences. Another is the monocentric view that metropolitan society as a whole maximizes its own welfare through a single metropolitan-wide government that therefore is able to give political attention to the social welfare of all individuals in the metropolitan area, including those without ability to pay for even the most fundamental goods that sustain life. A third view is the synercentric view, defined as a voluntarily entered, though possibly legally binding, networked system of cooperation that uses the self-interests of its partners from governments, firms, nonprofits, charities, citizens, faith-based associations, or locally unique sectors to provide public goods while moving toward a multiple bottom line.

Polycentrism concludes that living well within a metropolitan area is best accomplished with high numerosity of local governments, where many local governments are in market competition to provide different public goods under various prices to citizens in the region. Furthermore, in its pure theoretical expression, this particular metropolitan public economy sorts itself out to find the best public tax/goods package balance independent of any higher government's effort to influence that sorting. This theory has a single bottom line for each local government: delivering the right goods for the least taxes.

The bottom line is a reference to the last line in a corporate financial report, the space in which gross revenues appears and from which is subtracted expenses such as taxes and interest and depreciation, to yield the net profit or net loss. Governments, of course, do not have the objective of maximizing profits, but, according to polycentrists, governments do have the objective of maximizing low taxes to attract individuals to their tax/goods packages. The traditional economic approach is based upon a single bottom line (1BL); synercentrism can include multiple bottom lines (+BL); and other forms of regional governance may have a range in between (1BL, 2BL).[1]

The second school of thought, monocentrism, proposes that metropolitan living flourishes with a numerosity of one, where a metropolitan-wide government monopolizes public goods production for the benefit of the region's citizens. Within this monocentric view, there is centralized direction by one large metropolitan-wide government, one with the ability to affect the distribution of public goods, that is, to create that very policy interference rejected above. It is a more interventionist view, as Dennis Mueller instructs, "Just as the individual chooses bundles of commodities to maximize his utility, society must choose an allocation of commodities across individuals to maximize its welfare" (Mueller 2003, 582). Lacking competition, monocentric governments do not have the objective of maximizing low taxes to attract individuals to their tax/goods packages, because they are the only tax/goods package available, a situation where, in the extreme, the zero bottom line (0BL) applies.

A loggerhead of trends is engulfing local governments, pushing them into a new era where the third school, synercentrism, is emerging. This new era of partnership governance, or synercentrism, has a public economy model simultaneously evolving where scholars are developing supporting theoretical arguments (Feiock 2007; Goldsmith and Eggers 2004; Kettl 2002). Governing is no longer a domain occupied solely by governments. The nation's shift from reliance on governments as the sole deliverers of public goods to a system of partnership governance arises from ten trends that were in place at the turn into the twenty-first century, and that are rearranging the process of government (see Table 3.1). This new view of partnership regional governance proposes that metropolitan provision of public goods is best accomplished within a metropolitan area through the intersectoral cooperation of government, industry, nonprofit, charity, and locally unique sectors, and also individual residents or households, and to use sectoral self-interests to achieve these collective partnerships. An initial inventory of regional partnership organizations was completed in 1999 (Atkins, John, and Thangavelu).

Stephen Goldsmith and William Eggers explain why this shift from government to governance has occurred: "Government alone, for example, cannot thwart cyber attacks on telephone systems, power grids, financial systems, dams, municipal water systems, and the rest of our nation's critical infrastructure. Why? The private sector owns between 85 and 90 percent of the infrastructure. Recognizing this, the federal government has formed several

Table 3.1

Worldwide Twenty-First-Century Trends That Underlie Synercentrism

Nonprofit delivery and privatization of services

Multiple agencies and governments providing integrated services

Instant remote multiorganization communication and collaboration

Sophisticated consumers demanding high-quality public goods

Globalization of information

Globalization of economy

Public opinion influence on a mass scale

Diffusion of authority

Global environmentalism

National government distracted from domestic issues

Sources: Goldsmith and Eggers (2004), author.

multisectoral networks to coordinate cyber-security efforts" (Goldsmith and Eggers 2004, 9).

Of the ten trends in Table 3.1, Goldsmith and Eggers posit four trends that have led to "governance by network." These are: third-party government, meaning usage of private firms and nonprofit organizations to deliver services; joined-up government, meaning multiple agencies or multiple governments providing an integrated service; the digital revolution, meaning the ability of organizations to collaborate remotely with external partners in real time; and consumer demand, meaning increased citizen demands for more control over their own lives and more choice and variety in their governmental services to match the customized service provision that technology has spawned in the private sector. Two additional trends, globalization both of information and of the economy, have spurred another: millions of individuals who are impacting public opinion through postings of news and opinions on blogs and on Web sites, and, in turn, affecting public policies. These latter three trends contribute to another, diffusion of authority. The ninth trend is worldwide environmentalism. Global environmentalism, coupled with the earlier-mentioned economic globalization and mass public opinion trends, has ignited efforts within corporations and governments for a green bottom line. This translates into a double bottom line (2BL) or a triple bottom line (3BL), involving financial, social, and environmental net gains or net losses for business *or* municipal corporations, topics we will return to later in the chapter. Corporate social responsibility is an earlier version of this notion of a double bottom line. A tenth, concluding trend is a national government absorbed in wars overseas, less able to assist its domestic partners—the state and local governments.

Partnership regional governance is given the name synercentrism in this chapter, after the Greek word *syn,* which means "together" and *ergos* for "work," thus *syn + ergos,* for working together. Clarification of one more term is necessary before we proceed to the three schools of thought. Two other terms important to the discussion—fiscal disparity and fiscal capacity—already have been explained. A third is public goods.

Public goods are benefits jointly available to all members of a community. These include public services and public amenities. In popular usage, public goods most often are called public services. For the sake of clarity, the terminology of public goods is the adopted terminology throughout this chapter. It is an inclusive term that includes public services, public amenities, and public goods. Public services as a term is left unchanged in any quotes included within the chapter.

Public goods are distinguished from private goods in that all consumers can share in them without reducing any other individual's usage, and not, as the language may seem to suggest, by the fact that they are delivered by the public sector. Aaron Wildavsky argues "that the distinction between public and private goods is socially constructed. That is, *public goods* do not have characteristics that rule out private allocation. *Rather, they are public because and only because society chooses to put the goods in the public sector instead of the private sector*" (1998, 1).

Other terms that are used throughout this chapter—polycentrism, monocentrism, and synercentrism are often given different names by other researchers. Polycentrism popularly is called fragmentation or fractionization or complexity of governments within a metropolitan area. Monocentrism has as substitutable words amalgamation, monopolization, reformism, consolidation, aggregation, metropolitanism, and regionalism. What is meant in this chapter by synercentrism elsewhere has been called the networked polycentric megacity region, partnership governance, nestedness, governance by network, the complex network region, or new regionalism. However, in this chapter the terms of regional public economy, local public economy, and metropolitan public economy are used interchangeably.

Competition-Based Provision of Metropolitan Public Goods

Public finance economists were first to develop a formal and testable theory that describes how a metropolitan public economy functions, giving them the opportunity to establish the first rules and assumptions that guided the early theoretical discussions of metropolitan public economies. To date, countervailing approaches, including the monocentric approach, have not been as well grounded in a testable theoretical model as the polycentric approach. This polycentric approach also has been known as public choice theory, social choice theory, and as a subset of rational choice theory.

These pioneering urban finance theories, beginning with Charles Tiebout's account in 1956, define a metropolitan public economy through a private market rationale that specifies that the public economy is a marketplace among local governments, where each government is a producer of public goods provided at a cost to citizens. Each local government produces its own differentiated bundle of public goods financed by its own mix of taxes and fees; additionally the private market may generate more public goods. Each household in a region, based upon its ability to pay, then shops from among those bundles of public goods priced by the jurisdictions to find an affordable mix of taxes and fees that supplies the bundle of public goods it wants. Households, making their locational decisions, then efficiently sort across a metropolitan area to reside in the jurisdictions where public goods match their preferences at a price they can afford, that is, their ability to pay. Households have to balance preferences to their ability to pay. "The result is an equilibrium with individuals distributed among communities on the basis of public service demands, with each individual obtaining his own desired public service-tax bundle" (Rubinfeld 1987, 574).

The market is allocatively efficient when its households are matched to their preferred public goods at the price they can afford; in short, the right public goods for the right households at the right price. In theory, these markets practice productive efficiency because their public goods bundles are being produced at the lowest possible unit cost to a household. The corrective influences of the market approach, some political economists argue, make local governments in a polycentric metropolitan area more attentive to expenditures to maintain their individual governmental financial bottom line (1BL).

Local governments are the purveyors of public goods, but they may choose to provide public goods directly or through third-party provision by the private or nonprofit sector. For some public goods, such as prisons, government outsourcing to third-party vendors has become more prevalent in the United States, a trend that is transforming the public sector from a service provider to a service facilitator. The market-based approaches are creating a more differentiated public economy through contracts between government agencies, commercialization, public–private partnerships, outsourcing, concession arrangements, and privatization (Goldsmith and Eggers 2004, 10–11). Likewise, an individual household always has the additional option to select public goods through the private market, for example, religious schooling, or to provide them within its own household, as with home-schooling, although government maintains control over the delivery through promulgation of minimum standards and subsequent oversight. The end result of this process is household selection from an array of differing public tax/goods packages to maintain or upgrade the household's quality of life.

Alan Campbell explains this market concept as applied to the public sector, defining "maximum efficiency as occurring when each individual allocates his income between public and private goods according to his relative preference for these goods and their relative price. . . . Carried to its logical extreme, maximum efficiency in the no-externality case may be obtained when there is one local government for every different set of public-private preferences, i.e., for every person. Everyman a King" (Campbell 1976, 560). Probing further, efficiency arises for two reasons, both because "public goods are provided at minimum average cost and because each individual resides in a jurisdiction in which his demand is exactly satisfied" (Rubinfeld 1987, 574).

Polycentrists note that few consolidated metropolitan governments have materialized; citizens create new local governments based on rational choice, and metropolitan areas remain segregated, even those that have instituted consolidation-style governments (Rusk 1993, 35). In that they recognize that individuals will choose differently from among the public goods' bundles of local governments, polycentrists have redirected public policy design. Polycentrists have provided for theoretical inclusion of self-interest as a legitimate, nonstigmatized public policy driver, and the market-derived bottom line as a measure of success. This approach gained popular expression through the reinventing-government movement, initiated during the 1980s, thus "turning citizens into customers and making the customer's—not the bureaucracy's—needs the goal of government agencies" (Kettl 2002, 69).

Monopoly-Based Provision of Metropolitan Public Goods

The countervailing response to decentralization of public goods provision by the many competing local governments in a metropolitan area through a market approach is a monopolistic provision of goods by a single metropolitan-wide government. In this example, the public economy has a single government as the sole provider of public goods in the metropolitan area. Decisions about the production and distribution of public goods in the metropolitan area are made by elected representatives and government employees.

For a different set of political economists and policymakers, metropolitan-wide government provision of public goods is preferred to the polycentric approach. These theorists contend that monocentric government provision excels at distributive efficiency, externality reduction, and production cost savings, topics we will return to shortly. Because the public economy is a monopoly and exerts control over the distribution of public goods, it is able to direct public goods to whomever it chooses. Dependent upon legal constraints created by the government or its citizens, the metropolitan-wide government can choose to direct public goods to those who are most needy or to those who are the elite or to those who are in public office, or to any combination of households that monocentric government chooses. A poor choice on public goods dispensation, in the view of the majority electorate, however, can result in removal of political leaders from office. Ronald Oakerson explains that, "Under monocentric government citizens cannot choose their preferential bundle of public goods; and their option for change becomes election of a new government rather than exit. In turn, the lack of direct equivalence of differentiated public goods to a slate of elected officials reduces political accountability and the ease of ousting incumbents from office. Some suggest referendum usage as a mechanism to increase accountability" (Parks and Oakerson 2000, 176).

A large jurisdiction encompassing an entire metropolitan area, monocentrists contend, permits the local public economy to handle important functions of production cost savings, equitable redistribution, and externalities. The literature of the 1950s and 1960s was rich with proponents of large metropolitan governments (Bollens 1956, 132–36; Committee on Economic Development 1966, 17; Wood 1958, 232–41), though no pure theory emerged.

Sometimes residents of communities are able to receive benefits from neighboring communities without paying for the costs. They pay to receive the public goods of their own jurisdiction, but they also use the public goods of neighboring jurisdictions for free, a behavior called free-riding. Sometimes residents of jurisdictions where "what is, is good" as William Neenan (1968, 1970) notes, will support the continuance of this status quo and their free-riding behavior.

Polycentric metropolitan areas exhibit this condition. One solution to this problem is to sufficiently enlarge the local jurisdiction's boundaries so that all users of a particular public good live within the jurisdiction's boundaries. With some public goods, creation of a metropolitan-wide government would eliminate these externalities.

Few local governments are congruent to their metropolitan public or private economy. Thus public goods produced by a local government are not always contained within its boundaries nor used solely by its citizens. Barnes and Ledebur assert, "In the United States, the central problem is to overcome the lack of alignment between government and economics at the local level" (Barnes and Ledebur 1998, 142). Calthorpe and Fulton describe as "spatial suicide" "the manner in which many American metropolitan areas choose to

tear themselves apart rather than to adapt to the idea of an economic region."
They continue saying, "the mismatch between regional economic reality
and political fragmentation often leads to such severe social and economic
inequality across a region that it cannot function well either as an economic
unit or as a social unit" (Calthorpe and Fulton 2001, 21). David Rusk argues
that "separate but equal" cannot work, that ghettos and barrios create and
perpetuate an urban underclass, and that fragmented metropolitan areas facilitate the perpetuation of an urban underclass, necessitating metropolitan-wide
government (Rusk 1993, 121).

An externality violates Knut Wicksellian principles of egalitarian allocation of public sector preferences, according to Neenan, in that it "champions
a community which at any moment enjoys a welfare gain from a particular
constitutional provision, even though other communities may be suffering an
ongoing loss from it" (Neenan 1968, 170). Individuals with a relative wealth
advantage from this arrangement will continue to maintain the status quo, or
as earlier mentioned, Neenan's notion of "what is, is good."

Network-Based Provision of Metropolitan Public Goods

We have already reviewed the competitive or market-based polycentric form
of government system that favors the single bottom line, and monocentric
governments to which some ascribe a zero bottom line. Now we examine
synercentrism, or partnership governance, a system that meshes fiscal
proficiency with social welfare considerations through acquiescence to the
self-interests of the participating sectors. It is a form that is emerging as an
adaptation to the ten worldwide trends of the twenty-first century broached
earlier in the chapter.

There are three features that distinguish the monocentric, polycentric, and
synercentric governance systems from one another. The first is the number
and type of stakeholders, the second is the number and type of bottom-line
success measures, and the third is the motivation of the stakeholders (see
Table 3.2).

Stakeholders might be partners from governments, firms, nonprofits, charities, citizens, faith-based associations, or locally unique sectors to provide
public goods while moving toward a multiple bottom line. The bottom lines
might be, in addition to financial solvency, ones of social equity, environmental responsibility, and, recently, national security. "We are crossing new
bridges, connecting to the market, to the public sector, to people who think
about planning in ways we haven't before," according to Angela Glover
Blackwell. "It allows us to have a big conversation" (Pastor, Benner, and
Rosner 2006, 11).

Table 3.2

Comparison of Pure Forms of Three Governance Systems

	Monocentric	Polycentric	Synercentric
Number and type of stakeholders	One government	Many governments	Many sectors
Number and type of bottom-line success measures	Social equity	Economic efficiency	Social equity, economic efficiency, environmental reparation
Motivation of the stakeholders	Civic self-interest	Individual self-interest	Sector self-interest

When the goal of social equity is included with the traditional fiscal requirements imposed upon municipal and private corporations, the result is called the double bottom line. Efforts to use the double bottom line are efforts to introduce social welfare concerns into tax/goods packages. The double bottom line adds the goal of a net gain in social performance to the traditional business goal of financial performance. Social performance is taken to mean socially responsible (or irresponsible) business or government practices, for example, in investment, hiring, or workplace culture. By extension, the triple bottom line expands the ledger to include a third line that measures positive and negative environmental performance to compute a bottom line environmental sum (Elkington 1998). Thus the triple bottom line practice calculates financial, social, and environmental net gains or net losses for corporations or governments. A recent volume on regionalism invokes the possibility of a quadruple bottom line (4BL) through the computation of a security bottom line (Mansfield 1997).

Governments and corporations that include multiple bottom line calculations in their annual reports want to hold their organizations accountable to the environmental, social, or fiscal standards shown in their reports. They are introducing a way to annually attempt to measure and track aspects of their community's quality of life preferences.

Just as national governments now have gross domestic product calculations, local governance systems that are practicing 3BL in a metropolitan area would keep a gross regional environmental ledger that put on the books items such as the hidden economic costs of polluted beach closings to metropolitan park fee coffers. The local government functions with a fiscal- and collective-based agenda aligned with the self-interested preferences of its citizens, thus maximizing both efficiency and social welfare (Wolman 1990).

Synercentrism assumes that maximization of local self-interests and advancement of regional interests are not antithetical pursuits. Synercentrism posits that local governments and other sectors that are more advantaged regarding a particular public good will deed through agreements some of their advantage to less-advantaged governments or sectors under monopoly-based approaches or sell it under market-based approaches, so that the status quo, their own self-interest, is protected. The better-off government or sector has determined that, by not providing a satisfactory inducement to the less advantaged government or sector, there will be a change in the commodity that will be detrimental to their interests.

The smoothness of the deeding of some portion of public good from one jurisdiction to another is going to depend on the degree of transaction costs. "Given the transaction costs inherent in crafting voluntary collective agreements," Richard Feiock writes, "it is not surprising that much of the literature assumes governmental solutions such as centralization of authority and consolidation of units necessary for effective action" (Feiock 2007, 58). He posits that many situations exist where the transaction costs will exceed the benefits of cooperation.

The commodities under consideration may be fiscal, as through monopoly-based fiscal equalization mechanisms such as are used to level school district funding to induce better schooling in place, thus reducing migration from poorer-performing districts. They may be carbon-emissions commodities, as in the carbon-emissions cap and trade market-based program, the Regional Greenhouse Gases Initiative in the northeast United States, reviewed later in the chapter.

Scott A. Bollens, through his study of single-purpose regional districts in California, found that the districts acted in a self-interested fashion, but that social equity policies could be linked to those self-interests, observing that "if internal metropolitan divisions are truly self-defeating in an internationally competitive economy, then the introduction of social equity policies alongside infrastructure and physical resource policies within a comprehensive regional government would be consistent with economic self-interest" (Bollens 1997, 120).

Monocentric proponents, such as Ledebur and Barnes, are recognizing the emergence of the usefulness of following self-interests to improve the governance system, adopting one of the key features of synercentrism. They describe a situation where local government managers must understand that the world is a network of globally competitive regions and apply that knowledge "not just to cooperate with some other jurisdiction but also to better to [sic] serve the narrow interest of their [own] jurisdiction. Seeing the world more clearly and correctly and then acting accordingly to serve one's own purposes is the biggest initial payoff of the proposed paradigm shift" (Barnes and Ledebur

1998, 152). Urban scholars such as Scott Bollens conclude, "It is rational for these local officials operating in a regional forum to protect and enhance local interests to the possible detriment of regional goals and interests" (Bollens 1997, 118). Todd Swanstrom observes, "In place of regional governments, they [monocentrists] generally advocate regional governance—informal systems of cooperation between local governments that evolve over time" (Swanstrom 2001, 492).

Synercentrism requires a new imagery depiction of U.S. governance. Theorists in the twentieth century described federalism as resembling a layer cake, a marble cake, and other depictions. The twenty-first century governance system in metropolitan areas is better conceptualized as an emulsion where competitive entities are suspended within and networked through governance. These entities include philanthropic foundations, faith-based organizations, private industry, global internet communities of interest, public-interest organizations, traditional governments, and sectors unique to individual regions. An emulsion is the combination, in suspension, of any two or more liquids that do not ordinarily mix well. An emulsion is what is required for the twenty-first century, the melding of adverse self-interested entities through governance to enable collective action. "In doing their work," writes Donald F. Kettl, "American governments at all levels became increasingly interconnected with private corporations and non-governmental organizations (NGOs) that share in the task of delivering public services" (Kettl 2002, 118).

Examining the Debate on Monocentrism, Polycentrism, and Synercentrism

Critiquing Polycentrism

Charles Tiebout's formal elucidation of the metropolitan public economy caught regionalists' attention in 1956 because of the clarity with which he introduced market competition into the metropolitan public economy, because it proposed that self-interest was the force behind public goods distribution, and because it deemphasized centralized metropolitan polity. It shifted theorists' attentions from the supply-side economies of scale production to the demand-side prices and individual preferences of consumption (Tiebout 1956).

In his abandonment of larger metropolitan-wide government in favor of what he saw as more nimble and numerous smaller governments, Charles Tiebout unsettles both those who seek to implement social equity redistributive policies through metropolitan government, and those who contend that benevolent interests rather than self-interests are what motivate bureaucratic and political behavior. As political economist William Oakland observes, "Public officials cannot be supposed to ignore their own economic self-interests when formulating policy" (Oakland 1987, 530). The discussion of the application of economic models to explanations of political behavior continues today (Friedman 1996).

Tiebout's use of self-interest in individual public goods consumption challenged this common belief. Along with Vincent Ostrom and Robert Warren, Tiebout further developed the theory in 1961, precisely in time to fuel the ideological wars of the 1960s, where consolidation monocentrists went to work on the challengeable aspects of Tiebout's countervailing theory (Ostrom, Tiebout, and Warren 1961). Tiebout builds assumptions that are restrictive into his polycentric theory, just as do other public finance theorists, so as to describe an ideal situation and create pure theory. Others assume a finite number of jurisdictions, or a large number of jurisdictions for each set of preferences, or a limited number of preferences (Oakland 1987; Westhoff 1977). The unrealistic nature of Tiebout's assumptions (examples: individuals have perfect information or household mobility from one jurisdiction to another is costless) and the number of them (nine major ones) (Rubinfeld 1987, 575) means that, while this model describes theoretical metropolitan public sector production and consumption of goods, it has required major theoretical efforts over the past fifty years to increase its predictive power to describe empirical observations within metropolitan area public economies.

The application of Tiebout's theory to real-world regions, where we cannot ignore anomalies to achieve greater theoretical purity, reveals difficulties. A problematic key assumption of Tiebout's for some metropolitan areas is that there will be a sufficient number of local governments and a sufficient number of households in a metropolitan area to provide sorting of like-minded households into like-providing local governments. Some problematic real-world situations include: the imperfect information of households regarding public goods bundles, insufficient information within government about household preferences that leads to misallocation of households, household immobility, insufficient production of public goods, the distortions caused by property tax policies such as circuit breakers or tax limitations, externalities, and heterogeneity within a jurisdiction that distorts efficient choice (Friedman 1996; Ross and Yinger 1999).

Other theorists include competition that creates unexpected additional burdens on public services, transaction costs, erosion of trust between managers and subordinates, and rent seeking (Boyne 1998, 710). Others find more exceptions in Tiebout's theoretical assertions, for example, his assumption that competition will lead to lower public goods costs as households compare local governments' prices for public goods. Another criticism asserts that the structures of local governments do not fit well with the Tiebout assumptions; that is, large central cities and restrictions on mobility due to discrimination, or simply the inconvenience of moving one's household, undermine the relevance of the Tiebout mechanism (Oakland 1987, 529). One critic offered that the Tiebout mechanism contains assumptions so restrictive as to cast doubt on its validity (Oakland 1987, 530).

Discussions about distortions caused by political decisions, once considered extraneous to the Tiebout theory, are emerging in economics, with the realization that the process of providing for public goods will invariably involve distributional impacts, perhaps making economic efficiency of secondary importance in the political decision, and leading for the call to imbed political behavior into normative models of public good supply (Oakland 1987, 533). Nobel laureate James M. Buchanan of the polycentrist school has revised his analysis to acknowledge the importance of politics: "Any modern assessment must do more than lay down criteria for idealized structures that embody either equity or efficiency criteria. The feedbacks between any policy implementation and political behavior must be reckoned within any evaluative judgment" (Buchanan 2001, 1). Todd Swanstrom observes that public choice theorists have called for "second-generation models of rationality" that recognize that human beings are not narrow utility maximizers but can learn the value of norms of reciprocity and trust to overcome dilemmas of rational choice such as the prisoner's dilemma (Swanstrom 2001, 492).

Some in the polycentrist school are acknowledging the larger societal community recognized by monocentrists, "One important lesson of the research program on local public economies is that regionalism must always be complemented by localism, just as localism must always be complemented by regionalism. . . . Indeed, effective regionalism is actually built on effective localism; the history of metropolitan America provides a multitude of examples. Stressing either regionalism or localism to the exclusion of the other betrays the principle of nestedness that is the hallmark of successful metropolitan governance in America" (Parks and Oakerson 2000, 176, 177). Continuing that thought, Parks and Oakerson remark, "The strength of metropolitan governance in America is that it makes a place for both [regionalism and localism]" (169).

The present United States system fosters polycentrism, a fact noted by David Hamilton, writing: "No conclusive proof has been generated on either side. This debate, however, is nothing more than an academic exercise, as the majority of urban areas have chosen the more fragmented system championed by the public choice adherents, rendering moot the argument whether the fragmented or consolidated system is better" (Hamilton 1999, 202). Robert Bish explains that "the recommendations of the reform tradition [of metropolitan-wide government] do not appear consistent with an institutional structure [of polycentrism in the United States] designed to assist individuals to achieve an efficient allocation of scarce resources to meet their preferences" (Bish 1971, 155). Depending upon who is counting, about two dozen out of approximately 360 metropolitan areas have a core city that has consolidated with a county or counties; even still it is a consolidation that rarely encompasses the entire metropolitan area. This amounts to partial consolidation for only 6.7 percent of metropolitan areas.

Another criticism is that polycentric regions are unable to reach collective decisions (Lewis 1996), but polycentrists counter that it is wrong to assume that "whenever there are multiple governments, it is assumed that there is no co-ordination. The implication is that unless someone is in charge, problems will not be resolved and production managed in an efficient, coordinated manner" (Bish 1996, 8). The worst case scenario of failure to have someone in charge is Garrett Hardin's tragedy of the commons, a situation where a common public good is overused to extinction (Hardin 1968). Regional environmental resources, in particular, face this worrisome prospect, though some rational choice proponents will suggest that it can be remedied through the introduction of strict policing, or also through a net tax (Buchanan 2001, 5).

Worrisome as well is that equality of opportunity, a tenet of America's social contract, may be left behind. The polycentric perspective accepts inequities as by-products of the marketplace in action. There is no corrective collective social action, no 2BL or 3BL; simply household actions to shift themselves to another jurisdictional tax/goods package. This sidesteps government's role to represent collective social action.

Those who advocate for metropolitan-wide governments to provide public goods have focused on the value to society of equitable access to public goods and of provision of an adequate standard of living and equal choice for all residents in a metropolitan area. They base claims for adequate provision on Americans' ideas of social contract, which include fairness norms, protection of individual rights, and equality of opportunity, the latter of which does not happen if equitable access to public goods such as education is not provided to all citizens.

In a system of polycentrism at the metropolitan level, there will be some communities of wealth and some that are poor. The poorer communities will have more residents that need more services than those in the wealthier communities; furthermore, the poorer jurisdictions will have a smaller wealth base on which to raise the revenues to care for their populations who will need public services that individuals in wealthier communities are able to acquire on the private market. For a segment of the population, this is unfair, and the fairness with which public goods are provided and financed defines for them societal well-being. Political economist William Neenan believes Americans must place concern for equity before concern for efficiency, asserting "that an explicit equity judgment is required before central city-suburban public sector interactions can be analyzed in terms of efficiency" (Neenan 1968, 167).

Lynch notes that for those residents in the United States, "the principal basis of distribution is the ability to pay, a fact which does not usually offend us, unless it shuts off some basic goods such as political freedom or the resources essential for survival" (Lynch 1990, 225), meaning it falls below an adequacy standard. Because Americans believe that hard work and individual ability lead to personal income in a democratic capitalist society, "the money rule seems just to us" (Lynch 1990, 225). This is an important distinction, Lynch observes, the one between adequate levels of public goods and equal levels of public goods. As Robert Bish observes, "To determine that everyone should consume the same level of public goods would appear to be in conflict with most individuals' preferences" (Bish 1971, 153). Beliefs that hard work and individual ability lead to accumulation of personal income rest upon this assumption.

As with polycentric sorting of households into preferred jurisdictions, businesses choose their location in a metropolitan area. Peter Calthorpe and William Fulton explain that communities, whose political leaders see commercial and industrial development as a net gain and residential development generally as a loss leader, practice fiscal zoning, that is, the tendency to design their community to optimize tax income rather than to create a balanced community. Political leaders shun development of workforce housing and middle-income housing in favor of development of expensive homes, commercial buildings, and industrial facilities, and the latter two then languish because of the glut of such properties on the market (Calthorpe and Fulton 2001, 86). Their solution, examined in a subsequent section, is metropolitan tax-base sharing.

Monocentric adherents have failed to produce a theoretical public finance framework as formal and testable as Tiebout's, as witnessed by the school of thought's failure to generate a standard-bearer theorist. Monocentrism research lacks common threads and rests upon case studies. Because of these factors, monocentrism is less able to test new assumptions and thus to increase the sophistication of the approach.

Critiquing Monocentrism

As with polycentrists, monocentrists also ignore real world behaviors to improve their model. Some real world behaviors that their model minimizes include: government officials who have the same imperfect information problems that beset households, the subsidy of public goods by monocentric government, the short decision horizon for politicians pegged to the next election, distributional distortions introduced by favoritism to interest groups or other politicians, the regulatory capture of a monopoly bureaucracy by its regulated industry, the lack of technical expertise to manage a particular public good, lack of sufficient financial capital to invest in the public goods upgrade, inability to ensure management efficiency in the context of monopoly, other mechanisms studied within political science, public administration, and political economy.

According to the monocentrist view, metropolitan-wide government creates production-cost economies of scale through its centralization of planning and management, whereas polycentrism exhibits diseconomies (Rubinfeld 1987, 638–39). Because the monocentric approach emphasizes the production half of public goods provision, that is, the supply side, it makes sense that metropolitan areas that exhibit this approach will have economic output as a major goal. William Oakland presents this important distinction: "A particular government bureau is often the sole provider of a public good. Because it is in the public sector, however, the bureau's objective is not to maximize profits but to maximize output" (Oakland 1987, 530).

Cost economies inherent in the metropolitan scale of public goods delivery that could translate into lower taxes will be lost if efficiencies of operation are not maintained within the large government. A large local government must achieve, therefore, either of two conditions in order to best reap its inherent economies of scale. It must construct a work environment where the manager of each public good will operate it efficiently despite a monopoly on the good or despite political expediency to do otherwise. Robert Bish asks, "Do managers have an incentive to be efficient?" (Bish 1996, 12). A large local government that cannot devise policy mechanisms for efficiency in the context of monopoly and politics will erode its gains from economies of scale.

Research exists to counter the monocentrists claim of greater efficiency. "The preponderance of the evidence indicates that small local governments (and thus metropolitan areas characterized by fragmentation) are more efficient for labor-intensive services, whereas larger units are more efficient for capital-intensive services (because of economies of scale) and for certain overhead functions. . . . There is general agreement that consolidation has not reduced costs (as predicted by some reform advocates) and, in fact, may have even increased total expenditures" (Altshulter 1999, 106). "The most serious institutional rigidity in metropolitan America, however, is the monopoly power enjoyed by many central city governments. Bringing the benefits of a more highly differentiated local public economy to central cities ought to be a high priority for urban reformers" (Parks and Oakerson 2000, 176).

Critiquing Synercentrism

Synercentrism also has its critics. A comprehensive article by Wayne Norman and Chris MacDonald raises three criticisms of synercentrism. These are the lack of a rigorous definition of the concept of triple bottom line; the lack of a methodology or formula analogous to the corporate income statement bottom line, that is, a net social bottom line; and the necessity of making qualitative distinctions on social or environmental performance.

Unlike proponents of the triple bottom line (3BL), Norman and MacDonald do not believe there will be agreement on what a net social bottom line would look like or what the common measurement units would be, even if it were the case that methodological and measurement progress would enable such a task. They assert the difficulty of locating "the kinds of raw data . . . that will allow for a straightforward subtraction of 'bads' from 'goods' in order to get some kind of net social sum" (Norman and MacDonald 2004, 250). They note that agreement on financial accounting standards is controversial, and say "simply that inherently moralistic social accounting will be significantly more controversial" (Norman and MacDonald 2004, 260).

Norman and MacDonald continue, "Our conclusions are largely critical of this 'paradigm' and its rhetoric. Again, we are supportive of some of the aspirations behind the 3BL movement, but we argue on both conceptual and practical grounds that the language of the 3BL promises more than it can ever deliver" (Norman and MacDonald 2004, 245). They observe that social responsibility indicators "become vague enough that many mainstream executives would not find them terribly controversial (nor, perhaps, terribly useful)" (Norman and MacDonald 2004, 248).

Stephen Goldsmith and William Eggers level this criticism: "If structured poorly, they [private–public shared savings approaches] encourage cost cutting at the expense of service quality, distort behavior, limit the pool of potential vendors, or even bankrupt partners" (Goldsmith and Eggers 2004, 135). Partnership governance, because of the multiple chains of command within multiple agencies, needs to structure accountability and oversight with particular care.

Without rigorous accountability and oversight, synercentric governance systems that privatize will face problems with fiscal efficiency and social welfare. Within governments themselves, accountability and oversight are challenging goals. When government relies, for example, on private sector companies to manage juvenile offenders, then proper screening or training of the criminal justice employees becomes more difficult, and local councils or state legislatures need to ensure that legislation exists to require screening, that processes exist to enable screening and training, and that back-up systems exist to ensure that it happens. Donald Norris notes problems of governance systems such as synercentrism, ten of which he summarizes (Norris 2001, 562–66). These include state political traditions, race and class, and local government financing and tax structure, among others.

Applications of the Models

Experiments in Polycentrism—The Single Bottom Line of Local Governments

The research literature contains many efforts to empirically test Tiebout and his adherents' hypotheses. One of the most well-known research cases analyzed police function in eighty U.S. metropolitan areas, concluding that small- and medium-sized police agencies are more effective in producing direct services (Parks 1985).

A multiyear study of the San Francisco Bay Area's diverse array of transit service deliverers led the researcher to conclude, "Certainly, there is no clear evidence linking operating deficits with existing organizational arrangements and no reason to believe that consolidation would reduce such deficits" (Chisholm 1989, 214). George Boyne looked at existing academic research into competitive provision in nine areas in the United Kingdom, concluding, "All the results suggest that competition is associated with a reduction in expenditure" (Boyne 1998, 701). Some concerns with polycentrism include laxity in professional standards due to privatization, competitiveness that could be counterproductive, and unfair externalities.

A Case Example of Polycentrism—Regional Districts

Regional Districts in British Columbia have features that make them attractive to metropolitan areas in the United States because they do not supplant local governments or compete with them, are voluntary, are fiscally efficient, and work in conditions of polycentrism. Other provinces in Canada have regional districts that are different than in British Columbia and they operate more like metropolitan governments. In British Columbia, public goods are created for the regional level only upon the petition of a local government, and participation is discretionary for local governments. Writes Andrew Sancton, "The fact that the GVRD [Greater Vancouver Regional District] rests somewhere between the old regionalism and the new regionalism is just one of many reasons why it merits more attention from both Americans and Canadians who are concerned with the effective governance of our city-regions" (Sancton 2001, 554).

British Columbia contains twenty-seven regional districts (Ministry of Community Services 2006). Municipalities within them appoint representatives to the regional board, and rural area residents directly vote in their representatives. Thus the regional district is an aggregation of municipalities and rural areas. Regional districts are mostly voluntary organizations that provide public goods only upon the petition of member governments or residents. Their original purpose was planning, but the regional districts lost that function in the mid-1980s and shifted to their current management of bundles of services that are customized to local needs (Brunet-Jailly 2003, 21).

Regional districts face the situation where citizens outside of the requesting municipalities' or rural areas' boundaries could consume a particular public good without paying for it via taxes or fees, a situation economists term free-riding. To overcome this, local municipalities participating in a particular public good establish differential user fees, so citizens of nonparticipating municipalities pay a higher user fee. Regional districts undertake activities only at the request of their municipal members or the public, and extensive instructions exist for establishing that consent. Mutual agreements govern coordination of the public goods delivery among sharing jurisdictions. It is through the mutual agreements overseen by the regional districts that local interests get hammered into regional pacts.

Service delivery boundaries are fully elastic. A public good can be provided by a regional district to part of a municipality or rural area, to a single municipality or rural area, or any arrangement of municipalities and rural areas. Municipalities may provide other public goods and augment the regionally provided ones. Both have authority to contract out public goods provision. This flexible arrangement enables regional districts to adjust the boundary area of each public good to the size that is most optimal for economies of scale and externalities. In any case, "the same elected officials are responsible for the functions regardless of the level at which the activities are provided or produced" (Bish 2002a, 16).

Regional districts are required to match their costs to their revenues for each public good, a responsibility that is encouraged by separately accounting for each public good within the budget, similar to the situation of a special district within the United States. What is different about them, however, compared with U.S. special districts such as solid waste authorities is that regional districts in British Columbia are not the only source in the local government for a particular public good. Local jurisdictions and regional districts offer residents some of the same services, and residents are able to choose whether they want, for example, recycling service provided to them by a regional district or a local government. They may weigh the different prices of the two suppliers' costs against the frequency of pick-up, for example.

Over their forty-year history, having been established in 1965, regional districts have been legislatively amended numerous times. One of their add-on capabilities was to be the locus for municipalities to pool their assets to collectively approach the bond market so as to acquire more favorable borrowing rates for capital projects. Another change came through the decision to treat health care services differently than other public goods. Another problem that has occurred, mentioned earlier, is the internal competition for economic development between governments in polycentric metropolitan areas (Bish 1996, 12).

Provincial and local governments continue to adjust and refine the approach. Concerns have emerged, such as a need for a way to exit both the standard and the customized agreements, or to amend them. Problems with the functioning of mutual agreements arise when cooperating jurisdictions fail to draw up highly customized agreements, and problems ameliorate when agreements are highly detailed to include time limits, renewal provisions, notice provisions for exit, and a process for dispute resolution (Bish 1996, 12; Bish 2002a, 15–16; Bish 2002b, 5, 7). This strengthens the cooperating jurisdictions' coalition, and, under rational choice theory, thus reduces the incentive for a subset of consumers to undertake new collective action to form a coalition (Ross and Yinger 1999, 2020). Another concern is that Canadians do not understand regional districts; therefore an educational campaign should be undertaken (Bish 2002a, 16). Because privatization may reduce citizen input or oversight, questions about the future accountability of these regional districts must be answered if they are to become more prominent regional institutions (Brunet-Jailly 2003, 23).

A Case Example of Polycentrism—Six Metropolitan Areas

In the chapter's introduction, we observed that fiscal disparity is present in polycentric metropolitan areas. Theory suggests that regions with greater polycentrism will have greater jurisdictional disparity potential, though a literature review regarding the differing measurements, dependent variables, and, methodologies used in such studies found that overall conclusions are difficult (Altshuler 1999, 9). This section of the chapter discusses one recent effort to use the Representative Revenue System (RRS) (U.S. Advisory Commission on Intergovernmental Relations 1971) to test fiscal disparity as related to numerosity in six metropolitan areas: Baltimore, Las Vegas, Miami, Milwaukee, Richmond, and San Francisco (Bell et al. 2005). As mentioned in the introduction, very few intrametropolitan fiscal disparity studies have been completed. Usage of these techniques means that differences in capacity across jurisdictions reflect differences in economic circumstances, not differences in tax policies.

Table 3.3

Revenue-Raising Capacity Coefficient of Variation and Revenue-Raising Effort Coefficient of Variation for Six Metropolitan Areas, 2002

Metropolitan area	Revenue-raising capacity coefficient of variation	Revenue-raising effort coefficient of variation
Baltimore	0.690	0.73
Las Vegas	0.180	0.45
Miami	1.003	0.89
Milwaukee	0.770	1.16
Richmond	0.490	0.71
San Francisco	0.580	1.13

At the heart of RRS analysis is fiscal capacity, the potential ability of a local government to raise revenue from its own sources relative to its expenditure needs, that is, measuring equity in financing and equity in distributing public goods (Campbell 1976, 562). The two components of the measurement are local government's expenditure needs and its own-source revenue-raising capacity[2] and effort. Due to the intensive data requirements of RRS, this six-city research to date has examined only the local revenue-raising capacity[3] and effort, and not local expenditure outlays for public goods.

A revenue-raising capacity index was developed that measured each local government's potential revenue-raising ability compared with the average of all local governments in the metropolitan area. Thus, for example, local governments with a revenue-raising capacity index of less than 100 have below-average revenue-raising ability compared with the average of the local governments in their own metropolitan areas, and those with a revenue-raising capacity index greater than 100 have above-average revenue-raising ability. The notes section provides significant detail on the calculation of revenue capacity and its index, and revenue effort and its index, as well as the RRS method.

Our research found moderate support for the hypothesis that more highly fragmented, for example, polycentric, metropolitan areas will exhibit larger disparities in revenue-raising capacity among jurisdictions. A moderate relationship was found between the number of local governments with own-source revenues in a metropolitan area and revenue-raising capacity disparities, as shown in Table 3.3.

The coefficient of variation for revenue-raising capacity and for effort measures the deviation of each jurisdiction's index around the average. Appearance of a smaller coefficient of variation indicates less variation in

Table 3.4

Correlation Coefficients Between Indices of Revenue Capacity and Indices of Revenue Effort for Six Metropolitan Areas, 2002

Metropolitan Area	Correlation coefficient
Baltimore	−0.172
Las Vegas	−0.457
Miami	−0.225
Milwaukee	−0.276
Richmond	−0.466
San Francisco	−0.289

revenue-raising capacity or in revenue-raising effort among the jurisdictions in a metropolitan area. The Las Vegas metropolitan area jurisdictions have the smallest difference in revenue-raising effort with 0.45, and San Francisco with 1.13 and Milwaukee with 1.16 have a strong degree of variation among their jurisdictions in ability to raise revenue (see Table 3.3). Again, Las Vegas has the lowest revenue-raising capacity differential at 0.18, and Miami is highest at 1.003.

In both the instances of the coefficient for revenue-raising capacity and for revenue-raising effort, the Las Vegas metropolitan area had the smallest coefficient of variation, showing a greater equity in revenue-raising capacity and revenue-raising effort among the local jurisdictions in the Las Vegas region. This finding is conditioned in part by its having the fewest number of local governments in its region as compared with the other regions, which gives less opportunity for divergences than, for example, the 114 jurisdictions in Milwaukee comprising this calculation.

The Las Vegas metropolitan area relied least on the property tax, echoing fiscal experts' assertions that reducing property tax reliance promotes jurisdictional fiscal equity. When we generated a correlation coefficient between reliance on the property tax to the coefficient of variation for revenue-raising capacity, it was strongly significant at 0.57. In the Las Vegas metro area, 44 percent of own-source revenues were derived from the property tax, with Milwaukee at the high end with 69 percent, and the other four clustered around 59 percent.

Table 3.4 presents the correlation coefficients between the revenue capacity and revenue effort indices in each metropolitan area. All metropolitan areas show a negative relationship between fiscal capacity and fiscal effort indices. The Richmond and Las Vegas metropolitan areas have stronger inverse relationships between their fiscal capacity and fiscal effort indices, as their correlation coefficients are, respectively, −0.466 and −0.457, meaning the jurisdictions with lower than average revenue capacity are exhibiting a higher degree of revenue effort to raise regionally comparable revenues within these two metropolitan areas. The four remaining metropolitan areas have correlation coefficients that range between –0.172 and –0.289, indicating that the jurisdictions with significantly lower than average revenue capacity are not expressing a higher degree of revenue effort to raise regionally comparable revenues as is found in the Richmond and Las Vegas areas. Either sources other than own-source revenues are being tapped to meet expenditure needs or needs are going unmet due to services reduction within some jurisdictions.

This author hypothesizes that regions where synercentrism is increasing will see reductions in fiscal disparity because the inclusion of many interests in a partnership will create an averaging effect. Before this can be tested, new measurement mechanisms will be required for synercentrism, and such work is in its infancy.

A Case Example of Polycentrism—Three Tax-Base Sharing Programs

A criticism of polycentric metropolitan areas raised earlier in the chapter is their tendency to have greater fiscal disparity than regions with fewer governments. Consequently, some regions have begun to introduce mechanisms to lessen these fiscal disparities, and, in some cases, related social disparities.

The examination found a diversity in the forms adopted, a small-scale implementation, no explicit emphasis on the equity of the programs, and they were commonly stimulated indirectly by federal- or state-level programs "that may or may not be concerned primarily with social equity" (Bollens 2003, 646–47). This section presents formal agreements that establish region-wide tax-base sharing or special district tax-base sharing.

A well-known fiscal disparities example is the Minneapolis-St. Paul region's regional tax-base sharing program. The Fiscal Disparities Act of 1971 enabled metropolitan-wide revenue sharing of a portion of the property tax in the Minneapolis-St. Paul metropolitan area. Forty percent of the growth in value of each jurisdiction's commercial-industrial property acquired after 1971 is contributed to the regional pool, and funds are redistributed based upon inverse tax capacity and population.

The fiscal disparities program reduced property value disparities on a regional level from 50 to 1 to roughly 12 to 1, sharing about 20 percent of the regional taxable property value annually (Orfield 1998, 48). This policy recognizes that a jurisdiction with a low fiscal capacity lacks the ability with its own revenue sources to provide adequate levels of public goods for its residents. Some like the fact that wealth or incomes of residents will not equalize through tax-base sharing, since the wealth transfers are made between local governments rather than individual citizens (Martin and Schmidt 1983, 184).

A few other regions have fiscal tax-base sharing plans, though unlike Minnesota's, voluntarily initiated. One is a four-county region north of Research Triangle Park (RTP) in North Carolina that has completed an agreement for a super-industrial park that will benefit from proximity to RTP and disburse funds back to the four partnering counties through an interlocal agreement regardless of where in the super-industrial park the development occurs (Kerrtarhub 2007). As of February 2007, the project had attracted $6.2 million in grants from government agencies and private foundations, including Golden LEAF, Kerr-Tar Workforce Development Board, N.C. Department of Commerce, U.S. Department of Commerce Economic Development Administration, North Carolina Rural Economic Development Center, N.C. General Assembly, and the N.C. Department of Transportation. Another, established by Montgomery County, Ohio, in 1992, created a voluntary government equity fund that shares among the participating jurisdictions a portion of increased property and income tax revenues collected as a result of new economic development in Montgomery County.

Experiments in Monocentrism—The Zero Bottom Line of Local Government

Monocentric metropolitan areas have advantages that, despite shortcomings, proponents favor, including regional planning, economic competitiveness, equity, and environmentalism, among others (Freie 2005).

In polycentric areas, political leadership arguments for city–county consolidation based on economic competitiveness appeals are more successful than those based on other arguments, according to a comparison by Suzanne Leland and Kurt Thurmaier of twelve city–county consolidation movements, some successful and some not. They determined that the critical elements of a successful consolidation involved civic elites presenting an economic development vision, with the elites arguing the idea that the current political structure could not support the desired economic development, and convincing the public that consolidation was the solution to the economic development problem (Leland and Thurmaier 2005, 487).

The research found that elites who used arguments that emphasized the values of technical efficiency failed, and the arguments that centered around redistributive or equity benefits were also likely to fail. The success of an economic development message as an argument for metropolitan-wide government meshes with metro government's emphasis on the supply side of the public economy.

Research by David Rusk concluded of polycentric metropolitan areas that rivalry among jurisdictions inhibits a region's ability to respond to economic challenges (Rusk 1993, 39). Thus, while fractionalization might be an arrangement that promotes nimble and competitive local governments within a region according to Tiebout, Rusk states that it inhibits the competitiveness of the region as a whole as compared with other regions nationwide. Follow-up research recently completed by Rusk reinvigorates his thesis that elastic cities, Rusk's term for monocentric cities, provide a better economic base than smaller, inelastic cities. He found elasticity scores correlate at 0.86 (adjusted r-square) with Moody's municipal bond ratings (Rusk 2006, 7).

Regression analysis in 2001 by Jerry Paytas with 285 metropolitan areas supports Rusk's observation—polycentric metropolitan areas have a reduced level of metropolitan economic competitiveness (Paytas 2001, 22). British Columbia has instituted a purer polycentric local public choice model than in the United States, and Robert Bish found similar results in Canadian polycentrism in that province. "British Columbia has not shared in North American economic growth during the past decade," Robert Bish concludes, and he encourages the provincial government to institute policies for economic growth (Bish 2002b, 5). Likewise Sean McCarville's research leads to his conclusion, "it is clear that the more fragmented MSAs are less competitive" (McCarville n.d., 5). Finally, Herman L. Boschken found that, among forty-two transit agencies, those in monocentric regions provide a setting that facilitates both organizational and social-program effectiveness (Boschken 2000, 77).

Evidence that the private sector marketplace has accepted the contribution that metropolitan-wide government makes to a region's economic growth comes from Standard and Poor's change in its bond ratings policy. Standard and Poor's gives greater weight and higher bond ratings to those cities where annexation is easy, a governmental feature that enables growing monocentric regions to capture more of the wealth of their metropolitan areas (Rusk 2007).

A Case Example—CharMeck

Monocentric regions have found ways to introduce market-based mechanisms that create fiscal efficiencies. Charlotte, North Carolina, is an example of a functional metropolitan-wide government implementing market-based policies, policies that handle some of the issues related to monopolistic provision of public goods in a large polity. A 1960 annexation doubled the city territory from 32 square miles to 65 square miles. By 1980, it had doubled again to 138 square miles, and as of July 1, 2006, stands at 281 square miles. Charlotte utilizes a planned annexation policy permitted by the state of North Carolina, where annexation favors the core city in a metropolitan area.

Transfers of duplicative functions between the county and the city, so that each uniquely handles a particular activity, have achieved functional consolidation. Taking government efficiency further, in 1993, the city flattened its organization, reducing twenty-six city departments to thirteen and reducing management layers to no more than five—requiring even fewer in smaller departments; and it simultaneously created quality of life benchmarks to assess the progress of city programs toward departmental goals in (now) seventy-three neighborhoods. It advertises its low and uncomplicated municipal/county tax rate (Charlotte Chamber of Commerce 2007). Charlotte operates under city and county professional management with nonpartisan elections. Additionally, North Carolina has committed the state to professional public management through support of professional leadership training and certification programs for elected and public officials at the University of North Carolina–Chapel Hill and through its municipal fiscal oversight agency, the Local Government Commission.

Charlotte innovated within one of its agencies, the Department of Social Services (DSS), typically a hierarchical agency. The administrator of the Mecklenburg County Department of Social Services developed a variety of partnerships to address children and families in poverty. These cooperative ventures brought together business interests, the school system, health care systems, the state, the housing authority, other city departments, the nonprofit community, and the community college to create a partnered, integrated system for human services that works to move people from welfare to work, and to coordinate family safety nets (Jacobsen 2006, 6).

A key component was the establishment of an integrated, case-management–centered, social services information system, launched in the mid-2000s, through which to do coordinated assessment and case management. While the integrated social services information system has been careful to place multiple layers of privacy codes within the system, individuals with authorization are able to view family entries throughout the system. This enables the county to link truancy, arrest records, family employment, and other related family issues, and then to provide multiagency safety nets to fragile families.

Other successful applications emerged. DSS tracked seasonal fluctuations, learning that school district employees without a paycheck over the summer had to enroll in welfare, and worked with the school system. DSS worked with the Housing Authority to do online data matches with them, so they could determine who had jobs among the tenants. This meant the housing authority could adjust rents based on job holders, through accessing the common data base. An added value is that the system automatically figures out which federal program to draw from to do funding coding, selecting potential federal funding sources before moving on to state funding sources.

Stephen Goldsmith and William D. Eggers explain, "In today's interconnected world, where multiple programs interact with multiple levels of government and millions of individuals, [the] rigid, one-size-fits-all approaches
cannot effectively solve complex policy problems such as reducing youth crime
or rebuilding drug-infested communities" (Goldsmith and Eggers 2004, 33).
They describe a scenario where a networked social services delivery center
includes a range of providers from housing to counseling to workforce training
to be "a one-stop portal for myriad providers" (ibid.). While Charlotte is not
a pure metropolitan-wide government, it is close enough to be instructive.

A Case Example—Unigov

Indianapolis is a second monocentric region to have found ways to introduce
market-based mechanisms. Its Unigov has used privatization, contracting out,
and government agency competition with the private sector to address monopoly management problems. Unlike most metropolitan areas in the United
States, where airports are publicly financed and operated, Indianapolis boldly
privatized its airport in 1995, with the winning vendor promising Indianapolis
a guaranteed savings of $2.5 million before the company took its profit, a
goal it has met every year (Goldsmith and Eggers 2004, 134). However, the
terrorist events in the United States on September 11, 2001, have introduced
an unanticipated change with unexpected expenses, complicating the vendor's
contract fulfillment.

Experiments in Synercentrism—Sectoral Double and Triple Bottom Lines

As the global impact of environmental deterioration and economic competition
accelerates, some partnership governance networks are facing citizen pressures to expand local fiscal bottom lines to include social and environmental
net gains or net losses. Because synercentric governance is new and emerging, pure examples at the metropolitan level that include double and triple
bottom lines remain difficult to locate. More economic and environmental
collaborations will appear in the coming years in response to these two
trends. If we relax synercentric requirements, there are examples of double
and triple bottom line efforts. Partnership governance networks are handling
increasingly complicated regional intersectoral agreements. Mechanisms such
as collaborative regional initiatives (CRIs) "build a shared sense of region,
along with a common agenda for action. . . . Ordinary governance practices
emphasize sectoral concerns or localized issues within jurisdictions, but CRIs
bridge sectors and localities" (Innes and Rongerude 2005, 15).

A Case Example—The Chesapeake Bay Region

A multistate effort has married the fiscal bottom line to an environmental bottom line, while bringing in cross-sectoral stakeholders, features that identify the effort as synercentric. The Chesapeake Bay region has created the Regional Greenhouse Gas Initiative (RGGI), with governors of ten northeast and mid-Atlantic states together signing in 2007 a multistate memorandum of understanding (MOU) that pledges them to a regional carbon-emissions cap and trade program, one that uses a market-based approach to achieve the goal of greenhouse gas reductions. Environmental and electricity regulators from the participating states make up the Staff Working Group, counseled by a sounding board of twenty-four stakeholders including representatives from energy generators, trade associations, environmental organizations, academic institutions, multistate organizations, and others (RGGI 2007).

Agreement to the MOU pledges each state to a cap on the carbon dioxide its power plants are permitted to emit. Each state then is free to issue allowances for emissions that are distributed to its power plants and the market. Power plants that do not have enough allowances to cover their emissions have three options. They can reduce their emissions, buy unused allowances from cleaner power plants, or generate more allowances through an emissions offset project. Power plants that have excess allowances can bank them or sell them (RGGI 2005).

A Case Example—The Ministry for the Environment

Of interest is the effort by the Ministry for the Environment in New Zealand. Its 2002 annual report was an effort to quantify the ministry's own impact upon the environment, including annual full-time equivalent usage of electricity, paper products, and other environmental impacts. The ministry also looked at its social and cultural impact, for example, the average length of service of staff, the demographic makeup of staff, and recruitment and training of staff. The report indicates, "It has helped us clarify stakeholder relationships, demonstrate that we understand our own environmental impacts, and start assessment of the impact of our outputs on the government's economic, social and environmental outcomes" (New Zealand 2002a, 6).

Its pilot project, completed the December before, included a report that had the involvement of a number of city councils in New Zealand. The consensus was that 3BL could broaden existing performance measurement: "While many local authorities are already seeking social, economic and environmental outcomes and have some performance measures in these areas, it was felt by some that the majority of existing performance measures were financial"

(New Zealand 2002b, 28). Measurements within the ministry for social performance were sparse. The usefulness and benefit will lie in the skill of the definers. A participant in New Zealand's effort to produce a triple bottom line stated, "Communities are increasingly recognizing the links between the environment, sustainable economic development and the quality of life (health, safety, welfare). This raises expectations for information that links between environmental, economic and social aspects" (New Zealand 2002b, 29).

A Case Example—The Community Capital Investment Initiative

The Bay Area Alliance for Sustainable Communities began in 1997, reaching forty-five members from business, nonprofits, and regional agencies in the San Francisco area. Included in this group was the Bay Area Council, which would go on to establish the Community Capital Investment Initiative. With support from the Irvine Foundation, it began raising millions of dollars from investors for real estate development in disadvantaged neighborhoods. The fund adhered to a double bottom line, where investors received market-rate returns and disadvantaged communities received improvements without triggering gentrification.

A subsequent evaluation of the process found that the partners to the new approach had yet to adapt to the unusualness of the new effort. "Market rate of return seemed too high to the community people, and the business community has needed more help in choosing neighborhood investments than the CC [those in the community on the community council] has been able to offer. Learning has taken place on both sides, however" (Innes and Rongerude 2005, 13). It continues, "It is unique and ambitious in its effort to achieve the double bottom line and do so with cooperative governance from both the community and the business side" (14).

The project summary explains that the initiative was based upon the theory that untapped investment opportunities that could yield market-rate returns existed in disadvantage neighborhoods, thus attracting substantial private capital, and that knowledgeable community members could help investors find those opportunities in exchange for beneficial real estate development within the disadvantaged neighborhoods. It concludes that the adequacy of the theory remains to be determined (Innes and Rongerude 2005, 21).

Summary Lessons

The melding of trends mentioned throughout this chapter has brought into existence a new process for public goods delivery, and it is changing the way that local governments create policies to handle some of the basic challenges of public economies. This new process generates new sorts of approaches for public goods, summarized below.

- The monocentric form can devise and enforce policy mechanisms for efficiency in the context of monopoly and politics so that it will not erode its gains from economies of scale, as has been done by Unigov in Indiana and CharMeck in North Carolina.
- The monocentric form can create accountability by matching its costs to its revenues for each public good, facilitated by separately accounting for each public good within the budget as in Regional Districts in British Columbia.
- The monocentric form can introduce market-based approaches to create a more differentiated public economy through contracts between government agencies, commercialization, public–private partnerships, outsourcing, concession arrangements, and privatization, as Unigov in Indiana has done.
- The polycentric form can introduce regional equity, or regional fairness, into the local public economy through tax-base sharing, as the Twin Cities region in Minnesota and others have done.
- The polycentric form can reduce externalities through systems like Regional Districts in British Columbia that restrict resident usage of regional programs to those who are residents of participating jurisdictions.
- The synercentric form can accommodate numerous and diverse stakeholders, use a market approach, and mesh economic and environmental interests, following the example of the Regional Greenhouse Gases Initiative in the northeast of the United States.
- The modified synercentric form can quantify and attempt to benchmark multiple bottom lines, as with the Ministry of the Environment in New Zealand.
- The synercentric form can utilize a regional investment fund for disadvantaged neighborhoods, following a double bottom line goal as shown by the Community Capital Investment Initiative in the San Francisco area.

Conclusion

Numerous trends are redesigning how governments make policy in the twenty-first century. Local governments use private companies and nonprofit organizations to deliver their public goods to their residents. It may be the case that multiple sectoral partnerships are formed to deliver those goods, and they may deliver them in novel ways. Citizens and governments are able to collaborate externally and instantaneously, and citizens have greater sophistication in their expectations for governmental services, wanting both more control over and more choice in their governmental goods. Globalization of information and of the economy push those expectations up, along with the mass opinions of blogs and Web sites. Worldwide environmentalism creates more local activism, as does the national government's preoccupation overseas, making it less able to assist its domestic partners. This chapter provides a new term called "synercentrism" to capture this concept of partnership governance.

The two traditional views of metropolitan structure are polycentrism and monocentrism. Regions that are polycentric contain many local governments in their metropolitan area, while monocentric regions have single metropolitan-wide governments. Synercentrism is not tied to metropolitan structural form to the degree that polycentrism and monocentrism are.

Synercentrism assumes that local self-interests and advancement of regional interests can occur for the enhancement of both. Synercentrism describes voluntarily entered, though possibly legally binding, networked systems of cooperation that use the self-interests of their partners from governments, firms, nonprofits, charities, citizens, faith-based associations, or locally unique sectors to provide public goods while moving toward a multiple bottom line. The bottom lines might be, in addition to financial solvency, ones of social equity, environmental responsibility, and, recently included, national security. These synercentric approaches use privatization, accountability, contracting out, and competition as some of the features that introduce market mechanisms into governmental goods delivery.

Synercentrism posits that a local government or other sector that is more advantaged regarding a particular public good or fiscal capacity will deed through agreements some of its advantage to less-advantaged governments or sectors, so that its own self-interest is protected. Nobel laureate James Buchanan observes that the individuals in better-off jurisdictions have determined that, were they not to provide a satisfactory inducement to the less advantaged individuals for a particular behavior, there would be a change in the overall public good, which would be detrimental to their parochial interests. They thus purchase the willingness of those less well off to remain where they are (Buchanan 2001, 5). The flip side of this approach also shows up in policymaking, that of the less well-off jurisdiction using policies that would encourage individuals in the more privileged jurisdiction to migrate to the poorer jurisdiction.

This new view of government shifts government into partnership governance for some policymaking and public goods delivery. Governing for the public sector is no longer the sole domain of governments. Governing requires a multisectoral partnership where metropolitan provision of public goods is best accomplished through the intersectoral cooperation of government, industry, nonprofit, charity, residents, and locally unique sectors, and through inclusion of sectoral self-interests to bind these collective partnerships.

Notes

The author appreciates very useful feedback provided by David Brunori, research professor, George Washington Institute of Public Policy, on a draft of this fiscal chapter. Findings and interpretation remain the result of the author's efforts.

1. This notation is attributed to Wayne Norman and Chris MacDonald in "Getting to the Bottom of the 'Triple Bottom Line.'"

2. Local governments as the unit of analysis for the research presented here include municipalities, counties, and school districts. The research utilizes five major local own-source revenue sources utilized or potentially available to local governments: three taxes and two charges. The five revenue sources include: property tax revenues disaggregated into two categories—real property and personal property; personal income tax revenues; total sales tax revenues disaggregated into two subcategories of general sales and total selective sales (which, in turn, includes public utility sales and other selective sales); general user charges revenue with thirteen subcategories; and public utilities charges revenue including the four subcategories of water, gas, electric, and transit. Revenue sources traditionally under state purview, such as corporate income tax, motor fuels tax, death and gift taxes, estate and gift taxes, severance taxes, and occupational and business licenses are excluded.

3. A local government selects one of the tax rates (or user fees) in its metropolitan area that local governments are permitted to levy under state law, records the rate each local government has set for that tax, and computes the metropolitan area's average tax rate on that tax. The local government then uses that average tax rate, rather than its usual habit of applying its own tax rate, to the value of whatever it particularly was taxing, to compute a hypothetical amount of revenue-raising capacity. For example, it would determine—from all the local governments' individual sales tax rates in the metropolitan area—the average sales tax. Then it would apply that average sales tax to its own retail sales gross value—not its own sales tax rate, which it normally uses to collect its actual sales tax revenues—to figure out its hypothetical sales tax revenues. The jurisdiction repeats this for every single local tax in the metropolitan area, adds them together, and gets its own total hypothetical revenue-raising capacity. Continuing this exercise for all individual local governments in the metropolitan area, and dividing each local amount by the number of residents in the jurisdiction creates hypothetical revenue-raising capacity per capita value, which permits comparisons. Multiplying it by 100 creates a revenue-raising capacity index, a measure of each local government's potential revenue-raising ability relative to the average of all local governments in the metropolitan area. A local government that had all its tax rates set higher than its neighboring jurisdictions would generate a lower amount of revenue using the metropolitan average than using its own jurisdictional tax rates to compute its revenues. Thus, local governments with a revenue-raising capacity index of less than 100 have below-average revenue-raising ability compared with the average of the local governments in their own metropolitan areas, and those with a revenue-raising capacity index greater than 100 have above-average revenue-raising ability. The *revenue-raising effort* is the actual per capita collections for total own source revenue. The

revenue-raising effort index is calculated by dividing the actual per capita collections for total own source revenue by its per capita potential collections for each revenue source and multiplying by 100. The second part of fiscal capacity, not undertaken in this six case study example, involves the amount of money a local government expends to deliver its mix of public services. A standard approach to local government cost estimations, as described by Howard Chernick and Andre Reschovsky (2006), uses a regression that accounts for different local government and resident services preferences, then takes the first stage predicted values of services preferences outputs as controls for the second stage, the cost estimation regression.

References

Altshuler, Alan et al., eds. 1999. *Governance and Opportunity in Metropolitan America*. Washington, DC: National Academy Press.

Atkins, Patricia; DeWitt John; and Jennifer Thangavelu. 1999. *Emerging Regional Governance Networks*. Washington, DC: National Academy of Public Administration and National Association of Regional Councils.

Barnes, William R., and Larry C. Ledebur. 1998. *The New Regional Economies: The U.S. Common Market and the Global Economy*. Thousand Oaks, CA: Sage.

Bell, Michael E.; and Lindsay C. Clark with co-authors Joe Cordes and Hal Wolman. 2004. "Intra-Metropolitan Area Fiscal Capacity Disparities and the Property Tax." Cambridge, MA: Lincoln Institute of Land Policy. Working Paper.

Bell, Michael E.; Patricia S. Atkins; Leah B. Curran; Harold Wolman; and Joseph J. Cordes. 2005. "Intrametropolitan Area Revenue Raising Disparities and Equities." Washington, DC: George Washington Institute of Public Policy.

Bish, Robert L. 1971. *The Public Economy of Metropolitan Areas*. Chicago: Markham.

———. 1996. "Amalgamation: Is It the Solution?" Paper prepared for the conference on Coming Revolution in Local Government, Atlantic Institute for Market Studies, Halifax, NS, March 27–29.

———. 2002a. "Accommodating Multiple Boundaries for Local Services: British Columbia's Local Governance System." Paper presented at the Workshop in Political Theory and Policy Analysis, Indiana University, Bloomington, October 21.

———. 2002b. "The Draft Community Charter: Comments." Paper prepared for the Workshop on the Community Charter, Local Government Institute and the School of Public Administration, University of Victoria, Victoria, BC, June 14.

———. 2006–7. "Inter-Municipal Cooperation in British Columbia." *Public Manager* 35 (Winter): 34–39.

Bollens, John C. 1956. *The States and the Metropolitan Problem*. Chicago: Council of State Governments.

Bollens, Scott. 1997. "Fragments of Regionalism: The Limits of Southern California Governance." *Journal of Urban Affairs* 19, no. 1: 105–22.

———. 2003. "In Through the Back Door: Social Equity and Regional Governance." *Housing Policy Debate* 13, no. 4: 631–57.

Boschken, Herman L. 2000. "Urban Spatial Form and Policy Outcomes in Public Agencies." *Urban Affairs Review* 36, no. 1: 61–83.

Boyne, George A. 1998. "Competitive Tendering in Local Government: A Review of Theory and Evidence." *Public Administration* 76 (Winter): 695–712.

Brunet-Jailly, Emmanuel. 2003. "The Municipal Reshuffle: The Canadian Search for an Efficient Model of Local Government: Comparing the Reforms of Alberta, Ontario, and British Columbia." University of Victoria, School of Public Administration, Local Government Institute Working Paper Series. Available at http://web.uvic.ca/padm/cpss/lgi/pdfs/e_brunet_jailly_nov_2003.pdf. Accessed January 2007.

Buchanan, James M. 2001. "Fiscal Equalization Revisited." Speech presented at the Conference on Equalization: Helping Hand or Welfare Trap? Montreal, October 25.

Calthorpe, Peter, and William Fulton. 2001. *The Regional City*. Washington, DC: Island Press.

Campbell, Alan K. 1976. "Approaches to Defining, Measuring, and Achieving Equity in the Public Sector." *Public Administration Review* 35, no. 5: 556–62.

Charlotte Chamber of Commerce. 2007. "Fact Sheet: Prudent and Equitable Taxes." Available at http://www.charlottechamber.com/index.php?src=gendocs&refno=1495&category=taxes_incentives&search=taxes. Accessed May 2007.

Chernick, Howard, and Andre Reschovsky. 2006. "Fiscal Disparities in Selected Metropolitan Areas." Paper presented at the ninety-ninth annual conference on Taxation of the National Tax Association, Boston, MA, November 16–18.

Chisholm, Donald. 1989. *Coordination Without Hierarchy: Informal Structures in Multiorganizational Systems*. Berkeley: University of California Press.

Committee on Economic Development. 1966. *Modernizing Local Government*. New York.

Curran, Leah B. 2005. "Appendix D—Miami, Florida." In Patricia S. Atkins and Leah B. Curran, "Appendices B–G, Intrametropolitan Area Revenue Raising Disparities and the Property Tax." Washington, DC: George Washington Institute of Public Policy, November.

Elkington, John. 1998. *Cannibals with Forks: The Triple Bottom Line of 21st Century Business*. Stony Creek, CT: New Society.

Feiock, Richard C. 2007. "Rational Choice and Regional Governance." *Journal of Urban Affairs* 29, no. 1: 47–63.

Freie, John F. 2005. "The Case for Governmental Consolidation." Report prepared for Syracuse 20/20, September. Available at http://www.syracuse2020.org/LinkClick.aspx?fileticket=AlyA11jgEVo%3d&tabid=77&mid=406. Accessed May 2007.

Friedman, Jeffrey, ed. 1996. *The Rational Choice Controversy: Economic Models of Politics Reconsidered*. New Haven: Yale University Press.

Goldsmith, Stephen, and William D. Eggers. 2004. *Governing by Network: The New Shape of the Public Sector*. Washington, DC: Brookings Institution Press.

Green, Richard K., and Andrew Reschovsky. 1994. "Fiscal Assistance to Municipal Governments." In *Dollars and Sense: Policy Choices and the Wisconsin Budget—Volume III*, ed. Donald A. Nichols, 91–117. Madison: University of Wisconsin.

Hamilton, David. 1999. *Governing Metropolitan Areas: Response to Growth and Change*. New York: Garland.

Hardin, Garrett. 1968. "The Tragedy of the Commons." *Science* 162: 1243–48.

Innes, Judith, and Jane Rongerude. 2005. "Collaborative Regional Initiatives: Civic Entrepreneurs Work to Fill the Governance Gap." Berkeley: Institute of Urban and Regional Development, University of California.

Jacobsen, Richard. 2006. "Looking at Local Policy and Practice in Mecklenburg County from the Early 1990s to Present." Mecklenburg County, Department of Social Services, Powerpoint.

Kerrtarhub. 2007. Available at www.kerrtarhub.org. Accessed April 16.

Kettl, Donald F. 2002. *The Transformation of Governance.* Baltimore: Johns Hopkins University Press.

Ladd, Helen F. 2005. "Fiscal Disparities." In *The Encyclopedia of Taxation and Tax Policy,* 2d ed., ed. Joseph J. Cordes, Robert D. Ebel, and Jane G. Gravelle, 143–45. Washington, DC: Urban Institute Press.

Leland, Suzanne, and Kurt Thurmaier. 2005. "When Efficiency Is Unbelievable: Normative Lessons from 30 Years of City-County Consolidations." *Public Administration Review* 65 (July/August): 475–89.

Lewis, Paul G. 1996. *Shaping Suburbia: How Political Institutions Organize Urban Development.* Pittsburgh: University of Pittsburgh Press.

Lynch, Kevin. 1990. *A Theory of Good City Form.* Cambridge: MIT Press.

Mansfield, Edward D., ed. 1997. *The Political Economy of Regionalism.* New York: Columbia University Press.

Martin, Dolores Tremewan, and James R. Schmidt. 1983. "Expenditure Effects of Metropolitan Tax Base Sharing: A Public Choice Analysis." *Public Choice* 40: 173–86.

McCarville, Sean. N.d. "Metropolitan Fragmentation and Economic Competitiveness: Exploring the Relationship." Paper completed for the Center for Economic Development Working Paper Series, no. 1.

Ministry of Community Services, British Columbia. 2006. "A Primer on Regional Districts in British Columbia." Victoria, BC: British Columbia Ministry of Services.

Mueller, Dennis. 2003. *Public Choice III.* 3d ed. Cambridge: Cambridge University Press.

National Association of Regional Councils. 2000. *State of the Regions 2000: A Baseline for the Century of the Region.* Compiled by Patricia S. Atkins and William R. Dodge. Washington, DC.

Neenan, William B. 1968. *Political Economy of Urban Areas.* Chicago: Markham.

New Zealand Ministry for the Environment. 2002a. *Towards a Triple Bottom Line, A Report on Our Environmental, Economic and Social Performance, Summary Report, Year Ended 30 June.* Wellington (June).

———. 2002b. *Triple Bottom Line Reporting in the Public Sector, Summary of Pilot Group Findings, Summary Version 3 (Local Government Detail Included).* Wellington (December).

Norman, Wayne, and Chris MacDonald. 2004. "Getting to the Bottom of the 'Triple Bottom Line.'" *Business Ethics Quarterly* 14 (April), no. 2: 243–62.

Norris, Donald F. 2001. "Prospects for Regional Governance Under the New Regionalism: Economic Imperatives Versus Political Impediments." *Journal of Urban Affairs* 23, no. 5: 557–71.

Oakland, William H. 1987. "Theory of Public Goods." In *Handbook of Public Economics,* vol. 2, ed. M. Feldstein and A. Auerbach, 485–535. Amsterdam: Elsevier Science Publishers B.V., North-Holland.

Orfield, Myron. 2002. *American Metropolitics: The New Suburban Reality.* Washington, DC: Brookings Institution.

———. 1998. "Portland Metropolitics: A Regional Agenda for Community and Stability." A Report to the Coalition for a Livable Future. Portland, OR: Coalition for a Livable Future. July.

Ostrom, Elinor. 2003. "The Governance of Urban Ecologies: Why Consolidation Is Not a Panacea," University of British Columbia, March. Powerpoint.

Ostrom, Vincent; Charles Tiebout; and Robert Warren. 1961. "The Organization of Government in Metropolitan Areas." *American Political Science Review* 55 (December 1961): 831–42.

Parks, Roger B. 1985. "Metropolitan Structure and Systemic Performance: The Case of Police Service Delivery." In *Policy Implementation in Federal and Unitary States,* ed. K. Hanf and T.A.J. Toonen, 161–91. Dordrecht, Netherlands: Martinus Nijhoff.

Parks, Roger B., and Ronald J. Oakerson. 2000. "Regionalism, Localism, and Metropolitan Governance: Suggestions from the Research Program on Local Public Economies." *State and Local Government Review* 32 (Fall): 169–79.

Pastor, Manuel; Chris Benner; and Rachel Rosner. 2006. "Edging Toward Equity: Creating Shared Opportunity in America's Regions." Santa Cruz: Center for Justice, Tolerance and Community, University of California.

Paytas, Jerry. 2001. "Does Governance Matter? The Dynamics of Metropolitan Governance and Competitiveness." Carnegie Mellon University, Carnegie Mellon Center for Economic Development Working Paper. December. Available at http://www.smartpolicy.org/pdf/governancematter.pdf. Accessed January 2007.

Rafuse, Jr., Robert W., and Laurence R. Marks. 1991. "A Comparative Analysis of Fiscal Capacity, Tax Effort, and Public Spending among Localities in the Chicago Metropolitan Region." Paper prepared for the Regional Partnership. March.

Regional Greenhouse Gas Initiative (RGGI). 2007. "Stakeholder Process." Available at http://www.rggi.org/stakeholder.htm. Accessed September 2007.

———. 2005. "Frequently Asked Questions." Available at http://www.rggi.org/docs/mou_faqs_12_20_05.pdf. Accessed April 2007.

Ross, Stephen, and John Yinger. 1999. "Sorting and Voting: A Review of the Literature on Urban Public Finance." In *Handbook of Regional and Urban Economics,* ed. E.S. Mills and P. Cheshire, 2002–60. Amsterdam: Elsevier Science Publishers B.V., North-Holland.

Rubinfeld, Daniel L. 1987. "The Economics of the Local Public Sector." In *Handbook of Regional and Urban Economics,* ed. E.S. Mills and P. Cheshire, 571–645. Amsterdam: Elsevier Science Publishers B.V., North-Holland.

Rusk, David. 1993. *Cities Without Suburbs.* Washington, DC: Woodrow Wilson Center Press.

———. 2006. "Annexation and the Fiscal Fate of Cities." Brookings Institution, Survey Series, August.

———. 2007. Personal interview with the author, May 13.

———. N.d. Draft of North Carolina Report. Unpublished report for League of North Carolina Municipalities.

Sancton, Andrew. 2001. "Canadian Cities and the New Regionalism." *Journal of Urban Affairs* 23, no. 5: 543–55.

Sjoquist, David L. 1996. "Local Government Fiscal Report." FRP Report no. 96.5 (December). Atlanta: Georgia State University, Andrew Young School of Policy Studies, Fiscal Research Center.

Swanstrom, Todd. 2001. "What We Argue About When We Argue About Regionalism." *Journal of Urban Affairs* 23, no. 5: 479–96.

Tiebout, Charles. 1956. "A Pure Theory of Local Government Expenditures." *Journal of Public Economy* 64 (October): 416–24.

U.S. Advisory Commission on Intergovernmental Relations. 1971. *Measuring the Fiscal Capacity and Effort of State and Local Areas, Information Report,* M-58. Washington, DC: Government Printing Office. March.

Westhoff, Frank. 1977. "Existence of Equilibria in Economies with a Local Public Good." *Journal of Economic Theory* 14: 84–112.

Wildavsky, Aaron B. 1998. *Culture and Social Theory.* Contributors Richard M. Coughlin, Charles Lockhart, and Jesse Malkin. New Brunswick: Transaction Press.

Wolman, Harold. 1990. "Decentralization: What Is It and Why We Should Care." In *Decentralization, Local Governments, and Markets,* ed. Robert J. Bennett, 1–26. Oxford: Clarendon Press.

Wood, Robert C. 1958. *Suburbia: Its People and Their Politics.* Boston: Houghton Mifflin.

4

ALLAN WALLIS

Developing Regional Capacity to Plan Land Use and Infrastructure

Public choice theorists, such as Paul Peterson (1981), hold that since modern market-based societies offer a great range of choice in homes and communities, individual localities operate to produce a quality of life that will attract the businesses and residents they desire. Some of the basic ways they can do this are by organizing the use of their land and by investing public capital to produce a bundle of services that is priced attractively. Allowing local governments and their voters to make these decisions and compete with one another lets the market decide what the good life at a fair price is. Although this is an appealing notion in a democratic society, the principle of the tragedy of the commons (Hardin 1968), where common ownership of a resource results in overuse and loss of the resource, suggests that each community going it alone can result in collective environmental, economic, and social problems relating to land usage that none of them can independently solve or control.

One pressing aspect of the regional land use challenge concerns accommodating growth and territorial expansion. In the quest to find more land and housing at a better price, Americans have been converting agricultural lands and open spaces into urban and exurban uses at an unprecedented rate (Burchell et al. 2002). In many regions, new growth is occurring at half the density of development of just a few decades ago. Even in regions where population is not growing, such as in the old industrial "rustbelt," the conversion of land from agricultural to urban uses is occurring at a rapid pace.[1]

The resulting low density of new development makes efficient and timely provision of regional physical infrastructure difficult and costly. This is especially the case in states and localities where taxpayers have acted to fix or reduce rates and where they have repeatedly rejected capital bond issues while still inviting new growth (Mullins and Wallin 2004). Attempts to get new growth to pay its own costs have been difficult to calculate, no less to implement.[2] Even when physical infrastructure can be paid for, building it in a

92

coordinated and efficient manner is daunting when approval involves multiple jurisdictions that differ regarding what they want for their communities.

Another challenge of regional growth is that it generates the need to accommodate an increasing number of undesirable but essential land uses (so-called LULUs or locally undesirable land uses and NIMBYs for "not in my backyard"). Attempts to site power plants, landfills, sewage treatment facilities, prisons, transit lines, and the like are increasingly met with strong local resistance, except in poorer communities hungry for the potential economic development they might bring. The list of objectionable uses includes affordable or workforce housing, which many communities regard as a land use that fails to pay its own way, but it has also expanded to include opposition to any form of new housing simply because it adds density to a community (Pendall 1999). Most affluent localities use their land use regulations to exclude low- and moderate-income households.[3] As a result, those with more modest incomes must commute from outside the community in order to work there, spending a greater percentage of income to get to work. The lack of affordable housing can ultimately affect a region's economic competitiveness by making it a less desirable place to live.

The cumulative impacts of individual communities making their own land use and associated growth decisions threaten to produce a collectively unsustainable pattern of development. One in which open spaces will disappear, pollution will be increasingly hard to prevent, congestion will become more costly, and space-based social inequities more pronounced. The answer to these challenges would seem to be some form of regional land use planning; but despite decades of attempts to achieve such planning, the challenges seem to be mounting faster than the development and adoption of effective solutions.

Balancing Legitimacy and Authority

By tradition, local government is perceived as the most legitimate level at which to exercise public control over the use of private land.[4] People see this as a credible responsibility for local government. It is at this level that issues regarding what constitutes a nuisance between the uses and development of adjacent lands and structures can be sorted out. It is also at this level that shared aspirations for the future of a community can be defined, for example, determining what lands and resources should be preserved for common use.

Land use challenges at the regional level are inherently supra-local. At that scale, the proscriptive issues relating to nuisance are not between private owners but between local governments, each acting in the interests of their own citizens. One community's pig in a poke may be another community's pig in a parlor. Even more challenging is determination of shared aspirations. What assets should belong to all of the communities of a region and not just enjoyed by one because an asset happens to rest within its jurisdiction? Similarly, what deficits or liabilities should be shared by all and not fall unduly on those communities with the least power to reject them? A region is literally a community of communities, but with only weak traditions regarding the responsibilities and obligations each has to the whole.

The sorting out of these kinds of regional challenges inevitably results in tensions within the intergovernmental system. Growth management scholar John DeGrove observes that "[t]he intergovernmental approach automatically produces a situation of considerable tension between the state, regional, and local levels. . . . The question . . . [is] how much authority should reside at each level, and how that authority should be carried out" (Porter 1985, 169).

Local governments may hold the greatest perceived legitimacy in the exercise of land use planning powers, but their formal authority to plan is granted to them by their states. As Justice John F. Dillion concluded in his 1872 treatise on local government: "Municipal corporations owe their origin to, and derive their powers and rights wholly from the legislature" (Judd and Swanstrom 2006, 38). Fifteen states have mandated this power upon local governments through enabling legislation. Another twenty-five states make land use planning conditionally mandatory, and ten states leave the decision to plan to local communities. All three of these state land use planning devolution approaches make the assumption that local governments are best suited to set a pattern of land use that meets the needs of their citizens (American Planning Association 1999, 10). Nevertheless, when local governments use those powers to thwart state objectives—for example, to preclude the development of affordable housing in their community through zoning restrictions—they may have those powers withdrawn or their decisions overridden.

The federal government does not have the same direct authority over local land use decisions as the states, but it exercises enormous indirect power. It exercises this power through laws regulating specific aspects of the environment such as the quality of air and water, specific aspects of transportation facilities that connect states, ports, and waterways, and specific interest in numerous other built and natural elements. It exercises this power not only to eliminate nuisance, such as pollution, but also to achieve desired goals, such as connecting the nation's urban centers through a system of interstate highways. The federal government also exercises power through the purse, by attaching requirements to the use of federal funds. Consequently, when it is in the federal interest to see the community of communities that comprise a region act as a coordinated whole, it can set that as a condition for funding.

Although the state and federal governments have significant power and authority to direct the development of land use planning and development at the regional level, they typically lack the perceived legitimacy and credibility enjoyed by local government. Consequently, in their exercise of power they are often pressed to demonstrate an overriding interest, for example, that it is in the interests of the economy of a state to have its principal metropolitan region supported by efficient and effective transportation infrastructure even though some local communities object to its location or design. The exercise of state and local authority will also try to work through participatory processes to get local communities to sort out their differences and arrive at a voluntary consensus (Nunn and Rosentraub 1997). Today, in an increasing number of regions, communities and interest groups are coming together of their own accord to address challenges that they have come to regard as regional in scope. In these cases, they have sought grants of power from their states or through interlocal agreements to carry out their plans.

Regardless of whether the impulse to plan regionally comes from the top down or the bottom up, in order to be effective it must ultimately bring the authority and legitimacy to plan together at that regional level. Only then will communities feel that they have maintained control over their quality of life and only then will a region truly be a community of communities.

Waves of Development

In the United States, evolution of the capacity to develop and implement physical plans at the regional level has evolved in waves. Each wave represents a period of heightened activity in land development and associated demand for additional infrastructure. Each wave can be distinguished by a somewhat different focus for capacity building—for example, provision of infrastructure, protection of environment, addressing social equity issues—and each tends to attract distinctly different coalitions based on that focal interest. Although there is usually strong representation of government at multiple levels in each wave, leadership may also emerge from the private as well as the nonprofit sectors.

The first wave of regionalism emerged in the last quarter of the nineteenth century. The population of industrial cities and their manufacturing activities was growing rapidly. During this period cities were largely able to deal with territorial expansion through annexation or the incorporation of smaller municipalities. In effect, city and regional interests were one and the same. This period came to an end as more affluent suburbs lobbied state legislatures to create new barriers against the aggressive and largely unilateral central city expansion.

The second wave of regionalism emerged in the 1920s when cities confronted new and significant resistance to their territorial expansion by affluent suburbs that preferred to maintain control over their own quality of life. New forms of government and governance were developed at the local, state, and federal levels to try to address the increasingly fragmented jurisdictional structure of regions. The Depression followed by World War II delayed implementation of many ideas until the postwar period. During this wave, local planning capacity was greatly advanced through the widespread adoption of zoning, while regional capacity was advanced largely through the creation of service districts and authorities.

A third wave of regionalism developed in the 1960s and 1970s. It was characterized by strong federal efforts to impose regionalism. Initially, the emphasis of federal efforts was on coordination of infrastructure development, but this soon expanded to include concern for environmental protection and a variety of social equity issues. Overlapping the later part of this period was a fourth wave of regionalism led by individual states. Initially, states were interested in environmental protection, but over time focal concerns came to include the efficient and timely provision of infrastructure and, in some states, social equity issues such as affordable housing.

The most recent, fifth, wave of regionalism is characterized by leadership from strong and diverse, locally based coalitions of interest groups. These coalitions bring greater legitimacy to attempts to engage in strategically targeted regional planning. Often the legitimacy and capacity of these coalitions are reinforced by the engagement of local governments. Part of their approach is to develop sufficient support to gain enabling authority from their state governments or through interlocal agreements. However, in this wave there is less emphasis on building government capacity to plan and more on developing multisector, shared regional governance focused on strategic growth issues.

Although these waves are somewhat sequential, each has produced ideas and solutions that have become part of an ongoing set of options for achieving effective physical planning for urban regions. The following sections briefly describe the driving motivations, policy responses, and activities of each wave.

The First Wave: Central City Hegemony

The development and application of mass production technology, first in food processing and then in product assembly, created a tremendous demand for concentrated labor. In the period from 1870 through 1910, the number of jobs in the nation's largest industrial cities increased 7.5 times, with parallel growth in population. Accompanying demands for potable water, the disposal of waste, and the conveyance of people and goods all posed unprecedented technical and fiscal challenges.

Urban growth was typically accommodated by the extension of central city boundaries. This included annexation where parcels of land are brought into the larger adjacent political unit, city/county consolidations (e.g., San Francisco) where a city and a county merge, and agglomerations where a city joins with one or more counties to form a larger confederal union (e.g., New York City formed out of five boroughs or counties). Incorporation into a city meant that new suburbs could receive city services and infrastructure that were typically superior to what suburban municipalities could offer. Central cities, in turn, could achieve greater efficiency and effectiveness in the development of infrastructure. The benefit of this method of expansion was that the city and its immediate region remained one under a single government.

In the early part of this period, suburban life was regarded as inferior to city life in terms of access to services and amenities. However, the development of commuter rail suburbs allowed more affluent households to remove themselves from urban congestion and the working class masses (Jackson 1987). Affluent suburbanites preferred to maintain their autonomy rather than to be incorporated by their central city. One motivation for maintaining such autonomy was to exclude racial and ethnic groups that were perceived as undesirable (Hill 1974). The suburbs found support for the protection of their autonomy from state legislatures who distrusted the growth of political power of cities run by machines supported by immigrant voters. By the end of World War I, the nation's largest cities became surrounded by incorporated suburban municipalities. David Rusk describes the inability of many of these cities to continue their territorial expansion as a loss of "elasticity." As a result, most of these cities actually began losing population (Rusk 1993).

At the height of this wave, central cities exercised both the legitimacy and authority to plan their regions. The principal solution of the first wave— structural integration through city/county consolidation—continues to be pursued today but with rare success.[5] In addition to political resistance, the solution has become obsolete in most major urban areas because their growth has spilled over into multiple counties.

The Second Wave: Fragmentation and Experimentation

Although central cities were increasingly thwarted in absorbing and controlling their regions, the need to bring order to land use development along with the provision of physical infrastructure remained. As a result, the 1920s became a period of experimentation with different approaches to regionalism. One approach was to expand and coordinate the provision of strategic infrastructure by establishing a regional authority or district. A significant example of this is the Port Authority of New York and New Jersey, established through a bi-state compact in 1921. Creation of the authority ended decades of disputes between the two states regarding control of port development. More significantly, a single authority now had responsibility for planning, building, and operating the region's seaports and subsequently its airports. Districts and authorities facilitated development of regional physical infrastructure and associated services without encroaching on local sovereignty over land use decisions (Foster 2001).

During this period methods of local land use control were significantly transformed by the widespread adoption of planning and zoning methods. In 1916, New York City enacted a comprehensive zoning ordinance. By 1921, twenty-two states had acts endorsing some form of zoning. But the result was something of a hodgepodge of approaches raising numerous judicial challenges. Herbert Hoover, then secretary of commerce, observed that "the lack of adequate open spaces, of playgrounds and parks, the congestion of streets, the misery of tenement life and its repercussions upon each new generation, are an untold charge against our American life. Our cities do not produce their full contribution to the sinews of American life and national character. The moral and social issues can only be solved by a new conception of city building" (Knack, Meck, and Stollman 1996, 3).

Hoover formed a commission to survey emerging laws and practices of zoning with the objective of promulgating a national model. The Department of Commerce published the commission's Standard Zoning Enabling Act (SZEA) in 1924. Two years later, the U.S. Supreme Court's ruling in *Euclid v. Ambler* certified the authority of cities, duly enabled by their states, to engage in zoning.

The narrow but clearest foundation for zoning is nuisance law. The concept of nuisance, already well established in common law, holds that one person may not use property to the detriment of a neighboring property owner. What constitutes nuisance is largely relational or contextual. As Justice Sutherland observed in writing the opinion in *Euclid v. Ambler* (1926, 387–88): "A nuisance may merely be the right thing in the wrong place like a pig in the parlor instead of a pig in the pen." The concept of nuisance embedded in the SZEA holds that the most protected use is the single-family development. Even multifamily housing was not to be mixed in this zone. Ideally, each municipality would organize its land use to avoid nuisance caused by incompatible adjacent uses.

Although the model zoning code was not designed to regulate land use regionally, its widespread adoption had some powerful positive and negative effects on regional development. On the positive side, the potential use of large areas of undeveloped land was now assigned specified uses, thereby adding a degree of predictability to the development process. At the same time, nuisance was being interpreted broadly to include social class along with use segregation—an application of zoning that would be successfully challenged in the 1970s. At that time the idea of nuisance would also be redefined to address cases where a land use permitted by one local government could be challenged as a nuisance by adjacent local governments.

Building on earlier recommendations regarding zoning, in 1928 the Department of Commerce published the Standard City Planning Enabling Act (SCPEA). SCPEA called for establishing local planning commissions with responsibility for developing comprehensive plans to guide zoning. It also recommended establishing regional commissions that would be responsible for developing metropolitan-wide land use plans.

Although the regional plan recommendation in SCPEA was largely ignored, what such plans might look like was demonstrated in the eight-volume *Regional Plan for New York City and Its Environs,* published in 1929 by the Regional Plan Association (RPA). As described by the RPA's current executive director, Robert Yaro: "The plan suggested an extensive program of infrastructure investments to enable the region to achieve . . . the 'good life.' . . . It proposed the construction of vast new regional networks of commuter railroads, parks and parkways, bridges and tunnels, and other facilities to accommodate the projected more than doubling of the region's population" (2000, 56). The plan had been largely implemented by the mid-1960s through the entrepreneurial talents of Robert Moses who headed numerous public authorities and commissions (Caro 1974; Lewis 1980).

The RPA's vision of the region was challenged by a rival nonprofit, the Regional Planning Association of America (RPAA). The RPAA's most articulate spokesperson and cofounder, Lewis Mumford, opposed the vision contained in the *Regional Plan* because of its almost singular focus on structuring the region so as to support Manhattan's downtown business district. The RPAA argued for an alternative vision based on an ecologically oriented model in which the relationship of different elements of the region would be brought into a healthy balance with one another and with the natural setting (Luccarelli 1995). The principles behind this model reemerged decades later in approaches to regional planning[6] and design,[7] which most recently include the work of New Urbanists beginning in the 1990s.[8]

By the end of the 1920s, most of the basic approaches to regional land use management and infrastructure development still being employed today had been sketched out. A proscriptive foundation for planning was established through the SZEA, and a prescriptive model was offered by the RPA's plan for New York City. However, the actual implementation of those approaches was delayed by the onset of the Depression followed by World War II. Following the war, interest in regionalism revived. Several regions established authorities that included work on land use and infrastructure. For example, the first publicly supported regional planning commission (the Metropolitan Planning Commission, now the Atlanta Regional Commission) was established in Atlanta in 1947, in part to help coordinate regional land and infrastructure development (Atlanta Regional Commission n.d.).

Federal efforts to promote orderly land use regulation also resumed after the war, most notably through provisions of the Housing Act of 1954 (Kaiser and Goldschalk 1995). Section 701 of that act required local governments to adopt a long-range general plan in order to qualify for federal grants for urban renewal and other programs, and provided funds for the necessary technical work. While such plans offered some perspective on the long-range development expectations of local governments, they did not include any requirements for regional coordination.

By the end of the second wave, a strong technical and legal foundation had been established for land use and city planning. However, most application occurred at the municipal level. The option of providing infrastructure and services through service districts and authorities provided a way of meeting selected regional needs without encroaching on local autonomy, but resulted in increased jurisdictional fragmentation of regions. Finally, more holistic approaches to regional planning were developed that would reappear decades later when their alignment with urgent new regional challenges would give them greater legitimacy.

The Third Wave: Federally Induced Regionalism

In addition to the widespread adoption of zoning and planning during the postwar period, many urban areas began forming voluntary councils of government. These councils met to discuss mutual problems including: development of transportation infrastructure; flood control; water supply; refuse disposal; coordination of police, fire, and other services; and the development or protection of unincorporated land. Establishment of regional governmental coordinating bodies moved from a voluntary to an obligatory basis in the 1960s as the result of several major federal acts associated with transportation and urban redevelopment.

Transportation was the single largest federally funded program affecting urban areas in the 1960s, and as a result transportation legislation played a significant role in focusing attention on regional planning. The Federal-Aid Highway Act of 1962 required that the approval of any project supported by the act be based on a continuing and comprehensive urban transportation plan carried out cooperatively by states and local governments. Significantly, the act called for a planning process that would be carried out at the regional rather than at the municipal level. As implemented the act was used to tie freeway construction to impacts on the areas through which they pass. The act also supported a much higher level of transportation planning.

Regional planning was given further support through passage of the Urban Mass Transportation Act of 1964. The objective of that act was "to encourage the planning and establishment of area wide urban mass transportation systems needed for economical and desirable urban development" (Weiner 1997). Such planning was to include concern for using transportation investment to raise urban standards and enhance aggregate (regional) community values.

Under the Johnson administration, federal interest turned increasingly to the revitalization of central cities, especially those in the industrial Northeast and Midwest, which for decades had been losing jobs and population to their suburbs. Revitalization of these centers was seen as tied to their regions. The Housing and Urban Development Act of 1965 established the U.S. Department of Housing and Urban Development (HUD) with the objective of better coordinating urban programs at the federal level. Section 701 of the Housing Act of 1954 was amended to specify that, for the purposes of comprehensive planning, grants be made to " organizations composed of public officials . . . [who are] representative of the political jurisdictions within a metropolitan area or urban region" (Weiner 1997). The intent of this act was reinforced with passage of federal legislation the following year establishing the Model Cities Program.

With a growing number of federal grant programs directed at urban areas, *coordination* became an increasingly important objective. The Intergovernmental Cooperation Act of 1968 required the establishment of area-wide planning agencies. The effect of that requirement was to transform voluntary councils of government (COGs) into state-mandated agencies with prescribed rather than voluntary membership. In 1969, the Bureau of the Budget issued Circular A-95, titled "Evaluation, Review, and Coordination of Federal Assistance Programs and Projects." A-95 effectively gave COGs a clearinghouse function in reviewing and coordinating federal grants. The requirement for coordinated area-wide planning was subsequently incorporated in other major federal legislation affecting urban areas.

Despite the intent of this and related federal actions to, in the aggregate, achieve substantive regional planning, much of what resulted was procedural. Cities participated in coordinating councils but lobbied state and federal agencies and congressional representatives directly to try to ensure that their priority projects received federal support. Likewise, although transportation planning was to be coordinated with land use planning, transportation investments ended up increasing sprawl and accelerating the depopulation of central cities.[9]

In the late 1960s and early 1970s, environmental concerns became an additional and powerful focus of federal action. The National Environmental Policy Act of 1969 (NEPA) required development of environmental impact statements in connection with projects receiving federal funding. Amendments to the clean air and clean water acts tied transportation investment decisions to a review of environmental impacts. Provisions of NEPA were also effectively used to require social impacts. Social programs ranging from those addressing poverty to the needs of the elderly were also placed under an area-wide coordination requirement. By the end of the 1970s, there were forty-eight federal programs requiring some form of area-wide or regional coordination as a condition of funding, or giving preference to regional organizations within any pool of eligible funding recipients (Atkins and Wilson-Gentry 1992). Many states added their own regional requirements to such reviews.

An important characteristic of the later phase of the third wave was increased citizen participation in planning decisions. Coalitions of neighborhood organizations effectively mobilized to use provisions of federal legislation to halt or significantly alter major transportation and other capital improvement projects (Mohl 2004). The rise of community power gave new voice to groups that had been largely left out of direct and indirect discussions regarding the quality of life in their region. Although community power was used effectively to say "no" to undesirable projects, it raised a new challenge of how to harness that power to formulate aspirational visions for what communities would like their region as a whole to become.

The third wave of regionalism, shaped by federal legislation and fueled by significant funding for planning and capital improvements, took a sudden and significant reversal under the new federalism policies of the Reagan administration (Conlan 1998). Begun under the Nixon administration, the thrust of the new federalism was to "devolve" determination of coordinating responsibilities for most programs to states and, in turn, to localities. In the early 1980s, as funding was reduced or eliminated, the authority of designated coordinating agencies, such as COGs, was likewise reduced. Those agencies were left scrambling to demonstrate their legitimacy to local member governments.

The net effect of federal efforts during the third wave is difficult to assess. While many of its programs supported regional planning and coordination, especially in terms of adding technical analysis capacity, other federal initiatives intentionally or unintentionally resulted in greater regional fragmentation. Notably, the construction of the interstate highway system coupled with the availability of low-interest mortgages accelerated the depopulation of central cities while encouraging the spread of auto-dependent suburban communities. The resulting "sprawl" was first recognized and studied in the mid-1970s (Real Estate Research Corporation 1974).

The Fourth Wave: State Growth Management and Regionalism

Beginning with the first wave, states had supported the development of special purpose districts and authorities to help meet the infrastructure and service needs of metropolitan regions. During the third wave, state support for the formation of such districts strengthened in part to capture federal grants. Many states also passed enabling legislation that would allow regions to establish service districts without additional legislative action through interlocal agreements.

Minnesota has one of the most advanced examples of a state-enabled regional district. The Metropolitan Council of the Twin Cities was created in 1967 to address water pollution in the region's suburban areas resulting from widespread septic systems contamination. The power of the Met Council rests in combining both planning and operating responsibilities for several major services (Keefe 1992). It also administers one of the few regional revenue-sharing programs in the nation. Through its combined powers the council might have provided significant guidance in shaping the region's land use, but, perhaps fearing political backlash, its actions have been more reactive than proactive regarding physical growth.

While states continued to support special district formation during the third wave, their new area of action—constituting a fourth wave of regionalism—focused more broadly on managing growth. Initially, state efforts concentrated on land use development in relation to environmental protection and, in some states (Hawaii, Maryland, New Jersey, and Oregon), on the preservation of agriculture. By the 1980s, their focus expanded to include planning for the efficient and timely provision of physical infrastructure supporting growth. This concern arose in part out of cuts in federal programs that had previously supported capital development. Some states also incorporated social equity concerns in their growth management objectives, most notably in relation to affordable housing.

Adoption of State Growth Management Policies

To date, eleven states have passed growth management acts setting requirements for local government planning.[10] A few states tie local requirements for growth management to specific state goals, but others simply enable a process of multijurisdictional review where new development is likely to produce regional impacts (so-called developments of regional impacts or DRIs). Former

Vermont governor Howard Dean observes: "There is no magic formula that will work for every state. Each state has its own traditions, political structure, and level of tolerance for new forms of governance, and its growth management plans must fit within those confines" (Dean 1996, 141).

The first state to pass growth management requirements was Hawaii, which, in 1961, established four land use districts covering the entire state. Jurisdictions that did not plan would face legal sanctions. Hawaii's state planning act, passed in 1978, was never implemented. In 1970, Vermont passed Act 250, which enables DRI review. Under such reviews, if a local jurisdiction permits a development that would likely have spillover impact on neighboring localities—for example, regional shopping malls—those jurisdictions can review and condition the permit. In effect, DRI review takes the concept of nuisance and expands it to apply to land use decisions made by neighboring governments. Eight states now enable some form of DRI review. In 1988, Vermont greatly expanded its planning requirements with passage of Act 200. That act establishes state goals and provides funding for the voluntary development of local comprehensive plans.

Florida passed its first growth management act in 1972 with a strong emphasis on environmental protection. It soon added other planning requirements including DRI review. In 1985, the state greatly expanded its planning laws with a new emphasis on the provision of infrastructure to accompany growth. The most direct response to this concern was the "concurrency" requirement, which mandates that local governments provide for the adequate and timely development of physical infrastructure (including parks) to meet the needs of new development. Failing to do so could result in a state-imposed moratorium on development in the noncomplying jurisdiction. Although Florida requires the filing and state approval of local growth management plans that are consistent with state and regional plans, the state has no explicit comprehensive plan or goals.

In 1973, Oregon became the fourth state to pass a growth management law. Two innovations in Oregon's approach were establishment of explicit, measurable state goals and a requirement that incorporated cities and the metro-Portland region establish urban growth boundaries. To assure compliance with the law, the state can impose sanctions including the loss of state funds.

In 1985, New Jersey passed a growth management act with emphasis on reducing sprawl and concentrating growth to make more efficient use of infrastructure investments. A centerpiece of New Jersey's approach was the "cross acceptance" process in which all of the municipalities within a county must develop plans that are compatible with one another. Funding to local governments from state agencies was to be based on county certification that the compatibility requirement had been met.

In 1988, Rhode Island expanded its land use planning requirements with passage of the comprehensive Planning and Land Use Regulation Act, which requires that local plans be consistent with state planning guidelines. One year later, Georgia passed a comprehensive planning act that includes, but is not limited to, protecting the environment and building community capacity for growth. Local governments are provided incentives for filing comprehensive plans. Maine passed a Land Use Regulation Act in 1989, which built upon identified state goals. However, the legislature decided to weaken the act by making its planning requirements voluntary.

In the 1990s, three additional states added a growth management requirement. Washington passed growth management legislation (1990) mandating comprehensive planning in the state's fastest growing counties. Plans must be consistent between counties and their cities, and any modifications to zoning must be consistent with the comprehensive plan. The state's most populous counties are required to designate an urban growth area, which effectively serves as a growth boundary because urban-level services (including infrastructure) are not to be provided on the rural side of the boundary. Maryland, in 1992, established policies to guide growth while protecting natural resources including agricultural lands. In 1997, Maryland expanded its planning requirements by directing state funds to areas targeted for development. Tennessee, in 1998, established statewide growth management that basically requires every county to file a comprehensive plan or lose access to state transportation funds.

Other states, such as Utah, promote smart growth land use planning, but without legislatively mandated regulation. Rather the approach is to provide tools and limit incentives (e.g., planning grants and open space acquisition funds) to encourage voluntary planning.

While many states have passed growth management laws, it is far from clear that they have been effective in addressing the challenges of sprawl, especially in their major metropolitan regions.[11] Florida, for example, with one of the nation's strongest and most comprehensive growth management laws, has seen unabated sprawl despite that regulation. Likewise, efforts in Florida to tie the permitting of growth to local government obligations to fund and build the infrastructure necessary to support new development have yielded minimal success as evident in the recent passage of a "pay-as-you-grow" act attempting to address this challenge. Florida's successes have been largely in the area of environmental protection where a bright line has been drawn restricting development. Even in those cases, enforcement of a clear restriction on growth has been significantly reinforced by federal action, as in the case of protecting the Everglades.[12] Among the eleven states with some form of statewide growth management, only a few specifically designate requirements for regional level planning. The most explicit of these are Oregon and Washington with growth boundary requirements for metropolitan regions. The area where state-mandated growth management has been most effective is in environmental protection. The combination of state and federal proscriptions, at first supported by grants but then by unfunded mandates, helped clean the air and water and eliminate the most noxious uses of land uses.

The Undercurrent of Coalition-based Regionalism

Part of the contribution of the fourth wave, as well as the latter half of the third, was increased sophistication in the procedural aspects of planning, particularly with respect to citizen—and more specifically interest group—involvement. States were especially sensitive to this since their efforts to introduce top-down planning requirements seemed to contradict their grants of planning powers to local governments. Citizen involvement, whether invited or self-empowered, formed an increasingly significant undercurrent of activity during the third and fourth waves and subsequently became the foundation for the fifth. Arguably, some of the successes of the fourth wave result from this underlying involvement, which helped provide legitimacy to the planning process.

Among the states, Oregon—especially the Portland region—is regarded as an example of successful growth management. Although Portland's plan might at first appear to be largely top down and state driven—it is one of the few states with explicit planning goals and the only one that seriously benchmarks progress toward achieving them—in fact state authority was used to empower a local planning effort that was already under way. In addition, an existing administrative mechanism, the Metropolitan Services District, was already operating and could be expanded to administer new land planning policies.

Margaret Weir concludes that the factor most significantly accounting for the success of Portland's plan is that it was driven by a local coalition of strong urban, environmental, and agricultural interests that shared a common vision for their region (Weir 2000). The plan also benefited from the powerful and persistent leadership of Governor Tom McCall, who helped articulate that vision and got it enacted. When McCall left the governorship, he cofounded 1000 Friends of Oregon, a citizen group that continues to act as a watchdog guarding the intent of the plan through its ongoing implementation.

As mentioned earlier, a consistent problem faced by efforts to develop the capacity to manage growth and associated land development at the regional scale is the lack of perceived legitimacy. Regional power is seen as diluting local authority, which is the level of government at which most citizens believe land use decisions should be made. Although legitimacy and capacity are greatly increased when regional interests are narrowly focused—such as in

to win legislative approval for a regional government that would protect the environment while also enhancing its economic competitiveness. Although that effort failed by one vote, POS was successful in establishing special districts to preserve open space and protect fragile environments. In 1987, POS merged with the Greenbelt Congress to form the Greenbelt Alliance. With establishment of the alliance a more coherent strategy for addressing open space emerged: the idea of creating a greenbelt defining the Bay Area region. The alliance published a map showing its greenbelt and color coding the open spaces from "protected" to "threatened" thereby indicating where mobilization should be focused.

In 1990, the alliance partnered with the Bay Area Council to conduct Bay Vision 2020. Joe Bodovitz, who staffed the effort, had been the first head of the San Francisco Bay Conservation and Development Commission and was also instrumental in establishing the California Coastal Zone Commission. A principal goal of Bay Vision 2020 was to establish an enhanced regional planning capacity by combining several key regional planning and service authorities. Although the proposal made its way to the legislature, it died along with numerous other growth management bills when the state's economy sank into recession.

By this time the alliance had begun establishing subregional offices, beginning with the South Bay in 1988. The purpose of each office is to advance and preserve that part of the greenbelt that falls within its territory. To date, twenty-one urban growth boundaries have been established in the region, typically through incorporation in municipal or county comprehensive plans (Greenbelt Alliance n.d.). Because the preservation of open space is often seen as operating in cross purpose with affordable housing, the alliance has partnered in affordable housing efforts, endorsing compact housing developments.

The New York metropolitan region has also been pursuing the development of capacity to preserve a belt of open space to contain and define its growth. That work to date has focused on the New Jersey Highlands Coalition.

New Jersey Highlands Coalition

An East Coast counterpart to the Greenbelt Alliance in the Bay Area is the Highlands Coalition working in the northern and western parts of the New York region. The coalition advocates preservation of an open space buffer area that would help to define and contain urban growth. Such a buffer was in part envisioned in 1921 by Benton MacKaye, who proposed an open space system stretching from Georgia north to Maine.

The Highlands Coalition, established in 1988, is a grassroots association comprised of more than ninety local, state, regional, and national citizens' organizations formed to protect the vast Highland landscape covering parts of New Jersey, New York, and Connecticut. The Highlands include more than 200,000 acres of public open space that host 9 million recreation visits yearly. They provide clean drinking water for 12 million metropolitan residents and large stretches of contiguous forest critical to the survival of migratory songbirds.

The towns that encompass the Highlands are likely to grow by more than a quarter of a million people over the next two decades. Accommodating these new residents under current patterns of development could have the result that the Highlands will simply become a more mountainous part of the suburban sprawl north and west of New York City.

Coalition efforts have been based on several strategies. First, it has sought to build a common vision for the future within its constituency. A series of identity maps and the Forest Service assessment are providing the basis for getting conservationists and others to work collectively toward common goals. Second, the coalition has sought to develop initial strategies supported by a nucleus of important stakeholders. For the Highlands, one such strategy is obtaining access to federal land acquisition funding. Finally, the coalition has allowed various strategies to surface as needed. By taking state-level action, New Jersey is leading the charge in regional planning for the Highlands. In New York and Connecticut, where Highlands development is not yet a public issue, coalition members are moving more slowly toward regional solutions.

New Jersey's growth management law directs urban growth to already developed areas. This could help protect the Highlands, but existing communities would still be open to expansion. To help prevent growth that would compromise open space goals, the New Jersey State Planning Office has designated the Highlands as a Special Resource Area, and is now studying how to implement specific planning and implementation strategies to ensure coordination among federal, state, and local policies that protect the region's natural assets. Furthering planning efforts, in 1992, Congress directed the U.S. Forest Service to update the New York and New Jersey Highlands Regional Study, which includes an assessment of the region's natural resources and the projected impacts from urbanization.

The coalition estimates that it will require hundreds of millions of dollars over the next ten years to acquire valuable land. Consequently, a key element in the coalition's strategy has been to win federal funding for land acquisition in the region. In 2004, the coalition won a major victory with passage of the Highlands Conservation Act, which will provide $100 million over ten years for conservation buyouts in the Highlands of New Jersey, New York, Connecticut, and Pennsylvania.

The efforts of both the Greenbelt and Highlands alliances are to preserve open space as a boundary to regional growth. Cities in an increasing number of regions are also concerned with preserving the space that separates them so that they can maintain their distinctive identity while continuing to accommodate new growth. Idaho's Treasure Valley is one example of this type of effort.

Treasure Valley Partnership, Idaho

The Treasure Valley is located in southern Idaho with Boise as its population center. By 1990, rapid population growth was threatening to sprawl out across the Valley blurring the distinctiveness of its communities. In 1997, Mayor Brent Coles of Boise convened a meeting of the Valley's mayors and commissioners of its two counties to share common concerns. A summary of their meeting notes:

> They knew their citizens wanted good recreational opportunities, housing and a quiet, "small-town" feel to their communities. They wanted to provide these without sacrificing the traditional agricultural base that had supported the area for many years. The meeting resulted in the "Treasure Valley Partnership Agreement." As part of the agreement, the elected officials continued to meet monthly, and in 1998 they formalized their Treasure Valley Partnership (TVP) as a 501c(3).
>
> In 1999, TVP received a $510,000 grant from the Federal Highway Administration to develop a shared sense of the Valley's future. "Treasure Valley Futures" is designed to help decision makers from the public, private, and non-profit sectors understand and implement . . . [Valley] goals as well as the goals of local communities. This means that individual communities can decide what their future should look like. A variety of responses, or alternatives, are expected from the grant dependent on existing natural and man-made restrictions, structure of government and zoning ordinance implementation, existing transportation facilities, proposed future land use, proposed future transportation facilities, goals of the citizenry, how each community sees its future, and other relevant factors. (TVP n.d.)

In 2000, members of the TVP signed an agreement confirming their commitment to work toward a set of five common goals. The first of these goals is to "create coherent regional growth and development patterns," which includes joint review of individual comprehensive plans, comparing them against individual growth projections and community goals. Other goals link land use with transportation and open space protection.

The TVP has no legally binding authority; rather, it operates through voluntary consensus. Is such an arrangement sustainable, especially since it depends on who is in office at any particular time? With Brent Coles no longer mayor, and with the Valley's Future Grant spent, the future of the partnership is far from clear. Another test case of the use of voluntary regional growth management is offered by Denver's Mile High Compact.

Denver's Mile High Compact

Although Colorado has weak growth management requirements, in the late 1970s, it looked like a bellwether state for developing such policy (DeGrove 1984). Then governor Richard Lamm had issued an executive order, the Human Settlement Policy, which would prioritize the issuance of state grants based on whether communities had comprehensive growth plans embracing objectives stated in the policy. But Lamm withdrew his order in a showdown with legislative leaders from the opposing party. However, another part of Lamm's effort, a citizen-based initiative called the Front Range Project, remained and provided a foundation for interest groups to meet on a voluntary basis to shape a vision for their region's future.

In the spring of 1982, federal price supports for the development of oil shale and tar sands in the Rocky Mountain West were withdrawn. Practically overnight the energy went out of Colorado's economic boom. For years, new office buildings defining Denver's skyline remained largely vacant see-through towers. Faced with a deep recession, the economic development agencies in the counties comprising the metro area decided to pool their resources and form the Denver Business Network. The network markets the region as a whole to outside corporations looking to relocate or expand. When the network receives a request for proposals, it notifies its members, who are then free to send in competing proposals.

The Denver form of regional "coop-etition" (Lou 2004) has served it well and laid the foundation for similar efforts where collaborations are entered into without setting aside the reality that local jurisdictions continue to have strong incentives to compete with one another. In 1986, the region's mayors agreed to start meeting as a caucus. Although the region's Denver Regional Council of Governments (DRCOG) provides a formal mechanism for regional discussions, the mayors felt that they needed a more informal forum for peer-to-peer discussions of pressing regional issues.

An issue addressed by the caucus in the early 1990s, when growth began anew, was how to contain the region's sprawling land development. In the absence of state policies, managing growth is a community-by-community matter. But as with the case of forming a regional business network, the mayors saw advantages to collectively limiting growth in order to maintain the vitality of existing communities and to provide a basis for more efficient regional infrastructure investment. The caucus agreed that it wanted to explore the establishment of a voluntary regional growth boundary, but it lacked both the means and resources for developing a proposal (Wallis 1999).

Meanwhile, DRCOG was preparing to update its long-range transportation plan. The caucus, whose membership overlaps that of DRCOG, got approval to have the long-range transportation planning process redefined so as to include the development of an urban growth boundary and regional vision. Through a year-long series of public meetings involving a broad set of stakeholders, along with extensive technical analysis of growth trends and alternative growth scenarios, boundaries for the region were identified. The boundaries were based on the projected demand for developable land to the year 2020 and the allocation of that land across the region.

Certification of the boundary proceeded in two phases: first, adoption by the DRCOG board, then approval by individual municipalities and counties. To date over two-thirds of the region's municipalities and counties have adopted the boundaries presented in the Mile High Compact. Adoption typically means that the growth boundary is incorporated in the comprehensive plans of the signatory government. As an incentive to sign and comply with the compact, DRCOG has adopted a policy of allocating federal transportation infrastructure funding based in part on whether a community is a signatory in good standing.

In close connection with the Mile High Compact, DRCOG's *Vision 2020* plan promoted the idea of concentrating mixed use, higher density development along transit corridors. However, when originally proposed, Denver's rail transit system consisted of a single eight-mile line. In 2002, a referendum was defeated that would have supported bonds to expand the system, making it truly regional. However, in 2004, voters reversed themselves, passing a multibillion-dollar bond issue funding the expanded rail transit system. Planned and actual land use around proposed transit stops is already adopting transit-oriented development principles.

Trying to shape a regional agenda is most often associated with a central city and its surrounding hinterlands, but regionalism is also developing in areas with no dominant central city or in areas between central cities that want to establish an identity of their own. An example of this is southeastern Massachusetts.

Southeastern Massachusetts Vision 2020 Project

Southeastern Massachusetts is a region lying south of the metro-Boston area, west of Cape Cod, and north of Providence, Rhode Island. In the late 1990s, the region was experiencing growth at three times the state's rate, generating a wide range of challenges from expansion of development in once-rural areas and small towns to continued decline in the economies of several cities.

In 1997, the Planning for Growth Conference was convened jointly by the nonprofit Wildlands Trust of Southeastern Massachusetts and the region's three planning agencies. The conference resulted in a commitment to develop a vision for the region's future. The project was funded by a state grant, staffed by the three planning councils, but citizen driven. The fifty-person task force met throughout 1998 to find common ground on issues related to growth. In 1999, the process concluded with issuance of the report: *Southeastern Massachusetts: Vision 2020, An Agenda for the Future.* The report's recommendations stressed the importance of maintaining local autonomy over development decisions while working collectively to manage growth through alliances and cooperative ventures

After the report was published, the task force prepared the *New Mayflower Compact* committing signatories to cooperative action to manage growth. This is somewhat similar to the Treasure Valley Partnership agreement but involving many more local governments. Representatives of forty of the fifty-one participating towns and cities have signed the compact. The group developed proposals for designating "targeted investment" and "targeted protection" areas, sponsored additional conferences on growth issues, and conducted an extensive outreach and education program throughout the region. Compact members send representatives to special task forces targeting specific issues, such as the proposed widening of Route 3 and the reestablishment of commuter rail service to Fall River and New Bedford.

In early 2002, the task force moved to a new phase, under the name *Vision 2020: A Partnership for Southeastern Massachusetts.* It also adopted a new governing structure consisting of municipal officials working with the three regional agencies, and a new mission statement emphasizing education and advocacy for and with local cities and towns on growth issues. The partnership includes economic development as a key element of its work. In fact, one of the concerns that distinguishes "smart growth" from the earlier idea of "growth management" is a sustainability perspective that works to balance land use with economic development and social equity (Porter 2000).

The Partnership for Southeastern Massachusetts (srpedd.org n.d.) has agreed on five principal objectives:

- Establish a Center for Southeastern Massachusetts to provide outreach, education, technical assistance, and research to support growth management;
- Work to broaden the economic viability of the region's land-based industries;

- Use the legislative process to further Vision 2020 goals, particularly to enact statewide planning legislation, to develop incentives for targeted investments and protection, and to reform the zoning act and municipal revenue-generating powers;
- Develop detailed regional strategies for southeastern Massachusetts as proposed in the "Agenda for the Future"; and
- Assist cities and towns of southeastern Massachusetts to implement the New Mayflower Compact.

The case of southeastern Massachusetts suggests that regional approaches to land use are no longer primarily the concern of metropolitan areas with a defining core city or stewards of fragile rural lands, such as Lake Tahoe or the New Jersey Pinelands. Rather, it focuses on organizing what might be called the *between region,* a rapidly urbanized area that is working to maintain its identity and preserve its quality of life through collaboration.

Creation of the Cape Cod Commission located adjacent to southeastern Massachusetts offers another example of a collaboration of local governments and interests giving rise to a collective vision for that region. In that case, however, environmental concerns (water pollution from human waste) were a key driver. A similar example is offered in Santa Ana, California, a region brought together by concern for its watershed.

Cape Cod Commission

Cape Cod is a hook of land jutting out into the Atlantic. Its towns date back to colonial America. Armando Carbonell, first executive director of the Cape Cod Commission, and Dan Hamilton describe Cape politics as "marked by hundred of years of rugged individualism and often parochial town interests. . . . Yet that history has been recently capped by two exciting decades during which growth pressures and increasing awareness of groundwater issues, among other concerns, gave birth to a regionalist ethic that finally manifested itself in the creation of the Cape Cod Commission (1992, 148)."

The prime motive for beginning to think and act regionally on the Cape was a rate of growth that threatened water quality along with the local quality of life. Between 1980 and 1990, the Cape's population increased by 26 percent. The region's image of quaint colonial towns nestled near sea or bay was being undermined by new development. Since the Cape's communities are wholly dependent on groundwater pumped from the underlying aquifer, more people meant more pumping and the threat of saltwater incursion. The disposal of waste could also threaten both underground and surface water quality.

The federal Clean Water Act provided some funds to assess current and potential impacts of population growth on water quality and to educate officials and residents about the consequences of development. This assessment was conducted under the auspices of the Cape Cod Planning and Economic Development Commission (CCPEDC), an agency of Barnstable County, which covers the entire cape. In 1985, CCPEDC received support from several of the cape's private businesses to support an ambitious visioning and planning process called Prospect: Cape Cod.

Prospect: Cape Cod divided its work into task forces, one for each of three critical issues: the economy, the environment, and local institutions. Each task force was asked to consider how the cape should ideally look after another decade of development, and then craft strategies to arrive at that vision. Recommendations from the task forces were distributed and discussed cape-wide, both by elected officials and citizen forums. This process of engagement culminated in a day-long conference designed to arrive at some consensus about actions that should be pursued and implemented by 1992.

The discussion of land use development concerns under Prospect: Cape Cod gave rise to a recommendation for the formation of a new cape-wide planning agency: the Cape Cod Commission. Forming such a commission would require approval by the state legislature, but before the legislature could be approached it was essential to achieve local consensus for the idea. Initial response to the proposal by existing regional entities such as CCPEDC was chilly. Subsequent meetings before each of the town boards produced modifications and greater acceptance, but public opinion seemed to be stronger for the proposal than support from local elected officials.

Fortuitously, the proposal was kept from a slow death-by-process with a suggestion by former U.S. Senator Paul Tsongas that a moratorium on growth be enacted until growth controls could be put in place. As Carbonell and Hamilton (1992, 148) observe, "Tsongas succeeded in creating a sense of urgency about the issue of halting runaway growth." A ballot measure was proposed that would include formation of the commission. Subsequently, state legislators from the cape pulled together to support the proposal. After much local and state-level debate, refinement, and politicking, an act to create a Cape Cod Commission was passed and signed into law in January 1990. What the legislature had done was to enable communities of the cape to vote the commission into existence. This occurred in a special election in March, which garnered 53 percent support.

In its first year of operation the commission drafted a regional policy plan (RPP) to guide growth. In January 2002, a final draft plan was submitted to the Barnstable County Assembly of Delegates. The assembly held a public hearing on the RPP in early March 2002 and voted to approve the plan on

March 20, 2002. The final plan reflects input that the Cape Cod Commission received during a total of twenty-five public meetings, hearings, and workshops (Cape Cod Commission n.d.).

As recently updated, the overall goal of the RPP is to encourage a concentration of growth in downtowns and village centers and to reduce development in outlying areas. The chief mechanism for this is to suspend commission review of projects that would normally have to go through a DRI process if they are located in a designated growth center. Such projects are still subject to local review and permitting.

An innovative visioning process was key to the eventual formulation of the Cape Cod Commission. In fact, visioning has often been utilized in efforts to develop regional capacity in the fifth wave. One of the most ambitious and well-developed of such efforts took place in Utah.

Envision Utah

In 1987, the Coalition for Utah's Future, a nonprofit designed to address Utah's long-term critical issues, was formed. Over two decades, it has tackled numerous challenges including land use issues related to affordable housing, neighborhood and community development, wild lands protection, water, air pollution, and transportation. The approach of the coalition on all issues is "to seek to discover the common points of concern shared by leaders on all sides of the issue" (Envision Utah n.d.).

In 1995, the coalition began a visioning project designed to develop broad consensus around growth and development in the state. That initiative coalesced, in 1997, in the formation of Envision Utah, which functions as a public/private partnership. Members of the partnership include business leaders, developers, utility companies, state and local government, religious leaders, environmentalists, educators, and the media. Although the name suggests a statewide effort, the partnership focuses on growth in the area contained within the Wasatch Valley.

Instead of focusing on the physical structure of the region with elements such as growth boundaries and transit infrastructure, Envision Utah focuses on values. The coalition retained the services of an international marketing firm, Wirthlin International, to conduct research on the values underlying citizens' perception of growth and their quality of life. Wirthlin applied sophisticated marketing analysis techniques to determine what people valued in the region. That analysis showed that people most valued personal safety and security, followed by community enrichment (quality and convenient schools and recreation), and maximizing personal time and lifestyle opportunities. An Urban Land Institute report on regional visioning concludes: "Envision Utah found that regional visioning is about satisfying the market and removing barriers to the desired choices" (Cartwright and Wilbur 2005, 13).

Based on the value preferences revealed by the market survey, Envision Utah developed four scenarios representing realistic alternatives for the region's future. The vast majority of participants in the process favored development that included more transportation choices, more workable neighborhoods, and more parks and open spaces. Robert Grow, founding chair, and Alan Matheson, executive director, of Envision Utah describe the vision, not as a map of where new growth should occur, but as a set of goals and implementation strategies, which include a "toolbox" with model zoning ordinances, development tactics, and demonstration projects. They assert that: "The vision has influenced governmental approval processes in the greater Wasatch area, largely because it is backed by the public and by solid information. Local governments are gradually changing their approach to growth, and a number have reworked their general plans and zoning or- dinances to reflect the regional vision" (Grow and Matheson 2006, 64). The values analysis developed as part of the Envision Utah process provided the basis for successfully marketing a major transit bond issue that will help to support transit-oriented development.

*Coalitions and Regional Civic Infrastructure and
Urban Design*

The characteristic that most clearly distinguishes the fifth wave of regional growth management is the central role played by coalitions and the use of certain tools and methods, such as participatory visioning and voluntary com- pacts. The effectiveness of coalitions significantly reflects the strength of prior working relations among member organizations. Although these relationships are most immediately a reflection of the networking of individuals, the ability to maintain relationships over time and across issues is not dependent on spe- cific individuals but on what could be called the region's *civic infrastructure* (Wallis 1993). The term *infrastructure* is intended to convey something more enduring than a coalition, but somewhat less organized than what political scientists refer to as "urban regimes" (Stone 1989).

A region's civic infrastructure consists of organized interest groups that have a clear stake in their region's development, and that also have the capac- ity to collectively mobilize to formulate a regional agenda or vision and to develop the mechanisms necessary to implement that agenda (Foster 2000; Wallis 1993). While those mechanisms might include a comprehensive plan, more often they consist of narrower strategic initiatives that incrementally advance a single element of the agenda; for example, establishing an authority to build a new airport or developing a mechanism for the transfer of development rights to preserve open space.

Coalitions form out of and retreat back into their region's civic infrastructure. When there is a pressing challenge, a strong regional civic infrastructure can quickly generate a coalition to respond. In a few cases coalitions themselves may formalize (e.g., incorporate as a 501(c)(3), such as the Greenbelt Alliance in the Bay Area), but more typically they work to formalize the power needed to implement a strategic regional action (Porter and Wallis 2002).

Alexis de Tocqueville recognized civic involvement as a basic characteristic of governance in democracy. "Under . . . [democracy's] sway, the grandeur is not in what the public administration does, but what is done without or outside of it. Democracy does not give the people the most skillful government, but it produces what the ablest governments are frequently unable to create; namely, a superabundant force, and an energy which is inseparable from it, and which may, however unfavorable circumstances may be, produce wonders" (de Tocqueville 1956, 110). While the regional level might not have been anticipated by de Tocqueville, his observation helps explain the emergence of the fifth wave. It is still too early to tell if the fifth wave will produce more substantive results than previous efforts, but the case studies described above suggest that it holds promise.

A key element in the formation of regional civic infrastructure is a shared sense of values and a common vision of the desired quality of life. To the extent that regional planning has been a two-dimensional exercise, the vision element of a region has focused significantly on protecting valued natural assets that are strongly and widely associated with regional identity. But a more robust and integral example of a regional vision was offered during the second wave in the form of the *Regional Plan for New York City and Its Environs,* discussed earlier. That plan dealt not only with the location of regional infrastructure, but with the detailed design of neighborhoods and parks. The effect of the plan was to give citizens and decision makers images of the region that could help mobilize action.

That kind of detailed, three-dimensional planning has been renewed during the fifth wave through the efforts of designers and planners who collectively refer to their approach as the "new urbanism," though its roots seem firmly anchored in the regionalism of the 1920s. New Urbanists do not advocate for expanded regional government, rather they see their visions achieving implementation through the work of coalitions of interest (Calthorpe and Fulton 2001). In fact, New Urbanists' proposals have been broadly applied and implemented across the United States, but, rather than at the regional scale, these proposals have been implemented at a project or village scale. The images provided by New Urbanists seem to work well in communicating some of the agendas of regional coalitions in the fifth wave. What is not yet clear is whether their vision for regions can provide a sufficient basis for achieving regions with less sprawl and greater social equity (Downs 1994, 218–27).

Conclusions

Ultimately, if regionalism is to be effective, then regions need to be perceived as places where people see themselves conducting the real business of their daily lives. People already see this at the neighborhood level, and they rightly associate their neighborhood's destiny with local policies, but they are only beginning to appreciate regional ties to their local quality of life. Similarly, a sense of "home" needs to be attached to the regional scale of place, and from that identity a concern for stewardship of place must develop. Without identity and stewardship, calls for regionalism will lack legitimacy and hence capacity (Alliance for Regional Stewardship n.d.).

Capacity must also be supported by the proper application of authority. Authority detached from legitimacy is perceived as an unaccountable exercise of power; that is, accountability in a broader sense than simply having some type of elected representatives making decisions. Rather, it is accountability linked to the concept of stewardship.

With the relationships between capacity, legitimacy, and authority in mind, what lessons can be extracted from the five waves of regionalism? At least three generalizations are evident.

First, when there is an overarching public interest that can only be met at a regional scale, then top-down regionalism mandated at the federal and state levels gains a legitimacy claim over that of local communities. In relation to land use, such interests tend to be associated with shared nuisance, notably in the protection of natural resources such as clean water and air, and the banning or elimination of noxious uses. The remedy is typically proscriptive in nature, such as the strong restrictions associated with destruction of tidal wetland by development. Although there is a small set of such issues, they can develop a large penumbra or categorical creep, which, in turn, invites local-level challenges to legitimacy claims. Clean water is clean water, but how far should the sphere of environmental regulation extend to protect its purity?

Second, when the objective of regional planning is prescriptive— achieving a desired quality of life in its social, economic, and environmental dimensions—then bottom-up regionalism holds the greater claim to legitimacy. Quality of life issues will most immediately be determined at the local level, but creating an effective community of communities in support of local and aggregate objectives will also be perceived as legitimate. If local interests form an effective coalition, then they can make legitimate claims for a grant of authority from the state and even the federal levels. However, they may also choose to aggregate authority wholly at the local level through interlocal agreements or by having a program implemented one community at a time. This type of prescriptive planning may benefit from developing a broad vision, but implementation requires focusing on a narrow strategic objective within the vision.

The first generalization might be likened to drawing a line around a sensitive environmental area to preserve it against encroachment from without, while the second could be likened to drawing a growth boundary around a region to maintain its vitality within. Between these two there is a large middle ground in which much of the identity of a region is shaped. This includes decisions relating to the choice, location, and design of infrastructure—for example, whether a region should design and implement a sustainable energy policy. It also includes decisions relating to development of the collective cultural assets of a region. Addressing such decisions suggests a third generalization: more holistic regional policies must simultaneously involve top-down and bottom-up processes or what David Rusk (1999) refers to in the context of social equity planning as the "inside game/outside game." The fifth wave is characterized by the formation and action of precisely the types of coalitions needed to claim the middle ground: coalitions that work by drawing legitimacy from below while attracting authority from above.

Given these generalizations, is progress being made in developing sufficient and effective capacity to plan the regional environment? The answer is a qualified yes. Yes, because there is more widespread engagement across sectors in regional issues. Yes, because there is a far more sophisticated understanding of the interrelationship of issues. Yes, because pressures to think and act regionally are greater than they have ever been, providing stronger incentives to overcome fragmentation. Qualified, because the history of the first four waves suggests that efforts to achieve regionalism end up being stronger on process than substance, and qualified because the impulse of Americans to isolate themselves in lifestyle enclaves has so far proved much stronger than the aspiration to build a shared sense of home from our diverse regional scale of a place.

Notes

1. For example, metropolitan Cleveland has had virtually no population growth since the 1960s, but it now occupies twice the land area (see EcoCity Cleveland n.d.).

2. For example, a 1994 study in Loudon County, Virginia, estimated that a new home would have to sell at $400,000 in order to bring in sufficient property taxes to cover the cost of services provided by the county, but the actual selling price of homes at that time was slightly less than $200,000.

3. A well-known lawsuit successfully challenging such exclusions is the 1983 Mount Laurel II decision in New Jersey (South Burlington County N.A.A.C.P. v. Township of Mount Laurel, 92 NJ).

4. In *Democracy in America,* de Tocqueville (1956) observed that in the United States local government is sovereign.

5. The last city/county merger was in 2000 when Louisville and Jefferson County consolidated. This action took effect in 2003.

6. The ecological approach was brought back into professional practice with the publication in 1971 of *Design With Nature* by Ian McHarg.

7. Kevin Lynch argued for human-scale development in 1981 in his classic, *Theory of Good City Form.*

8. See the Congress for New Urbanism (www.cnu.org), also Peter Calthorpe's *The Next American Metropolis* (1993) and Calthorpe and William Fulton's *The Regional City* (2001).

9. This assessment was aired during discussions regarding the formulation of the Intermodal Surface Transportation Efficiency Act of 1991, notably by Senator Daniel Patrick Moynihan.

10. Calculating the number of states adopting growth management policies is difficult because definitions of what constitutes such policies vary. For example, is the requirement that all local governments plan for growth enough, or must that requirement be attached to enforceable state goals? For a comprehensive review of state growth management policies see DeGrove (2005).

11. Douglas Porter, in a review of state growth management initiatives, concludes that only one state (Oregon) has established a track record in meeting state goals through mandated local planning, and no state has succeeded in establishing a continuing state-level planning process (1992, 204–7).

12. How well current federal efforts to protect and restore the Everglades are faring is analyzed by M. Grunwald (2006).

13. For a discussion and statistics on this topic, see Atkins, John, and Thangavelu (1999).

References

Alliance for Regional Stewardship. N.d. Available at www.regionalstewardship.org (accessed September 12, 2007).

American Planning Association. *Planning Communities for the 21st Century.* 1999. Washington, DC: American Planning Association.

Atkins, Patricia S., and Laura Wilson-Gentry. 1992. "An Etiquette for the 1990s Regional Council." *National Civic Review* (Fall–Winter): 466–87.

Atkins, Patricia; DeWitt John; and Jennifer Thangavelu. 1999. *Emerging Regional Governance Networks.* Washington, DC: National Academy of Public Administration, and National Association of Regional Councils.

Atlanta Regional Commission. N.d. Available at www.atlantaregional.com (accessed September 12, 2007).

Bay Area Council. N.d. "Sixty Years of the Bay Area Council." Available at www.bayareacouncil.org/site/ (accessed September 3, 2007).

Burchell, Robert; George Lowenstein; William R. Dolphin; Catherine C. Galley; Anthony Downs; Samuel Seskin; Katherine G. Still; and Terry Moore. 2002. *Cost of Sprawl—2000.* Washington, DC: National Academy Press.

Calthorpe, Peter. 1993. *The Next American Metropolis.* Princeton, NJ: Princeton
  Architectural Press.
Calthorpe, Peter, and William Fulton. 2001. *The Regional City: Planning for the end
  of sprawl.* Washington, DC: Island Press.
Cape Cod Commission. N.d. "Regional Policy Plan." Available at www.capecodcom-
  mission.org/RPP/home.htm (accessed December 22, 2007).
Carbonell, Armando, and Dan Hamilton. 1992. "Creating a Regional Constituency on
  Cape Cod." In *State and Regional Initiatives for Managing Development: Policy
  Issues and Practical Concerns,* ed. Douglas Porter, 147–56. Washington, DC:
  Urban Land Institute.
Caro, Robert. 1974. *The Power Broker: Robert Moses and the Fall of New York.* New
  York: Knopf.
Cartwright, Suzanne D., and Victoria R. Wilbur. 2005. *Translating a Regional Vision
  into Action.* ULI Community Catalyst Report no. 2. Washington, DC: Urban Land
  Institute.
Congress for New Urbanism. www.cnu.org (accessed December 22, 2007).
Conlan, T. 1998. *From New Federalism to Devolution.* Washington, DC: Brookings
  Institution.
Dean, Howard. 1996. "Growth Management Plans." In *Land Use in America,* ed. Henry
  Diamond, and Patrick Noonan, 135–54. Washington, DC: Island Press.
DeGrove, John M. 1984. *Land, Growth and Politics.* Washington, DC: American
  Planning Association.
———. 2005. *Planning Policy and Politics: Smart Growth and the States.* Cambridge,
  MA: Lincoln Institute of Land Policy.
de Tocqueville, Alexis. 1956. *Democracy in America,* ed. Richard D. Heffner. New
  York: New American Library.
Downs, Anthony. 1994. *New Visions for Metropolitan America.* Washington, DC:
  Brookings Institution.
EcoCity Cleveland. N.d. "Smart Growth: Where Are We Now?" Available at www.
  ecocitycleveland.org/smartgrowth/intro/where_now.html (accessed September
  10, 2007).
Envision Utah. N.d. Available at www.envisionutah.org/cuf-whatis.phtml (accessed
  September 13, 2007).
Euclid v. Ambler Realty Co. 1926. 272 U.S. 365.
Foster, Kathryn. 2000. "Regional Capital." In *Urban-Suburban Interdependencies,*
  ed. Rosalind Greenstein and Wim Wiewel, 83–118. Cambridge, MA: Lincoln
  Institute of Land Policy.
———. 2001. *Regionalism on Purpose.* Cambridge, MA: Lincoln Institute of Land
  Policy.
Fulton, William. 2001. *The Regional City.* Washington, DC: Island Press.
Gerber, Elizabeth R., and Ken Kollman. 2004. "Introduction to Authority Migration:
  Defining an Emerging Research Agenda." *Policy Sciences* (July): 397–400.
Greenbelt Alliance. N.d. Available at www.greenbelt.org/about/history.html (accessed
  September 10, 2007).
Grow, Robert, and Alan Matheson. 2006. "Envision Utah: Laying the Foundation for
  High Quality Development." *Urban Land* (April): 64.
Grunwald, Mark. 2006. *Swamp: The Everglades, Florida, and the Politics of Paradise.*
  New York: Simon and Schuster.
Hardin, Garrett. 1968. "The Tragedy of the Commons." *Science* 162: 1243–48.

Hartman, Chester. 1986. *City for Sale.* Philadelphia: Temple University Press.

Hill, Richard Child. 1974. "Separate and Unequal: Governmental Inequity in the Metropolis." *American Political Science Review* 68, no. 4 (December): 1557–68.

Jackson, Kent T. 1987. *Crabgrass Frontier.* New York: Oxford University Press.

Joint Venture Silicon Valley. N.d. Available at www.jointventure.org (accessed September 8, 2007).

Judd, Dennis, and Todd Swanstrom. 2006. *City Politics: The Political Economy of Urban America.* New York: Pearson.

Kaiser, Edward J., and David R. Goldschalk. 1995. "Twentieth Century Land Use Planning," *Journal of the American Planning Association* 61, no. 3: 365–85.

Keefe, Steve. 1992. "Twin Cities Federalism." In *States and Regional Planning Initiatives for Managing Development,* ed. Douglas Porter, 81–142. Washington, DC: Urban Land Institute.

Knack, Ruth; Stuart Meck; and Israel Stollman. 1996. "The Real Story Behind the Standard Planning and Zoning Acts of the 1920s." *Land Use Law* (February): 3–9.

Lewis, Eugene. 1980. *Public Entrepreneurship: Toward a Theory of Bureaucratic Political Power.* Bloomington: Indiana University Press.

Lou, Yadong. 2004. C*oopetition in International Business.* Copenhagen: Copenhagen Business School Press.

Luccarelli, Mark. 1995. *Lewis Mumford and the Ecological Region.* New York: Guilford Press.

Lynch, Kevin. 1981. *Theory of Good City Form.* Cambridge: MIT Press.

McHarg, Ian. 1971. *Design with Nature.* New York: Doubleday.

Mohl, Raymond A. 2004. "Stop the Road." *Journal of Urban History* 30: 674–706.

Mullins, Daniel, and Bruce Wallin. 2004. "Tax and Expenditure Limitation." *Public Budgeting and Finance* 24 (December): 4.

Nunn, Samuel, and Mark S. Rosentraub. 1997. "Dimensions of Interjurisdictional Cooperation." *Journal of the American Planning Association* 63 (March): 205–17.

Partnership for Southeastern Massachusetts. N.d. Available at www.srpedd.org/2020index.html (accessed September 7, 2007).

Pastor, Manuel; Chris Benner; and Rachel Rosner. 2006. *Edging Toward Equity: Creating Shared Opportunity in America's Regions: Report from the Conversation on Regional Equity.* Santa Cruz: Center for Justice, Tolerance and Community at the University of California, Santa Cruz.

Peirce, Neal; Curtis Johnson; and John Hall. 1993. *Citistates: How Urban America Can Prosper in a Competitive World.* Washington, DC: Seven Locks Press.

Pendall, Rolf. 1999. "Opposition to Housing: NIMBY and Beyond." *Urban Affairs Review* 35 (September): 112–36.

Peterson, Paul. 1981. *City Limit.* Chicago: University of Chicago Press.

Porter, Douglas, ed. 1985. *Growth Management: Keeping on Target?"* Washington, DC: Urban Land Institute.

———. 1992. *State and Regional Initiatives for Managing Development: Policy Issues and Practical Concerns.* Washington, DC: Urban Land Institute.

———. 2000. *Practice of Sustainable Development.* Washington, DC: Urban Land Institute.

Porter, Douglas, and Allan Wallis. 2002. *Exploring Ad Hoc Regionalism.* Cambridge, MA: Lincoln Institute of Land Policy.

Real Estate Research Corporation. 1974. *The Costs of Sprawl.* Washington, DC: Government Printing Office.

Rusk, David. 1993. *Cities without Suburbs*. Washington, DC: Woodrow Wilson Center Press.

———. 1999. *Inside Game, Outside Game*. Washington, DC: Brookings Institution.

Schneider, Mark. 1989. *The Competitive City*. Pittsburgh: University of Pittsburgh Press.

South Burlington County N.A.A.C.P. v. Township of Mount Laurel. 1983. 92 NJ.

Stone, Clarence. 1989. *Regime Politics: Governing Atlanta, 1946–1988*. Lawrence: University of Kansas Press.

Treasure Valley Partnership. N.d. Available at www.tvfutures.org (accessed September 13, 2007).

Wallis, Allan. 1993. "Governance and Civic Infrastructure in Metropolitan Regions." *National Civic Review* (Spring): 125–39.

———. 1999. "Voluntary Coordination of Regional Growth." *Regionalist* 1, no. 2: 21–28.

Weiner, Edward. 1997. *Urban Transportation Planning in the United States*. Available at http://tmip.fhwa.dot.gov/clearinghouse/docs/utp/ (accessed September 13, 2007).

Weir, Margaret. 2000. "Coalition Building for Regionalism." In *Reflections on Regionalism*, ed. Bruce Katz, 127–53. Washington, DC: Brookings Institution.

Yaro, Robert. 2000. "Growing and Governing Smart: A Case Study of the New York Region." In *Reflections on Regionalism*, ed. Bruce Katz, 43–77. Washington, DC: Brookings Institution Press.

5

JAMES H. LEWIS

Race and Regions

One of the challenges facing urban regions today is to assure that the various benefits of living in a large, urbanized place, such as access to a variety of economic opportunities, cultural amenities, housing opportunities, and educational choices, accrue equally to members of different racial groups. As we shall observe in this chapter, structural forces, patterns of historical settlement, and individual decisions result in barriers to equal access to opportunity to at least some degree in most places. As a result, significant disparity exists in the experiences of place for members of different racial/ethnic groups.

While we might argue that an urban region should allow its residents to take advantage of the benefits its size offers without regard to race, one of the problems facing regions is that their very size permits people with economic resources to act on their personal preferences in ways that can privilege them. Historically, this has sometimes meant capacity to purchase housing in locations that reduce the chances of contact with members of races considered undesirable by the homebuyer; in other cases the operation of housing markets, combined with the high correlation between race and income, results in separation of people by race and diminished opportunity for some. The greater the size of a region the more ability individuals in one part of the region have to live independently of people in another part.

Consider, for instance, a white family in affluent Barrington or in any of the wealthy suburbs along the north lakefront of the Chicago area. The family's children will probably attend a high-quality school that has few black or Latino students. By riding an expressway or commuter train downtown, the family has easy access to world-class music, art, and restaurants. The entire region lacks truly good air quality because so many people drive so much, but the family is spared the stench of any nearby industrial plants or waste disposal facilities. Mom and Dad will spend more time commuting to work than they would like, but they are apt to do it on an expressway or commuter train either to the downtown area or to a new suburban office park. Mom and Dad will also complain about how high their property taxes are, and they are high in national comparison. However, because in Illinois local taxes account for most of the money spent on schools and municipal government, their total taxes paid are less than they would be if the structure of taxing bodies was such that they had to help subsidize the schools and municipal services of places where the residents have lower incomes than they do. The region, as a whole, delivers a high quality of life for them. The same may be said of residents of the elite suburbs of New York, Atlanta, or Los Angeles and many other places.

The region works a lot less well for a young black man living in one of the south Cook suburbs, also in the Chicago area. He may not have done well in school because he attended school in Chicago at a time when the schools were really poor, and his parents were not well educated either and so were of little help. Most of the manufacturing jobs that paid at least a lower-middle-class wage have left the south suburban region, and so now he needs to find a job in the western or northwestern suburbs. Because the commuter rail lines are not designed for that trip, he will have to use a car to get there. Because of the structure of the tax system described above, should his family own a home, they will pay about the same tax rates as the more affluent family, but because they have less income and their property is worth less, that same tax rate will generate only about half as much revenue for their schools and other city services, leading to lower-quality services, and in some instances, municipal bankruptcy. And because land is valued so much less in this part of the region, it is much more likely that he and his family will live near waste dumps that dispose of the refuse generated in other parts of the region.

Most large urban regions produce very different qualities of life for their black, Hispanic, Asian, and white residents owing to the correlation of race with income, and the institutional structures such as tax systems, zoning restrictions, housing markets, patterns of job growth, and transportation systems that translate that correlation into very different living experiences. In his 1987 book, *The Truly Disadvantaged,* William Julius Wilson argued that the severe disadvantage experienced by inner-city blacks was a result more of historic racial discrimination that had become institutionalized, than of ongoing overt racial discrimination, although he felt that to some degree it continued to exist.

The abundant data from employment and housing audit tests (Ayres and Siegelman 1995; Turner 1992; Turner, Fix, and Struyk 1991; Yinger 1986) and surveys (Krysan 2002; Kuklinski, Cobb, and Gilens 1997; Sniderman and Piazza 1995; Taylor 1998) show that many whites continue to harbor discriminatory attitudes toward blacks, and to a lesser extent members of other racial minority groups. It should be a concern to those who think that urban regions should function well for all residents regardless of race. But it is also important to understand how markets, infrastructure, and government finance perpetuate problems whose roots lie in earlier days.

In summary, it is problematic when the structure of government impedes the shared use of fiscal resources needed for the support of the less advantaged such as support for local schools or civic services, or when regional housing and job markets evolve so as to create opportunity for some, but limit it for others. The size of an urban region can allow its wealthier residents, who are predominantly white, to avoid living near areas of waste disposal, rail centers or airports, or industrial centers. As we shall see, urban regions have been severely challenged to benefit people of all racial groups equally. The following discussion considers the impact of various policy issues on minorities.

Income Opportunities

One of the largest racial problems facing urban regions is the spatial mismatch of jobs and housing. Since the 1950s, large numbers of blacks, and to a lesser extent Hispanics, have lived in central cities that once had high proportions of a region's manufacturing jobs. However, the deindustrialization of central cities, combined with the growth of light manufacturing and service industries in suburbs, has left many urban blacks isolated far from the sites of regional job growth. Raphael and Stoll (2002, 1–2) estimated that nationally about 44 percent of Hispanics and Asians and 53 percent of blacks would need to move for their populations to be perfectly aligned with city versus suburban job location. For whites, only 33 percent were misaligned. John Kain (1968) first, followed most prominently by William Julius Wilson (1987) and also many others, advanced the idea that many of the problems of the central city black underclass, and black men in particular, stemmed from the flight to the suburbs of manufacturing jobs from inner cities beginning in the 1950s. This transformation left inner cities largely devoid of well-paying employment opportunities that required only minimal skills and formal education. The exodus of those blacks that were more successful had the effect of concentrating poverty, as the least resourceful remained trapped by housing markets and discrimination in low-cost central city housing.

By the 1980s, ample evidence from case studies and quantitative studies existed for this thesis in most large metropolitan areas. In Los Angeles, the most rapid job growth had spread well beyond areas near to the black neighborhoods of south central Los Angeles to distant Orange and Riverside counties (Waldinger and Bozorgmeihr 1996). In Atlanta, the black population remained concentrated in the city and gradually spread south while remarkable job growth occurred to the north of the city (Kruse 2005, 243–44; Sjoquist 2000). In Boston, the "high-tech" so-called Massachusetts Miracle largely took place in the Route 128 corridor outside the city while the black population remained concentrated in the inner city Dorchester and Roxbury neighborhoods

(McArdle 2003). In Chicago, light manufacturing and the service industries grew rapidly in the northwest suburbs while blacks remained concentrated in the west and south sides of the city. As blacks increasingly populated the south Cook suburbs, the steel industry and other related manufacturers that had been located on Chicago's southeast side and in northwest Indiana closed plants (Wilson 1996).

Quantitative studies of the 1990s indicate that these patterns established in earlier decades have persisted (Raphael and Stoll 2002). Although the spatial mismatch between blacks and whites for jobs narrowed slightly during the 1990s, which is to say that at the end of the decade blacks lived relatively closer to sources of employment than they had a decade earlier, a significant black–white gap in geographic access to employment persisted. The degree of spatial mismatch remains a result of the residential segregation of blacks and whites, and economic development policies have done little to reverse the trend. Raphael and Stoll (2002) found that the 1990s' declines in mismatch were the result of movement of blacks into areas of urban regions where jobs were more plentiful, as opposed to the shift of jobs to locations closer to black communities.

The worst spatial mismatches are found in large metropolitan areas that have the highest degrees of racial segregation of housing—Chicago, Detroit, Miami, New York, Philadelphia, Los Angeles, and Cleveland. Each of these cities is plagued by highly impoverished central cities that house concentrated black populations. Six of the seven regions have lost significant numbers of jobs in their urban cores since the 1950s.

Levels of spatial mismatch are higher in the northeast and midwest regions of the United States than in the South and West, where spatial patterns of residence and employment were more recently established and loss of manufacturing jobs from urban cores has been less of a problem. Raphael and Stoll's (2002) analysis indicates that the problem may yet grow worse. During the 1990s, jobs continued to locate and relocate so as to exacerbate the mismatch of their location from where blacks live.

Concentration of Poverty

The spatial mismatch of jobs and residence, combined with high levels of racial segregation, contribute strongly to the concentration of poverty in cities, and it is concentrated poverty that is so strongly associated with high rates of crime, unwed pregnancy, poor schools, and business failures (Wilson 1987, 1996). Paul Jargowsky (2003) calculated that, in 1990, 3.4 million people lived in census tracts with poverty rates of at least 40 percent or more, most of these in urban regions. Of those people, 39 percent were

Table 5.1

Change in Concentration of Poor by Race/Ethnicity from 1990 to 2000 (%)

	1990	2000
White	7.1	5.9
African-American	30.4	18.6
Hispanic	21.5	13.8
American Indian	30.6	19.5
Asian	12.7	9.8

Source: Adapted from Jargowsky (2003).

African-American and 29 percent Hispanic. During the 1990s, the number of people living in high-poverty neighborhoods nationwide declined by 21 percent, and declines were higher among African-Americans. However, levels of concentrated poverty declined only 4 percent across suburbs. In the New York, Cleveland, Chicago, Miami, Atlanta, and Los Angeles areas, to name but a few, low-income blacks continued their migration from neighborhoods in the inner core to suburbs adjoining those central cities. As a result, urban poverty and its attendant problems have ceased to be a uniquely central city phenomenon (Jargowsky 2003).

In most urban regions, concentrated poverty has been more a black than a Hispanic or Asian problem. Although equally poor in many places, low-income Hispanics and Asians tend to be dispersed more widely across a region than are blacks. In the 1990s, most large urban regions across the nation, with the exception of southern California, saw significant declines in the proportion of Hispanic poor living in census tracts with poverty rates of over 40 percent. These patterns are a result of the increased integration of Hispanics into previously white and nonpoor neighborhoods in both central cities and suburbs (see Table 5.1).

Education

The racial composition of a region interacts with primary and secondary education systems in two fundamental ways. First, high levels of residential segregation combined with a high level of fragmentation of school districts result in fewer minority children attending school with whites than might be the case were districts less fragmented. Second, reliance on local property taxes, the high correlation of race and taxpayer capacity, combined with school district fragmentation, virtually ensures that, on average, black and Hispanic students will have less access to financial resources than will white students (Hoxby 2001; Kozol 1991; Lewis 1995).

School Segregation

Following the U.S. Supreme Court's decision in *Brown v. Board of Education* in 1954, supporters of integrated schools hoped that significant progress would be made toward integrating black and white children in the public schools. However, the movement to integrate schools triggered the flight of white families out of the public schools into sectarian and private schools, and contributed to the movement of whites from cities with substantial black populations into predominantly white suburbs. It also coincided with the beginning of the deindustrialization of cities and cheaper suburban home-building. As a result, school districts attempting to integrate under court order, consent decrees, or because of political pressure found fewer and fewer white students to integrate their black students with. It became immediately apparent that for the promise of the *Brown* decision to be fully realized, school integration plans would have to cross school district boundary lines.

In 1974, this option was effectively lost when the U.S. Supreme Court decided *Milliken v. Bradley*. Responding to a proposed desegregation plan in the Detroit area that would have resulted in busing among Detroit suburban school districts and central city Detroit, the Court ruled that mandatory cross-district desegregation plans could be implemented only where school district lines had been drawn to segregate schools intentionally, which, the Court said, had not occurred in Detroit. The decision effectively shielded most suburban school districts around the nation from any requirement that their students attend school with students from other school districts, which might be racially different. Parents concerned about the race of the students with whom their children attended school were assured that their schools would be only as integrated as the school districts within which they lived (Orfield 1996). White parents who opposed integration were enabled, if they so chose, to take advantage of fragmented political boundaries and the variety of housing options available in large urban regions, to select the children with whom their own children would attend school on the basis of race.

School Funding

The method of determining levels of funding for public school districts in the United States is governed principally at the state level. State legislatures establish the amount of state aid that will be distributed to districts based on formulas that account for attendance, number of students in poverty, students eligible for various categorical programs, and the like. These state aid formulas attempt to address disparate levels of need (fiscal and educational) of individual districts in various ways, and to varying degrees are successful at equalizing resources available to school districts.

However, the utilization of property taxes to support schools works against resource equality, and states with high reliance on local property taxes are prone to widely varying levels of per student funding between their school districts (Kozol 1991). In states with high local property tax reliance, individual school districts benefit disproportionately when they have large concentrations of commercial or industrial property that generate tax revenues without adding students, or large numbers of wealthy residents who have the capacity to pay taxes beyond the needs of their children alone and would otherwise be supporting the needs of the less fortunate if those children attend school in their district. The high correlation of race and poverty in urban areas means that where an urban region has numerous individual school districts that vary greatly in their racial composition, a strong correlation between race and level of educational resources often results (Kozol 1991; Lewis 1995).

Equalization across race is made easier in regions where school districts are countywide, or otherwise large, such that fewer district-level disparities exist. While conflict may continue to exist regarding fairness in the allocation of resources between schools of varying racial composition within districts, allocation problems within districts are easier to address than are allocation problems between districts. In the same way, urban fragmentation correlating with race and class results in fiscal overburden for municipalities (Coleman 2002; Hendrick 2004; Ladd 1994; Rusk 1993).

Environmental Hazards

Another way that location of different racial groups across a region impacts quality of life concerns exposure to environmental hazards. These might include various waste processing, holding, or disposal sites, industrial uses such as refineries, rail yards that produce noise, or social service functions such as homeless shelters, drug treatment facilities, or prisons that are generally considered socially undesirable. As a general rule, housing markets devalue the prices of homes closer to sites that generate noxious smells, industrial waste, or noise (Logan and Molotch 1987). By the same token, wealthier residents tend to live in places where land prices prohibit land use for waste disposal or manufacturing, and these residents have the political influence to block such uses if anyone were to attempt them.

While the problem of location of housing near environmental hazards may today be more a problem of class than of race, many continue to argue the persistence of what they call "environmental racism" (Bullard 1990). This theory argues not only that the intersection of race and class leads to racial minorities being placed at unfair risk, but also that policymakers continue to devalue the life and health of racial minorities when determining where to site waste disposal, industry, and civic infrastructure such as highways and rail.

A lively and, as yet, inconclusive debate has been conducted among scholars since the mid-1980s regarding whether, in fact, undesirable functions are disproportionately located near minority neighborhoods. In 1987, the Commission for Racial Justice (1987) of the United Church of Christ produced the first prominent study finding that environmental waste sites were disproportionately likely to be located in racial minority communities. However, a number of subsequent studies have found either that there is little relationship between race and siting or that race and class are inseparable in understanding the problem (Been 1994; Davidson and Anderson 2000; Krieg 1995; Weinberg 1998).

To some extent, the race versus class debate is a red herring in the urban context, for as long as the poorest residents of large urban regions tend to be members of minority groups, it does not matter whether they are disproportionately exposed to environmental hazard because they are discriminated against or because they are poor. It has been pointed out in the debate over the role of race in siting that in some instances hazards may have been initially sited in a race-neutral manner, only to have low-income minority residents move near the site in pursuit of cheaper housing (Been 1993). But whether or not the racially disparate result is intentional, the interaction of regional planning, job, and housing markets does appear to produce it (Pulido 2000).

Spatial Differentiation of Regions by Race

The use of space to differentiate land-use functions, and so produce higher quality of life for those who can afford it, has roots in America dating back to the early 1800s. From the mid-nineteenth century forward, urban regions have provided their residents with the opportunity to work, to play, and to be educated, while simultaneously allowing opportunities for whites of sufficient wealth to live in neighborhoods of their choice (Jackson 1985, 89–102; Massey and Denton 1993). The first American suburbs evolved from small towns located outside the cities of Boston, Philadelphia, and New York, many of which had been founded during the seventeenth century. By the end of the eighteenth century, local elites had established enclaves in some of them, which they used to escape increasingly congested inner cities and their ills (disease, noise, pollution), particularly in summertime (Binford 1988; Jackson 1985, 89–102).

In the antebellum South, those blacks who lived in cities tended to live among whites. But following the Civil War, Jim Crow practices physically separated blacks and whites in unprecedented ways (Lieberson 1980). When blacks moved into northern cities, in small numbers during the late nineteenth and early twentieth centuries, and in larger numbers during and following the Great Migration stimulated by World War I, they tended to live in enclaves in central cities. Harlem in New York and Bronzeville in Chicago are the most prominent examples (Lehman 1991). In addition to the black neighborhoods found in cities, Farley (1970) describes three types of black suburban communities that developed: (1) spillover from central city black neighborhoods located on the edge of cities (Yonkers, New York; Chicago south suburbs; Compton, California); (2) poor, semi-rural enclaves near cities (Kinloch, Missouri; Robbins, Illinois; Lincoln Heights, Ohio); and (3) suburbs with new housing (Richmond Heights, Florida; Yonkers, New York). By the mid-twentieth century, most large urban regions included all of these types of neighborhoods.

By the mid-twentieth century, millions of blacks had moved from the rural South to central cities in the North and South. Simultaneously, aided by low-cost Federal Housing Administration and Veterans Administration mortgages, many whites had begun to leave large central cities for new suburban developments. Whites moved to suburbs for a variety of reasons, including jobs, which had begun moving to the suburbs, the search for more space, a less "urban" environment, and flight from black neighbors (Farley, Richards, and Wurdock 1980; Jackson 1985, 238–45; Marshall 1979, 991). The specter of interdistrict school integration appeared to threaten the ability of those white migrants who were fleeing blacks to effectively do so, but the threat dissipated with the Supreme Court's decision in *Milliken* (1974). Blacks found their progression into white suburbs blocked by a variety of discriminatory real estate practices (Massey and Denton 1993). By the late twentieth century, most large regions included large numbers of low-income blacks, aging whites, and to varying degrees, middle- and upper-income whites in their central cities, and predominantly white suburbs that included growing concentrations of blacks.

The Hispanic residential pattern was different because in the western and southwestern United States, Hispanics were the indigenous population and were thus as likely to be found in cities as in rural areas during the nineteenth century and before. While certainly subject to housing discrimination, Hispanics did not face the degree of Jim Crow–inspired discrimination that blacks experienced. In many contexts, Hispanics were considered "white." Hispanic enclaves, or barrios, developed in and near urban areas, but to the extent they could afford it, Hispanics also lived much more among whites than did blacks. With the exception of Mexicans in Los Angeles and San Antonio, and Puerto Ricans in New York City, large urban Hispanic neighborhoods are a post-1960 phenomenon.

Asians began coming to the United States in the 1860s with the majority being Chinese recruited to build railroads in California and across the West. Chinese and Japanese immigrants settled in small enclaves on the West Coast and by the mid-twentieth century, most large cities—San Francisco, Los Angeles, New York, and Chicago in particular—had developed "Chinatowns" with large concentrations of Chinese residents, ethnic marketplaces, and offices of Chinese professionals. Only in California has Asian population growth been such that entire suburbs could take on an Asian character. Following the 1965 immigration reforms and the refugee migrations in the 1970s caused by the Southeast Asian conflicts, chain migration into the Los Angeles suburbs of Long Beach, Monterey Park, and other suburbs of Los Angeles and San Francisco began. By 2000, enclaves of various combinations of Chinese, Japanese, Vietnamese, Koreans, Asian Indians, and other Asian and Pacific Islander groups existed in most metropolitan areas across the nation.

The result of this history is a racially diverse set of urban regions. As Table 5.2 illustrates, while the average urban region nationally is about 75 percent white, the whitest 5 percent of urban regions in the country are about 95 percent white and the lowest 5 percent are less than 44 percent white. Half of all urban regions are under 7 percent black, but the top 5 percent are over one-third black. The Hispanic pattern is similar, but the most Hispanic regions in the country are more Hispanic than the blackest are black. Compared with numbers of blacks and Hispanics, no region in the country has as high a concentration of Asians.

Residential Separation by Race

Whether we consider the spatial mismatch of jobs and housing, access to schools, or degree of environmental justice, the discussion necessarily begins with the extent to which people of different races live among or apart from one another. It is this chapter's central contention that regions "work" in part to the extent that they facilitate the mingling of people of different backgrounds and "fail" in part to the extent to which they facilitate their separation. When they mingle, all residents of a region are more likely to share equally, and without regard to race, in economic opportunity determined by the location of commerce and industry, to share equally the benefits of schools and city services, and to bear more equally the burdens of environmental hazards.

Sociologists can assess the extent to which people who are members of different groups live together with statistical indices. The index of dissimilarity is one of the oldest and most commonly used measures of how together or apart two groups of people live in a geographic space such as a city or an urban region (Massey and Denton 1988b, 308). The index ranges from a maximum

Table 5.2

Distribution of Urban Regions by Race, 2000 (%)

	Mean	5th percentile	25th percentile	50th percentile	75th percentile	95th percentile
White	74.8	43.2	64.7	79.1	86	94.8
Black	10.3	0.6	2.4	6.8	15.1	33.6
Asian	3.4	0.4	0.8	1.4	2.65	8.7
Hispanic	9.9	0.8	1.9	4.5	10.7	40.4

Source: U.S. Bureau of the Census, Summary Files 3 and 4.

Note: Hereafter urban regions are defined as 331 Primary Metropolitan Statistical Areas (PMSAs) and Metropolitan Statistical Areas (MSAs) as defined by the Bureau of the Census.

score of 1 (here represented as 100) when two groups are completely separated (imagine two colored fields in a flag) to 0, when the members of two groups live completely mingled (picture the sixty-four squares of a chessboard). It can also be interpreted as the percentage of members of one group who would have to move in order to achieve complete mixing of the two groups.

The urban regions across the nation differ considerably in their levels of integration of residents by race with some regions (defined as 331 Primary Metropolitan Statistical Areas nationwide in the 2000 Census) experiencing nearly complete mixing of people of different races while others feature almost complete separation. In most places, African-Americans and whites live much more apart than do Hispanics or Asians and whites. Sociologists generally consider index scores of 30 or lower indicative of highly integrated places, and scores exceeding 70 as highly segregated. As Table 5.3 indicates, about 25 percent of urban regions have black/white segregation scores of 70 percent or higher. Almost no regions may be said to have true integration of blacks and whites. By contrast, few regions exhibit hypersegregation of whites from Asians or Hispanics.

To study regions is inherently to consider the effects of different types of space on how people live. We might, therefore, wonder whether racial groups mix differently in smaller or larger urban regions. In fact, larger geographic regions do tend to be a little more racially segregated than smaller ones. A small but significant correlation exists between the level of racial segregation of a region and the size of an urban region, with larger regions tending to have greater racial segregation (see Table 5.4). The effect is strongest for Hispanics ($r = 0.387$), followed by blacks ($r = 0.219$) and finally Asians ($r = 0.133$). Thus the degree of separation of Hispanics and whites is determined more by regional size than are levels of black and Asian separation. Hispanics and whites do not become segregated unless the region is very large, whereas blacks and Asians are more likely to be segregated—or not—irrespective of the size of the place. Regions where whites and blacks live separately tend toward separation of Hispanics and whites as well ($r = 0.314$).

The integration of racial minority groups with whites in urban regions is also related to their proportions in the region, but the relationship operates very differently for different groups. Across the nation's urban regions, the larger the percentage of the region's population that is black, the more likely blacks are to live among whites ($r = -0.215$). This occurs because the normative residential relationship of blacks and whites in urban areas is to live separately; therefore, as the black population of a region becomes particularly large, it becomes more likely to spill into neighborhoods that might otherwise be white, thereby integrating them, if only temporarily.

The Hispanic pattern tends to operate the opposite way. The higher the

138

Table 5.3

Distribution of Regions on Index of Dissimilarity, 2000 (%)

	Mean	5th percentile	25th percentile	50th percentile	75th percentile	95th percentile
White/black	60.3	39	51	60	69	83
White/Hispanic	36.4	20	27	35	44	59
White/Asian	40.0	28	34	40	46	53

Source: Lewis Mumford Center.

Table 5.4

Correlation of Index of Dissimilarity with Population of Regions, 2000

	Total population	White–black segregation	Percent of a region's minority
White–black segregation	0.219**		−0.215**
White–Hispanic segregation	0.387**	0.314**	0.311**
White–Asian segregation	0.133*	0.032	0.010

Source: U.S. Bureau of the Census; Lewis Mumford Center.
Note: * indicates probability < .05; ** indicates probability < .01.

Hispanic proportion of a region's population, the more likely Hispanics are to live separately ($r = 0.311$). Because Hispanics tend toward mixing with whites residentially, as more and more enter a region their density increases, particularly since the most recent arrivals tend to have poor English skills and are newer to the United States, and therefore find Hispanic enclaves socially and culturally preferable.

The proportion of a region's population that is Asian has no impact on whether they live among or apart from whites ($r = 0.01$). In most places, Asians make up a relatively small part of the overall population and so whether they are a small, or very small portion of a region, they tend to be integrated among whites.

Central cities and their suburbs tend to be similar in their patterns of racial separation between whites and the three major minority groups. Massey and Denton's (1988a, 621) comparative study of cities and suburbs during the 1970s found that blacks were highly segregated in central cities and only marginally less segregated in suburbs. Asians, conversely, were generally integrated among whites in central cities, in spite of the existence of "Chinatowns" and "Japantowns" in the largest cities, and tended to be fairly integrated in suburban areas as well. Hispanics showed the greatest difference in city–suburban experience, with less segregation in the suburbs than in central city neighborhoods.

Most- and Least-Integrated Regions

Blacks and Whites

Among the smallest places that we might characterize as independent urban regions, Primary Metropolitan Statistical Areas (PMSAs) with under 200,000 residents, a number have genuine black–white integration—which is to say they have dissimilarity scores under 40, and the most segregated places tend to have scores in the 60s. As regions become larger, fewer of them are integrated in any sense.

None of the largest metropolitan areas has truly high levels of black–white integration (see Table 5.5). Of PMSAs with more than 1.5 million persons, Las Vegas has the lowest dissimilarity score at 44 (although it does not appear in Table 5.5 because it is only 8 percent black). Of the regions with large black populations, Norfolk-Virginia Beach is the lowest at 47. The separation of blacks and whites across urban regions is simply a ubiquitous problem in the United States.

Few urban regions in the United States have truly low levels of white–African-American segregation. The lowest levels of segregation tend to be found in smaller southern cities that have expanded rapidly in population during the past forty years, well beyond their nineteenth-century residential structure, and so have absorbed large numbers of African-Americans who lived in small enclaves peripheral to earlier urban boundaries. In the North, in smaller places, the few blacks who live in those places may not have appeared to pose the threat that they were believed to pose in the South (Kuklinski, Cobb, and Gilens 1997; Oliver and Mendelberg 2000, 586).

The highest levels of black–white segregation are found in most of the nation's major urban areas, certainly in the older ones, and in smaller urban regions, particularly in the Northeast and Midwest. Faced in the late twentieth century with declining economic opportunity as they transitioned away from Fordist manufacturing, these places have traditional ethnic communities that shaped urban space both by their work and history. In the first decades of the twentieth century, black migrants from the South were not welcomed in these communities and as a result congregated in older, skid-row, or lower-working-class neighborhoods adjacent to industry that eventually became the slums of hollowing urban cores. The resultant white flight, as black chain migration from the South increased in the 1950s and since, led to highly segregated residential structures of inner cities and suburbs. Not unique to the Northeast, the pattern also characterized rapidly growing southern urban regions that have high racial disparity indices—notably Atlanta, Washington, DC, Houston, and Miami (Logan and Stearns 1981, 71; Shelton 1989, 76).

Blacks did not follow whites into the same suburbs in proportion to their overall population in each region for several reasons. Disparities in levels of income and savings between blacks and whites have limited the ability of the average black to live in the same neighborhood as the average white. Discriminatory real estate sales practices have discouraged and sometimes blocked blacks from moving into predominantly white places. Krysan and Farley (2002, 958) found that most blacks have not wanted to live in neighbor-

Table 5.5

Most Black/White Integrated and Segregated Urban Regions (Dissimilarity Index) by Size of Primary Metropolitan Statistical Area (at least 10 percent black), 2000

Most integrated	Index	Percent black	Least integrated	Index	Percent black
Under 200,000					
Jacksonville, NC	30	18	Albany, GA	61	51
Greenville, NC	33	34	Lake Charles, LA	62	24
Dover, DE	33	20	Danville, VA	62	33
Lawton, OK	35	19	Monroe, LA	66	34
Charlottesville, VA	37	14	Benton Harbor, MI	76	16
200,000 to 500,000					
Fayetteville, NC	34	34	Atlantic-Cape May, NJ	65	13
Lynchburg, VA	37	18	Chattanooga, TN	69	14
Gainesville, FL	38	19	Beaumont-Port Arthur, TX	70	25
Clarksville-Hopkinsville, TN	40	20	Bridgeport, CT	74	11
Tallahassee, FL	41	33	Flint, MI	77	20
500,000 to 1.5 million					
Raleigh-Durham, NC	44	22	Birmingham, AL	71	30
Charleston, SC	44	30	Toledo, OH	71	13
Greenville-Spartanburg-Anderson, SC	45	17	Dayton-Springfield, OH	72	14
Columbia, SC	51	32	Youngstown-Warren, OH	73	10
Wilmington, DE	52	17	Buffalo-Niagara Falls, NY	79	11
1.5 million and over					
Norfolk-Virginia Beach, VA	47	30	Newark, NJ	81	22
Orlando, FL	54	13	New York, NY	83	23
Dallas, TX	60	15	Milwaukee, WI	84	15
Fort Lauderdale, FL	61	20	Detroit, MI	85	23
Fort Worth-Arlington, TX	62	11	Gary, IN	85	19

Source: U.S. Bureau of the Census; Lewis Mumford Center.

hoods where they expect to experience discomfort. Finally, numerous studies have indicated that a majority of blacks prefer to live in neighborhoods where blacks are half, or more, of the residents.

Hispanics and Whites

Hispanics are far more integrated among whites than are blacks although, as with blacks, smaller places tend to be more integrated than larger ones. Among the smallest regions, the most integrated places have Hispanic/white dissimilarity index scores in the low 20s or below, and the highest scores are only in the 50s. However, among larger places, the lowest scores rise into the 30s and the highest into the 60s (see Tables 5.6 and 5.7). Still, we do not observe the hypersegregation between whites and Hispanics that is observed with whites and blacks.

Whites and Hispanics are most integrated in urban regions in the Great Plains and Northwest. Close behind them are the smaller and mid-sized regions of the Southwest, California, and Florida. In many of these places, Hispanics constitute 40 percent or more of the overall population.

Hispanics have tended to be most separated from whites in both large and small regions of the Northeast. The highest segregation occurs in smaller urban areas in Connecticut, Massachusetts, and Pennsylvania. Among the large cities, New York and Newark have the most separation. Puerto Ricans in New York City are the largest of these populations and are noted for their insularity from whites and low levels of separation from blacks. According to Massey and Bitterman (1985, 318), New York Puerto Ricans experience high social separation from whites, and their relatively high levels of poverty lead them to settle near blacks such that they become "bystander victims of Anglo prejudice against blacks."

In Florida, the Southwest, and California, Hispanics were indigenous to the places long before large urban centers existed there. Florida's large cities have existed only since the 1920s, when Miami expanded from around 30,000 people to over 200,000. Thus, when the first major Cuban migration occurred in the 1960s, urban Florida was only forty years old and many of the areas that were to become significant retirement centers began growing significantly at roughly the same time that Cubans began arriving. As a result, few long-established neighborhoods existed from which Cubans could be excluded. As the Miami area grew substantially, and the Cuban, and later Haitian, populations grew as well, enclaves developed based on chain migration that had the effect of separating greater numbers of Hispanics from whites residentially.

Most cities in California and the Southwest did not take on their current

Table 5.6

Hispanic/White Dissimilarity Index by Size of Region, 2000 (regions at least 5 percent Hispanic)

Most integrated	Index	Percent Hispanic	Least integrated	Index	Percent Hispanic
Under 200,000					
Redding, CA	12	5	Vineland-Milville-Bridgeton, NJ	49	19
Casper, WY	19	5	Richland-Kennewick-Pasco, WA	51	21
Bellingham, WA	20	5	Sioux City, IA	52	11
Pocatello, ID	20	5	Tyler, TX	56	11
Lawton, OK	22	8	New Bedford, MA	56	6
200,000 to 500,000					
Fort Collins-Loveland, CO	22	8	Lowell, MA	61	6
Anchorage, AK	25	6	Lancaster, PA	62	6
Gainesville, FL	25	6	Bridgeport, CT	66	12
Melbourne-Titusville-Palm Bay, FL	25	5	Reading, PA	73	10
San Luis Obispo-Atascadero-Paso Robles, CA	27	16	Lawrence, MA	74	14
500,000 to 1.5 million					
Brazoria, TX	26	23	Worcester, MA	61	7
Vallejo-Fairfield-Napa, CA	26	19	Allentown-Bethlehem-Easton, PA	62	8
Tacoma, WA	29	6	Hartford, CT	64	10
Colorado Springs, CO	30	11	Springfield, MA	64	13
Galveston, Texas City, TX	30	18	Providence-Fall River, RI	67	8
1.5 million and over					
Seattle-Bellevue-Everett, WA	28	5	Boston, MA	59	6
Portland-Vancouver, WA	30	7	Philadelphia, PA	59	6
Santa Rosa, CA	30	17	Los Angeles-Long Beach, CA	60	45
Fort Lauderdale, FL	32	17	Newark, NJ	65	13
Sacramento, CA	36	15	New York, NY	65	25

Source: U.S. Bureau of the Census; Lewis Mumford Center.

Table 5.7

White/Hispanic Dissimilarity Index Scores for Selected Other Regions with Large Hispanic Populations, 2000

Most integrated	Index	Percent Hispanic
Under 200,000		
Yuba City, CA	25	20
Pueblo, CO	32	38
Greely, CO	33	27
Yolo, CA	34	26
Las Cruces, NM	35	63
San Angelo, TX	37	31
Santa Fe, NM	43	44
500,000 to 1.5 million		
Bakersfield, CA	52	38
Tucson, AZ	47	29
Fresno, CA	45	44
Austin-San Marcos, TX	42	26
McAllen-Edinburg-Mission, TX	40	88
Albuquerque, NM	38	42
Stockton-Lodi, CA	35	31

Least integrated	Index	Percent Hispanic
200,000 to 500,000		
Salinas, CA	59	47
Naples, FL	53	20
Santa Cruz, CA	52	27
Yakima, WA	50	36
Brownsville, TX	45	84
Amarillo, TX	44	20
Corpus Christi, TX	44	55
Santa Barbara, CA	41	34
Lubbock, TX	41	27
Odessa-Midland, TX	41	36
Visalia-Tulare-Porterville, CA	38	51
Modesto, CA	34	32
1.5 million and over		
Ventura, CA	52	33
Houston, TX	52	30
Miami, FL	51	57
Orange County, CA	50	31
Dallas, TX	49	23
Phoenix-Mesa, AZ	49	25
San Diego, CA	48	27
San Antonio, TX	48	51
San Jose, CA	46	24
Jersey City, NJ	45	40
Riverside-San Bernardino, CA	41	38
Las Vegas, NV	38	21

Source: U.S. Bureau of the Census; Lewis Mumford Center.

urban forms until the twentieth century and thus similar patterns were obtained. The Los Angeles barrio dates back to the 1920s, but the city was also surrounded by smaller Hispanic farm-worker and grower communities that eventually were absorbed by the spread of greater Los Angeles. As Mexican immigration swelled the region's Hispanic population into the hundreds of thousands, they tended to aggregate in specific places defined by cultural affinity, discrimination, and ethnic competition for housing with whites, leading to the creation of East Los Angeles—the major statistical driver of Los Angeles's high dissimilarity score (Romo 1983, 21–23; Waldinger and Bozorgmeihr 1996). While many California cities date well into the nineteenth century as small population centers, it was not until the 1950s that most of them grew to their present character economically or demographically; residential space was thus less historically defined, which contributed to more integration. In the San Francisco Bay area, the Mexican barrio formed in the 1920s, but Mexicans were less likely to buy homes and were less successful at moving into the middle class than they were in Los Angeles, leading to patterns of greater population dispersion in the region (Pitti 2003, 89, 109). Additionally, while Mexican laborers were often despised and certainly discriminated against, they never encountered the enmity reserved for African-Americans—who were relative latecomers to California—or the Japanese and Chinese who suffered first from labor competition and later from vilification resulting from World War II.

In Massachusetts, Connecticut, and smaller industrial areas of the Northeast, Mexican immigrants of the 1980s and 1990s encountered very old (by American standards) cities and residential patterns and strong historical cultural norms. High degrees of residential segregation resulted as the migrants tended to occupy the lowest occupational rungs.

Asians and Whites

Asians are not found in large numbers in urban regions outside the Pacific coast and a few of the nation's largest regions. Outside of Honolulu, Hawaii, the San Francisco Bay area, at around 25 percent, constitutes the largest aggregation of Asians nationally. With the exception of the labor relations conflicts that followed the immigration of Chinese into California to work on railroads, and the fear of Japanese during and immediately following World War II, Asians have generally been viewed as the least threatening of the three major racial/ethnic groups (Rahn et al. 2003). Because Asian have done well economically for the most part, their residential patterns have been less defined by uneven housing markets than have those of blacks and Hispanics. Asians have not been associated with violence and are stereotyped as keeping to themselves and performing exceptionally well in school. As a result, while perhaps not always welcoming Asians as their neighbors, whites tend to view them far more favorably on average than they do blacks or Hispanics (Bobo and Zubrinsky 1996, 896; Link and Oldendick 1996, 157; Rahn et al. 2003; Wong et al. 1998). Since the nineteenth century, growing Chinatowns have not encountered the fear and the neighborhood defense that have greeted black migrants, and Southeast Asian refugees have benefited from extensive resettlement efforts sponsored by state and federal governments during the 1980s. Certainly local conflicts have developed as a result of migration, such as the Vincent Chin murder in Detroit and conflict between native and Vietnamese refugee fishermen in Louisiana. But these conflicts have never metastasized into the type of racial discrimination that has consistently burdened blacks and to a lesser extent Hispanics.

As a result, segregation levels of Asians from whites (see Table 5.8) are far lower than for blacks and generally lower than for Hispanics. In larger places, segregation increases less because of discrimination in housing than because of chain migration that has brought concentrations of refugees and recent immigrants to "ports of entry" in larger urban regions such as Los Angeles, San Francisco, or Chicago. Like recent Hispanic immigrants, the new Asian arrivals seek neighborhoods where their native language is spoken, and native foods, clothing, and religious institutions are nearby. Because Asians are disproportionately represented in professional occupations, they have also tended to aggregate in centers of new economic functions, common on the West Coast and some of the South.

Separation and Identity

Debate continues to exist regarding the utility of racial/ethnic identity for the accomplishment of American civic and cultural unity (Glazer 1997; Hacker 1992; Huntington 2005). Questions have been raised as to whether the nation's long-term interests are best served by a population with a common language, culture, and identity, or whether a more pluralistic and multicultural future is best and/or inevitable. Research does suggest a link between residential segregation and persistence of racial/ethnic identity. Bledsoe et al. (1995) in a study of the Detroit region found that living within the central city area of metropolitan Detroit raised levels of racial solidarity among blacks. Living in the suburbs, on the other hand, was associated with lower perceptions of racial solidarity. Across the region, blacks in segregated neighborhoods felt more solidarity than blacks who lived in more integrated neighborhoods. Kinder and Mendelberg (1995) found that racial prejudices continue to inform white opinion on various policy-related issues and that racial isolation enhanced their

Table 5.8

White/Asian Dissimilarity Index by Size of Region: Places Where Asians Are 5 Percent or More of the Population, 2000

	Index	Percent Asian
Under 200,000		
Yolo, CA	32	9
Champaign-Urbana, IL	46	6
200,000 to 500,000		
Merced, CA	35	7
Salinas, CA	37	6
Trenton, NJ	41	5
Lowell, MA	47	7
500,000 to 1.5 million		
Fresno, CA	34	7
Tacoma, WA	36	5
Honolulu, HI	36	45
Stockton-Lodi, CA	46	11
Vallejo-Fairfield-Napa, CA	47	10
Over 1.5 million		
Ventura, CA	28	5
Las Vegas, NV	31	5
Seattle-Bellevue-Everett, WA	35	9
Bergen-Passaic, NJ	36	8
Washington, DC	38	7
San Jose, CA	38	25
Oakland, CA	39	16
Orange County, CA	39	13
Jersey City, NJ	43	9
Chicago, IL	43	5
San Francisco, CA	44	23
San Diego, CA	45	9
Sacramento, CA	46	9
Boston, MA	46	5
Los Angeles, CA	47	12
New York, NY	47	9
Houston, TX	48	5

Source: U.S. Bureau of the Census; Lewis Mumford Center.

impact. Barreto, Segura, and Woods's (2004) study of Hispanics in California found that Hispanics in Hispanic communities were more likely to vote for Hispanic candidates than were Hispanics who lived in more integrated communities. In a national study, Chiswick and Miller (2005) found that immigrants living in enclaves appeared to acquire English somewhat slower than those living more dispersed among the English-speaking population. As noted above, high levels of racial segregation appear to contribute to racially motivated violence.

Economic Equity

One simple measure of regional racial equity in economic condition is a comparison of median incomes of whites with those of blacks, Hispanics, and Asians in each region. The measure does tend to understate disparity in total economic power because there are so many more very wealthy whites proportionally than there are blacks, Hispanics, or Asians, and because it fails to account for the tremendous white advantage in savings and intergenerational transmission of wealth.

Whites and Asians have roughly equal median incomes across the nation's regions, which are more than $10,000 higher than median incomes of blacks and Hispanics (Table 5.9). The highest of the white regional median incomes is approximately $16,000 higher than the highest of the black and Hispanic regional incomes. Asian communities vary more economically across regions than do white, black, or Hispanic communities. The richest Asian communities are more than three times wealthier than the poorest.

Blacks and Whites

While the pattern is not perfect, it is generally true that black–white income disparity is lower in newer, western communities that tend to have fewer African-Americans than do the older eastern and midwestern regions. Across the nation, ratios range from parity in a couple of regions (Parkersburg, West Virginia; Marietta, Ohio; Olympia, Washington; Brownsville, Texas; and McAllen, Texas) to less than half, which is far more common (see Table 5.10).

Parity is more likely to be reached in areas that have undergone rapid economic development and population expansion, and do not have large neighborhoods with multigenerational concentrated poverty. But it also occurs where people of all races are struggling together. While San Francisco and the Twin Cities have both done quite well economically, relatively speaking, they are older and have cores of urban poor that include the small numbers of blacks who live there. A review of the mid-sized regions finds a similar pattern with Vallejo-Fairfield-Napa, California; Colorado Springs, Colorado; and Tacoma, Washington, coming the closest to achieving parity and older places such as Galveston, Texas; Buffalo and Syracuse, New York; Mobile, Alabama; New Orleans and Baton Rouge, Louisiana, having the worst.

The sizes, ages, and demography of regions all play important roles in shaping levels of disparity between whites and blacks. There is a significant negative correlation ($r = -.355$) between the percentage of the population in a region that is black and the amount of disparity between black and white

Table 5.9

Distribution of Urban Regions by Median Income (dollars), 2000

	Mean	5th percentile	25th percentile	50th percentile	75th percentile	95th percentile
White	44,637	34,089	38,683	43,026	48,510	60,029
Black	28,991	19,181	23,569	27,310	32,662	44,281
Hispanic	32,905	22,357	28,221	32,515	36,826	45,312
Asian	45,666	23,118	36,817	45,344	52,321	70,910

Source: U.S. Bureau of the Census; Lewis Mumford Center.

Table 5.10

Ratio of Black to White Median Incomes: Urban Regions at Least 5 Percent Black and 1.5 Million Persons, 2000

	Ratio of black to white median incomes (lower indicates more disparity)	Percent black
Milwaukee-Waukesha, WI	0.50	15
San Francisco, CA	0.50	5
Minneapolis-St. Paul, MN	0.52	5
Cincinnati, OH	0.53	13
Newark, NJ	0.53	22
Houston, TX	0.55	17
Chicago, IL	0.56	19
St. Louis, IL	0.56	18
Philadelphia, PA	0.56	20
Oakland, CA	0.57	12
Denver, CO	0.64	5
San Antonio, TX	0.66	6
Orlando, FL	0.67	13
Jersey City, NJ	0.67	12
Sacramento, CA	0.68	7
San Diego, CA	0.70	5
Las Vegas, NV	0.75	8
Riverside-San Bernardino, CA	0.79	7
Nassau-Suffolk, NY	0.83	8
Middlesex-Somerset-Hunterdon, NJ	0.87	7

Source: U.S. Bureau of the Census, Lewis Mumford Center.

median incomes in a region. The greater percentage black a region is, the greater the level of income disparity. However, unlike with racial segregation in where people live, there is little correspondence between the size of a region and whether economic equity is obtained.

Hispanics and Whites

While relatively few Hispanics have attained the wealth or incomes typical of upper class whites, in a number of regions they have achieved rough parity at the middle class (see Table 5.11). In urban regions in Florida and California, where Hispanics have now lived for multiple generations and have built businesses, they have come closest to achieving economic parity. In these places, owing partly to multiple generations of family business presence, substantial Hispanic middle classes have penetrated the political and business communities. In the older eastern cities, significant Hispanic populations exist, but they

to prevent or slow school desegregation. In instances where desegregation became inevitable, opponents turned to private schools. While schools were eventually desegregated in most communities to some degree and black students appear to have derived some educational benefit, the policy can hardly be called a success. Likewise, in the Chicago region, the Leadership Council for Metropolitan Open Communities assisted thousands of poor blacks with relocation into affordable housing in Chicago neighborhoods and suburbs; yet the policy's implementation has been hindered by, among other things, landlord reluctance to accept housing vouchers, as similar programs have been hindered elsewhere.

Developing popular consensus that reduction of racial disparities at a regional level should be an important public goal will be difficult because of the persistence of racialized attitudes toward public policy (Sniderman and Piazza 1995). Taylor (1998, 531) found in national samples that whites in cities outside the South are more likely to adopt negative views of blacks as black population in their community increases. The concentration of blacks tends to heighten whites' levels of "traditional prejudice," "opposition to race targeting," and "policy-related beliefs." Levels of negative views toward Hispanics and Asians were not, however, influenced by their concentration in communities. Increased location of blacks in previously white suburbs could have the effect of creating opposition to various policies such as affirmative action and low-income housing development that have been targeted toward blacks in the past. Taylor suggests that heightened opposition may extend to public programs such as enterprise zones and targeted educational benefits, despite their wide support by whites.

Many people believe that the problems resulting from racial separation have minimal enough impact on them that they are better addressed by defending their own neighborhoods than by reducing racial differences. An extreme example that nonetheless sheds light on the problems of suburban integration is Lakewood, California. Lakewood fell under the national spotlight because of the revelation of the Spur Posse, a group of high school–age boys who engaged in gang behavior. Founded shortly after World War II as a white industrial suburb of Los Angeles, Lakewood was faced with prospects of school desegregation during the 1970s at the same time that industrial transformation began to cost the community jobs. The result was growth of a strong oppositional culture that viewed blacks as outsiders and fed on the fear that Lakewood would become "another Compton"—referring to the suburb adjacent to Los Angeles that resegregated into a black community fraught with poverty and violence. The result was a cohesive, and to some extent dysfunctional, white working-class community averse to change and opposed to racial integration (Brill 1996).

Examples such as these raise the question of whether the political will exists to accomplish the policy changes necessary to more fully integrate urban regions and improve racial equity in access to resources such as jobs, schools, and environmental amenities. Advocates for change often point out that social pathologies within a region have an impact on everyone in the region, and studies indicate interdependence between central cities and suburbs (Johnson 1999; Savitch et al. 1993). Yet, crime rates are lower in white neighborhoods, test scores are higher, and the heavy reliance on property taxes in many urban regions across the nation does effectively insulate residents of the more fiscally privileged school districts from the cost of educating often less-prepared minority students. While we may question the morality of so much racially correlated disparity within our regions, and everyone's quality of life is compromised to some degree, evidence has yet to be developed that a metropolitan region cannot remain sustainable despite significant social and economic disparities.

Evidence is also emerging that many blacks are stepping back from the integrationist vision that drove so much of social reform in earlier decades. Many blacks have tired of the idea that integration with whites residentially or in schools is required for them to progress and have provided new support for Afro-centric curriculum and schooling, and the development of middle- and upper-middle-class suburbs populated primarily by blacks. A majority of blacks continue to tell pollsters that they prefer to live in integrated neighborhoods, but remarkably few such neighborhoods exist for them to live in (Krysan 2002).

But these assertions of independence may work against the long-run interests of blacks if they provide defenders of the status quo with a rationale for avoiding policy changes that would result in greater integration and less disparate patterns of economic development. For the residents of Prince George's County (Maryland), the south suburbs of Chicago, and those central cities whose black majority or plurality populations eventually elected a black mayor, political independence can be a pyrrhic victory if sufficient resources do not accompany it to sustain healthy communities (Kraus and Swanstrom 2001; Preston 1976; Wiggins 2002, 770–76). In many instances, blacks achieved power in cities depleted of economic opportunity where concentrations of lower-wealth blacks have less capacity to pay property taxes. In Prince George's County outside Washington, DC, and in DeKalb County in metropolitan Atlanta, a strong perception exists that prominent upscale retailers have avoided locating stores in black suburbs either because of prejudices against the residents or underestimation of the neighborhood's true purchasing power and stability (Wiggins 2002).

Again the pattern has been somewhat different for Asians and Hispanics.

In Monterey Park, California, a suburb of Los Angeles undergoing significant increases in Asian population during the 1980s, older Japanese and newer Chinese residents joined whites in favor of managed development to elect Asians to the city council of a thriving community (Horton 1995). Hispanics who have become mayors of major cities (Pena in Denver, Cisneros in San Antonio, and Villaraigosa in Los Angeles) have been fortunate to govern cities in much better economic condition than those over which the first African American mayors governed twenty years earlier. Hispanics and Asians have no doubt been helped by the persistence of whites in neighborhoods they have entered that have stanched the potential racial tipping that led to segregated black neighborhoods.

For persons of Hispanic or Asian origin, greater acculturation, as measured by language acquisition, income, and citizenship, has brought movement into predominantly white communities and the suburbs. Alba and his colleagues (1999, 458) found that during the 1980s new immigrants were more likely to settle in suburbs in spite of low English proficiency, blurring historic urban–suburban distinctions. While ethnic enclaves will continue to exist in all large metropolitan areas, especially where immigrants new to the United States continue to arrive, the future likely holds more regional integration.

Housing integration would reduce employment inequity. Studies of the Moving to Opportunity (MTO) implemented in a number of cities, and the Gautreaux program in Chicago, show clear benefits to blacks who moved from central cities to suburbs (Rosenbaum 1991, 1995; Rosenbaum and Harris 2000). However, the development of public housing and related racial integration in suburbs has been difficult because of opposition in white suburbs, middle- and upper-income suburbs where there is fear of neighborhood deterioration, and even lower-income communities that fear that additional low-income housing will impede future development. From the late 1930s through the 1960s, public housing developments were concentrated in central cities and in black and Latino neighborhoods. Since the 1980s, there has been more dispersion of subsidized housing into suburbs and nonminority neighborhoods, but the trend toward location in minority, and particularly low-income, neighborhoods continues (Rohe and Freeman 2001, 289–90). Nonetheless, there is some evidence that location of Low-Income Housing Tax Credit subsidized units in metropolitan neighborhoods was associated with improvement of low-income neighborhoods in which they were sited (Freeman 2004, 1).

Still, NIMBYism (not in my backyard) has been a persistent problem. In Yonkers, New York, for instance, the persistent protests of white residents of middle-class neighborhoods consistently thwarted the intentions of the planning department to disperse sites for public housing across Yonkers, rather than concentrating them in blighted black communities near its downtown (*US v. Yonkers Board of Education,* 68–74). As the district court explained in a 1985 decision, "It is, in short, difficult to discern any plan at work in the City's site selection process during these years [1960s], except for an apparent determination to avoid, at virtually any cost, a confrontation with community opponents of public housing." Abundant research documents the same problems in Chicago (Hirsch 1983), St. Louis (Judd 1997, 232, 237), and elsewhere.

Because of local resistance to affordable housing development, many affordable housing initiatives have occurred at the state level. California and Illinois have passed legislation requiring each municipality to have at least a minimal quantity of affordable housing or produce a plan to accomplish it. Maryland's Smart Growth policy provides incentives for developers to produce new housing in areas designated by the state for development. Montgomery County, Maryland, requires between 12.5 and 15 percent of new housing development, whether detached homes or apartments, be moderately priced. The *Mount Laurel* cases in New Jersey resulted in state court–ordered mandates of construction of affordable housing (Bollens 1997, 16) resulting in more than 10,000 new units (Haar 1996).

Some of the most effective programs aimed at integrating urban housing have stemmed from the work of individual suburbs determined to preserve racial diversity. Oak Park, Illinois, and Shaker Heights, Ohio, are prominent examples. In Oak Park, the Regional Housing Center conducts affirmative marketing of rental housing so as to promote integration. Financial incentives are available to landlords who accept tenants from the center. Additionally, the village has operated a home Equity Assurance Program. Shaker Heights opened its housing office in 1967, marketing Shaker Heights as an integrated housing market. Below-market mortgages were offered from the Fund for the Future of Shaker Heights to buyers willing to move such that integration would be improved (Keating 1995, 301).

Breaking Established Patterns: Regional Governance, Markets, and Policy

While government plays a role in locating businesses and affordable housing, location patterns are still fundamentally determined by private markets and decisions that may or may not serve the specific interest of creating greater racial equity across a region. To make matters more complicated, through the operation of locally administered zoning, reliance on local property and sales taxes for funding so many educational and civic services, and the legal constraints of the *Milliken* ruling, the governmental structure has actually helped

to preserve racial disparity in many instances (Judd 1997; W⟨
administrative structures tend to isolate poorer, and often b⟨
people residentially, and hence fiscally. Finally, regiona⟨
the obstacle that many view regional planning as poten⟨
and counter to deeply rooted American traditions that value priva⟨ ⟨
distribution of jobs and housing as well as individual choice.

One approach to reducing disparity among regional subgroups is regional governance. Regional consolidations and governance were originally aimed at streamlining administrative functions and strengthening central cities, and, more recently, at helping individual regions to compete more effectively economically (Brenner 2002, 9; Hamilton 1999). The earliest forms of regional governance were the annexations of neighboring municipalities and land by central cities, and city–county consolidations. For the most part, these were undertaken in the interest of creating fiscal efficiency or promoting economic development. The most significant were the nineteenth-century consolidations in Boston (1821), Philadelphia (1854), the New York boroughs into present-day New York City (1898), and mid–twentieth-century city–county consolidations mostly in the South and West highlighted by Nashville, Tennessee (1962), Jacksonville, Florida (1967), and Indianapolis, Indiana (1969) (*Growth Within Bounds* 2000). However, high degrees of racial disparity weathered each of these consolidations, suggesting that consolidation, per se, will not solve the problem (powell 2004, 35–38).

Another approach has been to create regionwide special-purpose districts authorized to administer selected public functions so as to reduce the ability of enclaves to exist unaffected by their location. The most prominent example has been regional governance instituted in the Minneapolis-St. Paul area, which then implemented a policy aimed at reducing fiscal disparity among regional municipalities (Orfield 1997). But while consolidations and regional governance have been credited with facilitating economic growth in many urban regions, significant black–white income disparities continue to exist in the Twin Cities (0.71), Indianapolis, Indiana (0.80), Jacksonville, Florida (0.74), and Portland, Oregon (0.75). Economic development and job growth of a metropolitan region do not necessarily have a direct impact on low-income minority neighborhoods. As Galster and Mincy (1993, 327, 330) observed, poverty levels of black and Hispanic neighborhoods are related to labor market changes in the counties in which those neighborhoods are located, rather than to changes in the wider metropolitan area.

As a general principle, enlarging administrative boundaries so as to include whites and minorities within single jurisdictions makes it more difficult for whites who fear members of minority groups to flee them (Tiebout 1956). Alignment of local governmental functions such as administration of schools

with county lines can work to the same effect of broadening the administrative units and so creating at least the potential for eliminating enclaves of privilege within them. Particularly in the South, school districts and counties are coterminous, which in the 1950s and 1960s made possible court-ordered school desegregation plans. David Rusk (1995, 9–47) has argued that the best hope for reducing racial disparity in urban regions is the presence of what he has called "elastic" cities—places where the possibility of annexation persists so as to incorporate racially homogenous enclaves into the larger city. However, minorities can be shut out from power in at-large electoral districts because of difficulty getting elected or appointed to office where racial bloc voting persists or minority leaders are outside the established local power structure (Sanchez 2006, 7–9). The optimal configuration, therefore, would seem to be metropolitan-wide governmental districts with representatives elected from individual districts within them. This facilitates regional planning, but increases the likelihood of proportional minority-elected representation.

Ostensibly race-neutral policies such as the preservation of green space and low housing densities can make the dispersal of affordable housing and access to job growth more difficult. Portland, Oregon, Orange County, California, and other places have implemented growth control measures that work to preserve the environment and open space, but can drive up housing costs and so tend to discourage minority movers (Kling, Olin, and Poster 1991, 239; Pendall 2001, 30). Homes in New Urbanism communities, which have been designed purposefully to facilitate community, have been in such demand as to be priced out of reach of most black and Hispanic homebuyers.

Stronger regional governance will succeed in reducing racial disparities to the extent that reduced racial disparity is a goal of public officials (Goetz 1994, 103; powell 2004, 47; Rusk 1993, 118–19, 125). Efforts by regional planning bodies to manage growth, preserve green space, attract new industry, build more public transportation, or even develop more affordable housing, may or may not address problems of race, depending on the interests of the leaders. In many cases, attempts to create greater racial equity have engendered opposition. In Atlanta, for instance, Kruse (2005, 246–48) observes that suburbanites do not feel much connection to central city Atlanta. Adjoining suburbs opposed attempts to annex them, and when the Metropolitan Atlanta Rapid Transit Authority, was created, boards of neighboring counties voted to reject membership, concerned that mass transportation would become a vehicle for drawing them into school desegregation plans. Historically city–county consolidation plans are more likely to be rejected by voters than to be approved, and there has hardly been a rush to implement voluntary intersuburban school desegregation. Improved equity in school funding across districts has generally resulted not because a metropolitan area acted in a concerted, purposeful way, but because of the pressure of litigation, most often brought at the state level (Murray, Evans, and Schwab 1998).

Whether or not environmental racism operates in a systematic way, racial equity would be achieved in metropolitan regions by implementing processes that guarantee that the burdens of siting of facilities with unpleasant externalities, but from which broad benefit accrues across the region, are widely distributed. Been (1993) has identified a number of principles by which fairness in siting might be accomplished. To achieve fairness in the pattern of distribution, metropolitan areas might aim for equal division of sites across a region, or perhaps even "progressive siting," which would require accounting for deficits of particular populations. Been also proposes utilizing competitive bidding, adjusting taxes or user fees so as to fully internalize the true costs of undesirable sites. Decision-making processes need to avoid bias against particular communities and be transparent. Other possible approaches involve principles of "fair share" utilization of impact analysis.

Access to Quality Schools and Economic Opportunity

Although the tide is clearly running in the opposite direction by the early 2000s, metropolitan school attendance plans would aid in the desegregation of individual schools and districts and bring greater equity to educational opportunity across race (Orfield and Eaton 1997). Extensive transfers of students between city and suburbs exist in Raleigh-Durham, St. Louis, Milwaukee, Louisville, Indianapolis, and Boston, produced by city–suburban school-district mergers and federal court orders and state incentives. Countywide desegregation plans, common in Florida, where school districts are coterminous with county lines, resulted in greater exposure between black and white children (Frankenberg and Lee 2002, 13). However, since the U.S. Supreme Court's decision in *Board of Education of Oklahoma City v. Dowell,* which relieved the school district of many of its desegregation obligations, increasing numbers of districts are attaining unitary status and so ending court ordered or supervised desegregation plans.

Improved education would also seem to hold promise for reducing racial disparities, because better-educated people make more money and a much wider segment of the housing market becomes available to them. For Hispanics and Asians, substantial evidence indicates the success of this formula. Unfortunately, Logan and Alba (1993) have found that blacks derive significantly less locational benefit from education, as measured by the median income of a neighborhood, than do other racial/ethnic groups. But regardless of how it is accomplished, regions need to find ways to either equalize funding among school districts or assure that levels of adequacy are reached. This funding in turn must produce better teaching, quality facilities, and strong educational practices.

In theory, targeted economic development strategies aimed at locating new jobs in distressed, black, or Hispanic neighborhoods should improve racial equity in metropolitan regions. In practice, this is extremely hard to accomplish. Employers make the final decisions on where to locate their firms. The types of incentives they can be offered by local governments, such as assistance with site assembly and tax reductions, are far less important to them than are proximity to market, access to transportation, quality of workforce, and room for expansion—factors that local governments have little control over in the short run. While individual municipalities certainly succeed in attracting and retaining businesses, it is hard to plan at the metropolitan level given the lack of county and regional jurisdiction over the types of things listed above that businesses most value. As a result, it is hard to ensure that businesses will locate in or near municipalities with the greatest minority underemployment. Regional governments and special-purpose districts can attempt to target economic development to areas of need through progressive siting of transportation infrastructure, use of tax incentives, and brownfield redevelopment.

Conclusion

Most urban regions in the United States are characterized by high degrees of separation of black and Hispanic residents from white residents. Equally problematic are significant gaps in the average incomes of blacks and Hispanics, on the one hand, and whites. Separation is greatest in the nation's largest metropolitan regions, none of which can really be said to have integrated housing patterns, and it is in these places that residential segregation is most troublesome because, for many, neighborhood segregation leads to lack of access to areas in regions where employment is growing fastest. Housing segregation and related disparity in income in turn cause concentrated poverty and its related ills, environmental injustices, and undermine equity in the operation of school funding mechanisms.

The challenges are different for different groups. Places with greater proportions of black population are more likely to be integrated as blacks overflow historically segregated neighborhoods. Distressingly, from the point of view of those who value residential integration, blacks and whites of similar income level remain very likely to live in separate neighborhoods. Conversely, places with more Hispanics tend to greater white/Hispanic segregation as newly arriving Hispanics congregate among earlier Hispanic residents. Concentrated poverty can result when newcomers are low-skilled, low-educated immigrants.

Evidence indicates that racial identity is reinforced by residential seg tion. With each succeeding generation that remains, or becomes segregated, may come less willingness to work toward the racially integrated society that would allow our school funding formulas and market-based housing and economic systems to function well.

There are no examples nationally of sweeping improvements in the racial equity of an urban region. Where improvements have taken place, they have happened in incremental stages around particular issues—litigation that results in the construction of new affordable housing or a more equitable school funding system, or a local housing ordinance that attempts to stabilize a community expected to undergo racial change.

Economic disparity between blacks and whites is lowest in growing places where a relatively small proportion of the population is black. However, in the older cities of the Northeast, where neighborhoods are dense and retain their ethnic roots, both residential and economic segregation of blacks and whites remains high.

Ultimately, changes in racial attitudes on the part of members of all major racial groups are probably required to reduce racially based disparities in metropolitan regions. From the 1940s to the 1980s, Americans underwent a remarkable transition from widespread belief in inherent racial difference and a corresponding reluctance to grant equal rights, to general belief in racial equality and support for equality of rights and opportunity. But there is widespread disappointment that greater racial equality has not resulted from the rights revolution and the targeted social support policies that quickly followed.

At the regional level, this disappointment with racial equity progress would seem to argue for the development of a public commitment to moving beyond reliance on either equal rights or remedial social services to individuals, to addressing the systemic problems of educational access, integrated and affordable housing, the transparent and inclusive public decision making suggested here, as well as constantly working to improve basic race relations. Decision-making processes need to be transparent, and minorities who will represent the interest of low-income, segregated communities must have seats in public bodies. Funding formulas for schools and regional transportation must be amended as needed to account for the implications of economic and residential segregation as long as those conditions persist.

References

Alba, Richard D.; John R. Logan; Brian J. Stults; Gilbert Marzan; and Wenquan Zhang. 1999. "Immigrant Groups in the Suburbs: A Reexamination of Suburbanization and Spatial Assimilation." *American Sociological Review* 64, no. 3: 446–60.

Ayres, Ian, and Peter Siegelman. 1995. "Race and Gender Discrimination in Bargain-
ing for a New Car." *American Economic Review* 85, no. 3: 304–21.
Barreto, Matt A.; Gary M. Segura; and Nathan D. Woods. 2004. "The Mobilizing
Effect of Majority-Minority Districts on Latino Turnout." *American Political Sci-
ence Review* 98, no. 1: 65–75.
Been, Vicki. 1993. "What's Fairness Got to Do with It? Environmental, Justice and the
Siting of Locally Undesirable Land Uses." *Cornell Law Review* 78: 1001–85.
———. 1994. "Locally Undesirable Land Uses in Minority Neighborhoods." *Yale
Law Review* 103: 1383–1415.
Binford, Henry. 1988. *The First Suburbs: Residential Communities on the Boston
Periphery, 1815–1860.* Chicago: University of Chicago Press.
Bledsoe, Timothy; Susan Welch; Lee Sigelman; and Michael Combs. 1995. "Residen-
tial Context and Racial Solidarity among African Americans." *American Journal
of Political Science* 39, no. 2: 434–58.
Board of Education of Oklahoma City v. Dowell, 498 U.S. 237 (1991).
Bobo, Lawrence, and Camille L. Zubrinsky. 1996. "Attitudes on Residential Integra-
tion: Perceived Status Differences, Mere In-Group Preference, or Racial Prejudice?"
Social Forces 74, no. 3: 883–909.
Bollens, Scott A. 1997. "Concentrated Poverty and Metropolitan Equity Standards."
Stanford Law and Policy Review (Summer): 11–19.
Brenner, Neil. 2002. "Decoding the Newest 'Metropolitan Regionalism' in the USA:
A Critical Overview." *Cities* 19, no. 1: 3–21.
Brill, Alida. 1996. "Tomorrowland at 40 Lakewood California." In *Rethinking Los
Angeles,* ed. Michael J. Dear, H. Eric Schockman, and Gregg Hise, 97–112.
Thousand Oaks, CA: Sage.
Brown v. Board of Education 347 U.S. 483 (1954).
Bullard, Robert D. 1990. *Dumping in Dixie.* Boulder: Westview Press.
Chiswick, Barry R., and Paul W. Miller. 2005. "Do Enclaves Matter in Immigrant
Adjustment?" *City and Community* 4, no. 1: 5–36.
Coleman, Henry A. 2002. *Fiscal Stress: It's Not Just a Big City Problem.* New Jersey
Policy Perspective. Available at www.njpp.org/web2printer4w.php/ (accessed
November 2006).
Commission for Racial Justice. 1987. *Toxic Wastes and Race in the United States.*
New York: United Church of Christ.
Davidson, Pamela, and Douglas L. Anderson. 2000. "Demographics of Dumping
II: A National Environmental Equity Survey and the Distribution of Hazardous
Materials Handlers." *Demography* 37, no. 4: 461–66.
Farley, Reynolds. 1970. "The Changing Distribution of Negroes within Metropolitan
Areas: The Emergence of Black Suburbs." *American Journal of Sociology* 75, no.
4: 512–29.
Farley, Reynolds; Toni Richards; and Clarence Wurdock. 1980. "School Desegrega-
tion and White Flight: An Investigation of Competing Models and their Discrepant
Findings." *Sociology of Education* 53, no. 3: 123–39.
Frankenberg, Erica, and Chungmei Lee. 2002. *Race in American Public Schools:
Rapidly Resegregating School Districts.* Cambridge, MA: Civil Rights Project at
Harvard University.
Freeman, Lance. 2004. *Siting Affordable Housing: Location and Neighborhood Trends
of Low Income Housing Tax Credit Developments in the 1990s.* Washington, DC:
Brookings Institution.

Galster, George C., and Ronald B. Mincy. 1993. "Understanding the Changing Fortunes of Metropolitan Neighborhoods, 1980 to 1990." *Housing Policy Debate* 4, no. 3: 303–52.
Glazer. Nathan. 1997. *We Are All Multiculturalists Now.* Cambridge, MA: Harvard University Press.
Goetz, Edward G. 1994. "Expanding Possibilities in Local Development Policy: An Examination of U.S. Cities." *Political Research Quarterly* 47, no. 1: 85–109.
Growth Within Bounds: Report of the Commission on Governance for the 21st Century Structural Reforms in Municipal Government. 2000. Governor's Office: Sacramento, CA (January).
Haar, Charles, M. 1996. *Suburbs under Siege: Race, Space and Audacious Judges.* Princeton, NJ: Princeton University Press.
Hacker, Andrew. 1992. *Two Nations: Black and White, Separate, Hostile, Unequal.* New York: Scribners.
Hamilton, David K. 1999. *Governing Metropolitan Areas: Response to Growth and Change.* New York: Garland.
Hendrick, Rebecca. 2004. "Assessing and Measuring the Fiscal Health of Local Governments: Focus on Chicago Suburban Municipalities." *Urban Affairs Review* 40, no. 1: 78–114.
Hirsch, Arnold. 1983. *The Making of the Second Ghetto.* Cambridge: Cambridge University Press.
Horton, John. 1995. *The Politics of Diversity: Immigration, Resistance and Change in Monterey Park, California.* Philadelphia: Temple University Press.
Hoxby, Caroline. 2001. "All School Finance Equalizations Are Not Created Equal." *Quarterly Journal of Economics* 116, no. 4: 1189–1231.
Huntingdon, Samuel P. 2005. *Who We Are: The Challenges to America's National Identity.* New York: Simon and Schuster.
Jackson, Kenneth, T. 1985. *The Crabgrass Frontier: The Suburbanization of the United States.* New York: Oxford University Press.
Jargowsky, Paul A. 2003. *Stunning Progress, Hidden Problems: The Dramatic Decline of Concentrated Poverty in the 1990s.* Washington, DC: Brookings Institution.
Johnson, Elmer W. 1999. *Chicago Metropolis 2020: Preparing Metropolitan Chicago for the 21st Century.* Chicago: Commercial Club of Chicago.
Judd, Dennis R. 1997. "The Role of Governmental Policies in Promoting Racial Segregation in the St. Louis Metropolitan Area." *Journal of Negro Education* 66, no. 3: 214–40.
Kain, John. 1968. "Housing Segregation, Negro Employment and Metropolitan Decentralization." *Quarterly Journal of Economics* 82, no. 2: 175–97.
Keating, W. Dennis. 1995. "Open Housing in Metropolitan Cleveland." In *Cleveland: A Metropolitan Reader,* ed. W. Dennis Keating, N. Krumholz, and D.C. Perry, 300–310. Kent, Ohio: Kent State University Press.
Kinder, Donald R., and Tali Mendelberg. 1995. "Cracks in American Apartheid: The Political Impact of Prejudice among Desegregated Whites." *Journal of Politics* 57, no. 2: 402–24.
Kling, Rob; Spencer Olin; and Mark Poster, eds. 1991. *Post-Suburban California: The Transformation of Orange County since World War II.* Berkeley: University of California Press.
Kozol, Jonathan. 1991. *Savage Inequalities.* New York: Crown.
Kraus, Neil, and Todd Swanstrom. 2001. "Minority Mayors and the Hollow-Prize

Problem." PS Online. Available at www.apsanet.org (accessed November 2006).

Krieg, Eric J. 1995. "A Socio-Historical Interpretation of Toxic Waste Sites." *American Journal of Economics and Sociology* 54, no. 1: 1–14.

Kruse, Kevin M. 2005. *White Flight: Atlanta and the Making of Modern Conservatism.* Princeton, NJ: Princeton University Press.

Krysan, Maria. 2002. "Whites Who Say They'd Flee: Who Are They, and Why Would They Leave?" *Demography* 39, no. 4: 675–96.

Krysan, Maria, and Reynolds Farley. 2002. "The Residential Preferences of Blacks: Do They Explain Persistent Segregation?" *Social Forces* 80, no. 3: 937–80.

Kuklinski, James H.; Michael D. Cobb; and Martin Gilens. 1997. "Racial Attitudes and the 'New South.'" *Journal of Politics* 59, no. 2: 323–49.

Ladd, Helen F. 1994. "Fiscal Impacts of Local Population Growth: A Conceptual and Empirical Analysis." *Regional Science and Urban Economics* 24, no. 6: 661–86.

Lehman, Nicholas, 1991. *The Promised Land: The Great Black Migration and How It Changed America.* New York: Random House.

Lewis, James H. 1995. *Preserving Privilege Inequity of the Illinois Education Finance System.* Chicago: Chicago Urban League.

Lewis Mumford Center. N.d. Dimensions of Segregation: Race, Class and Nativity. Available at http//:mumford.albany.edu/census/segregation/ (accessed November 2006).

Lieberson, Stanley. 1980. *A Piece of the Pie: Blacks and Elite Immigrants Since 1880.* Berkeley: University of California Press.

Link, Michael W., and Robert W. Oldendick. 1996. "Social Construction and White Attitudes Toward Equal Opportunity and Multiculturalism." *Journal of Politics* 58, no. 1: 149–68.

Logan, John R., and Richard D. Alba. 1993. "Locational Returns to Human Capital: Minority Access to Suburban Community Resources." *Demography* 30, no. 2: 243–68.

Logan, John R., and Harvey L Molotch. 1987. *Urban Fortunes: The Political Economy of Place.* Berkeley: University of California Press.

Logan, John R., and Linda Brewster Stearns. 1981. "Suburban Racial Segregation as a Nonecological Process." *Social Forces* 60, no. 1: 61–73.

Marshall, Harvey. 1979. "White Movement to the Suburbs: A Comparison of Explanations." *American Sociological Review* 44, no. 6: 975–94.

Massey, Douglas S., and Brooks Bitterman. 1985. "Explaining the Paradox of Puerto Rican Segregation." *Demography* 64, no. 2: 306–31.

Massey, Douglas S., and Nancy A. Denton. 1993. *American Apartheid: Segregation and the Making of the Underclass.* Cambridge, MA: Harvard University Press.

———. 1988a. "Suburbanization and Segregation in U.S. Metropolitan Areas." *American Journal of Sociology* 94, no. 3: 592–626.

———. 1988b. "The Dimensions of Residential Segregation." *Social Forces* 67, no. 2: 281–315.

McArdle, Nancy. 2003. *Race, Place, and Opportunity: Racial Change and Segregation in the Boston Metropolitan Area: 1990–2000.* Cambridge, MA: Civil Rights Project, Harvard University.

Milliken v. Bradley, 418 U.S. 717 (1974).

Murray, Sheila E.; William N. Evans, and Robert M. Schwab. 1998. "Education-Finance Reform and the Distribution of Education Resources." *American Economic Review* 88, no. 4: 789–812.

Oliver, J. Eric, and Tali Mendelberg. 2000. "Reconsidering the Environmental Determinants of White Racial Attitudes." *American Journal of Political Science* 44,
no. 3: 574–89.

Orfield, Gary. 1996. "Forum: In Pursuit of a Dream Deferred: Linking Housing and
Education: Metropolitan School Desegregation: Impacts on Metropolitan Society."
Minn. L. Rev. 80: 825–73.

Orfield, Gary, and Susan E. Eaton. 1997. *Dismantling Desegregation: The Quiet
Reversal of Brown v. Board of Education.* New York: Norton.

Orfield, Myron. 1997. *Metropolitics: A Regional Agenda for Community and Stability.*
Washington, DC: Brookings Institution Press.

Pendall, Rolf. 2001. "Exploring Connections between Density, Sprawl, and Segregation by Race and Income in U.S. Metropolitan Areas, 1980–1990." Paper presented
at International Seminar on Segregation in the City (July 26–28). Cambridge MA:
Lincoln Institute on Land Policy.

Pitti, Stephen J. 2003. *The Devil in Silicon Valley: Northern California, Race and
Mexican Americans.* Princeton, NJ: Princeton University Press.

powell, john a. 2004. "Equity and Regionalism: The Impact of Government Restructuring on Communities of Color in Pittsburgh." Keynote address for Sustainable
Pittsburgh. Available at www.kirwaninstitute.org (accessed November 2006).

Preston, Michael B. 1976. "Limitations on Black Urban Power: The Case of Black
Mayors." In *The New Urban Politics,* ed. Robert Lineberry and Louis Masotti,
111–32. Boston: Ballinger.

Pulido, Laura. 2000. "Rethinking Environmental Racism: White Privilege and Urban
Development in Southern California." *Annals of the Association of American
Geographers,* 90, no. 1: 12–40.

Rahn, Wendy M.; Kwang Suk Yoon; Steven J. Lipson; and Michael S. Garet. 2003.
*Geographies of Trust: Examining Variation in Generalized Social Trust Across
Knight Communities.* Washington, DC: American Institutes for Research.

Raphael, Steven, and Michael A. Stoll. 2002. *Modest Progress: The Narrowing Spatial Mismatch between Blacks and Jobs in the 1990s.* Washington, DC: Brookings
Institution.

Rohe, William, and Lance Freeman. 2001. "Assisted Housing and Residential Segregation," *Journal of the American Planning Association* 67, no. 3: 279–92.

Romo, Ricardo. 1983. *East Los Angeles: History of a Barrio.* Austin: University of
Texas Press.

Rosenbaum, Emily, and Laura E. Harris. 2000. *Short-Term Impacts of Moving for
Children: Evidence from the Chicago MTO Program.* Cambridge, MA: National
Bureau of Economic Research.

Rosenbaum, James. 1991. "Black Pioneers: Do Their Moves to the Suburbs Increase
Economic Opportunity for Mothers and Children?" *Housing Policy Debate* 2, no.
4: 1179–1213.

———. 1995. "Changing the Geography of Opportunity by Expanding Residential
Choice: Lessons from the Gautreaux Program." *Housing Policy Debate* 6, no. 1:
231–69.

Rusk, David. 1993. *Cities without Suburbs.* Baltimore: Woodrow Wilson Center/Johns
Hopkins University Press.

Sanchez, Thomas W. 2006. *An Inherent Bias? Geographic and Racial-Ethnic Patterns of Metropolitan Planning Organization Boards.* Washington, DC: Brookings
Institution.

Savitch, H.V.; David Collins; Daniel Sanders; and John P. Markham. 1993. "Ties that Bind: Central Cities, Suburbs, and the New Metropolitan Region. *Economic Development Quarterly* 7, no. 4: 341–57.

Shelton, Beth Anne. 1989. *Houston: Growth and Decline in a Sunbelt Boomtown.* Philadelphia: Temple University Press.

Sjoquist, David, ed. 2000. *The Atlanta Paradox.* New York: Russell Sage Foundation.

Sniderman, Paul M., and Thomas Piazza. 1995. *The Scar of Race.* Cambridge, MA: Harvard University Press.

Taylor, Marylee C. 1998. "How White Attitudes Vary with the Racial Composition of Local Populations: Numbers Count." *American Sociological Review* 63, no. 4: 512–35.

Tiebout, Charles M. 1956. "The Pure Theory of Local Expenditures." *Journal of Political Economy* 64, no. 5: 416–24.

Turner, Margery Austin. 1992. "Discrimination in Urban Housing Markets: Lessons from Fair Housing Audits." *Housing Policy Debate* 3, no. 2: 185–215.

Turner, Margery; Michael Fix; and Raymond Struyk. 1991. *Opportunities Denied, Opportunities Diminished: Racial Discrimination in Hiring.* Washington, DC: Urban Institute Press.

United States of America et al. v. Yonkers Board of Education et al. No. 80 CIV 6761 (LBS) 624 F. Supp. 1276; 1985 U.S. Dist. LEXIS 13713.

U.S. Census Bureau, Summary Files 3 and 4. Available at http://factfinder.census.gov. (accessed December 22, 2007).

Waldinger, Roger, and Mehdi Bozorgmeihr. 1996. *Ethnic Los Angeles.* New York: Russell Sage Foundation.

Weiher, Gregory R. 1991. *The Fractured Metropolis: Political Fragmentation and Metropolitan Segregation.* Albany: State University of New York Press.

Weinberg, Adam S. 1998. "The Environmental Justice Debate: A Commentary on Methodological Issues and Practical Concerns." *Sociological Forum* 13, no. 1: 25–32.

Wiggins, Mary Jo. 2002. "Race, Class and Suburbia: The Modern Black Suburb as a 'Race-Making' Situation." *University of Michigan Journal of Law Reform* 35 (Summer): 749–807.

Wilson, William J. 1987. *The Truly Disadvantaged: The Inner-City, the Underclass and Public Policy.* Chicago: University of Chicago Press.

———. 1996. *When Work Disappears: The World of the New Urban Poor.* New York: Knopf.

Wong, Paul; Chienping Faith Lai; Richard Nagasawa; and Tieming Lin. 1998. "Asian Americans as a Model Minority: Self-Perceptions and Perceptions by Other Racial Groups." *Sociological Perspectives* 41, no. 1: 95–118.

Yinger, John. 1986. "Measuring Discrimination with Fair Housing Audits: Caught in the Act." *American Economic Review* 76 (December): 881–93.

6

DAVID K. HAMILTON

Affordable Housing Policies in Metropolitan Areas

Affordable housing policy has generally been absent from the discussion about regionalism policies. Regionalists have been concerned with sprawl, transportation issues, pollution, government structure, and only peripherally with housing issues. Planning for market-based housing provision was a local planning issue, while housing affordability was a federal concern involving issues on how to provide housing for the poor, mortgage loans and insurance, and related support. However, with the increasingly visible inequities in metropolitan areas, more attention has been given to regional housing policy (Downs 1994; Pastor et al. 2000).

The response has been a movement to deconcentrate poverty from the central city and to demolish the more massive public housing structures in central cities. Housing has become a regional agenda item, with an increasing number of states requiring suburban governments to absorb a percentage of affordable housing.

For most regionalists, the major issues relative to affordable housing policy are the mismatch of job locations to residential housing, and the concentration of minority and poor populations in high poverty areas in the inner city and selected suburbs. The solution to these problems, according to some regionalists, is a more equal distribution of people in poverty across the metropolitan area and location of affordable housing near jobs for easy commuting. They assert that this desired outcome can only be achieved through regional policy requiring suburbs to either establish a plan to accept their fair percentage of affordable housing units or to cede control over land use to a regional or state body.

In this chapter, the following research questions will be explored:

1. Is there an affordable housing crisis?
2. To what extent is affordable housing a regional problem?

3. Should the government become involved in housing policies?
4. What public policies have been instituted to address the problem of the distribution of affordable housing, and what is the impact of these policies?
5. What additional public policies, if any, should be instituted to ameliorate the regional affordable housing problems?

Information for this chapter was obtained by an extensive review of the literature, a review of a number of reports by government and nonprofit housing organizations, and by numerous interviews with political leaders and housing officials. Unless otherwise defined in the text, the author uses the terms "public housing," "subsidized housing," "affordable housing," and "low-income housing" to mean housing that is below market rate. The terms "public housing" and "subsidized housing" are used in reference to housing that is either owned or heavily subsidized by a government entity.

The Affordable Housing Crisis as a Problem of Location

The federal government has determined that low-income families that pay over 30 percent of their income for housing are cost-burdened, and those who pay over 50 percent of their income on housing are severely cost-burdened. According to 2000 census data (DataPlace 2005), 21.5 million households, over half of those with incomes 80 percent or less than the area median, spend 30 percent or more of their incomes on housing. Almost 11 million of these 21.5 million households spend 50 percent or more of their incomes on housing. This means that about one in ten of all U.S. households in 2000 were severely cost-burdened—about 11 million of 104 million households. The Millennial Housing Commission (2002, 2) reported that, in 1999, one in four households reported spending more than 30 percent of income on housing and one in nine households reported spending more than half of their income on housing. Furthermore, according to the commission, the gap between the supply and the demand from the poorest households stood at 1.8 million affordable housing units.

Housing affordability is an issue that affects workers in a variety of occupations across diverse income levels and occupation types. Government employees in essential city services such as paramedics, firefighters, police patrol officers, and public-school teachers face affordable housing challenges, often finding themselves priced out of the very communities that they serve. Residents working in service industry positions—janitors, childcare workers, retail salespersons, and school bus drivers—are usually the worst off, often unable to afford housing, even with two salaries.

For example, one study, using 2003 salaries and housing costs, found that, in the District of Columbia, firefighters, police patrol officers, elementary-school-teachers, and registered nurses would be required to pay well in excess of 30 percent of their average monthly salary to own a home. The study showed that in most cases, unskilled service workers such as janitors and retail salespersons would be required to pay in excess of 70 percent of their average monthly salary to own a home (Fox and Rose 2003). Another study by Stegman, Quercia, and McCarthy (2000) found that 3 million working families with crucial but low-paid jobs, such as teachers and police, are severely cost-burdened. These workers are essential to the functioning of the community and are often unable to afford to live in the communities they serve. In their search for lower cost housing, working families often locate far from their place of work, where housing is more affordable. This dramatically increases their transportation costs and commuting times. Indeed, many families who are not able to find affordable housing close to work find that their combined housing and transportation costs are equal to a family that is severely rent-burdened. A study of housing costs and commuting costs in twenty-eight metropolitan areas by the Center for Housing Policy found that families who were spending 50 percent and up of their income on housing spent about 8 percent on transportation for a total of 58 percent of their income. Conversely, those who spent 30 percent or less on housing spent 25 percent on transportation for a total of 55 percent of income (Center for Housing Policy 2006, 1). Of course, this does not calculate the cost of a person's time or the opportunity costs spent on commuting.

The number of available affordable housing units continues to decline. The Department of Housing and Urban Development (HUD) reported that the nation lost 400,000 low-income rental units during the four-year period from 1993 to 1997, in comparison with a loss of 425,000 units in the previous eight years. An example is Chicago where the lack of available affordable housing is particularly acute, with the demolition of selected Chicago Housing Authority (CHA) buildings and gentrification that is causing rents and housing prices to escalate in many neighborhoods (Irvine 2000).

A major problem is not just the loss of affordable housing but its location. Affordable housing is concentrated in the central cities and a few declining suburbs in the metropolitan area, while low-skilled jobs are increasingly located in growing suburbs that are not readily accessible without an automobile. It is estimated that 56 percent of all government-assisted housing is located in central cities and only 17 percent is in the suburbs (Haley 2005, 1). The spatial mismatch in Chicago is evident as 69 percent of the new jobs during the 1990s were located outside of Cook County in the suburban counties that have only 19 percent of the region's total rental housing (Chicago Metropolis 2020 2002).

Because poor families normally are unable to save the equity necessary to purchase their own homes, most remain in rental housing. Many jurisdictions have tight rental markets. For example, in the Chicago region during the 1990s, the population expanded by 500,000 while the number of available apartments shrank by 52,000 (Metropolitan Mayors Caucus n.d.). The Chicago region created more than 469,000 jobs between 1990 and 2000 while adding just over 7,000 new rental units. In 1991, there was one rental unit for every 2.95 jobs in the region. By 2000, that ratio had changed to one rental unit to 3.4 jobs. Cook County lost nearly 5,100 rental units during the 1990s due in large measure to condominium conversions and the demolition of Chicago Housing Authority buildings.

Many suburban jurisdictions have extremely tight housing markets, which exacerbates the housing/jobs mismatch. A rental vacancy rate of 6 percent or less is considered to be a tight housing market (U.S. Department of Housing and Urban Development 2005). In the Chicago region, the suburban municipalities that are experiencing economic growth have a rental vacancy rate between 3 percent and 4 percent, while the communities that have the highest vacancy rate are the poorest and most distressed. Moreover, the communities with the lowest percentage of rental housing are the ones with the highest median household income. The more wealthy communities have rental units that are less than 20 percent of their housing stock with most wealthy communities under 10 percent. In contrast, those communities at less than 50 percent of the county's median household income have 33 percent or more of their housing stock in rental units. It is also not coincidental that the communities with the lowest vacancy rate and the lowest percentage of rental housing have very little affordable housing (University of Illinois Building Research Council 2004).

Apparently, the problem is not a lack of supply of affordable housing but its quality and location. Approximately 100 housing units are left vacant for every 300 new units constructed. New construction in the United States between 1950 and 2000 created 30.8 million vacancies. Approximately 26 million units were demolished. The demolished units are generally abandoned structures in the poorest, least desirable areas (Lyons and Hardy 2003). According to one study in Chicago, 107,865 housing units were vacant in 1990 in the city. In 2000, the number had declined to 90,940 units, still a vacancy rate of 8.5 percent compared with the vacancy rate of less than half that in the economically growing suburbs.

Overview of Federal Housing Policy and Its Regional Effects

The federal government first became heavily involved in housing provision as a way to stimulate the economy during the Depression and also to subsidize housing for the poor. Prior to that time, housing was a private market enterprise. Housing needs for those in poverty were generally met by the private sector and in some cases by local governments if they were met at all. The private sector supplied a variety of options in low-cost housing, including tenements, low-rent hotels, apartments over stores, boardinghouses, apartments in basements and over garages, flats in back, and so forth. These options became less available with the emerging zoning laws that separated living space from commercial and industrial activity and with building regulations that set restrictions on building lot coverage (Norquist 1998).

When the federal government became involved in housing provision through the passage of the Housing Act of 1937, it injected politics into low-income housing, replacing the pragmatism of the private market and humanitarianism of local governments and private individuals. Since 1937 and especially since World War II, low-income housing has basically been driven by federal policies subjected to tremendous political maneuvering and by pressure from developers and local government political officials.

Politics has informed every aspect of federal policy regarding subsidized housing, including the types of housing units to be built and where to build them. Over the years, politics has caused experimentation in federally subsidized housing programs, including efforts to influence both supply and demand. Federal policies have included direct subsidies to private developers, and block grants and tax credits. Political pressures have abruptly changed housing programs. Federal government involvement has been problematic at best. In attempting to improve housing opportunities for those unable to afford market-rate housing, the federal government ultimately created a worse situation.

Suburbanization Policies

Overall, the federal housing policies established in the 1930s and 1940s to insure mortgages and build public housing contributed to a policy of selective suburbanization favoring white middle-class movement to the suburbs. The middle class demand for low-density living was reinforced by government-sponsored Federal Housing Administration- and Veterans Administration-insured mortgages and favorable tax policies, which reduced the relative price of the single-family, owner-occupied units largely concentrated in the suburbs.

Other federal policies inadvertently augmented the post–World War II suburbanization trends. These included infrastructure programs such as the federal highway program that initiated the interstate system and federal grants for water supply and treatment facilities.

By contrast, there were almost no federal subsidies for multiple-unit structures typical of apartment dwellings in central cities. The net result was a strong bias in favor of middle-class ownership of new homes in the suburbs. At the same time, within central cities, New Deal-initiated public-housing projects became an important concentration point for poor and minority populations, adding to the push factors contributing to rapid suburbanization (Hamilton 1999).

Fair-Share Policies

Discrimination has been a major problem in the concentration of minorities and poor people in inner-city neighborhoods. The Civil Rights Act of 1968, also known as the Fair Housing Act, was the first major piece of federal legislation to address discrimination in housing. The act made it illegal to discriminate in the sale or rental of housing on the basis of race, color, religion, or national origin. This act was the beginning of efforts by the federal government to promote fair-share affordable housing throughout metropolitan areas.

However, implementation was undermined by local political opposition, the lack of interest in enforcement by successive presidential administrations, and by inadequate staff to enforce the provisions of the act. In the years following the Fair Housing Act, the federal government briefly supported metropolitan dispersal of assisted housing. HUD's Open Communities Program, for example, provided water, sewer, and infrastructure funds based on local governments' compliance with fair-share housing concerns. Councils of governments (COGs) were required to review local applications for federal aid to ensure that proposed projects were consistent with regional development plans. The cities of Dayton, Chicago, San Francisco, Washington, DC, and others started fair-share programs. However, to disperse fair-share housing across the metropolitan area required the involvement of municipal governments throughout the region, a condition that did not exist at the time (Goetz 2003).

Due to the stiff suburban resistance, the federal government's fair-share housing programs of the early 1970s produced few results. Any federal government proposal that came close to "forcing" low-cost housing on suburban municipalities was defeated by fierce suburban resistance. Even certain programs not explicitly or implicitly designed to disperse subsidized housing ran into stiff suburban opposition. For example, Operation Breakthrough, a program aimed at facilitating manufactured housing in response to a housing shortage during President Nixon's first term, was fiercely resisted because it was viewed as an attempt to locate minorities and poor people in the suburbs.

Programs consciously designed to induce diversity fared even worse. HUD's brief efforts to open the suburbs during the Nixon administration were buried in an avalanche of suburban opposition. A proposal to have HUD administrators review local zoning was immediately killed in Congress. The wrath of suburban congressmen against HUD's practice of making water and sewer grants contingent on affordable housing progress brought an end to that practice. A 1972 plan to distribute housing subsidies through metropolitan agencies was also killed by suburban opposition. By 1973, it had become clear that Congress would initiate no regional housing legislation that was unacceptable to suburban interests. Metropolitan-wide affordable housing efforts came to a standstill at the federal level (Goetz 2003).

As the federal government withdrew its support, most fair-share programs did not survive unless they were required as a result of a court case. A notable example is the Mount Laurel case decided by the New Jersey Supreme Court in 1975. This case held that communities could not zone to exclude low-income housing. Two subsequent lawsuits were required to fully implement the court's mandate of regional fair-share strategies throughout the state. In 1985, the New Jersey legislature created the Council on Affordable Housing (COAH) to oversee statewide implementation of fair-share requirements. The council assigns communities low-income housing obligations based on the existing housing mix, present and projected employment, and the amount of open land. COAH also sets time limits for compliance and has the power to enforce its regulations. In the first six years, COAH facilitated development of 16,000 new affordable housing units in New Jersey suburbs. This program still receives substantial resistance in suburban jurisdiction; however, New Jersey continues to conduct the country's largest fair-share housing program (Goetz 2003).

Scatter-site Policies

Although fair-share affordable housing programs were discontinued at the federal level, federally subsidized housing programs continued to receive substantial funding support until the 1980s. From 1981 to 1988, the federal government cut funding for conventional public housing from $4.2 billion to $573 million, and decreased construction of new additional units from 18,003 to 3,109. The federal programs of the 1990s have moved from high-rise concentration to scatter-site housing, which is intended to deconcentrate affordable housing. Local housing authorities, using the HOPE VI program, have demolished or rehabilitated public housing in order to convert sites into mixed-income housing developments. The goal of the HOPE VI program, begun in 1992, was to tear down the most distressed, large-scale public housing developments and move the residents into scatter-site developments.[1] However, more units have been demolished than constructed. For renters with less than 30 percent of area median income, the number of affordable units dropped by 13 percent (750,000 units) between 1997 and 1999. According to a 1999 nationwide survey, there are only 40 units of affordable and available housing units for every 100 households at or below 30 percent of median income (Clampet-Lundquist 2003).

During the 1980s, a host of lawsuits were filed by minority residents of public-housing authorities alleging various types of discriminatory and segregationist practices. These lawsuits and the HOPE VI program provided increasing pressure to deconcentrate public housing. Most of the lawsuits were settled during the Clinton administration and involved the construction of scatter-site public housing and/or the issuance of Section 8 assistance to minority households in conjunction with mobility counseling.

The tenant-based Section 8 program (renamed Housing Choice Vouchers), passed in the 1970s, provides vouchers to qualified low-income people to find housing in the private market. The family pays not less than 30 percent and up to 40 percent of their income toward the government-approved fair market rent. The voucher covers the remainder of the rent. In some instances, there may be a court-mandated requirement that the voucher be used in low-poverty, low-minority neighborhoods (Galster et al. 2003; Orlebeke 2000).

Initially, Section 8 vouchers could be used only in the jurisdiction covered by the issuing public-housing authority. In 1987, Congress amended Section 8 to allow certificate holders to use their subsidies throughout the metropolitan area in which the subsidy was issued, or in a contiguous area. Congress then expanded the so-called portability provision in 1990, allowing statewide mobility by certificate holders. Most local housing authorities were slow to implement portability guidelines. A national survey in 1991 found that only 3 percent of Section 8 certificates and vouchers had been transferred across jurisdictional boundaries.

Local housing authorities did not vigorously adopt portability for at least two reasons: (1) many local authorities established residency preferences for admission to the Section 8 programs—an internal HUD survey of the 51 field offices found that 42 percent of 2,541 local public-housing authorities had such residency preferences; and (2) the program often resulted in a loss of administrative revenue to local authorities each time a family exercised portability (Goetz 2003).

Current Policies

The federal government's current policy is to demolish the worst of the public-housing units, spur the production of low-income housing through tax credits and selective subsidies, and provide Housing Choice Vouchers to low-income families to find housing on the private market.

The federal government's involvement over the years has resulted in a current estimated 1.1 million households living in public housing managed by some 3,200 public-housing authorities. There are another 1.4 million households living in HUD-subsidized, privately-owned projects, and 1.9 million households in the Housing Choice Voucher program (Haley 2005, 1).

Section 8 Vouchers and Scatter-site Housing

After decades of using public housing and other federally subsidized housing developments to shelter the poor and only the poor, federal housing policy increasingly emphasizes two approaches that deconcentrate poor households. The dominant method is to disperse poor households throughout a metropolitan region by providing them with rental vouchers for use in privately owned housing. The other approach is to combine low-income and higher-income households in the same development.

Although they share the objective of deconcentrating poverty, the two approaches operate in different ways. Dispersal strategies try to move those in poverty into more affluent neighborhoods, while mixed-income housing attempts to attract higher-income households to developments that are also occupied by the poor. By the late 1980s, dispersal strategies (Section 8 certificates and vouchers) constituted the major focus of federal housing assistance. Because the subsidy is tied to the household and not to a specific building, rental vouchers enable recipients to seek out housing in any neighborhood, provided the landlord accepts them and the rent does not exceed the area's fair market rent (Schwartz and Tajbakhsh 1997).

There is general consensus among affordable housing advocates that deconcentration of poor individuals into mixed-income housing is the best policy both for community acceptance and to improve their opportunities for a better quality of life. The Gautreaux program, a desegregation program resulting from a court order, has relocated some 6,000 low-income residents from Chicago to middle-class suburbs using vouchers. Research by Popkin, Rosenbaum, and Meaden (1993) on low-income families relocated through the Gautreaux program shows that those minorities who moved into middle-class suburbs achieved significant gains in employment and earnings and experienced less welfare dependence than those who relocated within the city. In addition, children in these families experienced greater gains in educational achievement and job opportunities than children whose families did not relocate to the suburbs.[2]

HUD has made efforts in the past ten years to disperse recipients of subsidized housing in a variety of ways. It has relaxed the rules governing the Section 8 housing allowance program to allow greater portability of vouchers across municipal boundaries. It instituted the Moving to Opportunity (MTO) program, a demonstration program in five cities (Baltimore, Boston, Chicago, Los Angeles, and New York).[3] Many studies of the experiences of MTO residents moving from their high-poverty neighborhoods to low-poverty neighborhoods confirm the findings of the Gautreaux movers. Compared with the control group, they experienced social interactions with neighbors that were not significantly different from their old neighborhoods. They had better physical health and fewer reports of depressive or anxious behavior. There were reductions in self-reported criminal victimization and lower rates of criminal offending and arrests for violent crimes for their young boys. There were also fewer instances of behaving punitively toward their children or engaging in restrictive parenting practices (Galster et al. 2003).

Moreover, neighborhood influences on educational attainment were astounding. Studies comparing families that moved to more affluent areas in the suburbs with those that stayed in higher-poverty areas showed substantial differences. For example, one study showed that children aged five to eleven in Moving to Opportunity and Section 8 groups were 18 percent more likely to pass reading tests for their age, roughly double the rate of the control group (Rosenbaum 2003, 83). MTO movers were more likely to be in the labor force or employed after the move. In addition, MTO families moved to neighborhoods that were significantly more advantaged than the areas to which Section 8 families moved. The improvement in family well-being from the additional support provided by program administrators and the requirement that the families move from their high-poverty to low-poverty neighborhoods indicates that the program has achieved remarkable success in the short term (Rosenbaum and Harris 2001).[4]

There are, however, a number of problems with the voucher programs, including lack of funding. Currently, the Section 8 waiting list in many metropolitan areas is extremely long. In Chicago, families must wait up to five years before receiving a voucher. In New York City, the wait is eight years and in Los Angeles, ten years. Families still complain of insufficient time to search for units, not enough landlords to choose from on the list, poorly trained housing staff, housing discrimination by landlords, and personal barriers that delay them in achieving self-sufficiency (Popkin and Cunningham 1999; Turner et al. 2002). There has been a decline in the number of available Section 8 units from 1.7 million in 1995 to 1.4 million in 2003. There are a number of reasons for this decline. One reason is the booming housing market and the movement to condominium conversions of rental housing. Another reason is that many landlords seek to avoid HUD's rigorous inspections and paperwork, or think that low-income tenants could be trouble. Finally, HUD has rent caps on the maximum rent they will subsidize, and these caps are often below market rate in some areas (Keilman 2004).

Another problem with vouchers and scatter-site housing is suburban opposition. Hysteria over Baltimore's MTO program in 1994, for example, brought swift congressional action. A Republican gubernatorial candidate called the program social engineering, while another statewide candidate made the program a main campaign issue, denouncing the prospect of public-housing families moving out of Baltimore and into the suburbs. Intense opposition also arose in a number of inner-ring suburbs (ironically, their poverty levels were too high even to qualify for any MTO families). The reaction, according to one observer, bordered on mass hysteria. Anti–MTO buttons and T-shirts were produced and distributed to people fearing an onslaught of inner-city blacks. In the end, Maryland Senator Barbara Mikulski, chair of the appropriations subcommittee responsible for MTO, killed further funding for the program. One HUD source was quoted as saying, "The congressional message was clear: We don't want to hear anything more about HUD programs to move poor blacks into white neighborhoods" (Goetz 2003, 65–66).

Other communities have also reacted violently to scatter-site public housing. A lawsuit settlement ended Dallas's scatter-site effort. In Allegheny County, Pennsylvania, a crowd of 250 protested the housing authority's purchase of three townhouses, and local government officials organized a petition to secede from Allegheny County rather than accept these three units of subsidized housing. In New Haven, several homes purchased by the housing authority for the scatter-site program were the targets of arson. Public hearings in New Haven and Omaha have been extremely contentious on the issue of developing affordable units in nonimpacted neighborhoods (Goetz 2003, 65–66).

Another problem is a reconcentration of poverty and segregation in the suburbs. Studies of relocation patterns in Chicago show that 93 percent of those who have relocated to the suburbs have settled in communities that are majority African-American, and three-fourths in neighborhoods that are considered high-poverty areas. In one suburban Chicago community, 8 percent of its households have vouchers. In comparison, Chicago has about 1 percent. Concentrating subsidized families in areas that already have high concentrations of low-income families only perpetuates poverty concentration. The former CHA housing tenants have been fiercely resisted. In one neighborhood that was starting to experience market-initiated development, the middle-class African-American homeowners protested. The mayor of one suburban municipality that is largely minority with one of every ten housing units already occupied by voucher holders, has indicated that he wants no more voucher holders in his community (Kotlowitz 2002, 17–18).

Voucher holders face significant obstacles in searching for housing options. These include financial barriers (the cost of transportation, credit checks, and security deposits); limited time to search, particularly for employed participants; large family sizes; and personal problems, such as lack of communication skills, substance abuse, family members with criminal backgrounds, illness, and disability. The paucity of support services makes affordable housing in the suburbs less desirable for low-income people. Needed health and welfare support services may be located only in the central cities. Public transportation in the suburbs is not as convenient or accessible for shopping, health care, work, and so on. An automobile is almost a necessity to live in the suburbs, adding another expense to a low-income family's limited budget.

Government regulations and bureaucracy can also be a hindrance. Housing providers who were interviewed do not find the Housing Choice Vouchers program very attractive, except in rental markets with higher-than-average vacancy rates and lower-than-average rents. Even property managers otherwise sympathetic to low-income residents complain about the voucher program's red tape, intrusive inspections, and low rent levels (Metropolitan Planning Council 2000a). The program requires a landlord willing to lease to a family with a housing voucher to wait until the unit is inspected and the rental payment is authorized, a process that may take from two to four weeks. The delay between a landlord's acceptance of a tenant and the housing agency's authorization can result in a loss of 8 percent of a landlord's annualized rent each month the unit remains vacant. If everything else is equal, the landlord will rent to the first person who can pay the rent and move in. Moreover, especially in a tight rental market, landlords can be selective and screen out tenants they deem undesirable. This makes it extremely difficult for racial minorities, large families, single-parent households, and tenants without established work, credit, and renting histories. Finally, providers complain that Fair Market Rents established by the housing agency are below the asking rents in many neighborhoods (Metropolitan Planning Council 2000b).

Despite research to the contrary, perceptions persist that government subsidized housing reduces property values or results in a blighted neighborhood. For example, research has shown that there is no consistent relationship between assisted housing and racial transition in surrounding neighborhoods or that the introduction of scatter-site low-income housing invariably has a negative impact on property values of neighboring nonsubsidized housing (Freeman and Rohe 2000). Galster and colleagues (2003, 134–41) report in a study of small public-housing units scattered throughout the Denver area that the Denver Housing Authority (DHA) facilities actually served to increase the value of housing in the vicinity. The price-enhancing impacts could be attributed to the types of property the authority purchased and renovated. It acquired vacant, often deteriorated single-family homes or buildings that had less than twenty units and renovated them. The improvement in the physical appearance of these properties and the return of vacant buildings to occupancy might have served to stem the decline of the areas where they were located. They also found that the long-term positive impacts on housing values from the location of the public-housing units was better in higher-value neighborhoods than in lower-value neighborhoods. Moreover, proximity of the properties to each other was also a factor. If there was more than one unit within a thousand feet of another unit in higher-value neighborhoods, the result was a negative effect on housing value. Galster and associates concluded from their study that the presence of DHA dispersed public housing generally enhanced the value of nearby single-family homes. There were also no discernable negative impacts on neighborhood crime rates. Finally, homeowner focus groups felt that the DHA maintained their dispersed units well and that their facilities and occupants blended well into the neighborhood.

The case of the Denver Housing Authority (DHA) is illustrative of the fact that scatter-site housing in low-poverty neighborhoods can be unobtrusive. The DHA operated a public-housing dispersal program and remained free of public opposition or political visibility for almost two decades. In 1988, HUD ordered DHA to inform the Denver City Council about details of its housing units and obtain council approval for any new dispersed-housing plans. Public notification of plans for further acquisitions resulted in extreme opposition in the community and restrictions placed on the DHA by the city council (Galster et al. 2003, 15–16).

Policy Issues in the Concentration of Affordable Housing

Housing and Segregation

The nation's poor and African-American populations in most metropolitan areas are concentrated in a few locations. This is not by accident but by racial and income segregation policies. During the rapid development of the suburbs in the 1950s and the 1960s, evidence indicates that poor individuals and African-Americans were excluded through exclusionary zoning, such as requiring large lots for homes, not adequately providing for multifamily housing, and engaging in racial steering and redlining practices. Based on a study of municipal incorporation during this time, Burns writes, "The evidence suggests, then, that the operative concern here was race, and not simply the presence of low-income populations. The founders' goal, it seems, was the exclusion of African Americans" (1994, 91).

The result of these exclusionary policies is evident today. One study of sixty-nine metro areas using 2000 census data found that where blacks are a dominant minority, more than two-thirds of whites live in areas that have less than a 5 percent black population. In these same urban areas, more than half of the black population lives in neighborhoods that are more than 50 percent black. The average white person in urban America lives in a community that is 80 percent white and only 7 percent black. The average black lives in an area that is only 33 percent white and as much as 51 percent black (Report Finds Crisis of Housing Segregation 2005).

Some observers claim that racial bias is the major impediment to dispersion of affordable housing throughout the metropolitan area. The general perception is that people in subsidized housing tend to be African-Americans. Indeed, over 91 percent of the users of Section 8 housing vouchers in Chicago are black (Dreier and Moberg 1996). Over 40 percent of Chicago Housing Authority residents who have used vouchers to move to the suburbs live in two contiguous south suburban zip codes in largely black and increasingly stressed communities (U.S. House of Representatives 1995). One CHA resident searching for a new apartment said, "You want to go somewhere nice, but landlords know you are from the projects, and they think you're bad" (Maney and Crowley 1999, V2). African-American movers have found it more comfortable to live in largely black communities where they feel they will be welcome. This is understandable, given the stereotypical image of the "hostile, discriminatory" white suburbs. Thus, most Housing Choice Vouchers end up being used in relatively few neighborhoods in the central city and select suburbs—areas with higher vacancy rates, lower rents, and higher concentrations of poverty than other parts of the metropolitan area. This concentration could also be because of limited tenant knowledge about the market.

Others claim that race is not the issue it once was in the suburbs. The suburbs in many metropolitan areas are more racially and ethnically diverse with East Indians, Asians, Latinos, African-Americans, and new immigrants moving into what were previously all white communities. They claim that discrimination is now based more on income level than on race. People with money who can maintain their housing are generally accepted in the community regardless of their race and ethnicity. People who are poor and landlords who do not maintain their housing are not welcome regardless of their race and ethnicity.

The result of the concentration of low-income residents in selected suburbs is profound for those communities. One Chicago suburban mayor complained that the influx of poor families into his community has required the diversion of school funds for "special needs" students. He claims that crime is up. The police force has been increased by 35 percent from twenty-six to thirty-five officers. He asserts that even with an increased youth population, the once popular youth football program has died because of the lack of parent support. With the school system in decline, the tax rate rising to fund the required increased services, property values declining, and stores closing, the mayor fears that the community is in a downward spiral. The reconcentration of poor individuals and families in some suburbs and the attendant problems have prompted some to call for a cap on the number of voucher holders in a census tract.

To some extent, the tight rental market, the high rents, and the lack of large rental units for families is the result of past local government policy. DuPage County, an affluent suburban county in the Chicago region, offers a good example of government policies that restricted the market supply of affordable housing. Before 1970, there were no government-subsidized housing units in the county. By 1980 there were only 4,154 units. The county had a zoning ordinance that prohibited the construction of multifamily developments without a zoning variation or special-use permit. This was granted only if the project did not increase the school population or would not increase taxes to current property owners. As a result, most multifamily housing consisted of one- and two-bedroom units with rents sufficiently high that low-income families could not afford them (Possley and Gould 1981; Ziemba 1981). These exclusionary policies were changed subsequent to a judge's ruling in a court case in 1981. Because of previous policies, the supply of affordable multifamily rental housing has been severely restricted. The DuPage Housing Authority has been able to use only about 1,800 of the 2,500 Housing Choice Vouchers it has at any one time (Grady 2000). This is alarming given the large number of families waiting for vouchers in many jurisdictions.

The problem is not so much the concentration of poor and minority populations in the central cities and a few poor suburbs, but the fact that it isolates them from the economic opportunities available in other parts of the metropolitan area. As of 1996, only 16 percent of the jobs in the average metropolitan area were within three miles of the central business district in areas usually well served by public transportation (Blackwell and Fox 2004). As employment continues to decentralize from the central city to growing suburban areas, there are increasing problems of job inaccessibility for inner-city and suburban residents who are excluded from housing near available jobs. There is, thus, a spatial mismatch between job availability and worker access.

Studies on the spatial-mismatch hypothesis show a direct correlation between limitations on residential choice and availability of low-wage workers (Fieldhouse and Tranmer 2001). A study of commuting patterns in the Pittsburgh area found that low-income workers (laborers, domestic and service workers), as a rule, have a shorter commute than others in higher-status occupations. The study found that almost 60 percent of low-income workers live within one mile of the work site and almost 90 percent live within three miles. Distances appear to be a major barrier for the low-income workers in the central city who are willing to work for firms located in the suburbs with low-skilled job openings. Indeed, there is growing anecdotal evidence that suburban employers in many large metropolitan areas are experiencing shortages of low-skilled workers (Hamilton 1999).

Opposition to Affordable Housing

Affordable-housing advocates have had minimal influence in local politics because of the ideological barriers, concerns regarding impacts on property values, and the traditional municipal orientation to economic development and the provision of property-related essential services. Developers feel that affordability mandates depress the value of their investments. Business interests are notorious for opposing most forms of regulation on principle. Segments of the public view the poor as lazy, and they oppose government assistance on the basis that it weakens any incentive for the poor to get ahead on their own (Calavita, Grimes, and Reynolds 1994).

The literature on subsidized housing indicates that people resist its introduction in their neighborhoods for many reasons. Freeman and Rohe (2000) have catalogued the following objections:

- It will upset the racial balance in the neighborhood and lead to racial transition.
- The social pathologies associated with people living in low-income housing, such as dysfunctional families, welfare dependency, criminal behavior, and so on, will not be contained within the boundaries of the assisted-housing developments.
- Introduction of assisted-housing leads to further concentration of poverty.
- People living in low-income housing are not desirable neighbors.
- Any neighborhood with assisted housing becomes stigmatized, leading to lower property values.

Despite the stigma and the negative stereotypes associated with subsidized housing, some surveys suggest that there is more support for it than might be expected. For example, a 1995 phone survey in metropolitan Chicago found that only 40 percent agreed that increases in subsidized housing would harm their community. Only 41 percent of suburbanites and 39 percent of white respondents felt that increases would harm their community, in comparison with 42 percent of black respondents and 43 percent of Latino respondents who felt that increases would be harmful to their community (Metropolitan Chicago Information Center 1998). These survey statistics contradict other evidence suggesting that people are generally opposed to subsidized housing and are bitterly opposed to its location in their communities. Indeed, the survey results suggest that blacks and Hispanics may be slightly more opposed than whites. It is also significant that a majority of the respondents did not oppose increased levels of subsidized housing. Although any analysis of this statistic is speculative, it may be that many people responding to a phone survey give politically correct answers.

In another phone survey of metropolitan Chicago residents, the respondents were asked whether they supported subsidized housing for low-income work-ers in their neighborhood. For this question, support was substantially lower. While 62 percent of city respondents indicated support, only 49 percent of suburban respondents did. Likewise, barely 50 percent of white respondents versus 65 percent of black and 66 percent of Hispanic respondents supported the statement (Metropolitan Chicago Information Center 2000). Neighbor-hood connotes a closer proximity to one's own house and environment, and people may be less supportive of affordable housing when they perceive its location as in close proximity to their own home. Indeed, depending on how the question is asked, the response may be different. For example, a National Low-Income Housing Coalition survey showed that most people react nega-tively to low-income housing issues. The majority in their survey did not agree that in a rich country such as the United States families should be guaranteed a decent place to live. Instead, most indicated that since they themselves work hard to pay for housing without a government handout, everyone else should be able to as well. A typical response came from residents in a Boston suburb; while they acknowledged the need for affordable housing for poor families, they opposed low-income housing in their suburb because it might bring crime and drugs into the community and lower property values (Power 1999b). The mayor of one Chicago suburb maintained that people generally agree with the concept of affordable housing but not with its implementation through government programs.

In many suburban communities, opposition to affordable housing may occur because it can introduce a different type of housing into the community. One suburban mayor felt that people did not want the character of their commu-nity to be changed. He stated that residents of a community or neighborhood with single-family, detached homes oppose not so much subsidized housing but the introduction of different types of housing (such as multifamily build-ings). In the eyes of these community residents, multi-unit structures lead to the deterioration of the community and lower housing values. Anecdotal evidence supports the mayor's contention. One councilman in an upscale suburban community was not reelected because she cast the deciding vote for a townhouse development with units that were more expensive than many of the single-family houses in the community.

Other reasons given for opposing multifamily housing developments are the fear of increased traffic, parking congestion, and the drain on community resources. However, research has shown that apartment dwellers place less demand on public services than do single-family households. The average apartment household requires just 70 percent of the amount of community services that a single-family household consumes. It is less expensive to provide public infrastructure and services, such as police and fire protection, to higher-density construction. Apartment households place less demand on local school systems, with 36.1 children per 100 multifamily households versus 55.6 across all kinds of homes (Colton 2003, 164–65).

It is difficult to change people's perceptions about contentious issues. Studies show that people take cues from sources they perceive as credible on issues about which they are not knowledgeable or do not have strong feelings. However, if people have strong feelings and perceptions, they are less susceptible to the influence of a respected source (Hamilton 1999). Mutz and Soss (1997) conducted a study of the influence of a newspaper on molding public opinion on the issue of low-income housing. One of the two newspapers in the metropolitan area consciously chose to emphasize the issue for a calendar year. The newspaper's goals were to heighten the general salience of the low-income housing issue within the area and promote support for a requirement that all new multifamily housing developments include some low-income housing units.

The researchers conducted surveys before the newspaper announced its agenda and at four different times during the year of the campaign. They found that readers of the newspaper were no more likely to change their opinions on low-income housing than were readers of the other newspaper or nonreaders. Those who supported the issue continued to support it, and those who were opposed continued to oppose. Also, the salience of low-income housing as a personal concern to individuals did not change significantly over the one-year period. However, on a collective level, citizens' perceptions of general public support for low-income housing did move in a more favorable direction during the year. In other words, while readers of the newspaper individually remained opposed, they believed that public support for affordable housing increased during the year. The end result was that the newspaper's low-income housing proposals met with substantial opposition and were not enacted. However, three years later the county executive worked with the two U.S. senators to amend federal legislation to provide funds for a pilot project for mixed-income housing. People surveyed at the close of the newspaper's campaign had favored the concept of a pilot program as a more acceptable alternative than the newspaper's original proposal to require low-income housing in all new developments. In this instance, it is impossible to determine whether the newspaper's crusade had any significant impact on the acceptance of this pilot program.

Inclusionary Zoning

Inclusionary zoning is the antidote to exclusionary zoning practices. These programs may require one or more of the following:

- A percentage of units in new developments to be set aside for low- and moderate-income occupancy;
- Opportunities for developers to appeal permit and zoning decisions by local governments as in Connecticut, Rhode Island, and Massachusetts; and
- State programs that require local communities to provide reasonable opportunities for the development of affordable housing as in California, New Hampshire, and Oregon (Blackwell and Fox 2004; Goetz 2003).

These objectives typically are achieved through incentives or direct regulation of the development process, and they shift the costs of supplying subsidized housing to developers and market-based homebuyers. Probably the best example of the impact of inclusionary zoning is Montgomery County, Maryland. When the ordinance was enacted in 1974, it took about two years for builders to realize that the county was serious about enforcing this requirement. To date, more than 12,000 affordable housing units have been built.

Montgomery County's policy requires all housing developments of 20 units or more to make at least 12.5 percent of the units affordable to low-income households. If the developer sets aside more than 12.5 percent as affordable, the county provides a density bonus of up to 22 percent. This density bonus allows developers to build more units than allowed under standard zoning rules. For example, in a 100-unit project, a 15 percent set-aside would allow the developer to build 122 units. Eighteen of these 122 would have to be affordable to families below 65 percent of the area median income for a family of four. The developer sells the other 104 units at market rate, which is 4 more market units than would have been permitted without the bonus. The county also grants the local Housing Opportunities Commission first right of refusal for purchasing up to a third of the project's affordable units (in this example 6 units), so that they may be rented or sold to even lower-income families, and made affordable indefinitely. Otherwise, affordability requirements on the inclusionary units stay in place for ten years for ownership units and twenty years for rentals (Fox and Rose 2003).

On the question of whether inclusionary zoning programs should be mandatory or should rely on voluntary programs with incentives, evidence indicates that voluntary programs have produced little affordable housing, while mandatory programs have been more successful. Whether inclusionary zoning programs are voluntary or mandatory, private developers will not build housing unless they can expect a reasonable return on their investment. It appears that there is little market incentive to build affordable housing without government subsidies and nonmonetary cost offsets such as density bonuses, unit size reduction, relaxed parking requirements, design flexibility, and reduced or waived impact and inspection fees (Fox and Rose 2003). For example, a recent survey of the housing market in the Chicago metropolitan area revealed that there was no private-sector-generated low-income housing planned and very few small, single-family affordable housing units. The focus for the building industry was on large-lot, upper-end housing (Chicago Metropolis 2020 and Metropolitan Mayors Caucus 2005).

The three states with the most experience in inclusionary zoning are New Jersey, Massachusetts, and California. Even though the law in these states requires inclusionary zoning if there is not sufficient affordable housing, few localities have actually adopted and implemented inclusionary zoning policies. Porter (2004) estimates that less than 100,000 units have been built through these programs in states that mandate them, which is only a fraction of affordable housing built under HUD-subsidized programs. Even though the numbers may be small, inclusionary zoning, as a tool to promote affordable housing, can work to increase the supply and dispersion of affordable housing. In a study of the impact of growth management policies on affordable housing, Carlson and Mathur (2004) reported that of the sample of four growth-management counties the amount of affordable rental housing in Montgomery County increased between 1990 and 2000 while it either decreased or stayed the same in the other counties studied.

Other states, in addition to the three mentioned, are joining the ranks of states with inclusionary zoning laws. In 2004, Illinois passed the Illinois Affordable Housing Planning and Appeal Act. It requires all counties and municipalities with insufficient affordable housing, defined as less than 10 percent of total housing stock, to adopt an affordable housing plan. Rental units must be affordable to households with incomes of 60 percent of area median household income, and owner-occupied units must be affordable to households with incomes of 80 percent of area median household income.

This act has resulted in substantial controversy and resistance by suburban municipalities identified as not in compliance. One community voted in home rule believing that home rule exempted it from the provisions of the act. A number of other home-rule and non–home-rule communities are mounting a legal challenge. However, one community reacted constructively. Highland Park, a wealthy suburban community in the Chicago region, established an affordable housing ordinance. With the 2002 median home sale price at $430,000, and the median sale price of new single-family construction at $1.1 million and the increasing property taxes, residents, especially senior citizens, could not afford to stay in the community. Moreover, children of residents could not afford to locate in the city. The ordinance requires 20 percent of all new multifamily residential construction with five or more units to be set aside as affordable housing for households earning between $56,000 and $90,000. To date, Highland Park is the only wealthy community in the region to establish a mandatory affordable housing ordinance. Even Chicago does not have a mandatory housing ordinance. Highland Park's ordinance does have an opt-out provision which allows developers of nineteen or fewer units to pay $100,000 to the city in lieu of the affordable housing requirement (Vogt 2003).

Despite some success with inclusionary zoning programs in a few jurisdictions, it is still resisted in most parts of the country. Obstacles include the following:

- Elected officials are concerned about the public's response to their support for inclusionary zoning and its impact on their own political future.
- Private sector builders are concerned that it will negatively affect the marketing of their developments. (This has not been the case in Montgomery County.)
- The fear that affordable housing will end up in one or a few locations, concentrating low-income people. (This can be avoided if the government enacting the inclusionary zoning covers a large geographic area, such as a county, and if the inclusionary zoning applies throughout the jurisdiction.)
- Inclusionary zoning does not supply affordable housing quickly enough to meet the needs (Meeting America's Housing Needs 1998).

Housing Affordability and Economic Development

Researchers are increasingly making the connection between housing affordability and economic growth. There are those who say that using public dollars to support affordable housing adds tax burdens to businesses and residents and therefore is counterproductive to economic development. However, the Fantus group, business relocation consultants, lists a good housing mix in terms of availability, affordability, and type of housing as one of the seven critical criteria that a relocating company seeks. Affordable housing should be viewed as a factor in the economic development of the community not just as a social and moral obligation (Kotval 2004).

Berry's (2003) research provides evidence that economic growth is fostered by population diversity, collaboration with and between the public and private sectors, and location of creative and entrepreneurial residents. Residential diversity, in turn, requires a range of housing opportunities, from affordable to the luxury level. Successful regional economies need to provide housing opportunities at the beginning of the careers of young creative workers, many of whom are struggling to get a foothold in the local housing market. Berry argues that investment growth and new jobs follow the location decisions of the creative class, not the other way around.

The efficiency of the regional economy suffers when low-paid service workers, entry-level workers, and professionals such as teachers, nurses, and government employees, are unable to afford to live near their work. High housing costs contribute to upward pressure on local wages and salaries, which tends to undercut the competitive position of businesses. High housing costs may also crowd out expenditures on other forms of consumption. The exclusion and lack of mobility of the unemployed and underemployed reduces the overall efficiency of the metropolitan economy. At its extreme, social exclusion results in the marginalization or disconnection of groups of people and can impact negatively on a region's competitiveness (Berry 2003).

Case Study of Affordable Housing in Massachusetts

Massachusetts passed the Comprehensive Permit Law (40B) in 1969 to address the shortage of affordable housing by reducing barriers created by local zoning and approval processes. Its goal was to obtain a minimum of 10 percent affordable housing in each Commonwealth jurisdiction. Under the act, developers of state or federally subsidized affordable housing apply to a zoning board of appeals (ZBA) for a comprehensive development permit in lieu of separate applications to individual communities. The ZBA notifies the communities, holds hearings, and makes a decision on the permit. It has the same power and authority as a community zoning board to grant or deny the permit and to set stipulations. If the permit is denied or the stipulations are unacceptable, the applicant can appeal to the state Housing Appeals Committee, which can overturn or modify the ZBA's decision if the municipality has less than 10 percent affordable housing (Meek, Retzlaff, and Schwab 2003, 142).

Chapter 40B has had some success in opening up the suburbs to affordable housing development. Many of the recently developed units are providing affordable housing in the Route 128 and I–495 communities where there has been significant job growth. However, only 31 of 351 communities, or less than 9 percent, have reached the state-mandated 10 percent affordable housing goal (Massachusetts Chapter 40B Taskforce 2003). Only 12 jurisdictions in the Boston region have achieved the 10 percent threshold. Inner-ring and urban core communities continue to account for a disproportionate share of the Boston area's affordable housing. These jurisdictions have produced one-third of the region's housing supply, but account for 60 percent of the total assisted inventory.

Criticisms of the law include developer abuse, high service and infrastructure costs, and the creation of negative environmental impacts. Resistance in many suburban jurisdictions has resulted in multiple attempts to weaken the legislation (Marsh 2003). Despite the problems, nearly 30,000 affordable housing units have been facilitated using the comprehensive permitting process, and the number of communities with no affordable housing has dropped from 173 to 54 (Massachusetts Chapter 40B Taskforce 2003). The Massachusetts Department of Housing and Community Development (2005) claims that the act has stimulated affordable housing production that would not otherwise have taken place. The number of affordable housing units in the state increased from 85,621 in 1970 to more than 205,000 units by 1999. Most of the communities that continue to have no subsidized housing units are very small, rural towns in the western part of the state, where housing costs and demand are relatively low, and, by 1997, only one Boston suburb had no affordable housing (Meek, Retzlaff, and Schwab 2003, 142–44).

The Community Preservation Act was passed in September 2000 to enable municipalities to add up to a 3 percent surcharge to property taxes to create a fund for acquisition and maintenance of open lands, preservation of historic facilities, and development and maintenance of affordable housing. The state matches the money raised by the local community. The act requires that a minimum of 10 percent be set aside for each of the three areas of the act. The remaining 70 percent can be allocated over the three areas as the community determines its priorities. So far, 103 of the state's 351 communities, or 29 percent, have enacted the act. This act has had limited impact on affordable housing because the act is not mandatory and communities that use the law are not required to set aside more than 10 percent of the revenue for affordable housing. However, of those communities that have approved the act, 42 percent of the revenue has been allocated to affordable housing (Community Preservation Coalition 2005; Kotval 2004).

The state is also taking a more proactive stance toward regional cooperation. It established the Office of Commonwealth Development in 2003 to coordinate policies and programs of the state offices dealing with environmental affairs, transportation, housing, and community development. To date, this office has had little impact on regional housing policies. Recent trends in the region have been toward a greater concentration of poverty. The most prevalent form of development continues to be single-family, owner-occupied homes on large lots. For example, 53 percent of the region's communities issued permits only for single-family housing in the years 2000 and 2001. Only 13 percent of new housing permits in the region since 1990 have been for multifamily housing, down from 40 percent in the 1980s. Over 50 percent of the multifamily housing permits were in just five municipalities, with 20 percent of the total in Boston.

Housing costs in suburban communities in the region have increased to the point that many municipal workers and children of residents looking for their first home cannot afford to live in the communities. For example, in Bedford, the median housing prices increased from $228,000 to more than $400,000 in the 1990s. Rental units have been lost to condominium conversions, and small homes on large lots have been replaced with large houses costing as much as $750,000 (Kotval 2004).

Given the Boston region's history of segregated settlement patterns, people of color remain spatially concentrated. Minimal access to public transit to reach new jobs in the outer suburbs or to reach jobs in central Boston from far-away communities has left many low-income and minority residents with the alternative of purchasing an automobile, enduring extremely long, multiple-transfer public transit trips, or limiting their job opportunities. For example, North Waltham has 77 employers that currently employ 3,000 entry-level workers, but a commuter traveling from a central-city neighborhood with a high concentration of welfare recipients must travel on three buses and walk more than a mile to get to those jobs (Kotval 2004). Rapid transit investments are often made to serve wealthier communities, sometimes purposely avoiding low-income communities of color. In Roxbury in 1987, the old elevated Orange Line, which served a predominately minority neighborhood, was moved to service the Southwest Corridor, a wealthier, predominately white community, leaving local residents with an inferior bus service. In a recent five-year period, the Massachusetts Bay Transportation Authority invested four times as much in commuter rail services than in the bus system, even though there are four times as many bus riders. The bus routes comprise the form of transportation that serves the predominately low-income communities of color (Kotval 2004).

Housing and Quality of Life

Housing is a major element in determining the quality of life. Quality-of-life issues refer to people's feeling safe and secure in their person and property, not living in substandard housing or in blighted neighborhoods. A home is more than shelter; when located in a community with resources and amenities, it is a critical determinant of opportunity. Living in quality affordable housing in an opportunity-rich neighborhood creates access to good schools, employment, social networks, quality public services, and opportunities for physical activity. As discussed earlier in the chapter, low-income families who reside in affordable housing close to good schools, employment centers, transportation systems, parks, grocery stores, civic institutions, and services are better positioned to succeed economically and socially. One's affluence or lack thereof is often evident by the quality of housing. Owning a home is how most Americans build wealth. Yet, despite some closing of the gap, significant racial disparities exist in homeownership rates. According to the 2000 Census, 73 percent of white households own their home, compared to 47 percent of African-Americans and 48 percent of Latinos. Housing is inextricably linked to access to jobs and healthy communities and the social behavior of the families who occupy the housing (Blackwell and Fox 2004, 8).

Studies show that low-income people living in low-poverty areas enjoy a higher quality of life. They are healthier and more satisfied. This was evidenced through studies of the Gautreaux and Moving to Opportunity participants discussed earlier in the chapter. The Gautreaux participants who moved to low-poverty suburbs were more satisfied with the curricular and extracurricular programs in schools than were those who moved to high-poverty areas. Moreover, they felt that they could control their life, plan for the future, and get ahead. Further, they perceived their environment as stable and predictable and were taking steps to improve their lives. In contrast, interviews of housing project residents demonstrated that they often had a fatalistic attitude toward life. They perceived their environment to be unpredictable and unstable due in large part to intimidation by gangs and those involved in drug dealing. The investigators concluded that the attributes of neighborhoods and experiences provided by neighborhoods have profound effects on people's capabilities, attitudes about their lives, and their ability to improve their lives (Rosenbaum, Reynolds, and DeLuca 2002, 81).

Similarly, studies of Moving to Opportunity families in Boston in low-poverty suburbs found that children had fewer mental health and behavioral problems, and adults had less anxiety than the control group that did not move. The largely black MTO group living in the mostly white suburbs was not more socially isolated than the control group as evidenced by similar numbers of friends for both groups. Finally, those who relocated from high-poverty areas to low-poverty suburbs felt more secure and safe. This feeling of being safer in the suburbs was despite racial harassment that many of those who relocated to the suburbs initially experienced. After a period of time, the harassment was no worse than that experienced in the city. Moreover, the harassment was not life threatening, as living in the city in crime-ridden poverty areas was (Rosenbaum 2003, 86).

The desirability of the neighborhood is also a reflection of the condition of housing. People living in blighted neighborhoods with deteriorated and abandoned buildings, vacant lots where buildings once stood, and high incidences of crime obviously experience a lower quality of life than those living in less poverty-concentrated areas. Residence in disadvantaged neighborhoods increases the risk of dropping out of high school, teen childbearing, and adolescent delinquency, among other negative outcomes. While such "neighborhood effects" tend to be smaller than the effects of family and background characteristics, their emergence, net of controls for individual-level attributes, supports the idea that people's life chances can be improved if they move to neighborhoods offering more and better opportunities. Not only does the quality of life improve for the residents of deconcentrated affordable housing, it improves for the region as a whole. Traffic congestion in the region is reduced when people live closer to work. Deconcentrated housing reduces crime that is higher in concentrated areas of poverty, which spills over into other areas of the region. Finally, the costs to the community of providing services to high-poverty areas are greater than for less-impoverished areas.[5]

Policy Recommendations to Deconcentrate Affordable Housing

State and Local Government Policies

Observers generally agree that local government building codes and approval processes add substantially to the cost of building housing (Downs 1994; Power 1999a). Although empirical evidence substantiates this, one affordable housing developer asserts that the major cost is the land and local inspectors' interpretation of the building codes. Any state laws establishing uniform and reasonable local building and fire safety codes would still require local interpretation. Not only overregulation but also the interpretation of regulations create problems and increase costs. However, it is also important to enforce codes and regulations to keep housing from becoming blighted. Although landlords providing Section 8 housing are required to have their units inspected at least once each year, an investigation of Section 8 housing in Chicago found that inconsistent inspections keep problem homes in the program, cheap repairs quickly crumble, and many renters are too busy or afraid of eviction to complain. This study found that 40 percent of the inspections in the previous five years cited violations, many serious (Olivo, Bebow, and Little 2005).

Developers indicate that they would build more multifamily housing if the communities were less resistant. Resistance ranges from not allowing multifamily development to inflexible building codes, lengthy permit review periods, and high land costs. There are also limited subsidies for affordable rental housing. These conditions limit rental-housing development of any type—including apartments for middle-income people. Given that middle-class apartments tend to "filter down" to less affluent renters over time, the lack of new rental units for middle- and upper-income groups will further constrain the number and location of apartments for lower-income tenants (Metropolitan Planning Council 2000b).

Adoption of inclusionary zoning would, over time, increase the supply of affordable rental units and disperse them throughout the region. Inclusionary zoning can be combined with the Housing Choice Voucher program to maximize the use of scarce resources through a provision that a percentage of the units be reserved for holders of housing vouchers. Alternatively, the public-housing authority could lease or purchase a number of units scattered throughout the region to manage so that voucher holders can be placed in them without the administrative process and delay involved in dealing with a private landlord. The housing authority in Montgomery County, Maryland, purchases up to 33 percent of a developer's affordable units to ensure they are available for voucher holders. Another possibility is to provide assistance to homebuyers for purchase of the inclusionary units. Some jurisdictions encourage people to purchase the inclusionary units by providing low-interest loans and no down payment (Fox and Rose 2003, 29).

State mandates overriding local government building regulations or zoning restrictions are strenuously resisted. Local land use control is a major article of faith for suburban communities. With substantial political power in the legislature in the hands of suburban legislators, most state legislatures find it politically difficult to impose such laws. For this reason, affordable housing incentives are the preferred approach; however, the state should intervene with mandates if incentives and voluntary efforts prove ineffective. Incentives can take various forms such as additional tax revenue sharing to those local governments where the housing stock includes a certain proportion in multifamily units with rents below the median. The state can also offer property tax incentives to landlords with well-maintained affordable housing, as determined by local government inspectors, and property tax penalties to landlords with housing-code violations. For example, Illinois has a law that landlords renting to voucher holders in any census tract with less than 10 percent of residents at the poverty level can receive a rebate on their property taxes (Yednak 2004). Property tax assessments could also be reduced for landlords who rent to voucher holders. Cook County, Illinois, reduces the property assessment rate on multifamily rental units that provide affordable housing from 26 percent to 16 percent for a ten-year period with the option to renew for additional ten-year periods.

Local governments can enact a number of policies to improve the percentage of low-income units. For example, in Oak Park, Illinois, the Regional Housing Center conducts affirmative marketing of rental housing to promote integration. Financial incentives are available to landlords who accept tenants from the center. Shaker Heights, Ohio, opened its housing office in 1967 to market the municipality as an integrated housing market. Its policies include below-market mortgages offered from the Fund for the Future of Shaker Heights to improve integration (Keating 1995). Local governments can also provide density bonuses and other incentives to encourage developers to include a percentage of low-income units within their developments. They can also provide incentives for landlords to set aside a percentage of their units for the Housing Choice Voucher program. Partnerships between governments and developers can also help to increase the supply of affordable housing. Moreover, a municipality could buy land and lease or sell it to a developer at an attractive interest rate as an incentive to build mixed-income housing. Since multifamily housing is being accepted in more and more suburbs, scattering affordable housing units into these developments would probably not raise opposition. Indeed, if they were well maintained, neighbors would not know that they were reserved for low-income families.

Education

Unlike central cities, there are few affordable housing advocacy groups in the suburbs to advocate for, and educate people about, affordable housing. Because of the opposition, a broad-based community coalition will be required to educate the community and lobby for policies promoting affordable housing. This coalition should include not just traditional advocates for poor families, but also working families, organized labor, church leaders, political leaders, and the business community. Creating and maintaining strong public–private coalitions and partnerships will reduce political impediments to the acceptance of low-income housing. Since local governments and the public are normally concerned with jobs and job creation, the private sector must play a key role in the coalition for affordable housing.

Provision of affordable housing must become part of a region's political and economic culture. A positive outreach to the community showing that affordable housing units can be as well kept as other units, if not better kept, would help to eliminate the negative image of subsidized housing. The opposition's issues should be immediately addressed, not by the affordable housing advocates, but by respected members of the community who are perceived as nonbiased. A campaign was recently launched in Chicago to build public support for affordable housing, correct misconceptions, and raise public awareness about the need for affordable housing. The message conveyed is that affordable housing is what allows teachers, nurses, police officers, and firefighters to live where they work. The message is also that affordable housing provides entry-level homes for young married people and opportunities for older adults to downsize without having to leave their communities (Grady and Yednak 2005).

Community acceptance of affordable housing depends on the credibility and preparation of the local housing agency, the support of political and community leaders, and the power and influence of the opposition. Private developers are a key component of any affordable housing plan. They should be represented on task forces and be involved in meetings as the plans are being created. Their commitment is essential to the success of affordable housing (Calavita, Grimes, and Reynolds 1994). San Jose's Department of Housing is an example of a successful housing agency. Since its inception in 1988, not a single affordable housing project has been rejected. Factors in its success include:

- City-financed affordable housing is often more attractive than the existing housing stock, effectively raising or stabilizing property values.
- The city works aggressively in the community to educate residents about the need for affordable housing and its relationship to economic development.
- The city has invested significant funds in developing and distributing agency and program marketing materials that bring a familiar face to housing by describing the kinds of people who need affordable housing (nurses, teachers, and so on).
- There are many avenues for the community to express its views about housing, from the Housing Advisory Commission all the way to the City Council.
- Housing costs in the area are high, meaning that affordable housing is clearly a benefit to moderate-income as well as low-income families (Association for Local Housing Finance Agencies and National Association for County Community and Economic Development 1997).

Nongovernmental Organization Involvement

Businesses should be actively involved in working with communities and their employees in order to provide nearby housing for their low-wage employees.

A growing number of companies provide assistance. A recent survey by the Society of Human Resource Management found that one in eight employers provided some form of mortgage or down-payment assistance. Assistance varies from rental subsidies or grants that cover closing costs to low-interest or forgivable loans. Assistance could also include matched savings, interest-rate buydowns, shared appreciation, and homebuyer education classes (Sichelman 2005). For example, Howard University bought and restored row houses in a nearby deteriorating neighborhood and provides forgivable loans equal to 7 percent of the purchase price to employees to move into the houses. The loans are forgivable if the employee stays for more than five years (Pugh 2000). Miami-Dade County has a program for county employees to assist them with counseling and home-buying assistance. They can receive below-market-rate loans and other benefits, which could include down-payment or closing-cost assistance, and homebuyer assistance. One hospital in suburban Chicago provides loans up to $5,000 for down payments, which are forgiven if the employee remains with the hospital more than five years. Businesses could also support affordable housing in other ways. One program sponsored by a civic organization recruits businesses to endorse a statement that they will not locate or expand in a community with policies that discourage the development of affordable housing. Over 100 companies have endorsed the concept.

Suburban community development corporations (CDCs) are needed to replicate in the suburbs their successes in improving housing and revitalizing inner-city neighborhoods in many cities. CDCs can access government grants and become involved in broad community development activities in addition to low-income-housing issues. Indeed, a reasonable strategy would be for a CDC to partner with a private developer to rehabilitate blighted housing and develop mixed-income housing to attract middle-class residents. At the same time, the CDC could work to attract business to the community, providing jobs for the residents.

An example of a successful initiative is the Charlotte/Mecklenburg Housing Partnership. This partnership was created in 1984 as a financial intermediary that worked with a CDC created by the Bank of America to develop financial packages and work with private developers to build housing in the low to moderate price range. The partnership, in essence, provided a financial package, a list of suppliers, plans, and a budget to the private developer. The result was a high production of market-based, affordable housing by the private sector with thousands of units built during the 1990s. The Housing Partnership also held ownership classes and worked with new homeowners to avoid foreclosures.

Federal Government Involvement

The federal government holds the most sweeping reallocative position in the federal system hierarchy. This places unique responsibilities on the federal government. These include efforts to assist in financing affordable housing, in regulating it, and in providing a metropolitan scope. Federal government housing programs are essential to provide funding support for various housing and community development initiatives. The federal grant programs should have guidelines and parameters but allow maximum flexibility for state and local discretion to tailor programs to meet local needs. These grants should be integrated with state and county programs to encourage dispersal of low-income families throughout the suburbs. Moreover, programs to encourage homeownership should be encouraged throughout the suburbs using government housing vouchers to help pay the mortgage and community development grants to subsidize the down payment.

Federal grants should be administered by housing agencies that cut across local government boundaries (Pastor et al. 2000). Housing agencies administering federal grants should have at minimum countywide jurisdiction and preferably regionwide jurisdiction. Although voucher recipients are allowed to use the vouchers anywhere in the United States, the current fragmented system of administering the vouchers discourages holders to go beyond the housing agency's jurisdiction. The portability process is administratively burdensome requiring agreements between the sending housing agency and the receiving housing agency. Moreover, housing agencies tend to focus their operations within their geographical boundaries.

A regional housing agency would be more aware of housing opportunities outside of the central city and have a greater incentive to assist low-income families to find rental housing in the suburbs. A regional housing agency would also have more incentive to develop mixed-income housing in the suburbs. Federal guidelines to the regional agency should provide incentives to move low-income families to low-poverty neighborhoods (census tracts where the poverty rate is below 10 percent) similar to the Moving to Opportunity program that has been operating as a small pilot program.

Affordable housing is usually located in disinvested neighborhoods or older suburban communities with a large minority population and high poverty rates. Therefore, Housing Choice Voucher households are steered by market forces to areas where affordable rents are allowable under HUD's fair market rent guidelines.

A regional housing authority with authority to administer the Housing

Choice Voucher Program would solve portability problems and improve service delivery in several ways. First, the housing authority can provide clients with up-to-date apartment listings from other communities that should increase the odds of families locating housing in racially diverse and moderate-income neighborhoods. Furthermore, a regional housing authority can influence policymakers to increase funding for vouchers, scattered-sites, and housing counseling. Finally, a regional housing authority can provide a unified voice to fragmented agencies, governments, social service providers, and advocates (Katz and Turner 2001).

There is precedent for regional housing authorities. In the late 1960s, HUD encouraged the development of multicounty regional housing authorities in more rural areas. The Housing Assistance Council, a private affordable-housing advocacy group, provided guidance and financial support, and in the 1970s several regional housing agencies were created. Since HUD did not distinguish between different types of housing authorities, no exact count is available. However, it is estimated that by 1978, there were forty-three regional housing authorities in nine states (Reid et al. 1980).

Conclusion

The overriding issue that has been the major focus of this chapter is the need to bring affordable housing to middle-class suburbs. As discussed in the chapter, most low-income families moving to the suburbs concentrate in only a few suburbs. The result is a reconcentration of poverty in already stressed communities. The goal of an affordable housing program should be to make affordable housing available throughout the suburbs and especially near jobs. Governments should use a combination of vouchers and mixed-income housing developments. Vouchers alone will not work in middle-class communities due to the paucity of affordable housing. Government incentive programs, such as those discussed above, for both the developer and the host community, should be instituted to encourage mixed-income housing with the use of mandates if incentives are not effective.

Progress has been made in bringing affordable housing to middle-class suburbs, even though it has seemed glacial in its slowness. However, looking back ten years, one can see progress. This progress can be accelerated through state fair-share legislation and the introduction of incentives and waivers to provide maximum flexibility in the use of housing funds and programs to meet the particular needs of the area. As well-maintained, multifamily housing becomes the norm, affordable housing in the suburbs will become more acceptable, and the pace of progress will quicken.

Notes

1. The George W. Bush administration has let the Hope VI program lapse (Broder 2006).

2. Recent research by Reed, Pashup, and Snell (2005) on Gautreaux movers did not come to the same conclusions on employment gains. In-depth interviews with women movers (most of the households in the Gautreaux program are woman-headed households) revealed that moving out of a highly segregated, high-poverty neighborhood into a more affluent and racially mixed neighborhood had little effect on increased or reduced employment, at least initially. Simply moving does not encourage greater labor force participation. Also the personal and health issues do not disappear when families move into a more affluent area. In fact, some issues, such as childcare problems may be exacerbated by the move because they no longer have a support network of family and friends.

3. Moving to Opportunity was designed to ascertain differences in mobility behavior and family outcomes for three groups: a control group residing in public housing in concentrated poverty neighborhoods, a group of former public-housing residents who receive standard Section 8 assistance, and a group of former public-housing residents who must use their Section 8 assistance in census tracts having 10 percent or lower poverty rates and who also receive extensive mobility assistance.

4. Recent research is also questioning some of the initial rosy findings of the MTO demonstration program. Clampet-Lundquist and Massey (2006) report that MTO movers often had a difficult time finding housing in the required low-poverty neighborhoods and would occasionally be allowed to locate in higher-poverty neighborhoods. They also report that the education attainment of the movers was not materially different from that of the group using regular Section 8 vouchers. About 40 percent of the experimental MTO group returned to high-poverty areas, indicating dissatisfaction with their situation.

5. Even though disadvantaged neighborhoods may not receive the same frequency of some services, such as street maintenance, and may have fewer neighborhood libraries and playgrounds than more wealthy neighborhoods, they receive more extensive social and police services. On balance, the community costs to provide services to these neighborhoods are higher than those in wealthier neighborhoods.

References

Association for Local Housing Finance Agencies and National Association for County Community and Economic Development. 1997. *Managing Local Opposition to Affordable Housing: Strategies and Tools.* Washington, DC.

Berry, M. 2003. "Why Is It Important to Boost the Supply of Affordable Housing in Australia—and How Can We Do It?" *Urban Policy and Research* 21, no. 4: 413–35.

Blackwell, A.G., and R.K Fox. 2004. *Regional Equity and Smart Growth: Opportunities for Advancing Social and Economic Justice in America.* Oakland, CA: Funders' Network.

Broder, D. 2006. "City Muscles up the Broad Shoulders." *St. Louis Post Dispatch,* August 7: B, 9.

Burns, N. 1994. *The Formation of American Local Governments: Private Values in Public Institutions.* New York: Oxford University Press.

Calavita, N.; K. Grimes; and S. Reynolds. 1994. "Zigzagging Toward Long-Term Affordability in the Sunbelt." In *Affordable City: Toward a Third Sector Housing Policy,* ed. J.E. Davis, 265–95. Philadelphia: Temple University Press.

Carlson, D., and S. Mathur. 2004. "Does Growth Management Aid Affordable Housing?" In *Growth Management and Affordable Housing: Do They Conflict?* ed. A. Downs, 20–81. Washington, DC: Brookings Institution.

Center for Housing Policy. 2006. *A Heavy Load: The Combined Housing and Transportation Burdens of Working Families.* Washington, DC (October).

Chicago Metropolis 2020. 2002. *The 2002 Metropolis Index.* Chicago.

Chicago Metropolis 2020 and Metropolitan Mayors Caucus. 2005. *Homes for a Changing Region.* Chicago: Chicago Metropolis 2020.

Clampet-Lundquist, S. 2003. "Finding and Keeping Affordable Housing: Analyzing the Experiences of Single-Mother Families in North Philadelphia." *Journal of Sociology and Social Welfare* 33, no. 4: 123–41.

Clampet-Lundquist, S., and D. Massey. 2006. "Neighborhood Effect, Race, and Poverty in the MTO Demonstration." Paper presented at the annual meeting of the Urban Affairs Association, Montreal (March).

Colton, K.W. 2003. *Housing in the Twenty-First Century: Achieving Common Ground.* Cambridge, MA: Harvard University Press.

Community Preservation Coalition. 2005. Available at www.communitypreservation.org (accessed November 2005).

DataPlace. 2005. Available at www.dataplace.org/area_overview/index.html (accessed October 2005).

Downs, A. 1994. *New Visions for Metropolitan America.* Washington, DC, and Cambridge, MA: Brookings Institution and Lincoln Institute of Land Policy.

Dreier, P., and D. Moberg. 1996. "Moving from the 'Hood: The Mixed Success of Integrating Suburbia." *American Prospect* 24 (Winter): 75–79.

Fieldhouse, E., and M. Tranmer. 2001. "Concentration Effects, Spatial Mismatch or Neighborhood Selection." *Geographical Analysis* 33, no. 4: 353–74.

Fox, R., and K. Rose. 2003. *Expanding Housing Opportunity in Washington, DC: The Case for Inclusionary Zoning.* Oakland, CA: Policy Link. Available at www.policylink.org (accessed October 2005).

Freeman, L., and W. Rohe. 2000. "Subsidized Housing and Neighborhood Racial Transition: An Empirical Investigation." *Housing Policy Debate* 11, no. 1: 67–89.

Galster, G.C.; P. Tatian; A. Santiago; K. Pettit; and R. Smith. 2003. *Why Not in My Backyard? Neighborhood Impacts of Deconcentrating Assisted Housing.* New Brunswick, NJ: Rutgers University Center for Urban Policy Research.

Goetz, E.G. 2003. *Clearing the Way: Deconcentrating the Poor in Urban America.* Washington, DC: Urban Institute Press:

Grady, W. 2000. "Rent Aid May Open Gate to Home Buying." *Chicago Tribune,* October 20: 2, 1.

Grady, W., and C. Yednak. 2005. "TV Ads Tout Need for Affordable Housing." *Chicago Tribune,* February 7: 2, 1.

Haley, B. 2005. "Guest Editor's Introduction: Cityscape." *Journal of Policy Development and Research* 8, no. 2: 1–4.

Hamilton, D. 1999. *Governing Metropolitan Areas: Response to Growth and Change.* New York: Garland.

444

Irvine, M. 2000. "U.S. Housing Crisis." *Chicago Sun Times,* March 29: 66.

Katz, L., and M.A. Turner. 2001. "Who Should Run the Housing Choice Program?" *Housing Policy Debate* 12, no. 2: 239–81.

Keating, W.D. 1995. "Open Housing in Metropolitan Cleveland." In *Cleveland: A Metropolitan Reader,* ed. W.D. Keating, N. Krumholz, and D.C. Perry, 300–309. Kent, OH: Kent State University Press.

Keilman, J. 2004. "Doors Shut on Needy Renters." *Chicago Tribune,* December 12: 1, 1.

Kotlowitz, A. 2002. "Where Is Everyone Going?" *Tribune Magazine,* March 1: 17–18.

Kotval, Z. 2004. "Preservation and Housing as Catalysts for Economic Growth." *Economic Development Journal* 3, no. 1: 43–49.

Lyons, A., and J. Hardy. 2003. "The Crises in Housing: Thinking the Unthinkable." In *Affordable Housing in the Chicago Region: Perspectives and Strategies,* ed. P. Nyden, J. Lewis, K. Williams, and N. Benefield, 4–27. Chicago: Housing Affordability Research Consortium, Loyola University and Roosevelt University.

Maney, B., and S. Crowley. 1999. *Scarcity and Success: Perspectives on Assisted Housing.* Washington, DC: National Low-Income Housing Coalition.

Marsh, D.S. 2003. *Promise and Challenge: Achieving Regional Equity in Greater Boston.* Oakland, CA: Policy Link. Available at www.policylink.org (accessed November 2005).

Massachusetts Chapter 40B Taskforce. 2003. *Report to Massachusetts Governor Mitt Romney, 30 May.* Available at www.state.ma.us/dhcd/Ch40Btf/ (accessed January 2006).

Massachusetts Department of Housing and Community Development. 2005. *Chapter 40B: What do the Numbers Show?* Available at www.state.ma.us/dhcd/Ch40B/Data. htm (accessed January 2006).

Meek, S.; R. Retzlaff; and J. Schwab. 2003. *Regional Approaches to Affordable Housing.* PAS Report 513/514. Chicago: American Planning Association.

Meeting America's Housing Needs. 1998. *Discrimination and Barriers to Equal Access to Housing.* A Habitat II Follow-up Project. Washington, DC. Available at www.nlihc.org/mahndiscrim.pdf (accessed August 2007).

Metropolitan Chicago Information Center. 1998. *1991–1998 Metro Report.* Chicago.

———. 2000. *Metro Survey: 1990–2000.* Chicago.

Metropolitan Mayors Caucus. N.d. *Northeastern Illinois Housing Endorsement Criteria.* Chicago.

Metropolitan Planning Council. 2000a. *Transformation Plan Update.* Chicago.

———. 2000b. *Regional Rental Market Analysis.* Chicago.

Millennial Housing Commission. 2002. "Meeting Our Nation's Housing Challenges: Report of the Bipartisan Millennial Housing Commission." Washington, DC.

Mutz, D.C., and J. Soss. 1997. "Reading Public Opinion: The Influence of News Coverage on Perceptions of Public Sentiment." *Public Opinion Quarterly* 61, no. 3: 431–52.

Norquist, J.O. 1998. "How the Government Killed Affordable Housing." *American Enterprise* July/August: 68–70.

Olivo, A.; J. Bebow; and D. Little. 2005. "Landlords Fail to Fix Poor's Housing Woes." *Chicago Tribune,* May 22: 1, 1.

Orlebeke, C.J. 2000. "The Evolution of Low-Income Housing Policy, 1949–1999." *Housing Policy Debate* 1, no. 2: 489–519.

Pastor Jr., M.; P. Dreier; J.E. Grigsby III; and M. Lopez-Garza. 2000. *Regions That Work: How Cities and Suburbs Can Grow Together.* Minneapolis: University of Minnesota Press.

Popkin, S., and M.K. Cunningham. 1999. "CHAC Section 8 Program: Barriers to Successful Leasing Up." Available at www.urban.org (accessed April 2003).

Popkin, S.; J.E. Rosenbaum; and P.M. Meaden. 1993. "Labor Market Experiences of Low-Income Black Women in Middle-Class Suburbs: Evidence From a Survey of Gautreaux Program Participants." *Journal of Policy Analysis and Management* 12, no. 3: 556–73.

Porter, R. 2004. "The Promise and Practice of Inclusionary Zoning." In *Growth Management and Affordable Housing: Do They Conflict,* ed. A. Downs, 212–64. Washington, DC: Brookings Institution.

Possley, M., and H. Gould. 1981. "Housing Bias in DuPage Must Stop, Judge Rules." *Chicago Sun Times,* October 2: 16.

Power, M. 1999a. "Housing America: The Government–HUD Speaks." *Builder* 22, no. 9: 84–87.

———. 1999b. "Housing America: The Obstacles—Scale the Drawbridge." *Builder* 22, no. 9: 82–83.

Pugh, T. 2000. "Benefits Package." *Chicago Tribune,* December 31: 16, 1.

Reed, J.; J. Pashup; and E. Snell. 2005. "Voucher Use, Labor Force Participation, and Life Priorities: Findings from the Gautreaux Two Housing Mobility Study." *Cityscape: A Journal of Policy Development and Research* 8, no. 2: 219–37.

Reid, Norman J.; Jerome M. Stam; Susan E. Kestner; and W. Maureen Godsey. 1980. *Federal Programs Supporting Multicounty Substate Regional Activities: An Analysis.* Economic Development Division. Economics, Statistics, and Cooperative Service. Washington, DC: U.S. Department of Agriculture.

"Report Finds Crisis of Housing Segregation." 2005. *Journal of Housing and Community Development* 62, no. 3: 23.

Rosenbaum, E., and L.E. Harris. 2001. "Residential Mobility and Opportunities: Early Impacts of the Moving to Opportunity Demonstration Program in Chicago." *Housing Policy Debate* 11, no. 2: 321–45.

Rosenbaum, J.E. 2003. "Places Matter; Research Findings on Neighborhood Influences on Poor People's Achievement and the Implications for Housing Relocation Programs, Welfare Reform and Other Policies." In *Affordable Housing in the Chicago Region: Perspectives and Strategies,* ed. P. Nyden, J. Lewis, K. Williams, and N. Benefield, 80–96. Chicago: Housing Affordability Research Consortium, Loyola University and Roosevelt University.

Rosenbaum, J.E.; L. Reynolds; and S. DeLuca. 2002. "How Do Places Matter? The Geography of Opportunity, Self-efficacy, and a Look Inside the Black Box of Residential Mobility." *Housing Studies* 17, no. 1 (January): 71–82.

Schwartz, A., and K. Tajbakhsh. 1997. "Mixed-income Housing: Unanswered Questions." *Cityscape* 3, no. 2: 71–92.

Sichelman, L. 2005. "Bipartisan Bill Pushes Employer-Assisted Housing." *Chicago Tribune,* July 14: 16, 14.

Stegman, M.A.; R.G. Quercia; and G. McCarthy. 2000. "Housing America's Working Families." *New Century Housing* 1, no. 1: 1–48.

Turner, A.M.; S.L. Ross; G. Galster; and J. Yinger. 2002. *Discrimination in Metropolitan Housing Markets.* Available at www.urban.org/urlprint.cfm?ID=7982/ (accessed October 2005).

University of Illinois Building Research Council. 2004. Report on Affordable Housing Planning and Appeal Act Public Act 93-595, as amended by Public Act 93-678 (July 23). Champaign, IL.
U.S. Department of Housing and Urban Development. 2005. Available at www.hud.gov/offices/cpd/affordablehousing/ (accessed November 2005).
U.S. House of Representatives. 1995. Subcommittee on Housing and Community Development; Hearing on HUD's Takeover of the CHA. Statement by Representative Weller, June 7.
Vogt, A. 2003. "Affordable-Housing Law Ok'd." *Chicago Tribune,* August 27: 2, 1.
Yednak, C. 2004. "Tax Break May Expand Housing-Voucher Options." *Chicago Tribune,* December 30: 2, 3.
Ziemba, S. 1981. "No Quick Change Seen in Suburban Housing Ruling." *Chicago Tribune,* October 12: 1, 19.

7

DAVID RUSK

Housing Policy *Is* School Policy

Let us look at recent school report cards for two schools in southern New Jersey. In Cranberry Pines Elementary in suburban Medford Township, 97 percent of third graders achieved proficient or advanced levels on the state language and math exams in 2005. By contrast, only 48 percent of third graders achieved proficient or advanced levels in Cooper's Poynt Elementary in Camden. What was the difference? Was a lot more money spent per pupil in Cranberry Pines? No. As a matter of fact, *per pupil expenditures in the Camden City District ($14,339) were 33 percent higher than in the Medford Township District ($10,722)*. Were class sizes smaller at Cranberry Pines? No. Cooper's Poynt had a slightly smaller average class size (nineteen) than did Cranberry Pines (twenty). Did Cranberry Pines have better prepared, more experienced teachers? No. By the only available measures, 35 percent of both schools' faculties had advanced degrees and all were state-certified teachers.

The big difference between the two schools was that only 2 percent of Cranberry Pine's pupils came from low-income families. By contrast, the proportion of low-income children at Cooper's Poynt was 87 percent. In short, Cranberry Pines's kids were overwhelmingly middle class (and upper-middle class at that). Cooper's Poynt's kids were overwhelmingly poor. It made a world of difference.

School Success and Family Income

The impact of the socioeconomic background of schoolchildren's families on academic outcomes was first documented by James Coleman in *Equality of Educational Opportunity* (1966), a massive study of American schools. For forty years there has been no more consistent a finding of educational research than this: the most powerful predictors of educational success or failure are family income and parents' educational attainment.

That certainly holds true for schoolchildren in the three-county Camden area's 207 elementary schools (divided among 92 different school districts).

In a multivariate regression, each school's proportion of low-income children explained, on average, 43 percent of the school-by-school variation in third-grade math scores and 55 percent of the variation in third-grade language scores in 2005.[1]

What was the explanatory influence statistically of expenditures per pupil (which varied by over 100 percent from $7,570 for Woodlynne Borough to $16,288 for Pemberton Township in 2005)?[2] *Zero.* How much influence could be attributed statistically to variations in average class size, ranging from eleven pupils per class (Washington Township's Green Bank Elementary) to twenty-six pupils per class (Mount Ephraim Borough's Mary Bray Elementary)? *Again, zero.*

In a multivariate regression, there was a slight but statistically significant correlation between test scores and a school's percentage of teachers with advanced degrees. (Fortunately, the relationship also carried a positive sign—that is, the better trained the teachers, the better the results.) However, the negative effect of low socioeconomic status was roughly four times more powerful than the positive effect of better teachers.

Finally, there was a very high correlation (81 percent) between a school's proportion of non-Asian minorities (i.e., African-Americans and Hispanics) and its proportion of low-income pupils. However, in the multivariate regression, minority status was completely subsumed by socioeconomic status—the issue is economic, not racial.

Spending more money and having smaller class sizes in school A than in school B would probably produce somewhat better results for school A *when both pupil populations have almost identical socioeconomic backgrounds.* But when there are significant socioeconomic disparities, the effects of poverty and low parental education just wipe out other factors.

Discovering this phenomenon is not rocket science—though some rocket scientists from the Rand Corporation have weighed in with a recent study. The Rand study found that the most critical factors associated with the educational achievement of children appear to be socioeconomic ones. These factors include parental education levels, neighborhood poverty, parental occupation status, and family income (Lara-Cinisomo et al. 2004).

In this era of the school-accountability movement, however, we do not need the Rand Corporation with its Ph.D. researchers and mainframe computer banks to do such a study. All the information we need is right on the Internet: annual school-by-school report cards that anyone can copy down and plug into a desktop computer spreadsheet with a standard regression analysis package that can be analyzed without employing the Rand Corporation. I am not trained as a professional educational researcher, but I have done such analyses many times to make a point for my audiences. To illustrate, a correlation of 1.00

means an absolute and unvarying rate of change between a dependent variable (e.g., test scores) and an independent variable (e.g., socioeconomic status). Computerized archives revealed that the correlations between a school's percentage of low-income pupils and standardized test scores were:

- 0.77 for each school's percentage of students that achieved proficient and advanced levels on third-, fourth-, and fifth-grade reading, writing, and math tests of the Colorado School Assessment Program (CSAP) for 2000, 2001, and 2002 in all 391 public elementary schools in metro Denver's seventeen school districts;

- 0.74 for the fourth-grade battery of Connecticut Mastery Tests (CMT) for all 518 elementary schools in 149 school districts in the state of Connecticut in 2000–2001; the correlation between CMT scores and five "school-based" independent variables (average class size, pupil–staff ratio, average years of teacher experience, percentage of teachers with master's degrees, and percentage of noncertified teachers) was 0.04;

- 0.87 for fourth-grade test scores for twenty-two elementary schools in the Alachua County Public Schools (Gainesville, Florida) in 1994–96; the correlation between test scores and three "school-based" independent variables (expenditures per pupil, average class size, and percentage of teachers with more than ten years' experience) was 0.46, seemingly very explanatory as well until one realizes that more spending per pupil and smaller class sizes were *negatively* related to pupil performance. (Clearly, with federal aid targeted on low-income pupils, greater spending and smaller classes were simply proxies for the pupils' low socioeconomic status.);

- 0.65 for third-grade test scores at fifty-one elementary schools in 1991 and 0.62 for third- and fourth-grade test scores at sixty-one elementary schools in thirty-four school districts in the three-county Peoria-Pekin, Illinois, area in 1996;

- 0.85 for the battery of ISTEP tests for all grades in sixteen Lake County, Indiana (Gary-Hammond-East Chicago), school districts (plus statewide averages) in 1998–99; 0.85 for the percentage of students achieving math and English standards in 1998–99; and 0.89 for SAT scores in 1998–99. The correlations between two school-based "inputs" (expenditures per pupil and average teacher salary) and these three academic "outputs" were –0.09, –0.09, and –0.05 (all *negatively* related, so they were proxies for socioeconomic status as well);

- 0.81 for three-year average composite results of second- and fourth-grade math and reading scores on the Comprehensive Test for Basic Skills in 373 elementary schools of the seven school districts of Baltimore, Maryland, in 2000–2002;

- 0.82 for three-year average composite results of second- and fourth-grade math and reading scores on the Comprehensive Test for Basic Skills in 125 elementary schools of the Montgomery County, Maryland, Public Schools (the thirteenth wealthiest county in our nation) in 2000–2002;
- 0.50 for four-year average composite results of fourth- and fifth-grade reading, writing, math, and science exams of the Michigan Educational Assessment Program (MEAP) at 483 elementary schools in an eighteen-county area of southwestern Michigan from 1994 to 1998. That region of the state included many schools in farming communities where nominal family cash incomes were low (thereby qualifying more children for subsidized meals) but parental educational attainment was relatively high. (That same phenomenon was at work in farming communities of the three-county Peoria-Pekin, Illinois, area. Children from family-owned farms score higher than their family's income level would predict if they were from urban settings.);
- 0.75 for eight-year composite results for third graders and 0.78 for eight-year composite results for fifth graders on the Iowa Test of Basic Skills battery in seventy-eight elementary schools of the Albuquerque, New Mexico, public schools from 1983–84 to 1991–92;
- 0.77 for three-year average pass rate of fourth graders on a five-test battery at 110 elementary schools in the three-county Toledo, Ohio, area from 1999 to 2001. The correlation between two school-based "inputs" (total expenditures per pupil and average teacher salary) and academic "output" was 0.41, which implies successful strategic deployment of scarce public resources; however, higher per pupil expenditures were negatively associated with test scores and greater proportions of low-income pupils were associated with lower teacher salaries;
- 0.67 for two-year averages in fifth-grade math and reading scores for forty-three elementary schools (in sixteen school districts) of York County, Pennsylvania, in 2000–2002;
- 0.66 for three-year averages on the Texas Academic Achievement System (TAAS) tests for 189 school districts in the five largest metro areas of Texas (Austin, Dallas, Fort Worth, Houston, and San Antonio) in 1994–97;
- 0.75 for three-year averages for achieving Advanced and Proficient (A&P) thresholds on the five-test battery for fourth graders in sixty elementary schools in Dane County (Madison), Wisconsin, in 1999–2001. At the level of the sixteen school districts, the correlation between the district's percentage of low-income pupils and A&P-level performance was –0.67; the correlation between test performance and two school-based inputs (education cost per pupil and pupil–teacher ratio) was –0.18.

The association of higher expenditures per pupil and smaller class sizes with lower test performance demonstrates again that more money and smaller class sizes flow toward lower-income pupils because of federal mandates for education aid; and

- 0.80 for four-year averages in achieving Advanced and Proficient (A&P) thresholds in third- and fourth-grade reading at forty-three elementary schools in eight school districts in Brown County (Green Bay), Wisconsin, in 2000–2004.

My fourteen studies (amid scores of such analyses done by others) are cited to hammer home a point. All consistently document one of James Coleman's central findings: "The educational resources that a child's classmates bring to school are more important than the educational resources that the school board provides." So important are fellow students, the report found, that "the social composition of the student body is more highly related to achievement, independent of the student's own social background, than is any school factor" (Kahlenberg 2001, 26).

Poor Cities/Poor Schools

I have been a speaker and consultant in over 100 metro areas. In about half of them, the proportion of poor children in the central city school district is over 60 percent. From Allentown to Youngstown, from smallish Muskegon to giant New York City, the stories I hear always seem the same: "The city schools are terrible . . . the school board is always fighting . . . superintendents come and go constantly . . . we must fix the city schools before the city can make a comeback." After several dozen repetitions, one begins to suspect these complaints are just symptoms, not causes. The *primary* cause is the high concentration of poverty in city schools. The schools must grapple with the various problems and minimal home support that many poor children bring to school.

Does Money Solve the Problem?

Perhaps we are just not spending enough extra money, many school reformers argue. Even in New Jersey, as I have discussed above, where the state Supreme Court in *Abbott v. Burke* has ordered state government to spend $7.3 billion to rebuild school facilities in thirty-one poverty-impacted, urban school districts, court-ordered annual subsidies (amounting to $1.5 billion in 2005–6) translate into per pupil expenditures that are only 35 percent higher in the *Abbott* districts than in New Jersey's 519 *other* districts. Reform advocates contend that much more must be spent to overcome the complex, negative environment of poverty-impacted schools.

Well, how about spending almost twice as much money? In 2000–2001, I served as an itinerant Visiting Professor of Urban Planning at the University of Amsterdam. In the context of carrying out a study for the Dutch government on sprawl and segregation, I learned a good deal about the Dutch educational system (Rusk 2001). Since 1919, the Dutch national government provides 100 percent of the funding not only for all nonsectarian public schools but also for all Catholic, Protestant, Jewish, Muslim, and other private schools. Moreover, all parents are constitutionally guaranteed total freedom of choice in where to send their children to school.

Recognizing the special problems that low-income children must often overcome, the national funding formula provides a 25 percent bonus per student for "low-income" ethnic Dutch students (so-called 1.25 students) and a 90 percent bonus per student for "low-income" ethnic minority students (so-called 1.90 students), whose parents have emigrated primarily from Turkey, Morocco, Surinam, and the Dutch Antilles.

In America, conservative reformers now champion "school choice" to provide tax-supported vouchers for low-income children to attend both private nonsectarian and private religious schools. The controversies that wrack the American political scene about tax-funded vouchers, freedom of choice, and tax support for religious educational institutions have been settled public policy in the Netherlands for almost a century.

School choice is hardly the cure-all that American conservatives envision. When compared to their closest American counterparts, neighborhoods in Dutch metropolitan areas are about as ethnically segregated as neighborhoods in similar American metropolitan areas. However, Dutch neighborhoods are substantially less *economically* segregated than American neighborhoods because of the widespread dispersion of "social housing." ("Social housing" accounts for about 40 percent of the Dutch housing supply whereas less than 5 percent of the American housing supply is dedicated to "public housing" and federal housing vouchers.)

After all parental "choices" about where their children attend school are sorted out, Dutch *schools* are substantially more segregated than the norm for Dutch *neighborhoods* and even more segregated—both ethnically *and economically*—than their American counterparts. This has led to the emergence of "black schools" (i.e., majority low-income immigrant schools) in several larger Dutch cities. Academic performance at "black schools" is particularly low and resistant to the influence of more funds. Most recent Dutch educational research confirms similar socioeconomic effects as in the United States. In effect, the benefits Dutch society gains from having more economically integrated neighborhoods are substantially nullified by having more economically segregated schools.

A recent report by the Dutch Court of Audit concluded that it is unclear whether or not an annual expenditure of 1.2 billion guilders in compensatory education for 1.25 and 1.90 students has had any positive impact. Educational goals are not clearly established nor are adequate administrative controls in effect, the Board of Audit complained. After thirty-five different evaluation studies over the course of two decades, the Board concluded, the results of substantial compensatory funding are unclear.

In America, "education reform is out there trying to make 'separate but equal' work." Progressives have embraced a variety of modest steps: reducing class size, adopting voluntary national standards, ending social promotion, ensuring better teacher training, promoting so-called "charter schools," and equalizing state school funding. However, "increased spending on school inputs has not been shown to be an effective way to improve student achievement in most instances" (Burtless 1996, 40).

What Can Be Done?

What can be done is to pay serious attention to the second major finding of James Coleman's monumental study four decades ago: *Poor children learn best when surrounded by middle-class classmates.* My own studies of several metro areas have shown that:

- In an Albuquerque study of 1,108 individual pupils, the average pupil from a public housing household increased Iowa Test of Basic Skills (ITBS) scores by 0.22 percentile points for every 1 percent increase in middle-class classmates (Rusk and Mosley 1994); the difference between a public housing child's attending Cochiti Elementary (80 percent low-income classmates) and that child's attending John Baker Elementary (80 percent middle-class classmates) would be, on average, a 13-percentile points improvement in the child's ITBS ranking;
- In a study of 373 elementary schools in metropolitan Baltimore, for every 1 percent increase in middle-class classmates, a low-income pupil's scores improved, on average, 0.18 percentile points on the Comprehensive Test of Basic Skills (Rusk 2003). The difference between a low-income pupil's attending Mosher Elementary in Baltimore City (80 percent low-income classmates) and that child's attending Rivera Beach Elementary in Anne Arundel County (80 percent middle-class classmates) would be, on average, an 11-percentile points improvement in the child's CTBS ranking;

- In a study of 186 school districts in the five largest metro areas of Texas, for every 1 percent increase in middle-class pupils, low-income pupils increase their chances of achieving a passing rate on the Texas state exams (Texas Assessment of Academic Skills, or TAAS) by 0.27 percentage points: the difference between a low-income child's attending a typical elementary school in the Southside Independent School District (80 percent low-income classmates) and a typical elementary school in suburban Alamo Heights Independent School District (80 percent middle-class classmates), on average, would be a 16-percentage point improvement in their chances of achieving a passing rate in TAAS; and
- In a study of 60 elementary schools in Madison-Dane County, for every 1 percent increase in middle-class classmates, a typical low-income, fourth-grade pupil would see an average improvement on his/her state WINSS tests of 0.64 percentage points in reading; 0.50 percentage points in language; 0.72 percentage points in math; 0.80 percentage points in science; and 0.74 percentage points in social studies (Rusk 2002). In other words, the difference between a low-income pupil attending a school with only 45 percent middle-class classmates (e.g., Lincoln or Mendota) and that pupil attending a school with 85 percent middle-class classmates (e.g., Crestwood or Northside) would typically be a 20- to 32-percentage point improvement in that low-income pupil's probability of achieving A&P thresholds.

In September 2002, the Century Foundation issued *Divided We Fail,* the report of its Task Force on the Common School (Kahlenberg 2002). Chaired by former U.S. Senator and Connecticut Governor Lowell P. Weicker Jr., the Task Force was composed of two dozen distinguished educators, researchers, civil rights attorneys, and former public officials. I served as a member of the Task Force and wrote one of the studies, "Trends in School Segregation," that it commissioned. The Task Force report was drafted by Richard D. Kahlenberg, its staff director, and author of *All Together Now: Creating Middle-Class Schools Through Public School Choice* (2001). The Task Force's report deserved far more public attention than it received. I cannot do better by the issue than to quote extensively the report's introductory words:

> Nearly forty years ago, Alabama Governor George Wallace declared in his inaugural address, "Segregation today, segregation tomorrow, segregation forever." Today, almost no American would embrace what was once the reigning ethos, but the everyday reality lived by millions of schoolchildren is not too far from Wallace's vision. No longer segregated by law, our nation's schools are increasingly segregated in fact—both by race and ethnicity and,

increasingly, by economic class. Our nation made great strides to eradicate segregated schooling from the early 1970s to the mid-1980s, but since then we have seen increasing racial and economic segregation, and almost no one—from either political party—has articulated a clear plan for addressing this disastrous trend.

Trend

The past twenty years have seen an explosion of education policy debates, over issues ranging from raising academic standards to lowering class size, from improving teacher training to promoting after-school programs. But current discussions largely ignore the central source of school inequality: segregation by race and class. All of history suggests that separate schools, particularly for poor and middle-class children, are inherently unequal. A child growing up in a poor family has reduced life chances, but attending a school with large numbers of low-income classmates poses a second, independent strike against him or her. While some look at the link between poverty and achievement and conclude that failure is inevitable, the members of the Task Force believe that poor children, given the right environment in school, can achieve at very high levels.

There exists today a solid consensus among researchers that school segregation perpetuates failure, and an equally durable consensus among politicians that nothing much can be done about it. Education reformers take as a given that schools will reflect residential segregation by class and race and therefore any solutions are narrowly conceived to make separate schools more equal. We believe that this approach is seriously flawed. (Kahlenberg 2002, 11)

Written for a national audience, this introduction, it seems to me, aptly characterizes our self-created national educational failure. In 1954, the U.S. Supreme Court (the Warren Court) unanimously (9–0) declared that racial school segregation was unconstitutional in its epochal *Brown v. Board of Education.* Just twenty years later, in 1974, a bitterly divided U.S. Supreme Court (the Burger Court), by a 5–4 vote in *Milliken v. Bradley,* declared that suburban school districts had no obligation to cooperate with central city districts in area-wide racial desegregation plans unless each suburban district could be proved to have intentionally segregated. Twenty-one years after that, in 1995, the U.S. Supreme Court (the Rehnquist Court), by a 5–4 vote in *Missouri v. Jenkins,* rejected state responsibility for segregation in schools and neighborhoods; the Court placed the blame for the deterioration and segregation of city schools on "normal pattern[s] of human migration." The majority opinion never discussed the history of housing discrimination, lending bias, public housing construction, federal home loan mortgage practices, exclusionary zoning, or other governmental causes of racial and economic segregation.

But as legal scholar john powell has written, "The efforts of the federal courts to treat housing and school segregation as independent are counterfactual. State courts and policy makers, however, are not bound by the federal approach to segregated schools and housing. Policy makers have it within their power to address the interrelationship of housing and education" (powell, Kearney, and Kay 2001, 19).

Housing policy *is* school policy. Over the past thirty years, while housing barriers based on race have been slowly coming down, housing barriers based on income have been steadily going up. In most American housing markets, Jim Crow by income is replacing Jim Crow by race. As a result, schools are more economically segregated than ever before.

This next section will explore what local school boards, as state-authorized policymakers, can achieve to create greater economic integration—the heart of the matter. It will explore briefly what three communities (La Crosse, Wisconsin; Wake County, North Carolina; and Cambridge, Massachusetts) have done. Then I will model the degree of economic integration that could be achieved if local school boards within two major metropolitan areas (Baltimore and Camden-South Jersey) would pursue socioeconomic status (SES) integration policies within each school district.

Three Examples of Economic School Integration

Each of these case studies is developed in greater detail in *Divided We Fail* (Kahlenberg 2002). I have edited them substantially to reduce their length while retaining what I believe is the core of the story. However, whenever I felt that any paraphrasing of mine would not improve upon the original authors' words, I have included such sections without quotation marks, reserving those for important statements of local officials, educators, and parents.

La Crosse, Wisconsin[3]

La Crosse is a city of 52,000, surrounded by a suburban area of about 37,000. Hemmed in by the Mississippi River on the west (forming the Wisconsin state line) and suburban townships along the bluffs to the east, the city has annexed land modestly; since about 1970, the city's population has been stagnant, and new subdivisions, shopping malls, and office complexes rose exclusively in its suburbs.

The region had few minorities until a large immigration of Hmong refugees from Vietnam occurred in the 1980s. The Hmongs were better known as the Montagnards, the hill peoples of Laos who were staunch American allies during the Vietnam War. By 2000, the La Crosse area was still 94 percent Anglo, but two-thirds of all minorities and almost 70 percent of Asians lived within the city of La Crosse. The records of the La Crosse Hmong Mutual Assistance Association showed 3,491 Hmong residents of La Crosse County rather than the 2,282 reported by Census 2000. Suburbanization of more affluent families and concentration of low-income minorities in the city brought city per capita income down to 76 percent of suburban levels by 1999.

In the La Crosse public schools, however, minorities were proportionally greater; in October 2000, there were 1,070 Asian students (13.9 percent), 255 black students (3.3 percent), 85 Native Americans (1.1 percent), and 73 Hispanic students (0.95 percent). Anglo students made up 80 percent of the total 7,605 students in the district.

By the late 1980s, school leaders were worried about concentrations of low-income students (often minority) that were developing. District-wide, 30 percent of students qualified for free lunches. However, in 1991–92, Jefferson Elementary had 69 percent and Hamilton Elementary had 63 percent qualifying for free lunches. By contrast, State Road School in an affluent neighborhood had only 4.8 percent.

Faced with the need to redistrict because of the construction of two new elementary schools to meet the rising, immigration-driven enrollment, Superintendent Richard Swantz and his staff saw an opportunity to correct the big poverty imbalances in La Crosse's elementary schools. In May 1991, school board members approved ten guidelines for redistricting, including "redistricting shall attempt to establish a socio-economic percentage of poverty students in each school that represents the district's average; . . . when re-assigning students to achieve a socio-economic balance, an attempt shall be made to place them in the closest school."

Realizing that achieving a 30 percent target in each school would be impossible, school officials set a goal of a range from 15 percent to 45 percent low-income students in each school. Under the proposed plan, 45 percent of the district's 3,700 elementary school students would have to be bused to another school for the 1992–93 school year.

After months of deliberations and three public hearings, on January 7, 1992, the La Crosse School Board voted 8–1 to approve the plan to achieve socioeconomic balance in its eleven elementary schools through boundary changes and busing. On January 22, a group named the Recall Alliance announced that it would soon begin collecting signatures for the recall of board members that supported the plan and that a new board would fire Superintendent Swantz. A counter group, the Coalition for Children, was formed the next day. At the regular election already scheduled for April, two pro-plan incumbents were defeated and a third did not stand for reelection. All were replaced by busing opponents.

With the recall campaign heating up, the *New York Times, Washington Post,*

Boston Globe, news magazines, and TV networks descended upon La Crosse. They broadcast far and wide the news that, on July 14, three incumbents were defeated and replaced by busing opponents. Then the national news media disappeared and failed to report (to borrow radio commentator Paul Harvey's phrase) "the rest of the story."

First, the new board could not fire Superintendent Swantz, whose contract had been extended for three years by the old board with a $250,000 buyout provision. Second, with school about to begin, the board found that rolling back the busing plan would be too disruptive. They contented themselves with adding a choice provision to the plan. Any parent who did not want to send a child to a different school for SES balance could opt out. Less than 200 (of the 1,700 chosen for reassignment) refused the new assignment under the parental choice option during the first year. All but two schools met the SES targets that first year. Third, most remarkably, just nine months after the recall election, in April 1993, three antibusing board members were defeated, and were replaced by two members of the Coalition for Children and a Hmong candidate (who supported the SES balance plan)—the first Hmong elected to public office in La Crosse.

Fourth, the busing plan progressed. Most parents and children adjusted to their new schools. As one board member said, "People got to experience it, that it wasn't awful. Moving to different schools wasn't awful. Leaving your neighborhood school wasn't awful. The kids benefited from it. People backed off. The staff at all the different schools made sure that it worked." Fifth, public support for the SES balance plan has grown. In 1994, just two years after the recall election, 60 percent of district residents surveyed said they favored "the idea of attempting SES balance in the schools" and 29 percent said they opposed it. In a follow-up survey in April 2001, 64 percent favored SES balance; only 21 percent were opposed.

Finally, SES balance has been an academic success. La Crosse has a fairly high poverty rate, with only Milwaukee County and two Native American reservations higher in Wisconsin. Yet, according to former Superintendent Swantz, the district's test scores are at 83 percent of the national average.

In 1992, La Crosse was in the forefront of a movement to look at the impact of SES balance in the schools and to create schools in which the majority of students were middle class with middle-class education values. However, parents were allowed to use school choice to opt out of the program, making SES balance potentially more difficult to achieve. Demographic changes over the years allowed some schools to slip back to high percentages of low-income students, and Hamilton School's small and dense attendance made that school's income makeup particularly difficult to change. The impact of La Crosse's socioeconomic balance plan was immediately evident in metropolitan segre-

Table 7.1

Average Segregation Indices for La Crosse, Wisconsin, Selected Years

	Segregation index	
Period	Low-income	Asian
1988–92	33	61
1992–93	4	35
1993–95	21	40
1995–99	27	41

gation indices (which cover seven school districts) in the mid-1990s as well as the slow erosion since then because of parents opting out and continuing neighborhood changes. Table 7.1 lists annual averages for three time periods and a transition year. On a scale of 0 to 100, a score of "0" would mean that all schools would have the same proportion of low-income pupils; a score of "100," by contrast, would mean than all low-income children (and only low-income pupils) attended certain schools—in other words, total economic apartheid. An economic segregation index of 4 for 1992–93 (the first year of the plan) is so low that it raises the possibility of missing data. The impact of the La Crosse district's changing enrollment policies is reflected in declining metropolitan segregation trends both economically and socially.

La Crosse's new superintendent, Thomas C. Downs, sums up La Crosse's continuing challenge, "We've got to do what we need to do to support socio-economic balance. It raises the achievement of the lower-income kids and doesn't in any way hurt the achievement of the more advantaged kids. I believe that it's a higher value for me now."

Wake County, North Carolina[4]

With 105,000 students, Wake County Public Schools is one of the nation's premier "Big Box" school systems. It has also been one of the nation's most racially integrated systems since local officials merged the county school system with the separate Raleigh city system in 1974 and instituted a county-wide policy of busing and magnet schools to achieve racial balance. By 1999, however, Wake County school officials could see the handwriting on the wall regarding their explicit student assignment policies to promote racial balance. The federal Fourth Circuit Court of Appeals (which includes the Raleigh area) was moving to strike the racially based assignment policies in Arlington County, Virginia, and in Montgomery County, Maryland. In the adjacent Cir-cuit Court district, the federal judge was dismantling Charlotte-Mecklenburg's racial balance plan that had been implemented since the historic *Swann v. Charlotte-Mecklenburg School District* case in which the U.S. Supreme Court first authorized district-wide busing to achieve racial balance.

Reflecting on a tense meeting seeking a workable alternative, one school official recalls: "What I remember most intensely was that a number of people would say, 'It makes us sick to our stomachs because we are walking away from 20 years of doing something that had been good for the school system and good for the community.'" A legal analysis summarized the evolving new federal judicial policy:

> In essence, the new decisions forbid all school boards (unless they are operating under federal desegregation decrees) from considering race or ethnicity as they assign children to public schools. The prohibition holds even if it leads to desegregated schools, even if most parents desire their children to attend racially diverse schools, and even if school boards are acting in good faith to ensure that students receive the educational benefits that may come from a diverse school environment.

School leaders had reviewed extensive local and national research regarding the linkage between socioeconomic status and educational achievement. They decided to replace the system of student assignment to achieve racial balance with a system of student assignment to achieve socioeconomic balance. For the 1999–2000 school year, the school board adopted new student assignment criteria designed to assure that no school would have more than 40 percent low-income pupils or more than 25 percent of students with low academic performance levels (see Table 7.2).

The Wake County Public School system has a tough challenge to attain its goals in the face of a regional housing market that promotes more and more economic segregation. Though Raleigh itself has expanded its boundaries rapidly (from 11 square miles in 1950 to 115 square miles in 2000), it continues to be home to 60 percent of Wake County's African-Americans. Meanwhile, the white population is exploding in four towns in western Wake County—most importantly, Cary, the bedroom community for Research Triangle Park. Their schools are geographically distant from minority neighborhoods in south Raleigh.

The early academic returns from Wake County's new pupil assignment policy are encouraging. In 2001, 64 percent of Wake County students eligible for free and reduced-price meals (FARM) performed at or above grade level, a rate that outpaces most low-income students in urban districts. While free and reduced-price eligible students have had a steady improvement in math proficiency prior to 2001 (when racially integrated schools also meant sub-

Table 7.2

Racial and Economic School Segregation in Raleigh Area Elementary Schools, 1999–2000

1999–2000 pupil group	Metro Raleigh	Wake County
Elementary pupils	136,442	55,844
Anglo	58%	63%
Black	34%	28%
Hispanic	5%	4%
FARM*	28%	22%
Segregation indices		
Black segregation index	32	21
Hispanic segregation index	40	32
FARM segregation index	35	30
Average pupils and classmates		
Non-FARM	70%	77%
FARM	50%	36%

*Free and reduced-price meals
Note: The figures cited for Metro Raleigh include Wake County.

stantially economically integrated schools), improvement in reading levels bumped subsequent to the new pupil assignment policy. Figures 7.1 and 7.2 provide the 1998–2003 trend lines.

As Wake County Superintendent of Schools Bill McNeal explains, "The reason that you want to create middle class schools is expectations as much as anything. How do you know what excellence is without seeing it? You've got to be able to touch it and feel it."

Cambridge, Massachusetts[5]

In December 2001, the Cambridge School Committee adopted a policy of controlled school choice to achieve SES balance in the district's fourteen elementary schools. With 48 percent of elementary school pupils qualifying for subsidized meals, starting with kindergarten, the school board set a goal of having each school fall within fifteen percentage points of the district-wide average (that is, between 33 percent and 63 percent FARM) for 2002–3. The permissible range would be narrowed to ten percentage points for 2003–4 and to five percentage points for 2004–5.

The new policy builds on twenty years of experience in implementing a controlled choice policy to achieve *racial* balance in the city's schools. (Cambridge's elementary schools cover K–8, and the district has a single high school.) No school had a majority of any one racial group except Fletcher/

Figure 7.1   **Percentage of All Grade 3–8 Students at/above Grade Level in Reading by Free and Reduced-Lunch Status, 1998–2003**

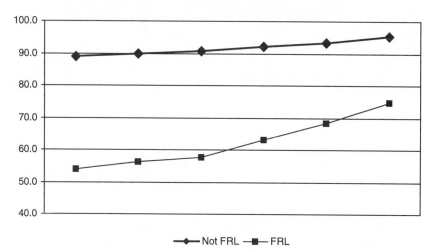

Source: Dulaney, Chuck, and Roger Regan. 2003. *Measuring Up, End-of-Grade Multiple-Choice Test Results: 2002–03.* Raleigh: Wake County Public School System, July.

Figure 7.2   **Percentage of All Grade 3–8 Students at/above Grade Level in Math by Free and Reduced-Lunch Status, 1998–2003**

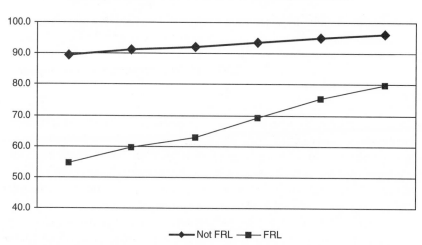

Source: Dulaney, Chuck, and Roger Regan. 2003. *Measuring Up, End-of-Grade Multiple-Choice Test Results: 2002–03.* Raleigh: Wake County Public School System, July.

Maynard Academy, which was 52 percent black in 2000–2001. (One-quarter of the Academy's black enrollment was not African-American, but African immigrants, Haitians, and West Indians.) Overall the district's elementary schools were 40 percent Anglo (non-Hispanic whites), 34 percent black, 14 percent Hispanic, 11 percent Asian, and 1 percent Native American. Table 7.3 calculates the familiar segregation indices for 2000. The following four facts stand out:

- First, though the residential segregation of blacks (ages five to seventeen) was the highest (46) of any group, the controlled school choice program brought school segregation of black pupils down to an astonishingly low index of 13. Many black parents clearly sought out "better" schools beyond the boundaries of the moderately segregated neighborhoods in which they lived.

- Second, Hispanic and Asian enrollments mirrored neighborhood patterns.

- Third, Anglo pupils were grouped in certain schools rather than in neighborhoods—again, a function of more aggressive parents utilizing the controlled choice system to their advantage. However, one-third of Anglo school-age children were not attending Cambridge Public Schools. (Over 90 percent of school-age children from all other groups attended the public schools.)

- Fourth, economic segregation was not diminished by the racially based controlled choice policy. Schools were as economically segregated (35) as neighborhoods (36). The schools' economic imbalance ranged from a low of 19 percent low-income pupils (Cambridgeport) to a high of 79 percent (King).

It is important to note that the comparison between school and neighborhood is somewhat of an apples-to-oranges comparison. The two age groups are not identical as the schools' K–8 range is compared with Census 2000's five to eleven age grouping (roughly K–6). Of potentially more consequence, the residential calculation is based on children under the poverty line, while FARM eligibility for partial subsidies cuts off at 185 percent of the poverty line. Nonetheless, it was this last disparity plus concern about the uncertain legal status of a race-based controlled choice plan and the growing understanding of the linkage between SES and academic outcomes that caused the district to shift to controlled choice for SES balance in December, 2001.

Table 7.3

School and Neighborhood Segregation Indices for Cambridge, MA, 2000
(0 to 100; 100 = total apartheid)

Group <17 years of age	School	Neighborhood
Anglo	15	10
Black	13	46
Hispanic	36	36
Asian	28	30
Native American	29	41
Low-income	35	36*

*This index is calculated for ages five to eleven (in effect, Grades K–6).

Since that time, the minority population within Cambridge elementary schools has increased as the proportion of Anglo pupils has declined slightly (from 40 percent in 2000–2001 to 37 percent in 2004–5)—a nationwide trend. However, the proportion of low-income pupils has dropped more markedly (from 48 percent in 2000–2001 to 40 percent in 2004–5). Though they have missed the board's ideal targets, the range between "regular" elementary schools has narrowed from Peabody and Tobin (27 percent low-income pupils) to King (59 percent low-income pupils). Ironically, the most poverty-impacted schools are two charter schools, special academies set up at parents' behest: Amigos (68 percent Hispanic; 61 percent low-income) and Fletcher-Maynard (58 percent black and 23 percent Hispanic; 73 percent low-income). By a substantial margin, these two academies have the lowest test scores in the system (a reminder of the old adage: "Be careful what you wish for; you may get it").

The impact of the district's policies on economic integration can be clearly seen in Table 7.4, which compares segregation indices between 2000–2001 and 2004–5 (the latter listing separately "all elementary schools" and then only "regular" elementary schools, excluding the two special academies). The comparison shows that Cambridge schools continue to be very balanced in terms of racial diversity and that the district's SES policies significantly improved economic integration (shown in the bottom row). Considering all elementary schools, the economic segregation index was cut from 35 to 23—a 35 percent improvement. Setting aside the two academies where many black and Hispanic parents were electing to enroll their children without regard to the school district's SES policy, the economic segregation index among "regular" elementary schools was halved from 35 to 17. In the process, average test scores improved modestly. Third graders who achieved advanced and proficient levels on the Stanford 9 reading test increased from 44 percent in 2000–2001 to 51 percent in 2003–4.

Table 7.4

**School Segregation Indices Pre- and Post-Socioeconomic Status
Integration Plan in Cambridge, MA, 2000–1 and 2004–5**
(0 to 100; 100 = total apartheid)

Group	All 2000–2001	All 2004–2005	Excluding Academies 2004–2005
Anglo	15	20	16
Black	13	19	16
Hispanic	36	38	18
Asian	28	24	23
Native American	29	23	21
Low-income	35	23	17

Cambridge Public Schools and La Crosse Public Schools are relatively small school districts in "little boxes" regions. The La Crosse, Wisconsin-Minnesota metro area (126,838 residents in 2000) has 7 school districts, while the Boston, Massachusetts-New Hampshire metro area (3,406,829 residents) has 105 school districts. Absent constitutional compulsion, achieving greater integration among multiple "little boxes" school districts through school board action is an impossible task. The next section will examine, however, the potential for local school board action in the Baltimore area, which, like Raleigh-Durham-Chapel Hill, is a "Big Box" region. What are the limits of what could be achieved if local school boards in the Baltimore and South Jersey areas adopted SES balancing plans within each district?

SES Integration in Baltimore and South Jersey

Over the past several years I have worked intensively on housing reform campaigns in the Baltimore region and the three-county Camden area (Burlington, Camden, and Gloucester counties). The two regions could not be more dissimilar in terms of governmental structure.

The 2.5 million-person Baltimore area is the quintessential "Big Box" region. Its seven county governments (counting Baltimore City as its own county) are the basic local governments; its twenty-one municipal governments house less than 5 percent of the region's population. Many such municipalities lack any planning and zoning authority under state law; county governments control planning and zoning for 97 percent of the population.

By contrast, the 1.2 million person Camden area is totally divided among 101 "little boxes" municipalities; county governments have little role, and no land use planning and zoning powers whatsoever.

Table 7.5

Simulated Socioeconomic Status Integration of Free and Reduced-Price Meal (FARM) Pupils in Baltimore Area Elementary Schools by School Board Action Within Each District in Percents, 2002

School district	FARM	Current range	Projected range	Pupils reassigned
Baltimore City	84	99–29	90–69	4.0
Anne Arundel County	19	78–0	34–12	11.4
Baltimore County	33	79–1	48–21	15.8
Carroll County	9	28–2	24–4	1.2
Harford County	19	72–3	34–11	12.4
Howard County	—	45–0	25–4	3.8
Queen Anne's County	—	31–8	31–8	0.0

The Baltimore region has fewer school districts (seven) than any comparably sized, multicounty region in the country. In 2002, the economic segregation index for metro Baltimore's elementary schools, I have calculated, was 61.7. What would the result be if each school board adopted a common policy to achieve maximum economic integration *within* each of the seven districts? The goal would be to have FARM enrollment in every school equal to their district-wide average (plus or minus fifteen percentage points).

I have simulated the effects of such a policy for the Baltimore metro area. Table 7.5 lists the current and simulated distribution of pupils by SES. For all schools I maintained their 2002 enrollment levels. However, within each district, I replaced FARM pupils with non-FARM pupils in high-poverty schools until I had brought each school to within fifteen percentage points of the district-wide FARM percentage. Then I shifted enough FARM pupils into low-poverty schools until all transfers within the district balanced out. (The floor for the lowest FARM schools may be closer to the district-wide FARM average than fifteen percentage points.)

Substantial realignment occurs within Anne Arundel County, Baltimore County, and Harford County. A modest realignment occurs within Howard County. Little realignment occurs within Carroll County, and none within Queen Anne's County. With only one elementary school below 50 percent FARM, such an SES policy would not be worth implementing in Baltimore City, but I carried out the mathematical exercise anyway.

The net effect of having school boards maximize socioeconomic integration within each district in this way would be to lower the economic school segregation index from 61.7 to 53.5—about a 13 percent improvement.

Let's turn to the "little boxes" Camden area. Its 101 municipalities contain 92 independent school districts. Its three-county economic school segregation index was 49.3 in 2005. While that is substantially better than the Baltimore region's 61.7 index score, it reflects the fact that the three-county area is really a suburb of Philadelphia, whose tremendous concentration of poor children is not counted in my calculation as is Baltimore City's. While Camden is technically still recognized by the U.S. Census Bureau as a "central city," it is less than 7 percent of its three-county area's population. However, the disparities in the socioeconomic profile of its 92 school districts are tremendous. One hundred (100) percent of the pupils in Davis Elementary in the Camden City School District were low-income in 2005, while Samuel Mickle Elementary in wealthy, suburban East Greenwich District had zero low-income pupils.

What would the result be if each of the ninety-two school boards adopted a common policy to achieve maximum economic integration *within* their ninety-two districts? Within each district, I replaced FARM pupils with non-FARM pupils, or vice versa, until I had brought each school *to the exact district-wide FARM percentage*. The result was only a negligible improvement in the region-wide economic school segregation index—from 49.3 to 48.0. In other words, in this "little boxes" region, economic segregation is much greater among school districts than within school districts.

Inclusionary Zoning: Mixing Up the Neighborhood

To achieve much greater racial and economic integration, we must act on a metropolitan-wide basis through changes in the housing market. More racially and economically integrated neighborhoods will produce more racially and economically integrated neighborhood schools. But producing more economically integrated neighborhoods (with their concomitant greater racial integration) requires changing local governments' traditional practices in shaping their housing markets.

Where and what kinds of housing are built are not the result of the workings of some unfettered "free market." Such a "free market" is a myth. Public policy dictates where development occurs. Local governments' zoning decisions regulate the allowable uses of land: what can be built and at what density of development. Building and engineering codes set standards that private developers must follow. Public taxes (sometimes without developer cost sharing) install the utility systems, create the street network, and provide the parks, schools, fire stations, and other public facilities that are essential for most urban development.

Many suburban governments carry out these policies and programs in ways that seek to exclude low-income households from their communities: large minimum lot sizes for new homes; severe restrictions (even outright bans) on townhouse and apartment development; mandated deep building setbacks from lot lines; excessive off-street parking requirements. All of these contribute to a pattern of what is typically termed "exclusionary zoning." Over 135 local communities, however, have adopted "inclusionary zoning" policies that deliberately seek to create economically diversified new housing. These communities seek to assure that housing for modest proportions of moderate- and low-income families will be provided in any new, market-rate housing developments.

For more than thirty years, Montgomery County, Maryland, has had the United States' most comprehensive inclusionary zoning policy. Complying with the near-countywide policy adopted in 1973, private, for-profit homebuilders have delivered over 12,000 moderately priced dwelling units (MPDUs) as integral parts of new subdivisions and apartment complexes. Carrying out another provision of the county law, the county's public housing authority, the Housing Opportunities Commission, has purchased 1,700 highly scattered MPDUs and rents another 1,500 for very low-income families. The basic provisions of the MPDU are:

- Any new housing development of twenty or more units must include at least 12.5 percent MPDUs that are affordable for households at no more than 65 percent of the county's median household income (the lowest one-third of the income scale);
- As a cost offset for providing up to 15 percent MPDUs, the county offers density bonuses of up to 22 percent (in effect, removing all land costs for both MPDUs and for bonus market rate units);
- Resale prices and rents of MPDUs are controlled for thirty years; and
- The county's public housing authority is directed to buy or rent one-third of the MPDUs in order that the program will assist very low-income households. (Nonprofit agencies can acquire another 6 2/3 percent.)

The MPDU policy is the most innovative centerpiece of Montgomery County's 40,000 mixed-income housing units. Its progressive policies have facilitated a remarkable social and economic transformation. In 1970, Montgomery County had the look of a classic suburb: wealthy and white (92 percent). By 2000, Montgomery County had a "rainbow look": 16 percent black, 12 percent Hispanic, and 12 percent Asian. It still was the thirteenth wealthiest county in America while becoming one of the more racially and economically integrated communities in our nation. Over three decades, its residential economic segregation index hardly changed from 27.2 in 1970 to 27.9 in 2000—low and stable.

By providing housing for all occupational levels, the county helped promote a diversified local economy centered on its I-270 "Technology Corridor." In a generation, Montgomery County has become the global center of biomedical and genetic research. Adopting a Montgomery County–type inclusionary zoning law would be the most important single step that any metro area—including greater Baltimore and Camden—could take to reverse trends toward greater economic segregation.

Inclusionary Zoning for the Baltimore and Camden Areas

I have simulated what might have been the results of adopting Montgomery County's type of inclusionary zoning laws by all local governments (primarily the seven county governments) in metro Baltimore for the past twenty years. Some 316,000 new housing units were built from 1980 to 2000 (about 30 percent of the total housing stock). A region-wide MPDU policy would have produced 15,800 units of workforce housing for modest-income workers (young teachers, police recruits, sales clerks, etc.) and another 7,900 units of "welfare-to-workforce housing" (for very low-income households). Less than 10 percent of the MPDUs (1,650 units) would have been located in Baltimore City. Most MPDUs would have been integrated into new, middle-class subdivisions and new, market-rate apartment complexes in newly developing communities.

The Urban Institute has calculated that 95,225 poor persons would have had to move from high-poverty to low-poverty census tracts to have totally eliminated economic segregation in the Baltimore region in 2000 (i.e., to reach a segregation index of "0"). The 18,375 poor persons that could have been moved through a regional MPDU policy would have achieved 20 percent of that ideal goal. Hypothetically, metro Baltimore's residential economic segregation index for 2000 would have been reduced from 43.3 to 34.6—15 percent below the economic segregation index of 40.1 recorded three decades earlier.

The calculations above focus only on the relocation of families eligible for public housing ("welfare-to-workforce housing"). However, setting the MPDU eligibility ceiling at 65 percent of median household income approximates the ceiling for FARM eligibility. In other words, all 23,700 MPDU units built during our twenty-year period would have come into play.

I have simulated what would have been the impact on school economic integration if the school boards' SES policy had been reinforced by an MPDU policy implemented by county and municipal governments. I have assumed that 75 percent of the MPDUs built would have been available to low-income families with children and that such families would have had one child enrolled in public elementary school. Furthermore, the number of low-income pupils "transferring" (i.e., moving into new attendance zones) would have been limited so that no suburban district would have been lifted above the regional average of FARM pupils (35.8 percent in 2002). Effectively, this would have limited the number of newcomers to Baltimore County (33.1 percent FARM), which was already close to the regional FARM average by 2002.

The effects would be dramatic. Progressive enrollment policies like those in Cambridge and Wake County, if adopted by area school boards, would hypothetically reduce economic school segregation by 15 percent from 61.7 to 53.5; *adding a region-wide MPDU policy like the one in Montgomery County for twenty years would further reduce economic school segregation to 25.8—a 60 percent reduction!*

The consequences for Baltimore City would be impressive. From a system with 83 percent FARM pupils, the district average would be reduced to 53 percent. Meanwhile, no suburban district would exceed the regional FARM average (35 percent). No suburban elementary schools would have majority FARM enrollments. While the schools attended by the "designer clothes" set would no longer be the former preserves of near-exclusive privilege, they would typically have about 25 percent FARM pupils—many of them the children of the public employees, retail and service workers whom the "designer clothes" class sees and relies upon within their communities every day.

For the Camden area, I was able to use a forward-looking methodology. In 1975, the New Jersey Supreme Court issued its epochal *Mt. Laurel* decision; the court declared that each of the state's 566 "little boxes" municipalities has a constitutional responsibility to provide for its "fair share" of low-income housing based not just on needs of low-income residents within the town's boundaries but based on the *regional* need.

Unfortunately, the court's courageous doctrine lacked any significant political support. After eight years of inaction, the state legislature substantially watered down *Mt. Laurel*'s potential impact through the cynically titled Fair Housing Act of 1985. One of the most outrageous loopholes the legislature created was Regional Contribution Agreements by which wealthy suburbs could sell back up to half their designated fair share of low-income housing to poor cities.

Nevertheless, however inadequate, the state Council on Affordable Housing (COAH) has now promulgated its "growth share" formula; 10 percent of all new housing built in every town must be affordable to low-income households. In addition, the growth share formula provides that an additional affordable unit must be built for every twenty-five new jobs created.

Using a data-based Municipal Opportunity Index, I have divided the Camden area's 101 municipalities into six categories: 8 maximum-opportunity towns, 28 high-opportunity towns, 22 medium-opportunity towns, 20 low-opportunity towns, 22 minimum-opportunity towns, and Camden, the central city. The COAH projects that over a ten-year period (2005–15) some 3,600 affordable housing units must be built in the maximum-, high-, and medium-opportunity towns in compliance with its growth share formula. I have simulated that one-quarter of those housing units would be occupied by low-income families relocating from Camden and another quarter would be occupied by other low-income families moving out of another twenty-two poverty-impacted school districts in older, inner suburbs of Camden. (In Camden's case, I assumed that pupils leaving were not replaced; in the case of the low- and minimum-opportunity communities, I assumed that non-FARM families did indeed move in.)

The result of this simulation is that, combined with each school district's policy of equalizing the socioeconomic profiles of all its schools at the district-wide average, the regional economic school segregation index would drop from 48.0 to 37.6. In short, *in the "little boxes" Camden region, implementing a mixed income housing strategy would have ten times the impact of achieving greater economic integration within the public schools than would just district-wide socioeconomic balancing policies.*

Summing Up

Some may view the preceding analysis as simply an exercise in "fantasy math," based on uniform policies across all jurisdictions and flawless implementation (which is rarely achieved). Montgomery County's MPDU program, however, has come very close to hitting its policy targets. The 12,000 MPDUs built by private, for-profit homebuilders represent 7.4 percent of 162,000 units built. The Housing Opportunities Commission has bought or rents 29 percent of the MPDUs (close to its one-third target allocation). Nonetheless, this analysis frames the outer limits of what could be achieved by such policies.

Critics usually argue, however, changing housing patterns as you recommend would take too long. Should all efforts not be concentrated on providing low-income children with the best possible quality education in their current neighborhood schools? I agree that we have a responsibility to do the best that we can to educate low-income children wherever they are right now. I would not advocate simply abandoning such efforts. But, at the federal level, we have been following a conscious remediation strategy for almost forty years, principally through $7.2 billion a year in Chapter 1 support for poverty-impacted schools. The most comprehensive, federally sponsored evaluation of Chapter 1, tracking the progress of 40,000 students over four years, found that Chapter 1 intervention failed to narrow the learning gap between the low-income students it served and non–low-income students (Hoff 1997).

"High-poverty schools put disadvantaged students in double jeopardy," the researchers concluded. "School poverty depresses the scores of all students in schools where at least half of the students are eligible for [federally] subsidized lunch, and seriously depresses the scores when over 75 percent of students live in low-income households." To the response that some high-poverty schools do succeed, "the authors warned that the sample of successful schools was too small to be scientifically reliable."

A recent book, *No Excuses,* published by the Heritage Foundation of Washington, DC, focused on case studies of twenty-one high-poverty schools around the country that were succeeding in raising low-income children's academic achievement (Thernstrom and Thernstrom 2003). "Quite true," the Century Foundation's Richard Kahlenberg commented to me. "They usually reflect special circumstances where an inspired principal, given a largely free hand, has recruited a corps of talented, highly motivated teachers, corralled additional resources, and successfully engaged parents in school activities. But if that magic could be bottled and spread throughout whole school districts," he concluded, "there wouldn't be a need for books like *No Excuses.*"

That conclusion was confirmed several years ago when *Education Week* dispatched a reporter on a nationwide tour to find an "urban" school district with more than 60 percent low-income pupils, *which was successful*. The reporter's conclusion: "Unfortunately, there are none."

The most effective educational reform is to mainstream poor children in middle-class schools—not just as classmates six hours a day, 185 days a year (which school board policies on social class can achieve) but also as playmates 365 days a year through creating mixed-income neighborhoods. Inclusionary zoning is a key tool to achieve the goal of an inclusionary society. A little bit of everything built goes a long way. In the 100 largest U.S. metro areas, 30 million new houses and apartments were built in the past twenty years. Metro-wide inclusionary zoning laws would have produced 3.6 million affordable housing units. That is almost three times as much subsidized housing as now owned by the 3,300 U.S. public-housing authorities. That is producing affordable housing at twice the annual rate supported by federal Low-Income Housing Tax Credits. Unlike most public housing and tax credit projects, inclusionary zoning reverses economic segregation because affordable units are integrated into market-rate developments. Economically integrating neighborhoods would economically integrate neighborhood schools.

The Coleman Report's findings have been both consistently reconfirmed and even more consistently—I would say, deliberately—ignored by most politicians and many educators, who will not challenge the racial and class structure of American society. That challenge is now being taken up by grass-roots groups in many communities, spearheaded by faith-based coalitions affiliated with the Gamaliel Foundation. Baltimore's BRIDGE, Empower

Hampton Roads, New Jersey Regional Coalition, and others are champion-
ing inclusionary zoning ("opportunity-based" housing) before city councils,
county commissions, and state legislatures.

The campaigns' rallying cry: "Anyone good enough to work here is good
enough to live here. And their children are good enough to go to our good
schools."

Notes

1. Student test scores are notorious for having a high degree of almost random
variation. My study of Albuquerque Public Schools found only a 51 percent correlation between third-grade test scores and fifth-grade test scores for 431 pupils for
whom I had both scores—that is, for the same kids just two years apart! Averaging
school-by-school test scores for two consecutive years would smooth out such swings
and raise the correlation into the mid-60 percent range; the correlation between test
scores and socioeconomic status would probably top 70 percent by averaging three
years of test scores.

2. In *Abbott v. Burke,* the New Jersey Supreme Court ordered the state to provide
compensatory financial aid to thirty-one high poverty, low tax-base, urban school districts. As an *Abbott* district, Pemberton Township received over $32 million in *Abbott*
aid in 2005–6—about $5,000 per elementary school pupil. Though quite poor, the
Woodlynne Borough District received no special *Abbott* aid. Because of *Abbott* aid
($1.5 billion in 2005–6), there is actually a *negative* statistical relationship between
expenditures per pupil and test scores.

3. The source for the information in this section is Mial (2002). Material from
this case and the cases noted in notes 4 and 5 below are drawn and adapted from R.D.
Kahlenberg, ed., *Divided We Fail: Coming Together through Public School Choice:
The Report of The Century Foundation Task Force on the Common School* (New York:
Century Foundation Press, 2002). Copyright © 2002 The Century Foundation, Inc.
Used by permission.

4. The main source for information in this section on Wake County Public Schools
is Silberman (2002).

5. The source for the information in this section is Fiske (2002).

References

Burtless, G. 1996. *Does Money Matter? The Effect of School Resources on Student
    Achievement and Adult Success.* Washington, DC: Brookings Institution Press.
Coleman, J. 1966. *Equality of Educational Opportunity.* Washington, DC: National
    Center for Educational Statistics, Government Printing Office.
Dulaney, C., and R. Regan. 2003. *Measuring Up, End-of-Grade Multiple-Choice
    Test Results: 2002–03.* Raleigh: Wake County Public School System (July), 15.
    Available at www.wcpss.net/evaluation-research/reports/2003/0317eog2003.pdf
    (accessed February 2007).
Fiske, E.B. 2002. "Controlled Choice in Cambridge, Massachusetts." In *Divided We
    Fail, Coming Together Through Public School Choice: The Report of the Century*

Foundation Task Force on the Common School, ed. R.D. Kahlenberg, 167–208. New York: Century Foundation Press.

Hoff, D.J. 1997. "Chapter 1 Aid Failed to Close Learning Gap." *Education Week* 16, no. 27: 1–2.

Kahlenberg, R.D. 2001. *All Together Now: Creating Middle-Class Schools through Public School Choice.* Washington, DC: Brookings Institution Press.

———, ed. 2002. *Divided We Fail: Coming Together through Public School Choice: The Report of The Century Foundation Task Force on the Common School.* New York: Century Foundation Press.

Lara-Cinisomo, S.; A.R. Pebley; M.E. Vaiana; E. Maggio; M. Berends; and S.R. Lucas. 2004. "A Matter of Class: Educational Achievement Reflects Family Background More Than Ethnicity or Immigration." *RAND Review* 28, no. 3: 10–15.

Mial, R. 2002. "La Crosse: One School District's Drive to Create Socioeconomic Balance." In *Divided We Fail, Coming Together Through Public School Choice: The Report of the Century Foundation Task Force on the Common School,* ed. R.D. Kahlenberg, 115–40. New York: Century Foundation Press.

powell, j.a.; G. Kearney; and V. Kay. 2001. *In Pursuit of a Dream Deferred: Linking Housing & Education Policy.* New York: Peter Land.

Rusk, D. 2001. *Inside Game/Outside Game: Segregation and Spatial Planning in Metropolitan Areas.* Available at www.gamaliel.org/strategic/StrategicpartnersRuskNIROVdoc.htm (accessed November 2006).

———. 2002. *Classmates Count: A Study of the Interrelationship Between Socioeconomic Background and Standardized Test Scores of 4th Grade Pupils in the Madison-Dane County Public Schools.* Available at www.gamaliel.org/DavidRusk/Unified%20final%20report.pdf.

———. 2003. *Housing Policy Is School Policy: An Analysis of the Interaction of Housing Patterns, School Enrollment, and Academic Achievement in the Baltimore Area Schools.* Available at www.gamaliel.org/DavidRusk/Abell%202%20school%20final%20report.pdf (accessed November 2006).

Rusk, D., and J. Mosley. 1994. *The Academic Performance of Public Housing Children: Does Living in Middle Class Neighborhoods and Attending Middle Class Schools Make a Difference?* Washington, DC: Urban Institute. Available at www.gamaliel.org/Strategic/StrategicpartnersRuskCarnege.htm (November 2006).

Silberman, T. 2002. "Wake County Schools: A Question of Balance." In *Divided We Fail, Coming Together Through Public School Choice: The Report of the Century Foundation Task Force on the Common School,* ed. R.D. Kahlenberg, 141–66. New York: Century Foundation Press.

Thernstrom, S., and A. Thernstrom. 2003. *No Excuses: Closing the Racial Gap in Learning.* New York: Simon and Schuster.

8

JAMES H. LEWIS AND DAVID K. HAMILTON

Poverty and Urban Regions

Poverty as a Regional Problem

Central to the work of the pioneering school of University of Chicago sociologists who sought to understand the process by which urban regions grew
and developed was understanding why various forms of urban dysfunction
occurred, such as crime, gang activity, prostitution, and other forms of social
deviance. A key tool in their conception was Ernest Burgess's theory that cities
developed a set of concentric rings that bounded different types of places and
functions (Burgess 1923). Under this theory, poverty occurred most prevalently
in the second innermost ring, located between the downtown area, where most
industry was located and commerce transacted, and the third ring, where industrial workers typically lived. Occupying the outermost areas of the region,
on the central city's edge or in the suburbs, were the highest-income residents.
Within the circles, so called "natural areas" would emerge where residents of
common class and culture would settle, and a variety of social groups would
contend for influence over these spaces. For Burgess, urban poverty would
largely be confined to areas adjacent to the downtown area. This theory of
urban organization accurately described most large cities that grew around
heavy industry dependent upon rivers and lakes for transportation and where
workers were expected to commute only short distances to work.

By the late twentieth century, a competing theory of urban organization
emerged, espoused by the L.A. School, so named for Los Angeles, the proto-
typical city for this new pattern of urban growth that was becoming evident in
the U.S. West and Southwest. The theory described urban subregions characterized by residents of varying economic levels located in multi-nucleated sites
of postmodern light industry rather than in concentric circles outward from
the core of a city; and along the location of interstate highway systems rather
than rivers or lakefronts (Dear 2001; Scott and Soja 1998). The poor would
not locate in a second innermost concentric circle, but might be consigned to
the oldest, innermost circle, or to communities located throughout a region.

While the L.A. School describes a multi-nucleated, less ordered urban regional environment, important elements of Burgess's theory of neighborhood succession continue to operate, only not necessarily within the confines of concentric circles. In the Chicago area, for instance, south suburban neighborhoods that once housed the middle-class steelworkers who worked in the mills encircling the southern shores of Lake Michigan in Chicago and northwest Indiana have gradually been reoccupied by lower-income residents, many of whom are impoverished. In Chicago's northwest suburbs, apartment complexes inhabited by lower-middle-class workers have largely transitioned to even lower-income immigrant workers who escape the poverty line only by including two and sometimes three near-minimum-wage workers in the same household. Thus, even in a multi-nucleated regional setting, neighborhood invasion and succession continue to operate as local elites and new migrants contest control of suburban space.

The cycles of competition and stasis, so well described by Burgess and Park eighty years ago and modified by more recent theorists, continue to describe where and why low-income persons tend to concentrate in particular communities in urban areas, and the policy implications of where they live. We discuss in this chapter how the differentiation of space in urban regions creates concentrations of poverty and its attendant problems, the scope of the problem, and the strengths and weaknesses of strategies that might be used to mitigate the problem. We commence with a discussion of some of the reasons why urban regions exhibit high poverty. These include migration of low-skilled people to urban regions, lack of low-skilled jobs that pay a living wage, discrimination, and lack of personal resources.

Migration and Urban Poverty

The vast majority of poor in most large cities today are a product of two major waves of migration, and the urban structures those migrants entered. The first wave was the migration of African-Americans and some whites from the rural American South into cities from the 1920s through the 1950s, and second, the immigration of Latinos from Mexico and Central America into urban regions from the 1970s through the 2000s. The basic template for settlement of African-Americans into northern cities was established between 1900 and 1920 when their migration from southern rural areas into both northern and southern cities began. Blacks were attracted to northern cities first as labor that could be used to break strikes, and soon thereafter as substitutes for white workers fighting World War I. These migrants settled in segregated neighborhoods, which increased in density with chain migration (Drake and Cayton 1993; Kusmer 1978; Osofsky 1965). Blacks were hemmed into these highly impoverished central city neighborhoods by the neighborhoods' proximity to jobs, and by restrictive covenants and other tactics of racial discrimination in housing markets. Black migration into northern cities continued at near-geometric rates in the 1950s and 1960s, and persistent discrimination in housing and employment continued to limit blacks largely to inner-city neighborhoods (Lemann 1992).

The arrival of large numbers of low-income Hispanics in urban regions is a more recent story. In the Southwest and in California, low-income persons of Mexican lineage lived in and around cities for centuries, and migrant farm workers were a persistent presence, living in barrios that may or may not be located in the central city (see Lewis, in this volume). In the North, with the exception of Puerto Ricans in New York City, Hispanic immigrants began arriving in large numbers only in the 1970s. Settling initially in central city neighborhoods where housing markets steered them to low-cost housing, by the 1990s they had penetrated suburbs in most major urban areas, attracted by jobs and concentrated in affordable housing (Frey 2001). These households were typically composed of multiple wage earners who, individually, would have lived beneath the poverty line but, collectively, raised households to, or above, the poverty line. The presence of these immigrants, both documented and undocumented, first in central cities, and then in suburbs, stimulated fears among some in communities that poor immigrants would absorb too many public benefits and dilute the English-language culture (Ramirez 2002; Tolbert and Hero 1996).

Deindustrialization and the Service Economy

At the same time that millions of low-educated and low-skilled blacks and Hispanics were migrating into urban regions from the 1950s to 1980s, the nation's economy was beginning to undergo fundamental changes that would immediately disadvantage these migrants. Incited by lower cost overseas competition, rising costs of union labor, especially in northern cities, and the need for more space for expansion, manufacturing firms that had paid their workers a living wage began deserting northern cities (Bluestone and Harrison 1982). In the United States, the chief beneficiaries of this transition were cities in the Sunbelt and California, which offered lower labor and energy costs, and abundant inexpensive space for expansion. In some instances, firms relocated production overseas; in other instances, such as the auto and steel industries, foreign competitors simply supplanted them in the marketplace, forcing them to downsize, or worse.

Between 1967 and 1987, Detroit lost 51 percent of its manufacturing jobs, New York—8 percent, Chicago—60 percent, and Philadelphia—64 percent.

Most manufacturing jobs did not disappear completely; rather, they relocated from the older central cities to the suburbs, south and overseas (Teaford 1990). A study of job location and change in the sixty largest primary metropolitan statistical areas (PMSAs) indicated that the central city had 52 percent of the jobs in 1975 and 47 percent in 1986. Two-thirds of all jobs created in these PMSAs after 1976 were outside central cities. These areas captured 93.5 percent of manufacturing jobs added in the metropolitan areas from 1976 to 1980 and all of the jobs added from 1980 to 1986. For example, Chicago had 58.4 percent of the jobs in the metropolitan area in 1970. In 1990, Chicago's share of jobs in the metropolitan area had fallen by 20 percent (Hamilton 1999).

These transitions increased the concentration of poverty in older Rustbelt urban regions while poverty rates declined in southwestern cities during the 1970s and 1980s (Jargowsky and Bane 1991). Northern cities attempted to recoup their losses by reconceptualizing their inner cores around information technology, managerial functions, and recreational industries such as sports and arts. Suburbs competed for high-tech manufacturing in which the United States continued to be able to compete globally, as well as corporate managerial functions (Kasarda 1985).

In the Midwest and Northeast, these transformations impacted working-class communities located both in central cities and in blue-collar suburbs. The entire transformation contributed to urban poverty by replacing union-scale manufacturing occupations with millions of new service jobs in light manufacturing, office work, and hospitality industries that paid barely above the minimum wage and are rarely unionized (Bound and Holzer 1993; Kodras 1997). The urban cores of Detroit, Cleveland, St. Louis, and other northern manufacturing cities have not yet fully recovered from the transformation. But it also has left impoverished "inner-ring" suburbs in many places.

The loss of manufacturing jobs in the central city was especially devastating for the black labor force because of the high concentration of African-Americans in manufacturing. From 1968 to 1970, over 70 percent of blacks working in metropolitan areas had blue-collar jobs. Between 1968 and 1970, 80 percent of African-Americans in the central city with less than a high school education were working, compared to under 50 percent of similarly educated African-Americans in the central cities between 1990 and 1992 (Kasarda 1993). As central cities lost relatively well-paying manufacturing jobs, they gained jobs in the service sector. High-paying service-sector jobs require skills and education not readily available in the black and immigrant population. This transformation has brought greater attention to the problems of the working poor employed in minimum wage jobs that are insufficient to support themselves or their families or raise their incomes above the poverty line (Newman 1999; Shipler 2004).

Although the decline in manufacturing was traumatic for older central cities, almost equally devastating was the loss of retail jobs. Retail employment declined in most of the older cities of the Northeast and Midwest while it increased for the nation as a whole. For instance, in the Milwaukee metropolitan area between 1979 and 1994, retail and wholesale jobs declined by 11,000 in the central city and increased by 28,000 in the suburbs (Hamilton 1999). Retail employment in the central business districts (CBDs) was especially hard-hit, declining by over 25 percent in Chicago, Detroit, Baltimore, St. Louis, Buffalo, Cincinnati, and Minneapolis. This occurred despite efforts to revitalize shopping in the CBDs of many central cities such as Renaissance Center in Detroit, Harborplace in Baltimore, Quincy Market in Boston, and the State Street Mall in Chicago. Major department stores in CBD after CBD closed their doors during the 1980s. Not only did the closing of department stores contribute to the loss of retail jobs, but the empty stores added to the perception of decline in the CBD (Teaford 1990).

Detroit is the ultimate example of the debilitating effects on central cities when businesses relocate or industries change, although the same pattern can be observed in New Jersey, southeast Chicago, and northwest Indiana. Highland Park, a community inside Detroit's boundaries, once housed Henry Ford's Crystal Palace, the world's showplace for mass production. It was called the "city of trees" and possessed beautiful neighborhoods and vibrant institutions. The community's schools were so good that suburban students flocked to attend. Over the years the community deteriorated as businesses moved out. Forty-five percent of Highland Park's residents now receive some form of public assistance. Suburban Auburn Hills is becoming the Highland Park of earlier times. Job growth was phenomenal during the 1990s. The contrast between Highland Park and Auburn Hills also reveals how economic restructuring is redirecting the flow of capital away from Detroit's central city and into the northwest Oakland County suburbs. In 1960, Detroit held 50 percent of the region's assessed valuation; Oakland County's share was 14 percent. By 1980, the city's share had plummeted to 18 percent while Oakland County's share had grown to 38 percent (Hill 1990).

Discrimination and Poverty

Racial discrimination has contributed to the problem of poverty in urban regions in several ways. Employment discrimination, particularly against blacks, narrows the employment market for blacks and has prevented them from accessing job opportunities, particularly in predominately white suburbs. Considerable evidence suggests that the practice is less widespread than it once was (Wilson 1987), but evidence also indicates that it persists. Tester studies conducted in a number of major cities (Turner, Fix, and Struyk 1991) continue to indicate that employers fail to interview and hire blacks and Hispanics who are presented as equally qualified for jobs as whites. Kirschenman and Neckerman (1991) revealed how white suburban employers often utilize the travel time from city to suburb, or even city residence alone, as a pretense for discriminating against black job applicants that they prefer not to hire.

Persistent housing discrimination also contributes to poverty because, as Massey and Denton (1993) have demonstrated, normal downturns in the business cycle have disproportionately negative effects on neighborhoods where poor blacks are isolated. Like employment discrimination, discrimination in housing is less prevalent than it once was. Yet, tester studies continue to reveal its presence in a directly observable way, and the persistence of racially segregated housing patterns across regions, although caused by a variety of factors, indicates that at least some housing discrimination continues to exist (Turner 1992). Across urban regions, the poor are segregated by housing markets, leading to concentrations in inner-city neighborhoods as well as suburban neighborhoods. Race, and being black, in particular, is a stronger predictor of housing segregation than is economic class, but nevertheless income still plays a major part in determining where people will live.

General Theories to Explain Poverty

The sociologists of the "Chicago School" theorized that poverty and mobility would be dynamic conditions—zones of transition surrounding urban cores would cycle through periods of invasion and succession as new immigrant groups competed with older ones and most people eventually assimilated into the American culture and economy. Eventually, they thought, either they or their children would move to more stable and affluent neighborhoods. And for the most part, this pattern was born out by the successive groups of European immigrants arriving before 1920. They did not foresee the seemingly permanent state of African-American poverty that came to characterize the inner cores of most large midwestern and eastern cities, and that also exists in the Southwest and West to a lesser degree.

Debate among sociologists as to what best explains the persistence of poverty in urban regions, and particularly for African-Americans, has coalesced around two general theories. Wilson (1987; 1996) has argued that inner-city poverty was caused principally by loss of well-paying jobs, largely in manufacturing, that left black men with diminished job prospects. Simultaneously, middle-income blacks, freed to pursue housing outside the central city by improvements in the nation's civil rights climate, did so, thereby emptying inner-city neighborhoods of their leavening presence. The result was inner-city neighborhoods devoid of economic resources.

Massey and Denton (1993) have argued that the principal cause of concentrated poverty is found in racial segregation. Blacks found themselves isolated in inner-city neighborhoods by discriminatory housing markets, location of public housing, and other public policies and private practices. Because blacks on average have lower education and resources, and were in lower-paying jobs to begin with, the periodic dips in economic cycles have had a disproportionately damaging effect on these neighborhoods because the absence of a middle class in these neighborhoods meant that neighborhood businesses could no longer remain viable during downturns. The result has been a continuous downward spiral into concentrated poverty.

Quillian (1999) evaluated and synthesized these two arguments, finding that during the late 1970s and 1980s the number of nonpoor blacks moving into nonpoor white neighborhoods in cities and suburbs accelerated, leaving isolated poor blacks behind. In the suburbs, many whites responded by deserting their neighborhoods for others seemingly more likely to remain white. In many cases, poor blacks have followed nonpoor blacks into these suburbs. Because Quillian did not find increasing rates of poverty among blacks who remained behind in poor neighborhoods, he tended to downplay deindustrialization as a major reason for concentrated inner-city poverty. Of course, not all concentrated urban poverty is African-American. About 29 percent of people in high-poverty neighborhoods nationwide are Hispanic, and 24 percent are white.

The Regional Structure of Poverty

Because of their diverse economic functions, large regions are less prone to the boom and bust of economic change than are smaller regions. Across the nation, the highest and lowest rates of poverty are found in smaller regions, with the nation's largest urban regions occupying the middle ground. Larger regions generate sufficient economic activity to absorb increasingly large populations. As a result, many have become magnets for immigration. The largest urban regions with the highest poverty rates have about half as much poverty as the most impoverished smaller regions because their size guarantees sufficient economic diversification to support more people. However, even the most prosperous regions have poverty rates of at least 6 percent, indicating that however economically strong a region is, a number of residents, for reasons of low skills, low wages, disabilities, or discrimination, will be impoverished. The data also indicate that places with high levels of poverty have large numbers of either Hispanics or blacks while regions with low poverty are generally mostly white. Table 8.1 shows the regions with the highest and lowest poverty rates by major population groupings.

Table 8.1

Poverty Rates by Size of Region in Percents, 2000

Regions with highest poverty rates	(%)	Regions with lowest poverty rates	(%)
Regions under 500,000			
Brownsville-Harlingen-San Benito, TX	33.1	Sheboygan, WI	5.2
Laredo, TX	31.2	Appleton-Oshkosh-Neenah, WI	5.4
Bryan-College Station, TX	26.9	Rochester, MN	6.4
Las Cruces, NM	25.4	Cedar Rapids, IA	6.5
Visalia-Tulare-Porterville, CA	23.9	Wausau, WI	6.6
Regions 500,000 to 1.5 million			
McAllen-Edinburg-Mission, TX	35.9	Salt Lake City, UT	7.7
El Paso, TX	23.8	Colorado Springs, CO	8.0
Fresno, CA	22.7	Harrisburg-Lebanon-Carlisle, PA	8.1
Bakersfield, CA	20.8	Fort Wayne, IN	8.2
New Orleans, LA	18.4	Grand Rapids-Muskegon-Holland, MI	8.4
Regions over 1.5 million			
Los Angeles-Riverside-Orange County, CA	15.6	Minneapolis-St Paul, MN	6.7
Miami-Fort Lauderdale, FL	15.3	Washington D.C.-Baltimore, MD	8.3
San Antonio, TX	15.1	Kansas City, MO	8.5
Houston-Galveston-Brazoria, TX	13.7	Seattle-Tacoma-Bremerton, WA	8.5
New York-Northern NJ-Long Island	12.9	Denver-Boulder-Greeley, CO	8.6

Source: Computed from Bureau of the Census, Summary File 3 (2000).

Table 8.2

Percentages of Households with Public Assistance and Persons Below Poverty Line by Region, 2000

	Total population	Total persons in poverty	Percentage public assistance	Percentage poverty
New England	9,582,629	881,773	3	9
Mid-Atlantic	37,667,669	4,486,158	4	12
East North Central	34,734,821	3,563,825	3	10
West North Central	11,812,873	1,049,053	3	9
South Atlantic	39,465,451	4,390,215	3	11
East South Central	9,462,112	1,251,234	3	13
West South Central	24,273,275	3,643,015	3	15
Mountain	13,328,254	1,471,788	3	11
Pacific	39,290,040	5,272,365	5	13

Source: Computed from Bureau of the Census, Summary File 3 (2000).

Due to the variety of reasons that people become poor, and the variety of reasons poor people move to different regions, regional differences in the incidence of poverty are not as great as one might suppose. While the Rust-belt has been hit hard by deindustrialization and the neighborhood effects of concentrated inner-city poverty, the more prosperous Southwest and California urban regions have absorbed huge numbers of low-skilled immigrants and their families. California has a history of providing some of the nation's most generous welfare benefits, which have had the effect of attracting many poor people. As Table 8.2 shows, in 2000, despite doing well on the whole economically, the Pacific states had the highest percentage of population using public assistance, and the Pacific, West South Central, and East South Central areas of the nation had the highest percentages of populations in poverty. The lowest incidence of poverty was found in New England and in the West North Central states.

City–Suburban Allocation of Poverty

In the vast majority of regions, central city poverty is deeper than suburban poverty. To determine the extent of the difference between central city and suburban poverty, we computed the ratio of the percentage of residents in poverty in a region's central city to the percentage in poverty in its suburbs. Thus, the smaller the number, the greater the poverty of the central city relative to its suburbs; a number greater than "1" indicates that the percentage of persons in poverty in the suburbs is larger than the percentage in the central city. Across the nation, the mean ratio between central cities and suburbs is 0.58, indicating that central city residents are almost twice as likely as suburban residents to be poor. But urban regions vary tremendously in their central city to suburban ratios. The greatest extremes are found in Milwaukee, Wisconsin (ratio 0.18) Reading, Pennsylvania (ratio 0.18), Topeka, Kansas (ratio 0.19), and York, Pennsylvania (ratio 0.20), where a resident of the central city is about five times more likely than a suburban resident to be in poverty.

On the other hand, in Naples, Florida (ratio 1.81), Laredo, Texas (ratio 1.63), the McAllen-Edinburg-Mission, Texas MSA (ratio 1.60), and El Paso, Texas (ratio 1.44), a suburban resident is about 150 percent as likely as a central city resident to be poor.

In general, larger urban regions have more disparity between their central cities and suburbs than do smaller regions. Regions over 1.5 million in population average a ratio of 0.44, regions 500,000 to 1.5 million average a ratio of 0.54, and regions with fewer than 500,000 people have ratios averaging 0.62. The difference between the largest and smallest regions is statistically significant. This pattern exists because in larger regions, the distinction between living in a suburb and the central city is more meaningful than it is in the smallest regions. Because the zones of specialization, to borrow from Burgess's vocabulary, are much nearer one another in smaller places, any given place is more affected by what borders it. Other evidence suggests that in smaller places, local elites have felt more ability to control local political processes and so have had less incentive to flee central cities for suburbs. Conversely, in the first half of the twentieth century, in larger places, people with money reacted to waves of new population and industry in large cities spinning out of their control by moving to suburbs where they could maintain a lifestyle more to their liking. Similarly, by virtue of being smaller, smaller regions are more likely to have a single countywide school district, or at least fewer districts, thereby reducing the incentive of wealthier people to flee the central city for suburbs where their children can attend school in a school district isolated from the diversity of the central city. Thus among the very large regions—those with populations over 1.5 million people—none of them had a city–suburban poverty ratio greater than 1, meaning that, in all of them, a person living in the central city was more likely than a suburbanite to be poor.

Table 8.3 indicates that the largest city–suburban differences are found in older eastern and midwestern cities, while the large cities that reached maturity after the mid-twentieth century, and are located in the West and in Florida, have much smaller city–suburban differences. Las Vegas, the large metropolitan area with the least city–suburban difference, is the one that enjoyed the greatest population gain between 1990 and 2000.

Even among the small regions, there is a tremendous difference in ratios,

Table 8.3

Largest and Smallest City–Suburban Poverty Ratios for Regions of More Than 1.5 Million Persons, 2000

Urban region	Ratio
Milwaukee-Racine, WI	0.18
Minneapolis-St. Paul, MN	0.24
Detroit-Ann Arbor-Flint, MI	0.25
Philadelphia-Wilmington-Atlantic City	0.25
Cleveland-Akron, OH	0.27
Orlando, FL	0.63
Los Angeles-Riverside-Orange County, CA	0.63
Phoenix-Mesa, AZ	0.72
San Diego, CA	0.74
Las Vegas, NV	0.90

Source: Computed from Bureau of the Census, Summary File 3 (2000).

indicating that it is not their size alone that determines where their rich and poor live. Small regions such as Yuma, Arizona, and the Visalia-Tulare-Porterville, California MSA, have ratios greater than 1, yet Bloomington-Normal, Illinois, and many other small regions, have a city to suburban ratio of 0.25, meaning the region's poor are far more likely to be found in the central city area.

Size alone does not determine the allocation of poverty between central cities and suburbs. Clearly, there are regional differences as well. As Table 8.4 indicates, suburbs are much more relatively wealthy in the northeast and midwestern states, where central city residents are about twice as likely to be poor, than they are in the southern and western states where suburban residents are only on average one-third as likely as city residents to be poor, a finding similar to that of Nathan and Adams (1989) for the 1960s and 1970s. The worst city–suburban ratios, noted above, are all located in the northeastern and Atlantic seaboard states. Conversely, in New England, the greatest city–suburban parity is found in Bangor, Maine, with a ratio of only 0.70, and in the Middle Atlantic States, the best are Jamestown, New York, and the Scranton-Wilkes-Barre-Hazleton, Pennsylvania MSA, with a ratio of only 0.62. In these national subregions, there are no urban areas where poverty is more likely in the suburbs than in the central city.

Differences in the dates of settlement of the cities, and their geographies, explain many of the regional differences. For most of the southern and western cities, small urban cores existed from the nineteenth century, and in some cases even earlier. It was not until the mid-twentieth century, and in the case of Las Vegas even later, that huge migrations of Americans, and foreign immigrants, made these southern and western cities the metropolises they are

Table 8.4

Ratios of Percentage of Suburban Residents in Poverty to Percentage of Central City Residents in Poverty, 2000

Region	Mean	Minimum	Maximum
New England	0.45	0.24	0.70
Middle Atlantic	0.38	0.18	0.62
East North Central	0.39	0.18	1.25
West North Central	0.50	0.19	0.98
South Atlantic	0.65	0.25	1.81
East South Central	0.60	0.34	0.95
West South Central	0.73	0.32	1.63
Mountain	0.76	0.29	1.60
Pacific	0.72	0.25	1.39

Source: Computed from Bureau of the Census, Summary File 3 (2000).

today. These migrants moved into places far less defined by the riverfronts, ports, and heavy industry of the late nineteenth-century industrial revolution than by the multi-nucleated postindustrial highways and airports of the 2000s. As a result, rapidly expanding cities in these environments created less city–suburban differentiation of housing markets and the poor were much more likely to be located in suburbs. In many of the smaller urban regions, in California and Texas in particular, urban regions incorporate more semi-rural areas than do the older, more densely built-out eastern metropolitan areas. As a result these southern and western regions tend to have far larger populations of poor, migrant farmworkers living in their suburban peripheries than do eastern and midwestern cities.

The more poverty in an urban region as a whole, the more likely some of it is to be found in the region's suburbs. This is evident by the sixty-seven urban regions that have poverty rates of over 15 percent with the most equivalent city–suburban ratios, averaging a ratio of 0.72 with a ratio of 1 being equal distribution between city and suburbs. Regions with low poverty almost uniformly had extreme city–suburban differences, with ratios averaging 0.47, while the high-poverty places had much more variation in ratios. Thus, it was comparatively rare for a low-poverty region to have much poverty in its suburbs.

Strongest Predictor of City–Suburban Poverty Allocation

Which, then, is the strongest predictor of allocation of poverty between city and suburbs: the impact of a region's size, where it was located and when it developed, or its recent prosperity? A multivariate analysis weighing the relative impact of these factors on patterns of regional poverty identifies four key factors. The most important of these is the per capita income of a region, which correlates highly with concentration of poor in the central city. Thus, the wealthier an urban region, location and size accounted for, the more likely poor are to be located in the central city rather than the suburbs. Cities located on the West Coast or in the Mountain States were more likely to have poor in their suburbs, and cities in the Mid-Atlantic region were more likely to have poor in their central cities. The analysis suggests, therefore, that it is not the size of a region alone that determines whether the poor are more or less likely to locate in suburbs; rather, location within the nation and the urban region's prosperity mediate the influences of size.

These observations have important implications for policies aimed at reducing poverty in that they suggest that one size probably does not fit all. Increasing the wealth of any given region is likely to reduce the number of poor people living in it, but the analysis suggests that those living in the inner city will likely be the last to benefit from that economic growth. Strategies aimed at reducing poverty must be different in different parts of the country as the city–suburban mix of rich and poor clearly differs by when regions grew and the geography of their locations. Reducing poverty in places that are relatively new with a sprawling, auto-dependent development pattern is a different problem than doing so in places where the poor tend to be concentrated in a central city that has an aging infrastructure.

Concentrated Poverty

From the 1970s through the 1990s, the concentration of poverty in American cities increased (Jargowsky 1997). These increases were the result of flight of the nonpoor from low-income neighborhoods, combined with increasingly large numbers of poor urban residents (Quillian 1999). However, from 1990 to 2000, the number of high-poverty neighborhoods in U.S. cities declined significantly. According to Jargowsky (2003), nationwide the number of persons living in census tracts with over 40 percent poverty declined by 24 percent during the 1990s, falling from 10.4 million persons to 7.9 million in 2000. Metropolitan areas in the Midwest and the South experienced the steepest declines, neighborhoods in the Northeast changed the least, while the number of high-poverty neighborhoods in the West increased somewhat. Studies show that the economic well-being of suburbs is linked to the economic well-being of their central city (Ledebur and Barnes 1992; Savitch et al. 1993). Pastor and colleagues (2000) concluded that concentration of poverty and joblessness can constitute a drag on overall regional growth.

In part, the decline in concentrated poverty recorded in the 2000 Census was a result of the strong economy of the 1990s, but in the cases of Detroit and

Chicago, the two cities with the greatest decreases in people living in tracts over 40 percent poor, declines were more the result of depopulation of many inner-city tracts rather than the redevelopment of those neighborhoods. In Los Angeles, the city with the greatest increase in poor neighborhoods, the increase was largely attributable to the rising low-income Latino population.

As both Wilson (1987) and Massey and Denton (1993) point out, whether poverty is distributed evenly across many of a region's communities or concentrated in relatively few can have a dramatic impact on the health of a region. Concentration of the poor makes it more likely that poverty will be transmitted intergenerationally as parents and neighborhoods fail to provide the supports needed for children to attain the education, skills, and motivation to work productively.

Interrelationship of Poverty and Crime

One of the critical debates in sociology is the argument over the extent to which a resident's neighborhood affects the person's likelihood of committing a crime (Case and Katz 1991; Glaeser and Sacerdote 1999; Sampson and Raudenbush 1999), doing well in school (Brooks-Gunn et al. 1993), holding a job (Borjas 1995), or becoming an unwed mother (Crane 1991; South and Crowder 1999; Sucoff and Upchurch 1998). Neighborhood effects may operate in a number of ways, including providing material resources that make possible quality education or finding a job, such as good schools or contacts with potential employers (Sampson, Morenoff, and Gannon-Rowley 2002). They may also work more indirectly, as in the case of the role models children observe and with whom they interact, who may model different types of behavior such as committing crimes as opposed to obeying the law, or having children out of wedlock, or at an early age, as opposed to marrying or deferring parenthood. Arguments such as Wilson's account of the perpetuation of highly disadvantaged neighborhoods depend on the operation of neighborhood effects to explain why the out-migration of middle-class residents from poor neighborhoods has the deleterious effects that it appears to have.

Studies differ in their estimates of the amount of variance in resident behavior that may be attributable to neighborhood characteristics, but there is consensus that neighborhood characteristics have a measurable effect on residents. While the correlation of low educational outcomes, teen pregnancy, crime, and poor health with poverty is not in itself an issue relevant to the study of regional development, the fact that these problems are exacerbated by how regions differentiate economic and housing functions, and so allocate the poor spatially, is an issue. Land use decisions, unregulated housing markets, indifference to race relations or other public policies that have the effect of concentrating poverty, contribute, however unintentionally, to creation of criminals, the low-skilled, and the low-educated. Galster and Santiago (2006) conclude from a review of the literature that high concentrations of poverty lead to weaker social cohesion and lack of informal social controls and norms, lack of positive role models, increased crime, single-parent and dysfunctional families, lack of institutional resources and public services, spatial mismatch with jobs, and exacerbated racial and class differences.

The differentiation of space in urban regions that tends to locate and concentrate poverty in specific places creates areas where various types of crime are either more or less common. Most urban regions across the country display substantial differences in the crime rates between their central cities and their suburbs. These range from a few places where rates are close to equal to others, primarily located in the northeastern states, where central cities experience crime rates as much as seven times higher than their suburbs.

The original scholars of the Chicago School of sociology assumed that high-crime areas would be created by zones of transition or disorganization that would be located near the inner core of central cities. These areas, characterized by slum housing conditions, transient populations, and violent competition between residents and newly arrived immigrants, would experience high levels of street crime, homicide, gang activity, and prostitution. Because these theorists anticipated that cities would grow in accordance with a set of concentric circles, the outermost, or suburban one with the wealthiest citizens would have the least crime.

This model fairly well described cities and the location of crime for much of the twentieth century, but by the 1980s and 1990s, as we have discussed above, areas of high poverty, immigration, and concentrations of African-Americans were no longer confined to the central city, but were commonly found in the suburbs. What Ernest Burgess would have termed "natural areas" or zones of "disorganization" emerged in any number of patchwork patterns across suburban America.

Whether viewed as causes or correlates of levels of crime in suburbs, poverty, increases in black population, and increases in the number of Hispanic immigrants have all been associated with higher levels of crime. Poverty appears to be an underlying factor explaining much of crime in any number of studies. One study in Philadelphia found that, for every percentage point increase in the neighborhood poverty rate, the major crime rate increased by 0.8 percent. Another study in Columbus, Ohio, showed that in a neighborhood where the poverty rate was under 20 percent, the violent crime rate was around 7 per 1,000, whereas neighborhoods where the poverty rate was over 40 percent, the crime rate was 23 per 1,000 (Massey 1996). Galster (2002) found that a tipping point seems to emerge when neighborhood poverty reaches around 20 percent such that negative impacts reach a maximum level at around 40 percent poverty.

These studies indicate, then, that the concentration of poverty has the greatest negative effect on crime rates. With the highest concentrations of poverty in the central cities, crime rates in the central cities continue to be much higher than in the suburbs. A Bureau of Justice Statistics study using data collected through the annual National Crime Victimization Survey reported that central city dwellers accounted for 29 percent of the U.S. population and 38 percent of all violent and property crime victimizations in 1998. The study reported that the average annual violent crime rate in central cities from 1993 to 1998 was about 37 percent higher than the suburban rate. Central city dwellers over the age of twelve have a population that is 58.2 percent of the suburban population, yet they experienced 80 percent of the metropolitan violent- and property-crime victimizations. The study reported that central city dwellers were victims of personal theft at a rate twice that experienced by suburbanites, and property crime rates were 36 percent higher than the rate for suburban households (Duhart 2000). Although Brown (1982, 260) found that criminals did travel long distances to commit property crimes in commercial or manufacturing areas, most violent crimes are committed in the home of the perpetrator, or nearby.

Even though suburbs with increasing concentrations of poor, African-Americans, or immigrants do experience some increases in crime, almost 62 percent of the crimes of violence per 1,000 population and almost 60 percent of the property crimes per 1,000 households were committed in central cities in 2004. This ratio has increased as the central cities accounted for 59 percent of the violent crimes and 57 percent of the property crimes in 1996.

The rate of violent crime in the United States reached its highest recorded rate in the twentieth century in 1990 and was double the rate just twenty years earlier (Downs 1994, 79). However, since that time crime rates have fallen. Since 1993, the rate of every major violent and property crime measured by the federal government's National Crime Victimization Survey has fallen and by the early 2000s had reached a thirty-year low. The FBI's Uniform Crime Reports, which compiles data on violent and property crime reported by law enforcement authorities, has also recorded a drop of more than one-third in violent crime from 1994 to 2004 (Thomas 2005). Between 1994 and 1995, violent crime declined 12 percent nationwide, the largest yearly decline in more than twenty prior years.

Crime rates have continued to decline in both central cities and suburbs except for a slight increase for crimes of violence in central cities in 2004. Even though crime has decreased in both the central cities and the suburbs, it has decreased faster in the suburbs. Tables 8.5 and 8.6 give comparisons be-

Table 8.5

Urban–Suburban Violent Crime Rates per 1,000 Population over the Age of Twelve and Property Crime per 1,000 Households, Selected Years

Year	Property crime[a]	Burglary	Vehicle	Crimes of violence[b]	Rape	Robbery	Assault
1996 Urban	335.8	64.3	20.3	55.2	1.9	10.8	42.8
1996 Suburban	252.6	37.9	13.1	38.6	1.3	3.3	33.9
1998 Urban	274.2	49.3	17.8	46.3	1.7	6.5	38.1
1998 Suburban	204.5	32.5	10.2	35.5	1.4	3.2	30.9
2000 Urban	222.1	40.9	13.1	35.1	1.5	6.0	27.6
2000 Suburban	163.7	27.2	8.1	25.8	0.8	2.6	22.4
2002 Urban	215.3	40.5	17.1	33.1	2.2	4.3	26.7
2002 Suburban	145.3	22.4	7.5	20.0	0.7	1.8	17.6
2004 Urban	214.7	41.9	13.4	29.0	1.5	4.0	23.6
2004 Suburban	143.2	23.2	8.8	18.0	0.8	1.4	15.8

Source: Calculated from U.S. Department of Justice. Bureau of Justice Statistics, 1996–2004.

[a]Property crime includes burglary, larceny-theft, and motor vehicle theft.
[b]Violent crime includes murder, rape, robbery, and aggravated assault.

tween central cities and suburbs. Table 8.6 shows statistics on twelve selected cities and their suburbs with 2003 metropolitan populations over 2 million. According to the data presented in Table 8.5, the rate of crimes of violence has been cut by almost 50 percent in central cities and by over 50 percent in the suburbs. The drop in property crime has not been quite as dramatic, but has also been significant, declining by 36 percent in central cities and almost 43 percent in the suburbs. A Bureau of Justice Statistics report on crime perceptions between central city and suburban residents indicated that central city residents were three times more likely to identify crime as a significant neighborhood problem (DeFrancis and Smith 1998).

Poverty-related Influences on Crime Rates

Rather than crime spreading across suburbs evenly, self-perpetuating mechanisms produced by racial segregation and income disparity seem to operate together to concentrate commission of crime. In a study of the New York region, Alba, Logan, and Bellair (1994, 427) identified the percentage of a suburb's population that was black, level of poverty, and population size as "powerful" predictors of levels of exposure to crime. Liska, Logan, and Bellair (1998, 37) found that as more blacks moved into neighborhoods, robbery rates increased, but increasing robbery rates were an even stronger predictor of increase in black population. This suggests that in the suburbs, white flight from resegregating suburban communities is closely tied to crime rates such that increasingly dense minority neighborhoods often deteriorate. The link between poverty and crime is further validated by Shihadeh and Ousey's finding (1998) that reduction in income and loss of entry level jobs raise urban murder rates.

Most middle- and upper-class suburbs have responded to the problems of poverty by establishing strict zoning laws that restrict construction of low-cost housing, leaving the poor isolated in communities that have supplies of affordable housing. Complementing this isolation of the poor, the affluent have developed an additional way to isolate themselves through gated communities. More than 10 percent of new housing constructed across the nation is in the form of gated communities designed to accord residents a specific type of lifestyle (retirement or golfing for instance) or simply to provide safety from crime (Blakey and Snyder 1997). These new communities have been particularly prevalent in the Southwest and West, where abundant land remains in suburban areas to develop and suburban areas tend to be more heterogeneous economically than they are in the Midwest and the East (Blakey and Snyder 1998, 55).

Critics argue that this response to crime only further fragments regions,

Table 8.6

Crime Rates per 100,000 Population for Selected Central Cities and Their Suburbs, 1995 and 2003

MSA and CC* 2003 population	2003 CC Violent crime[a]	2003 CC Property crime[b]	2003 MSA Violent crime	2003 MSA Property crime	1995 CC Violent crime	1995 CC Property crime	1995 MSA Violent crime	1995 MSA Property crime
Atlanta MSA 4.595 million CC 0.431 million	1,970.1	8,870.3	361.6	3,849.0	3,646.5	13,421.2	374.3	5,471.4
Cincinnati MSA 2.046 million CC 0.325 million	1,123.3	7,452.1	243.7	3,509.5	1,290.0	6,196.3	226.3	3,308.9
Baltimore MSA 2.626 million CC 0.645 million	1,735.0	5,813.3	605.9	3,169.0	3,018.1	10,300.3	658.2	4,427.0
Dallas MSA 5.569 million CC 1.230 million	1,370.8	7,957.4	358.3	4,272.4	1,532.4	7,931.7	408.0	4,495.6
Denver MSA 2.303 million CC 0.566 million	624.0	5,135.9	314.5	4,116.9	861.3	6,012.4	380.6	4,721.3
Detroit MSA 4.497 million CC 0.928 million	2,018.3	6,986.0	922.3	3,367.0	2,407.6	9,531.2	424.4	3,986.4

Houston MSA 5.064 million CC 2.041 million	1,175.3	5,879.5	443.6	331.7	1,860.1	6,304.5	483.2	3,445.1
Los Angeles MSA 12.879 million CC 3.839 million	1,271.9	3,537.1	487.5	2,706.6	2,034.4	5,645.5	1,052.5	4,158.8
Phoenix MSA 3.580 million CC 1.403 million	692.8	6,971.3	386.4	5,131.4	1,067.5	9,812.6	528.7	6,740.7
Pittsburgh MSA 2.424 million CC 0.335 million	1,061.4	4,901.6	246.8	2,007.5	803.8[c]	4,492.1	217.1	1,994.7
Portland MSA 2.038 million CC 0.545 million	813.5	7,693.6	195.7	3,961.6	1,926.0	10,142.3	286.9	4,495.6
San Francisco MSA 4.223 million CC 0.772 million	741.5	4,943.0	492.2	3,860.5	1,476.6	6,713.6	406.5	3,527.2

Source: Calculated from Federal Bureau of Investigation. Uniform Crime reports, 1995–2003.
*MSA (metropolitan statistical area); CC (central city).
[a]Violent crime includes murder, rape, robbery, and aggravated assault.
[b]Property crime includes burglary, larceny-theft, and motor vehicle theft.
[c]Statistics are from 1996; 1995 statistics were not available.

making public problems harder to address as substantial portions of the population effectively try to avoid addressing them at all. Furthermore, many serious types of crimes—drug use, types of domestic violence, and white-collar crime—are at least as common, and in some cases even more common, among affluent rather than poor people, meaning that gated people are often less "safe" than they might imagine.

There appears to be a direct relationship between how well urban regions provide equal economic opportunities to all of their residents and how much crime will occur within the region. Blau and Blau (1982, 122) identified relative deprivation, measured by income inequality, as a strong predictor of levels of crime within large metropolitan areas. While levels of poverty within metropolitan areas also correlated with levels of crime, the extent of inequality was the more important of the two measures. Likewise, levels of economic inequality between blacks and whites were a stronger predictor of levels of crime than was the proportion of the region that was black.

Poverty Impacts on Education, Neighborhood Disinvestment, and Fiscal Distress

Concentrated poverty has substantial deleterious effects on education, neighborhood decline, and a community's ability to fund services. These areas are covered in other chapters of this volume, particularly Chapters 5, 6, and 7, and are thus discussed only briefly here. There is a high correlation between poverty, poor school performance, and high dropout rates. Thus, poor central city neighborhoods and poor suburbs have high concentrations of low-skilled residents. As a result, the low-skilled labor market can become highly segmented, making some communities attractive to businesses, and other communities distinctively unattractive.

Most state education finance systems continue to rely heavily on local property taxes. These systems severely disadvantage school districts that have large numbers of poor residents and children, if funding received from the state is insufficient to equalize school quality. Large numbers of poor children can be more expensive to educate, and low-income residents have fewer financial resources to contribute to the support of their schools. This problem particularly impacts suburban school districts that cover small, impoverished geographical areas, but can also be problematic in larger districts, such as central cities, that have experienced substantial disinvestment.

The fortunes of declining neighborhoods are very difficult to reverse because of a self-reinforcing mechanism whereby the poor can afford to live only in dilapidated housing, homeowners and landlords may either be unable to make needed repairs or may choose not to. Then the condition of housing becomes increasingly bad, reducing rental values and ensuring that only more low-income people will be attracted to the neighborhood. The exceptions to this downward neighborhood spiral are gentrifying neighborhoods, but this gentrification is most likely in neighborhoods that have avoided high concentration of high school dropouts, female-headed families, and unemployment, and have had more "vintage" housing stock. Homeownership is also associated with greater chances of improvement.

Galster, Quercia, and Cortes (2000) found that various social indicators, including poverty, exert threshold effects on low-income urban neighborhoods such that when they reach a certain point, further neighborhood decline is predicted. Fogarty (1977) found that, for lower-income places, income inequality and larger numbers of elderly contributed to neighborhood decline. High levels of poverty also lead to loss of businesses, which in turn costs neighborhoods their jobs, further reducing their attractiveness for residential location. Despite some studies that have sought to show that low-income communities have substantial wealth to spend on consumer goods, equal densities of middle-class and poor people produce very different patterns of consumer spending. With the exception of small, ethnic family-operated establishments, few businesses choose to locate in low-income neighborhoods.

In the fragmented metropolitan area largely dependent on local property and sales taxes for funding local services, deteriorating property values and loss of local businesses translate to less revenue for public services or, alternatively, a higher tax burden on low-income people. Studies indicate that impoverished communities, particularly those in the suburbs that have a small property tax base, lack the resources to fund even basic services, a topic analyzed further in Chapter 3.

Moreover, concentrations of poor require additional government expenditures in increased welfare, health, police, and other services. To the extent that these costs are not financed by federal and state aid, they must be borne through the city's tax revenue, putting an unequal burden on taxpayers in the municipality relative to taxpayers in other municipalities with lower percentages of poverty. In addition, heavy concentrations of poverty result in property deterioration, which reduces property tax revenue. Thus, the additional taxes required to support poverty-related services, and the increased costs associated with blighted neighborhoods, dysfunctional families, drugs, and crime must increasingly be borne by a declining property tax base. The result is that taxes increase or services decrease. This encourages a population exodus of middle-class taxpayers to avoid the higher taxes and the deterioration of the impoverished neighborhoods. This exodus leads to further neighborhood deterioration.

Public Policies to Deconcentrate and Reduce Poverty

We consider two broad ways of addressing the problem of poverty. The first, and clearly most desirable, outcome is to find ways to reduce the number of poor individuals living in metropolitan regions by helping them raise their standards of living. But a second possible objective would be to concede that significant numbers of low-income individuals will remain in urban areas, and so to develop a public policy aimed at mitigating the negative effects of concentrated poverty through dispersal of the poor across the region. While it is self-evident that reducing the number of poor would have positive impacts, less consensus exists around dispersing the poor. Of course when the question moves from whether it is good to reduce poverty, to what are acceptable ways of doing it, or what are acceptable costs, consensus around taking measures to reduce poverty also fades.

The American public is sharply divided over both the fairness and effectiveness of policies that have been utilized historically to fight poverty, such as welfare, universal health care, civil rights enforcement, equalized school funding, and affirmative action. At the local level, residents must decide whether or not to allocate tax revenues to infrastructure that would lead to more economic development in poor neighborhoods or whether to share tax revenues across rich and poor municipalities.

Poverty-dispersal Policies

Although there is substantial controversy surrounding policies aimed at reducing poverty, far more widespread and heated opposition is raised to policies that would disperse the poor. In practice, this often means desegregating both city and suburban communities, and helping low-income people to live among the middle and upper classes. In spite of this opposition, a number of considerations, many enumerated above, argue for dispersing low-income people more widely. The concentration of poverty contributes to crime, poor educational outcomes, and other dysfunctional behavior. Concentrated poor are less likely to live near jobs, which are more likely to be located in or near more affluent areas. Individuals who live in neighborhoods where most residents are poor have less access to social capital that can accrue to them educationally, economically, and socially. Indeed, poor people who do have access to social capital, and who live near work, have less chance of remaining poor. It can also be argued, from the point of view of simple justice, that if the economic structure and policies regarding how to allocate public resources such as money for schools inevitably lead to significant numbers of people being poor and if those people tend to incur more social costs in the form of welfare, housing, medical subsidies, or crime, then people across the region should shoulder those burdens equally (Been 1993).

In addition to regional strategies to reduce poverty, deconcentration strategies should be pursued. For instance, Galster (2002) found that a uniform distribution of poor households throughout a metropolitan area, ensuring that neighborhoods remained below 20 percent of poverty, would result in less negative behavior. Deconcentrating poverty would address many of the problems created by neighborhood effects described by Wilson (1987); and Massey and Denton (1993).

Public policies that would contribute to the spatial dispersion of poor individuals across the metropolitan area include the availability of affordable housing. Availability of low-cost housing is an essential part of any policy to reduce racial and economic segregation. Spatially dispersed low-cost housing would bring low-income people in closer proximity to jobs and reduce the negative effects of high concentrations of poverty. The ability to reduce concentrated poverty depends in part on levels of segregation in metropolitan regions. South and Crowder (1997, 1078) found that blacks were less likely to escape poor neighborhoods than were whites, even after controlling for income. Black inability, or unwillingness, to leave low-income neighborhoods was exacerbated by high levels of metropolitan segregation and high proportions of blacks in a region. In part, this results from black hesitancy to move to neighborhoods that are predominantly white if they have a choice, which they do as regions gain black population (Krysan and Farley 2002).

Poverty-reduction Policies

Poverty reduction has historically been either a municipal function or a federal one. In only rare instances has it been a regional one. It is beyond the scope of this chapter to recount at length the ebb and flow of federal antipoverty strategies, from the emergence of welfare, jobs programs, and housing associated with the New Deal, to the Great Society programs of the 1960s, and to the partial retreat from federal involvement characterized by revenue sharing (Nixon), tax cuts (Reagan), and welfare reform (Clinton). Likewise, literally tens of thousands of economic development initiatives have taken place in America's cities, either utilizing federal dollars for local programming or undertaking initiatives funded locally. These include infrastructure, business development, housing, education, crime prevention, sports and tourist venues, and transportation projects. Galster and Mincy (1993) found that the fortunes of individual poor neighborhoods were tied to the overall economic fortunes of the region, so economic growth of a region as a whole has positive impacts on the lives of the poor.

It is rare, however, for regional initiatives to embrace poverty reduction as an explicit mission. The original city–county consolidations were done in the interest of promoting the economic strength of those places. Unigov and other regional governance systems were motivated in part by economic considerations, but not expressly to reduce poverty. In Pittsburgh, the Allegheny Conference on Community Development was initially formed to sustain the Pittsburgh region by focusing on the environment, economic development, and downtown preservation. "By cleaning the environment, redeveloping the downtown, modernizing the industrial base, improving air service, selectively implementing downtown-oriented road improvements, avoiding the construction of a beltway, and fighting a rear-guard action to counterbalance the growing appeal of suburban living among the city's middle class, the Pittsburgh Renaissance achieved relative regional stability" (Gleeson and Paytas 2005, 206).

More recently, intraregional cooperation has emerged as a new strategy aimed at enabling urban regions to compete more effectively in the global marketplace. One prominent advocate of regional cooperation operating in the Chicago area, Chicago Metropolis 2020, states its mission thus: "Our unifying vision is that the region's governments, businesses, and residents must work together to make the kinds of informed choices that will make the region attractive and economically competitive 10, 50 and 100 years from now. . . . We can choose a better future. We can spend less time in traffic. We can live nearer to our jobs. We can protect more open space. We can build communities that are friendlier to walking and biking—and, therefore, healthier for the people who live in them. We can make economic opportunity available to more of our region's residents" (promotional brochure 2003). To the extent that reducing poverty is a goal of the organization, it appears to be subsumed under the broader categories of attractiveness and competitiveness, suggesting that while quality of life for residents may be important, at least in their mission it appears subordinate, at least in the short run, to being attractive (to investors) and, therefore, competitive.

However regions organize themselves to address problems of economic competitiveness and poverty, two of the fundamental issues they face are how to implement strategies or practices that would reduce poverty and how to stop doing things that have the effect of increasing, or at least preserving, levels of poverty.

One major strategy to decrease poverty is to provide an effective, affordable public transportation system. Many large cities have effective rail and bus grids in their central cities, but travel times and access to transit stops are problematic in the suburbs. With the increasing number of entry-level jobs in the suburbs and the poor heavily concentrated in the central cities, public transportation is not a viable solution to the spatial mismatch. Additionally, suburban residents have not always welcomed inner-city, minority workers in their neighborhoods and have thus discouraged expansion of public transit systems from central cities into their neighborhoods. Regional transportation issues are covered at length in Chapter 9.

Another strategy to address poverty is to site economic development convenient to low-income residents. Although businesses ultimately decide for themselves where they want to locate, public policy can play a key role in helping them to make that determination. Assistance with site assembly, land clearance, tax incentives, infrastructure, and job training funds can influence business location. Cities create industrial parks so as to structure, manage, and intentionally benefit from agglomeration effects that tend to occur naturally. Unfortunately, from the point of view of those seeking to reduce poverty, the dominant paradigm in siting of businesses has been for municipalities to compete with one another to attract them by offering financial incentives that ultimately cost the winner tax revenue that either could have been levied or resources that could have benefited residents rather than businesses.

The other major strategy for business development is utilizing the siting of major public works such as airports, stadiums, or the arts to stimulate compatible economic development such as restaurants, hotels, and shopping in the case of stadiums, and a wide variety of light industry in the case of airports. In Indianapolis, Cleveland, and other cities, new downtown stadiums have been credited with reviving failing downtowns; however, critics have argued that rather than creating new wealth and jobs, they have tended to simply relocate them (Noll and Zimbalist 1997; Spirou and Bennett 2003). Jobs generated by the "consumption" sector tend to be low paying, and while arguably better than no jobs, often do not pay well enough or are too seasonal to move workers over the poverty line.

Rarely, if ever, are these economic development decisions made with regional health in mind, as opposed to the well-being of the specific location of a new industrial site. For instance, over the past decade, the siting of new airport capacity in Chicago, whether a new south-suburban airport, or expansion of runways at O'Hare International Airport, has been plagued with political contention and litigation, characterized by anything but regional cooperation. Historically, central city political leaders have partnered with business leaders or created other coalitions to enable mega projects. In the past, projects with regional impact such as Boston's central artery, or any number of Robert Moses's New York projects were as likely to pave over poor neighborhoods as to help them (Caro 1975). According to Altshuler and Luberoff (2003) more recent projects such as Denver's new airport or Boston's "Big Dig" continue to be initiated by central city interests rather than regional planning.

Another public policy solution would be to improve the distribution of funds for public services and especially for public education. As discussed above and elsewhere in this volume, one of the key means of reducing poverty is to improve educational outcomes. Given the disparities among municipalities in metropolitan areas, as long as the major source of revenue is own-source taxes, achieving sufficient and equitable funding for schools and municipal services will be impossible. The municipalities with wealthy residents and strong tax bases have a lighter tax burden per capita than the less-well-off communities. These wealthy communities are able to raise disproportionate amounts of public revenue compared with poorer communities. Wealthy school districts and municipalities have been loath to surrender these advantages voluntarily. Indeed, state action, often as the result of litigation, is required to make any attempt to reduce disparities among school districts in metropolitan areas (Hoxby 2001, 1192). An example of a successful regional initiative to reduce fiscal disparities is the Minneapolis-St. Paul area, where a state law requires that a portion of revenue generated from commercial and industrial property growth across the region be redistributed to resource-poor communities (Orfield 1997).

Regional Governance and Poverty Strategies

Part of the challenge of reducing the concentration of poverty involves combating suburban sprawl. In a study of poverty, Yang and Jargowsky (2006) found that suburbanization plays a role in economic segregation, and concluded that concentrations of poverty in metropolitan areas would have decreased even more during the 1990s absent continued suburbanization. A corollary of sprawl has been the proliferation of local governments, each charged with defending their communities from unwelcome change. Ironically, to the extent that suburbanites feel safe in their suburban communities, regionalism and fair-share distribution of low-cost housing may become even more difficult (Orfield 1997). One study in the Twin Cities found that people's fears of being a victim of crime in the central city were, in many instances, more than six times their true likelihood of becoming a victim. Yang and Jargowsky (2006) also found that government fragmentation tends to correlate with increased concentration of poverty. The larger the number of governments in a metropolitan area and the more homogeneous the housing values in these communities are, the less likely that communities will be economically integrated.

Leading advocates of regional governance such as Myron Orfield (1997) and David Rusk (1993) argue that regional governance is necessary to deconcentrate poverty. However, some observers argue that even regional approaches may not be sufficient. In Portland, Oregon, one model for regional planning and city–suburban collaboration, a "fair-share" provision requires each municipality to provide affordable housing. However, stocks of affordable housing in the region have been threatened by the same upward price pressure that has affected other major cities since the 1990s. Analysts debate whether Portland's urban growth boundary contributed to rising housing costs by limiting supply and altering the usual patterns of filtering older housing (Abbott 1997, 35–36). In Indianapolis, Unigov has had but marginal success in reducing poverty in Indianapolis and Marion County, performing only a little better than neighboring Detroit and Cleveland (Rusk 1994, 3–5). As Lucy and Phillips (2000, 249) explain in describing failed efforts to strengthen Minnesota's Metropolitan Council, regional governance requires extensive compromises between interests, making the measures needed to fight concentrated poverty difficult to adopt.

In some respects, the very logistics of being poor have also argued against dispersal of low-income people. Low-income people benefit from access to a concentrated grid of bus and train routes and will thus tend to locate where these are more available. Likewise, some have argued that social services are most available, and delivered more efficiently, when their users are located nearer to one another (Allard 2004). The bonds of community operate both in neighborhoods where residents "defend" their communities by resisting location of affordable housing and low-income people, and in low-income neighborhoods where there are community and family networks. Poor African-Americans in particular, have rejected relocation to white suburbs as public housing is reconstructed, and often prefer that their children attend racially segregated black neighborhood schools rather than be bused to racially segregated white schools. They often choose to live among other blacks, even if it means living in a lower-income neighborhood. Surveys indicate that most blacks do not wish to live in neighborhoods that are over 50 percent white, fearing for their security and comfort (Krysan and Farley 2002). Thus, the high correlation between race and poverty makes the integration of the poor among the more affluent doubly difficult to achieve, requiring persuasion at both loci of change.

Conclusion

Reducing poverty begins with jobs that pay living wages, and regions thus need to undertake strategies that will help them to compete effectively economically, both nationally and globally. Suburbanization and the fragmented government system are not conducive to reducing economic segregation. Indeed, suburbanization and the fragmented government system are used as a means to support economic segregation. Public policies designed to reduce the negative effects of the fragmented government system and the increasing decentralization of our metropolitan area should also serve to promote economic integration. Finally, decreasing poverty and economic segregation requires the involvement of the private sector. Businesses must be willing to work with the public sector on policies that promote development and the revitalization of blighted areas. Through economic growth and public policies designed to disperse people living in blighted areas and policies to revitalize blighted neighborhoods, poor people will be able to participate in the quality of life enjoyed by other residents of the region and the entire region will benefit from increased prosperity.

Because wherever they live, the poor require subsidized social services and tend to produce more social costs, municipalities housing disproportionate numbers of poor need to be relieved of the threat of municipal overburden. As long as concentrations of affordable housing and the poor exist, this can be achieved only by redistributing resources across the metropolitan area. As discussed above, the municipalities in the Twin Cities region share a portion of property taxes derived from commercial and industrial property. However it is accomplished, it is essential that affluent taxpayers, whether corporate or individual, not be able to escape contributing their fair share to support antipoverty programs.

Dispersing those who are poor across a region can have the effect of reducing poverty by improving access to job opportunities, but also helps spread the cost of supporting low-income people more evenly across municipalities that do not share tax resources sufficiently. It also reduces the cost of poverty by reducing the concentrations of poverty that are so highly associated with crime, violence, and social isolation. Achieving relocation of poor individuals and families to create more even distribution within a region has proved extremely difficult nearly everywhere because of the tendency of markets to concentrate lower-rent housing, affluent people to defend their neighborhoods, and high levels of racial segregation to persist.

Where poverty exists crime exists and, as discussed previously, concentrated poverty concentrates crime. Fear for personal safety is a critical element in the enjoyment of the quality of life. When residents are afraid to venture onto their streets and sidewalks, when families will not allow their children to walk to school unescorted, when homes and stores are routinely burglarized or robbed at gunpoint, concern for personal safety and the safety of family and friends trumps all other issues. These conditions grotesquely mock the personal freedoms a democratic society supposedly guarantees. If people cannot walk outside their homes without fear of robbery, attack, or injury, they are not free. Deconcentrating poverty will reduce the incidence of crime and improve the quality of life.

Setting aside any moral requirement to assist the poor, poverty reduction is essential for regional economic competitiveness, both to maximize the productivity of a region's population and to minimize the expense of mitigating the effects of concentrated poverty. Thus, we believe it is in any region's interest to establish mechanisms that facilitate regional planning and governance aimed at reducing and deconcentrating poverty. While no regional system in this country has yet been successful, regional approaches have produced some improvements.

References

Abbott, Carl. 1997. "The Portland Region: Where City and Suburbs Talk to Each Other and Often Agree." *Housing Policy Debate* 8, no. 1: 11–51.

Alba, Richard D.; John R. Logan; and Paul E. Bellair. 1994. "Living with Crime: The Implications of Racial/Ethnic Differences in Suburban Location." *Social Forces* 73, no. 2: 395–434.

Allard, Scott W. 2004. *Access to Social Services: The Changing Urban Geography of Poverty and Service Provision.* Washington, DC: Brookings Institution.

Altshuler, Alan, and David Luberoff. 2003. "The Changing Politics of Urban Mega-Projects." *Land Lines Newsletter* 15, no. 4. Lincoln Institute of Land Policy. Available at www.lincolninst.edu/pubs/ (accessed November 2006).

Been, Vicki. 1993. "What's Fairness Got to Do with It? Environmental, Justice and the Siting of Locally Undesirable Land Uses." *Cornell Law Review* 78: 1001–1085.

Blakey, Edward J., and Mary G. Snyder. 1997. *Fortress America: Gated Communities in the United States.* Washington, DC: Brookings Institution Press.

———. 1998. "Separate Places: Crime and Security in Gated Communities." In *Reducing Crime Through Real Estate Development and Management*, ed. Marcus Felson and Richard B. Peiser, 53–70. Washington, DC: Urban Land Institute.

Blau, Judith R., and Peter M. Blau. 1982. "The Cost of Inequality: Metropolitan Structure and Violent Crime." *American Sociological Review* 47, no. 1: 114–29.

Bluestone, Barry, and Bennett Harrison. 1982. *The Deindustrialization of America: Plant Closings, Community Abandonment, and the Dismantling of Basic Industry.* New York: Basic Books.

Borjas, George, J. 1995. "Ethnicity, Neighborhoods, and Human-Capital Externalities." *American Economic Review* 85, no. 3: 365–90.

Bound, J., and Harry J. Holzer. 1993. "Industrial Shifts, Skills Levels, and the Labor Market for White and Black Males. *Review of Economics and Statistics* 75, no. 3: 387–96.

Brooks-Gunn, Jeanne Duncan; Greg J. Klebanov; Pamela Kato; and Naomi Sealand. 1993. "Do Neighborhoods Influence Child and Adolescent Development?" *American Journal of Sociology* 99, no. 2: 353–95.

Brown, Marilyn A. 1982. "Modeling the Spatial Distribution of Suburban Crime." *Economic Geography* 58, no. 3: 247–61.

Burgess, Ernest W. 1923. "The Growth of the City: An Introduction to a Research Project." *Publication of the American Sociological Society* 21: 178–84.

Caro, Robert. 1975. *The Power Broker: Robert Moses and the Fall of New York.* New York: Vintage.

Case, Anne C., and Lawrence F. Katz. 1991. "The Company You Keep: The Effects of Family and Neighborhood on Disadvantaged Youths." NBER working paper, 3705 (May).

Crane, Jonathan. 1991. "The Epidemic Theory of Ghettos and Neighborhood Effects on Dropping Out and Teenage Childbearing." *American Journal of Sociology* 96, no. 5: 1226–1259.

Dear, Michael J. 2001. From Chicago to LA: Re-Visioning Urban Theory. Thousand Oaks, CA: Sage.

DeFrancis, C.J., and S.K Smith. 1998. *Perceptions of Neighborhood Crime, 1995.* Washington, DC: Bureau of Justice Statistics. U.S. Department of Justice. Available at www.ojp.gov/bjs/pub/pdf (accessed March 2006).

Downs, Anthony. 1994. *New Visions for Metropolitan America.* Washington, DC: Brookings Institution.

Drake, St. Clair, and Horace Cayton. 1993. *Black Metropolis: A Study of Negro Life in a Northern City.* Chicago: University of Chicago Press.

Duhart, R. 2000. *Urban, Suburban, and Rural Victimization, 1993–1998.* Washington, DC: Bureau of Justice Statistics, U.S. Department of Justice. Available at www. ojp.gov/bjs/pub/pdf (accessed March, 2006).

Federal Bureau of Investigation, Uniform Crime reports. 1995–2003. *Crime in the United States,* Table 6. Washington, DC. Available at www.fbi.gov/ucr/cius/ (accessed March 2006).

Fogarty, M.S. 1977. "Predicting Neighborhood Decline Within a Large Central City: An Application of Discriminant Analysis." *Environment and Planning* 9: 579–84.

Frey, William H. 2001. *Melting Pot Suburbs: A Census 2000 Study of Suburban Diversity.* Washington, DC: Brookings Institution.

Galster, George C. 2002. "An Economic Efficiency Analysis of Deconcentrating Poverty Population." *Journal of Housing Economics* 11: 303–29.

Galster, George, and Ronald Mincy. 1993. "Understanding the Changing Fortunes of Metropolitan Neighborhoods, 1980 to 1990." *Housing Policy Debate* 4, no. 3: 303–52.

Galster, George C., and A.M. Santiago. 2006. "What's the 'Hood Got to Do with It? Parental Perceptions About How Neighborhood Mechanisms Affect Their Children." *Journal of Urban Affairs* 28, no. 3: 201–26.

Galster, George C.; Roberto G. Quercia; and Alvaro Cortes. 2000. "Identifying Neighborhood Thresholds: An Empirical Exploration." *Housing Policy Debate* 11, no. 3: 701–32.

Glaeser, Edward L., and Bruce Sacerdote. 1999. "Why Is There More Crime in Cities?" *Journal of Political Economy* 107, no. 6: 225–58.

Gleeson, Robert E., and Jerry Paytas. 2005. "Pittsburgh: Economic Restructuring and Regional Development Patterns, 1880–2000." In *Sunbelt/Frostbelt: Public Policies and Market Forces in Metropolitan Development,* ed. Janet Rothenberg Pack, 182–218. Washington, DC: Brookings Institution Press.

Hamilton, David K. 1999. *Governing Metropolitan Areas: Response to Growth and Change.* New York: Garland.

Hill, R.C. 1990. "Industrial Restructuring, State Intervention and Uneven Development in the United States and Japan." In *Urban Policy and Economic Restructuring in Comparative Perspective,* ed. J. R. Logan and T. Swanstrom, 67–92. Philadelphia: Temple University Press.

Hoxby, Caroline. 2001. "All School Finance Equalizations Are Not Created Equal." *Quarterly Journal of Economics* 116, no. 4: 1189–1231.

Jargowsky, Paul A. 1997. *Poverty and Place: Ghettos, Barrios, and the American City.* New York: Russell Sage Foundation.

———. 2003. *Stunning Progress, Hidden Problems: The Dramatic Decline of Concentrated Poverty in the 1990s.* Washington, DC: Brookings Institution.

Jargowsky, Paul A., and Mary Jo Bane. 1991. "Ghetto Poverty in the United States, 1970–1980." In *The Urban Underclass*, ed. Christopher Jencks and Paul Peterson, 235–73. Washington, DC: Brookings Institution.

Kasarda, John. 1985. "Urban Change and Minority Opportunities." In *The New Urban Reality*, ed. Paul Peterson, 33–67. Washington, DC: Brookings Institution.

———. 1993. "Cities as Places Where People Live and Work: Urban Change and Neighborhood Distress." In *Interwoven Destinies: Cities and the Nation*, ed. H.G. Cisneros, 70–95. New York: Norton.

Kirschenman, Joleen, and Kathryn M. Neckerman. 1991. "We'd Love to Hire Them, Out: The Meaning of Race for Employees." In *The Urban Underclass*, ed. Christopher Jencks and Paul E. Peterson, 155–74. Washington, DC: Brookings Institution.

Kodras, Janet E. 1997. "The Changing Map of American Poverty in an Era of Economic Restructuring and Political Realignment." *Economic Geography* 73, 1: 67–93.

Krysan, Maria, and Reynolds Farley. 2002. "The Residential Preferences of Blacks: Do They Explain Persistent Segregation?" *Social Forces* 80, no. 3: 937–80.

Kusmer, Kenneth. 1978. *A Ghetto Takes Shape: Black Cleveland from 1870 to 1930.* Champaign: University of Illinois Press.

Ledebur, L.C., and W.R. Barnes. 1992. *City Distress, Metropolitan Disparities, and Economic Growth.* Washington, DC: National League of Cities.

Lemann, Nicholas. 1992. *The Promised Land: The Great Black Migration and How It Changed America.* New York: Vintage.

Liska, Allen E.; John R. Logan; and Paul E. Bellair. 1998. "Race and Violent Crime in the Suburbs." *American Sociological Review* 63 (February): 27–38.

Lucy, William, and David Phillips. 2000. *Confronting Suburban Decline: Strategic Planning for Metropolitan Renewal.* Washington D.C.: Island Press.

Massey, Douglas S. 1996. "Concentrating Poverty Breeds Violence." *Population Today* 24 (June/July): 82–91.

Massey, Douglas S., and Nancy Denton. 1993. *American Apartheid.* Cambridge, MA: Harvard University Press.

Nathan, Richard P., and Charles F. Adams. 1989. "Four Perspectives on Urban Hardship." *Political Science Quarterly* 104, no. 3: 483–508.

Newman, Katherine S. 1999. *No Shame in My Game: Working Poor in the Inner City.* New York: Knopf and Russell Sage Foundation.

Noll, Roger, and Andrew Zimbalist. 1997. "Sports, Jobs, and Taxes: Are New Stadiums Worth the Cost?" *Brookings Review* 15, no. 3: 35–39.

Orfield, Myron. 1997. *Metro Politics: A Regional Agenda for Community and Stability.* Washington, DC: Brookings Institution.

Osofsky, Gilbert. 1965. *Harlem: The Making of a Ghetto: Negro New York, 1890 to 1930.* New York: Harper and Row.

Pastor Jr., M.; P. Dreier; J.E. Grigsby II; and M. Lopez-Garza. 2000. *Regions That Work: How Cities and Suburbs Can Grow Together.* Minneapolis: University of Minnesota Press.

Quillian, Lincoln. 1999. "Migration Patterns and the Growth of High-Poverty Neighborhoods, 1970–1990." *American Journal of Sociology* 105, no. 1: 1–37.

Ramirez, Ricardo. 2002. "Race, Social Context and Referendum Voting." Working paper no. 14. Los Angeles: Center for the Study of Law and Politics, USC Law School and California Institute of Technology.

Rusk, David. 1993. *Cities without Suburbs.* Washington, DC: Woodrow Wilson Center Press.

———. 1994. "Unigov's Unfinished Business." Unpublished paper. Sterling Tucker Associates.

Sampson, Robert J., and Raudenbush, Stephen W. 1999. "Systematic Social Observation of Public Spaces: A New Look at Disorder in Urban Neighborhoods." *American Journal of Sociology* 105, no. 3: 603–51.

Sampson, Robert J.; Jeffrey D. Morenoff; and Thomas Gannon-Rowley. 2002."Assessing 'Neighborhood Effects': Social Processes and New Directions in Research." *Annual Review of Sociology* 38: 443–78.

Savitch, H.V.; David Collins; Daniel Sanders; and John P. Markham. 1993. "Ties That Bind: Central Cities, Suburbs and the New Metropolitan Region." *Economic Development Quarterly* 7 (November): 341–57.

Scott, Allen J., and W. Edward Soja. 1998. *The City: Los Angeles and Urban Theory at the End of the Twentieth Century.* Berkeley: University of California Press.

Shihadeh, Edward S., and Graham C. Ousey. 1998. "Industrial Restructuring and Violence: The Link Between Entry-Level Jobs, Economic Deprivation, and Black and White Homicide." *Social Forces* 77, no. 1: 185–207.

Shipler, David. 2004. *The Working Poor: Invisible in America.* New York: Knopf.

South, Scott J., and Kyle E. Crowder. 1997. "Escaping Distressed Neighborhoods: Individual, Community, and Metropolitan Influences." *American Journal of Sociology* 102, no. 4: 1040–1084.

———. 1999. "Neighborhood Effects on Family Formation: Concentrated Poverty and Beyond." *American Sociological Review* 64 (February): 113–32.

Spirou, Costas, and Larry Bennett. 2003. *It's Hardly Sportin': Stadiums, Neighborhoods and the New Chicago.* DeKalb: Northern Illinois University Press.

Sucoff, Clea A., and Dawn M. Upchurch. 1998. "Neighborhood Context and the Risk of Childbearing among Metropolitan-Area Black Adolescents." *American Sociological Review* 63, no. 4: 571–85.

Teaford, J.C. 1990. *The Rough Road to Renaissance.* Baltimore: Johns Hopkins University Press.

Thomas, J. 2005. *Crime Rates in U.S. Remain at 30-Year Lows.* Washington, DC: U.S. Department of State. Available at http://uninof.state.gov/eur/archive/2005/sep/29/ (accessed March 2006).

Tolbert, Caroline J., and Rodney E. Hero. 1996. "Race/Ethnicity and Direct Democracy: An Analysis of California's Illegal Immigration Initiative." *Journal of Politics* 58, no. 3: 806–18.

Turner, Margery; Michael Fix; and Raymond Struyk. 1991. *Opportunities Denied, Opportunities Diminished: Racial Discrimination in Hiring.* Washington, DC: Urban Institute Press.

Turner, Margery Austin. 1992. "Discrimination in Urban Housing Markets: Lessons from Fair Housing Audits." *Housing Policy Debate* 3, no. 2: 185–215.

U.S. Department of Justice. Bureau of Justice Statistics. 1996–2004. *Criminal Victimization in the United States.* Washington, DC. Available at www.ojp.usdoj. gov/bjs/abstract/cvusst.htm (accessed June 2006).

Wilson, William Julius. 1987. *The Truly Disadvantaged.* Chicago: University of Chicago Press.

———. 1996. *When Work Disappears: The World of the New Urban Poor.* New York: Knopf.

Yang, Rebecca, and Paul A. Jargowsky. 2006. "Suburban Development and Economic Segregation in the 1990s." *Journal of Urban Affairs* 28, no. 3: 253–73.

9

DAVID K. HAMILTON, LAURIE HOKKANEN,
AND CURTIS WOOD

Are We Still Stuck in Traffic?
Transportation in Metropolitan Areas

Anyone who has driven on the roads in the same metropolitan area over a number of years can attest to an increase in traffic. Anthony Downs (1992) gave expression to the frustration of most metropolitan commuters with his book, *Stuck in Traffic*. Twelve years later he revisited the topic and found that little had changed and that Americans are *Still Stuck in Traffic* (Downs 2004). We have not built capacity fast enough to keep up with the increased number of vehicles on our metropolitan roadways. Data from the Texas Transportation Institute's study of seventy-five metropolitan areas confirm what the users of the metropolitan roadway systems experience on a daily basis. The institute found that daily traffic subject to congestion almost doubled from 17 percent in 1982 to 33 percent in 1999 (Downs 2004). These percentages simply give hard data to what users of the metropolitan roads know from firsthand experience. Traffic congestion is not some obscure concept. Everybody who travels the metropolitan roadways experiences it. It is not restricted to those whom society might marginalize, the poor or minorities. Indeed, middle-class, white Americans encounter it more than any other socioeconomic group because of their suburban lifestyles. It is interesting that this group usually determines public policy and, so far, no viable public policy has been forthcoming to significantly alleviate congestion. It has simply worsened as metropolitan America continues to sprawl and the number of vehicles on the roadways continues to multiply.

Transportation is the lifeblood of regions. Moving people and goods within and outside metropolitan areas and having access to raw materials and markets are critical to the growth and development of regions. This chapter is about transportation problems in metropolitan areas. It covers government transportation policies and the effect of those policies. A focus of the chapter is on public transportation and issues of mobility for low-income people.

266

Finally, some recommendations are made for improving mobility. A thesis of this chapter is that a holistic, regional approach to transportation is essential to coordinate and facilitate the movement of goods and people around the metropolis, and to achieve an acceptable quality of life.

Traffic Congestion

Traffic congestion and increased time spent in automobiles are considered major social costs of sprawl and negatively affect the quality of life as well as the environment. Due to the sprawl pattern of development, America is uniquely dependent on the automobile as the main mode of transportation. In the United States, 84 percent of total trips are by automobile, compared with 74 percent in Canada and 40 percent in Western Europe. Only 3 percent of all urban trips in the United States utilize public transit, while the percentage is four or five times that much in Canada and Western Europe (Lincoln Institute of Land Policy 1995, 7). Dependence on the automobile and distances between activities are increasing as metropolitan areas continue to decentralize. America has 232 million automobiles, 17 percent more than just ten years ago. Air pollution is a major issue in our metropolitan areas. In 2004, the Environmental Protection Agency (EPA) designated 474 counties in 31 states as being noncompliant with federal air quality standards of the 1990 Clean Air Act for smog-causing ozone. Some 150 million people, just about half the population, live in these areas (Katz and Puentes 2006, 7).

Governments cannot build roads fast enough to keep up with the increase in automobile use. Since 1986, car travel has increased almost 40 percent while highway capacity has barely grown (Hamilton 1999, 290). Nationwide, the total highway mileage between 1980 and 2001 increased by only 4.2 percent while the number of vehicles registered rose by 45.7 percent and total miles driven rose by 82.1 percent. Considering just urban areas, the increase in lane miles was a more respectable 41 percent. However, it was still approximately half of the increase of 74.5 percent in total daily vehicle miles traveled according to one study of seventy-five metropolitan areas (Downs 2004, 51, 103). The Chicago region is an illustrative example. Between 1980 and 1990, vehicle miles traveled outpaced new roads in the region sixfold. Highway construction increased the number of miles by 5 percent while the number of miles traveled increased by 33 percent (Hamilton 1999).

Although traffic congestion seems to get worse each year, the average commute to work as reported by the U.S. Census Bureau (2000; 2005) only increased from 21.7 minutes to 22.4 minutes between 1980 and 1990 and to 25.5 minutes by 2000. The average commute time dropped to 25.2 minutes by 2005 possibly as a result of continuing decentralization of businesses to the suburbs and the increasing suburb-to-suburb commuting patterns as opposed to traveling from the suburb to the central city, or it could be the result of reporting differences. It must be remembered that these data are nationwide averages with residents in the larger metropolitan areas experiencing the longest commutes. New Yorkers topped the list with an average commute of 36.2 minutes in 2005, an increase from 34 minutes in 2000. The metropolitan area with the shortest commute time was Great Falls, Montana, with an average commute of 14 minutes, less than 40 percent of the commute experienced by New Yorkers. Miles driven also rose during this period, which might help to explain the increase in travel time. Average miles driven were 8.5 in 1983, 10.6 in 1990, 11.6 in 1995, and 12 miles in 2001. The estimated annual delay per rush hour traveler grew from 16 hours in 1982 to 47 hours in 2005 (Katz and Puentes 2006).

Average commute speed increased in the early 1990s but decreased by 2001. It was approximately 28 miles per hour in 1983 in metropolitan areas with 3 million or more inhabitants and rose to about 33 miles per hour in 1995 before falling back to about 28 miles per hour in 2001. The commuting speed was not much different in metropolitan areas of between 500,000 and 1 million people, which exhibited the best speeds. These areas increased from approximately 29 miles per hour in 1983 to 35 miles per hour in 1990 before dropping to about 33 miles per hour by 2001 (Downs 2004, 21; U.S. Department of Transportation 2005). Over one-third of all commuters traveled 30 minutes or more to their jobs in 2000, an increase of 30 percent from 1990. In Chicago, for example, the average commute increased from 25.4 minutes in 1980 to 31 minutes in 1990, where it remained in 2005 (U.S. Census Bureau 2005). On balance, average commute times have not increased dramatically although there is an overall upward trend.

Speculation as to why the average commute time has not increased substantially points to additional expressways and improvements in existing roads as well as the expansion of public transportation systems in U.S. metro areas. It may also be the institution of flex time in some organizations, which allows workers to travel at times other than during the normal rush hour, and new telecommuting technology, allowing workers to work some days at home or from a work site closer to home. In any event, whereas downtown employment once dominated, over 40 percent of all commute trips are now suburb to suburb. The result is that major highways leading from suburb to suburb are regularly congested (Hamilton 1999).

Critics opposed to government intervention to control or direct growth and limit sprawl suggest that the market is working and that spontaneous relocation decisions by firms and households do the job of achieving balance and keeping commuting times within tolerable limits without costly planning interventions.

They suggest that local governments and planning agencies should not attempt to regulate private market decisions but should relax zoning restrictions that limit commercial land uses in residential communities. Further, they suggest that government should help in land assembly to provide economic infrastructure and discourage growth control initiatives (Hamilton 1999, 289).

Federal Transportation Policies with a Regional Impact

The Federal Highway Act of 1956 firmly established the federal government's involvement in transportation policy. The act provided for the federal government to bear 90 percent of the costs of a limited access highway system spanning the nation. Included in the provisions of the act were high-speed roads around and through metropolitan areas. The implementation of this act provided city–suburban access as never before and was a major factor in the relocation of people and jobs from the central cities to the suburbs. Recognizing the need for coordination of roads within metropolitan areas, Congress passed the Highway Act of 1973. This act required states to dedicate a small portion of their federal highway funds in urbanized areas over 50,000 in population for new regional planning entities to conduct metropolitan planning activities. These metropolitan planning organizations (MPOs) were a significant development. Many observers and practitioners saw the new MPOs as a means to counter or at least to put metropolitan areas on more equal footing with the domineering influence of state transportation departments. However, the MPOs in most metropolitan areas became essentially advisory bodies, with the state highway department continuing to dominate decision making on setting priorities and allocating funds. Although the Reagan administration in the 1980s sharply reduced or eliminated federal funding for most metropolitan planning, MPOs continued to be required to prepare a regional transportation improvement plan, but this activity generally consisted of nothing more than compiling projects developed and recommended by the state departments of transportation (Puentes and Bailey 2003, 3).

By the close of the twentieth century, as the Interstate Highway System neared completion, the federal highway program refocused, moving away from a pure interstate program to one that put an emphasis on all modes—not just highways—providing greater flexibility to states and localities in determining how transportation grants were to be used. Previous to the laws of the 1990s, transportation was an affair of federal and state highway departments. With the new laws, representatives from metropolitan areas became an important part in the process. Spending shifted from an almost total focus on highway and road building and maintenance to a small portion allocated for mass transit and other forms of transportation. Federal laws commencing in the

1990s spurred holistic transportation planning in many metropolitan areas. The major highlights of the new direction in transportation policy are:

- The legislation shifted MPOs away from their advisory roles with the state departments of transportation. They were given more authority and responsibility for making transportation decisions to meet metropolitan needs. Representation on MPOs was also broadened to make them more representative of the regions they served.
- The laws provided a substantial increase in funding, and the federal highway trust fund dollars were redistributed based more on source of contribution and not on need.
- The laws stressed systems maintenance instead of construction.
- The states and regions were given greater flexibility in determining their own needs and objectives and using federal funds to meet those needs. Funds could be shifted from highways to public transit.
- New initiatives were targeted, such as reverse commuting programs and projects to reduce congestion and improve air quality.
- The laws required that projects consider regional social, economic, and environmental impacts.
- The laws required greater citizen participation in the decision making on projects (Katz, Puentes, and Bernstein 2003).

These changes were emphasized in the first federal highway law of the 1990s, the Intermodal Surface Transportation Efficiency Act of 1991 (ISTEA). ISTEA required that MPOs develop a twenty-year long-range metropolitan transportation plan, and a short-range transportation improvement plan (TIP). The purpose of developing these plans was primarily to aid in the selection of projects by requiring an inclusive and regionally representative process that gave adequate consideration to all modes of transportation. The TIPs from MPOs throughout each state are collected and, without modification, incorporated into the statewide transportation improvement plan (STIP) (Puentes and Bailey 2003, 3). Then came the Transportation Equity Act for the 21st Century (TEA-21), enacted in 1998. The most recent transportation act, Safe, Accountable, Efficient, Transportation Equity Act: A Legacy for Users (SAFETEA-LU) was enacted August 10, 2005, for the five-year period 2005–9. This is the third renewal of the new federal direction in transportation policy replacing the 1998 law that expired in 2003. Each renewal maintained the basic principles of the 1991 act while substantially increasing federal funding available to the states. For example, the 1998 act increased funding by 40 percent. The 2005 act increased funds for earmarks by almost three times over the 1998 law (Katz and Puentes 2006).

The power of the MPOs has been substantially enhanced by these acts. Although most of the funds were still allocated to the state departments of transportation, MPOs were given direct authority over a portion of the funds and were able to make transportation decisions affecting about ten cents of every federal transportation dollar (Puentes 2004). Representation on the MPOs was also expanded to include local government leaders, agencies operating public transportation systems, and state officials. Although the authority of MPOs was strengthened, states continued to play the primary role in most transportation decisions in metropolitan areas. There is also great variability among states in the amount of funds MPOs directly control and the structure of the boards (Sanchez 2006).

As indicated, the federal highway programs commencing with the 1991 act provided flexibility to state and local decision makers to transfer federal transportation dollars between highways and public transit. This flexibility allowed states and MPOs to fund a more integrated transportation system. These were profound changes from previous federal policy. With these changes came the recognition that the metropolitan transportation challenges were best addressed through decentralized decision making. Many states took advantage of this provision. During the period 1992–99, 12.5 percent of available federal highway funds were transferred to public transit use. However, the use of the transfer provision varied widely among the states. The more rural states, such as Wyoming, South Dakota, and North Dakota transferred no money. However, some states with metropolitan regions also transferred few or no funds from highways to public transit. For example, Delaware, Kansas, and Mississippi transferred no funds and Arkansas, Kentucky, Iowa, and Hawaii transferred little more than 1 percent. On the other end, the District of Columbia and Massachusetts transferred 40 percent or more (Puentes 2000).

While the highway acts have been lauded, they have also been criticized. Criticism of the laws includes poor implementation in that the states have not devolved sufficient powers and responsibilities to the MPOs and metropolitan transportation needs are not being adequately addressed. States receive and manage all of the federal transportation money as well as the majority of state transportation money, and have transferred only about 6 percent of the federal funds to the MPOs for their priorities. Federal transportation policy and state control of funds and projects continue a bias that favors roads over transit and other alternatives to traditional highway building. For example, although the policies call for a federal 80 percent match for the cost of road and transit projects, Congress recently directed the Federal Transit Administration (FTA) to approve only a 60 percent match for public transportation projects. Highway projects remained at an 80 percent federal match (Katz, Puentes, and Bernstein 2003, 6). The acts are criticized as lacking accountability and performance measures to determine whether the funds are meeting local or national policy goals. Furthermore, the most recent law has been severely criticized as a way to spread transportation projects to favored congressional districts in an unprecedented fashion.

Even while devolving greater powers and flexibility to metropolitan areas, each act has provided more targeted projects. The 5,145 earmarks in the 2005 acts are a 40 percent increase over the 1,849 earmarks in the 1998 law and add up to $14.8 billion. However, the "pork" was spread around so well that 90 percent of the Senate and 95 percent of the House voted for the final bill. The earmarks usually do not fund the entire project and require state or local participation. This is an example of reducing the flexibility in state and local decision making that was supposed to be a hallmark of the transportation legislation (Katz and Puentes 2006).

A Government Accountability Office (GAO) study of implementation of the ISTEA laws found that state governments resist any effort to reduce their control over funding or decision-making responsibility. Although state opposition to greater MPO authority is beginning to wane, several states continue to oppose greater roles and responsibilities for MPOs. Unlike state departments of transportation (DOTs), MPOs are not operational organizations. The governor and state DOT still have veto authority over MPO-selected projects. Although large MPOs (in areas with populations over 200,000) also have authority to veto projects, the states control the majority of the funds and have far greater political leverage than the MPOs. In fact, a GAO report found that the state domination of MPOs ranges from the extreme of the state DOT being the effective MPO to the Chicago and New York areas where MPOs are only advisory bodies to the state DOT. While federal transportation spending increased from ISTEA to TEA-21, the share of funds suballocated to MPOs actually declined as a share of total highway spending (Katz, Puentes, and Bernstein 2003, 5). Many MPOs are still struggling between parochial local interests and regional interests that are more interlocal in nature. Within many regions, local governments continue to compete with one another for their share of the metropolitan pie. Finally, both MPOs and state capacity remain uneven. State transportation planning has largely remained the province of transportation professionals versed in engineering and concrete pouring rather than urban planning, environmental management, or economic development (Puentes and Bailey 2003, 9).

State transportation fund distribution formulas are uneven and often biased against urban areas. Some states have developed distribution formulas based on transportation-related needs, or based on resident population, registered motor vehicles, and highway miles. However, other states (Tennessee, Ohio, Arkansas, and Alabama) allocate a portion of funds evenly among their counties, regardless of their size, needs, and contribution to state funding pools (Puentes and Bailey 2003, 9). There is no doubt that interest groups have had and continue to have a major impact on federal transportation policies. The automobile companies, the oil companies, and the road builders dominated the national conversation on policies that shaped federal transportation funding. The public transit lobby had no strong voices to fight for public policies supportive of public transportation. Thus, mass transit was largely neglected as our metropolitan areas grew and the automobile became the vehicle of choice and necessity in the sprawling metropolis.

Public Transportation Overview

Public transportation systems utilize any one or a combination of bus, light rail, subway, and commuter rail. Buses can operate on a dedicated roadway system or on the regular roads. Most central city public transit is a combination of bus and light rail while suburban systems may include these modes plus commuter rail systems operating over regular railroad tracks. The major purpose of mass transit is to provide a means of moving people around the urban area efficiently and expeditiously at a cost both the commuter and the government can afford. The major use of public transportation is to transport people to work. If the system is successful, automobile congestion and road building or expansion pressures are mitigated.

However, public transportation has not been able to provide efficient and cost-effective service within the sprawling metropolis. Some combination of the convenience of the automobile, the inconvenience or unavailability of public transit, the generally shorter commute by automobile, and the acceptable difference in cost keeps most commuters in their cars. There may be other factors as well, such as concerns about crime and personal safety with mass transit and the privacy and comfort afforded by the automobile. Although many suburban areas are not served or are underserved, central city public transportation is a viable means of transportation. Because central cities have higher population densities, they can offer much more convenient and cost-effective public transit. Most suburban areas do not have sufficient density to support a public transportation system. One study concluded that buses need residential densities of 4,200 people per square mile and fixed rail systems need higher densities to be cost efficient. In 2000, 457 of the nation's 476 urbanized areas had average densities below 4,000 people per square mile (Downs 2004, 52).

Ridership Statistics

The statistics on the use of public transit are stark. Although the major use of public transportation is for the commute to work, with 54 percent of riders using it for that purpose (American Public Transportation Association 2006), the vast majority of workers do not use public transportation. In 1990, only 5 percent of all rush-hour commuters used public transit, 86 percent used private vehicles, and 73 percent drove to work alone. The heavy reliance on the automobile actually increased in 2000 to 87.9 percent with 75.7 percent driving alone. Although the number of commuters using public transportation increased in 2000 over 1990, due to the increase in the workforce, the proportion of workers commuting via public transit actually declined to 4.7 percent (U.S. Census Bureau 2000). In 141 metropolitan areas out of 280, or approximately half the total, less than 1 percent of all workers over age sixteen used mass transit in 2000. In 2000, a total of seven regions (New York, Chicago, Washington, DC, Boston, Philadelphia, Nassau and Suffolk counties [N.Y.], and San Francisco) contained 55.7 percent of all public transit commuters. When New York City is excluded, the share of all workers over age sixteen using public transit declined to 3.5 percent (Downs 2004, 118, 123).

In 2000, 10.5 percent of all central city workers and only 2.9 percent of all suburban workers commuted by public transit. In 2000, in only six cities (New York, Chicago, Philadelphia, San Francisco, Boston, and Washington, DC) was public transportation utilized by more than 20 percent of all city workers. In another nine cities (Los Angeles, Baltimore, Seattle, Oakland, Portland [Oregon], Atlanta, Cleveland, Minneapolis, and Miami), between 10 percent and 20 percent of the city workers used public transportation (ibid., 123).

The Chicago region is a good example of the difficulty of getting people to abandon their automobiles for public transportation. Despite a large increase in the workforce in the region and one of the best public transportation systems in the country, fewer Chicago-region employees used the public transportation system in 1990 than in 1975. Indeed, between 1980 and 1990 public transit ridership decreased by almost a third. Ridership on public transportation in the Chicago region continues to spiral downward at the same time that the number of workers in the Chicago area continues to increase. In 1990, 13.7 percent or 524,756 of the 3,049,431 workers over the age of sixteen took public transportation. In 2000, that number had dropped to 484,835 or 11 percent of a workforce that had increased to 4,218,108. The actual numbers and the percentage continued to drop and in 2005 stood at 465,057 or 10.8 percent of the metropolitan workforce (U.S. Census Bureau 1990; 2000; 2005).[1] One reason for the decline is that the system is oriented toward taking workers downtown, and jobs are increasingly dispersed throughout the suburbs. One example is the relocation of Sears's headquarters from the Sears Tower in Chicago's central business district to suburban Hoffman Estates. Prior to its relocation, 92 percent of Sears's workers used public transportation. Since its relocation, public transportation is used by only 5 percent of the workforce (Hamilton 1999).

Innovations and Upgrades

To attract and keep riders, public transit systems have made vigorous attempts to upgrade and expand their systems. For example, public transportation agencies in the Chicago metropolitan area have developed an ambitious project to better serve the region. This plan is known as the Suburban Access Transit Route (STAR) line that would link the suburbs with each other. This project was been approved for funding in the 2005 SAFETEA-LU federal transportation bill. STAR would consist of two segments, linking sixteen Chicago suburbs to each other. Planners expect the system to be used by approximately 100 communities. A commuter could travel from a northwest suburb to a southwest suburb without having to journey into Chicago, significantly reducing commuter time. Currently, these types of trips are feasible only by automobile and occasionally by bus.

Many transit systems have built or expanded light rail systems with little long-term success in enticing substantial numbers of people to abandon their automobiles in favor of public transportation. Commencing in the 1970s, the federal government provided significant subsidies for capital investments for public transit systems, including building light rail systems, expanding bus routes into the suburbs, and purchasing modern equipment. This resulted in a slight increase in ridership in the 1970s, but rising fuel costs and wage demands in the inflationary economy of the late 1970s made it impossible for many transit systems to balance their budgets even with the federal and state subsidies. Facing increased political resistance from tax-revolt-conscious legislators and other political actors, the public transit systems once again had to begin cutting back operations and raising fares in the late 1970s and early 1980s (Harrigan 1993, 300). Public transit ridership started falling again in the 1980s. The federal subsidies to the transit systems had little or no effect on reducing traffic congestion.

More recently, many metropolitan areas have embraced public transportation concepts that were previously confined to the older, more densely populated, industrialized cities of the Northeast and Midwest. Problems with ridership and high costs have not kept other cities from developing light rail systems, especially with heavy federal subsidies available. Federal transportation policy has allowed metropolitan areas to significantly develop or expand their public transit systems. Light rail systems have been or are being built in diverse areas such as Salt Lake City, Charlotte, Las Vegas, Dallas, and San Jose. Since the opening of the San Diego rail system in 1981 (the Tijuana Trolley), additional systems have been built or are being seriously considered in at least twenty-two other metropolitan areas, with the federal government providing substantial subsidies. For instance, the St. Louis system, which opened in 1993, cost $351 million, of which the federal government provided $345.6 million.

With the new and expanded service, the number of public transit riders is slowly increasing. The American Public Transportation Association (2006) reports that from 1995 through 2005, total public transportation ridership increased by 25.1 percent, a growth rate higher than the 11 percent increase in U.S. population and higher than the 22.5 percent growth in use of the nation's highways over the same period. It was estimated in 2000 that approximately 13 million people used mass transit each workday. The result is that transit ridership is at its highest level since 1960. Even though the percentage of workers using public transit to commute to work is down, the overall number of riders is up, reflecting population growth in our metropolitan areas, the expansion of service to underserved areas, and increased use of the public transit system for purposes other than the journey to work.

A number of recently built or expanded light rail systems have been successful in meeting ridership projections. Lyndon Henry and Samuel J. Archer (2001) conducted an analysis of six service expansions and found that only the Hudson-Bergen (New Jersey) line failed to meet projections. The other five communities—Dallas, Denver, Portland (Oregon), St. Louis, and Salt Lake City—exceeded their projections by 10 percent to 67 percent, with the average being 52 percent. One of the most noteworthy accomplishments was that of the St. Louis system, where ridership on the MetroLink light rail system exceeded its initial forecast of 12,000, or 67 percent, by carrying 20,000 riders its first year. In 2001, after eight years, annual ridership was 40,000, exceeding the twenty-year projection of 37,000. Ridership on the Portland system now accounts for 3.6 percent of all trips in the Portland area, up from 3 percent in 1980. Due to the high ridership, San Diego has doubled its rail miles since it first opened, and Portland is adding a second rail line.

Portland's experience demonstrates that linking light rail with land use planning can shape regional growth. In 1990, Portland's voters entrusted the regional government with the legal power to require local governments to comply with the Region 2040 Plan, the long-range transportation and land use plan, which focuses on promoting development along public transit lines and containing urban sprawl through its urban growth boundary. According to Arrington (1998, 8), "By any objective standards, the Portland metro area has been quite successful in integrating land use and transit." The region's most aggressive venture in marrying transportation and land use is the Westside Light Rail Project. Even before the project was opened in 1998, about 7,000 new residences were underway. The decision of where to locate the light rail project was made not based on where the riders were but on creating a new corridor and putting the train where the riders will be (Arrington 1998, 15–20).

The Portland success demonstrates that an overall regional approach integrated with an overall land use development plan is necessary in order to make mass transit and particularly rail systems viable. Portland's system is working because it is one component of an overall regional comprehensive plan. The goal of the plan in the three-county urbanized Portland area is to make a majority of new jobs and housing within a five-minute walk of a transit line. Public transit cannot be justified solely as a means to move people but as a way to maintain and strengthen the viability of the downtown and as part of a regional growth strategy (Henderson 1996).

Public Transportation and Low-Income People

The goals of public transportation systems are diverse and go beyond moving people. One such purpose is to provide an alternative for those who cannot afford an automobile or who are disabled. Public transportation is the only alternative for many low-income or disabled people. Transportation is the second largest household expense, consuming nineteen cents out of every dollar. This transportation burden disproportionately affects the poor and working poor. Households earning between $12,000 and $23,000 spend twenty-seven cents of every dollar they earn on transportation. For the very poor (households that earn less than $12,000), the transportation burden rises to thirty-six cents per dollar earned (Katz, Puentes, and Bernstein 2003, 7–8). Almost 50 percent of all users of bus and light rail transit in 2000 had annual household incomes below $20,000. This is in contrast to 40 percent of the suburban riders on commuter rail systems who make over $100,000 annually (Blumenberg and Waller 2003).

Without public transportation, many low-income people would have no means of transportation. In Atlanta, 66.4 percent of transit users are transit dependent in that they do not have access to an automobile, and almost 72 percent of these transit-dependent riders have household incomes that are less than $35,000 per year (Corporan 2005). In Chicago, 63 percent of regular Chicago Transit Authority riders have household incomes less than $40,000. In Phoenix, the proportion of persons using public transportation because they do not own a car rose from 22 percent in 1986 to 58 percent in 2001

(LKC Consulting Services 2001). These trends are echoed to varying degrees across the country. Thus, public transportation makes it possible for the most dependent in the metropolitan region to access jobs and services and remain contributing and independent citizens.

Public transportation, however, is not available or service is lacking in large parts of many metropolitan areas but particularly in the suburbs where many of the jobs are. Suburban sprawl with its low-density levels does not lend itself to cost-effective public transportation systems. With public transportation historically oriented from the suburbs to the central city in a hub and spoke pattern, the movement of central city workers to suburban jobs is problematic. As employment continues to decentralize (57 percent of all jobs in metropolitan areas are located in the suburbs), a spatial mismatch exists between jobs and low-income workers. The commuting pattern changed as employment decentralized. In 1960, travel from suburb to suburb comprised only 10 percent of all commutes. Today, travel from suburb to suburb is 46 percent of all commutes. Many suburban employers report that low-skill and entry-level jobs are difficult to fill. One survey of 700 employers found that 36 percent were not accessible by public transit, although the percentage varied by metropolitan area. For example, only 13 percent of the employers sampled in the Los Angeles area were not accessible compared to versus 30 percent in Milwaukee (Blumenberg and Waller 2003, 4).

The decentralization of employment and the inaccessibility of public transportation to jobs are particularly problematic for low-income families. The Government Accountability Office reported that almost three-fourths of all welfare recipients lived in the central cities during the 1990s while three-fourths of all jobs in over 100 metropolitan areas were located in the suburbs (Waller 2005). Examples of the difficulty of inner-city workers traveling to suburban job locations by public transportation are numerous. In one example in the Boston area, North Waltham has 77 employers with 3,000 entry-level positions. A commuter traveling from a low-income central city neighborhood would be required to travel on three buses and walk more than a mile to get to those jobs (Kotval 2004). In another example, a commute from the inner city to a suburban job in Chicago by public transportation required two hours and four bus or train changes (Hamilton 1999, 203).

One alternative for inner-city workers commuting to the suburbs is express bus service. Express bus service is more costly than regular bus service covering short distances with frequent stops to take on and discharge passengers and, therefore, requires either greater subsidies or higher user charges. Another alternative is para-transit service—flexibly organized vanpools and shuttle services that are provided on request. Experience with para-transit service has been largely confined to the elderly and the disabled. This service is extremely convenient but, again, extremely costly. Studies placed the operating expense in 2000 for demand-responsive service at $16.74 per passenger trip, approximately eight times more expensive than fixed-route bus service at $2.19 per passenger. Para-transit service is also substantially more expensive than express bus service. Despite the high cost of owning and operating an automobile, it is the major mode of transportation, with 88 percent of low-income workers traveling by private automobile to the work site (Blumenberg and Waller 2003, 8).

Although inner-city buses are the least costly to operate and carry the highest percentage of riders, the vast majority of which are low income, the focus of many mass transit agencies has been on suburban commuter rail service. One study revealed that the operating subsidy per passenger for commuter rail was at least three times more than for bus services. Despite the high cost of rail service in comparison to bus transportation, much of the capital public investment has been for rail services rather than buses. In Los Angeles, bus riders successfully challenged the transit agency's decision to spend 70 percent of its budget on rail service when 94 percent of its users were bus riders (Waller 2005). The Massachusetts Bay Transportation Authority invested four times as much on commuter rail services between 1999 and 2004 than on bus systems, even though there are four times as many bus riders. Service to one low-income neighborhood was moved to enable service to a wealthy suburban area (Kotval 2004).

Benefits of Public Transportation

There are personal and societal benefits from effective public transportation systems. One personal benefit is that it costs less to use public transportation than to own an automobile. The personal cost of owning an automobile, including purchase price, maintenance, registration, gas, insurance, parking, and so on, is much higher than the use of public transportation. Table 9.1 compares the cost of automobile expenditures with public transportation expenditures for seven regions. The household annual savings from public transportation ranges from $1,518 in Chicago to $7,887 in Houston, and the average annual household annual savings amount to $4,456 in the seven regions. The estimated savings are conservative in that the annual household expenditures for public transportation reflect 2006 rates while the household automobile expenditures reflect 2003 costs, the latest available at the time of this writing, which are considerably lower than 2006 transportation expenses. The projected savings would be realized only if the household did not own an automobile. In most metropolitan areas, access to an automobile is a necessity for a variety of reasons. However, the expansion of public transportation could

Table 9.1

Comparative Annual Expenditures for a Household ($), 2003 and 2006

Metropolitan area	Total automobile expenditures (2003)	Total public transportation expenditures* (2006)	Estimated annual savings from public transportation
Houston	9,891	2,004	7,887
Phoenix	8,659	1,585	7,074
Atlanta	7,400	1,632	5,768
Portland, OR	6,807	2,238	4,569
Denver	9,652	7,273	2,379
Washington, DC	7,853	5,859	1,994
Chicago	7,961	6,443	1,518

Sources: Bernstein, Makarewicz, and McCarty (2005) and information obtained from the public transportation agencies of the cities listed.

*The calculation of the annual household cost for public transportation is based on the 2000 Census household estimate of 2.59 persons and the assumption that each person in the household purchases an unlimited use pass, and the most expensive fare, for each mode of transportation available in their system. For example, in Denver we assumed that 2.59 persons purchased one light rail express pass at $99 per month and one regional bus pass at $135 per month for twelve months.

mean that more households would have the option to reduce their reliance on the automobile.

Public transportation is also environmentally friendly. Using public transportation reduces air pollution. The National Safety Council (1998) states that one person using mass transit for an entire year, instead of driving to work, can keep an average of 9.1 pounds of hydrocarbons, 62.5 pounds of carbon monoxide, and 4.9 pounds of nitrogen oxides from being discharged into the air, and one full, forty-foot bus also takes fifty-eight cars off the road. A 10 percent nationwide increase in transit ridership would save 135 million gallons of gasoline a year.

A study in Atlanta demonstrated the health benefits of the reduction of automobile pollution (Farren 2003; Replogle 2002). In 1996, Atlanta was host to the Olympics, providing researchers at the Centers for Disease Control and Prevention a chance to test the effects of reducing vehicle emissions on air quality and rates of asthma. During the 1996 Olympics, Atlanta residents and businesses engaged in a variety of tactics to reduce traffic congestion and single-occupancy-vehicle trips, including flex hours, telecommuting, ridesharing, and increased public transit options. The effort was so successful that auto commuter traffic was reduced by 25 percent during the Olympics, even as the region accommodated over 1 million additional visitors. By tracking traffic counts, hospital visits for asthma and nonasthma events, concentrations of major air pollutants, and meteorological events, researchers documented significantly lower incidents of child asthma. Additionally, there were no violations of the one-hour air quality standards during the games.

The effort to reduce pollution by increasing the use of public transportation is working in the Portland region. The EPA has designated the Portland area as one of the twenty metropolitan areas with the least ozone air pollution. The high air quality in Portland is not an accident. "Maintaining livability" is one of TriMet's (the regional public transportation authority) main goals. TriMet claims that 70 percent of the system users are riders who have a car available to them but choose to utilize transit. The result is the elimination of 62.5 million car trips and 1,500 tons of smog-producing pollutants a year (TriMet 2005).

Increased public transportation availability and usage can also increase the quality of life by reducing traffic congestion and shortening commuting times. Public transportation thus reduces traffic congestion by offering an alternative to the automobile. As more people switch from the automobile to public transportation, commuting times for commuters who continue to use the automobile are reduced. Research by Kenneth Small and José Gómez-Ibáñez (1999) found that if public transportation service was discontinued and the riders traveled in private vehicles, the eighty-five urban areas in the Urban Mobility Report would experience an additional 1.1 billion hours of delay in 2003, or an increase of 30 percent.

Small and Gómez-Ibáñez's findings are not surprising. The National Capital Region Transportation Planning Board (2005) determined that public transportation in the Washington, DC region has removed 325,000 commuter trips per day from the roadways and eliminated the need for 1,400 lane-miles of highway construction. A 1984 study estimated that without Tri-Met, six new forty-two-story parking structures would have been needed in the downtown area in addition to two additional lanes to every major highway entering the downtown (Arrington 1998, 9). Table 9.2 shows the annual delay per person (in hours) in 2005 in six selected regions and each region's national traffic congestion ranking. The annual per person delay for these regions ranges from 39 hours in Portland to 93 hours in the Los Angeles metropolitan area. Without public transportation, annual per traveler delay due to increased traffic congestion would increase about 30 percent (using the results of the Small/Gómez-Ibáñez study), or about 12 hours in Portland, 15 hours in Phoenix and Denver, 17.4 hours in Chicago, 20 hours in Atlanta, 21 hours in Washington, DC, 22 hours in San Francisco, and 28 hours in Los Angeles.

In many instances, it is less expensive to build a public transportation system than it is to build highways. An examination by E.L. Tennyson (2004)

Table 9.2

Most Congested Metropolitan Areas, 2005

Metropolitan area	Annual delay per traveler in hours	National ranking (1 = most congested)
Los Angeles	93	1
San Francisco	72	2
Washington, DC	69	3
Atlanta	67	4
Chicago	58	7
Denver	51	13
Phoenix	49	18
Portland, OR	39	26

Source: Texas Transportation Institute, Urban Mobility Report (2005).

compared the cost of building light rail transit (LRT) to the cost of building highways. Tennyson studied light rail construction in Denver, Portland, Sacramento, Salt Lake City, and St. Louis. He concluded that LRT built in vacant right-of-way costs an average of $20 million per double track mile. Costs rise to $30 million per double track mile if it is necessary to rebuild streets, and $60 million if an elevated structure is necessary. By comparison, Tennyson found that highway construction averages $17 million per lane mile, for a total of $68 million per mile for a four-lane highway with interchanges. Tennyson's analysis shows that, even in the worst-case scenario, constructing light rail is more cost effective than constructing a highway of equal capacity.

The Macon–Atlanta commuter rail line illustrates the cost savings of building and operating commuter rail relative to highway construction. The Georgia Department of Transportation (n.d.) estimates that adding two highway lanes to the adjacent roadway (I-75 and US 19/41) would cost $700 million. Capital costs for a 103-mile Atlanta–Macon rail line that would carry the same amount of traffic as the two additional lanes (7,600 peak-period trips) are estimated at $299 million, about 43 percent of the cost to construct a highway. The Georgia Department of Transportation estimates that the annual operating costs for the rail line would be $15.9 million (1999 dollars) or about $318 million over twenty years. Using a 3 percent discount factor, the present value of the annual operating costs of the rail line would be about $236.5 million. The total present value of the rail line (capital and operating costs) would be about $535.5 million, or about $165 million less than just the construction of the highway. If the maintenance costs of the highway over twenty years were included, the difference in savings of the rail system relative to the highway would dramatically increase.

Public Transportation in a Sprawling Metropolis

Most regions are experiencing significant population growth that will chal-lenge these regions to meet citizens' needs without adversely impacting the quality of life. Rising populations in metropolitan regions will mean more traffic congestion, urban sprawl, and pollution unless these regions can offer a high level of comprehensive (accessible) and integrated (seamless) public transportation services. By 2030, the Atlanta region (thirteen counties) is projected to increase to 6 million people, an increase of about 2.3 million people over thirty years (Atlanta Regional Commission 2006). The Chicago region is expected to add about 1.9 million people during the next thirty years (Regional Transportation Authority 2006). The population in the Denver region is expected to grow to 3.26 million in 2020, an increase of 25 percent in the next fifteen years (Regional Transportation District 2006). The Portland region is expected to grow by 645,000 people during the next twenty years (Arrington 1998). The DC region expects to add 1.6 million new people to its pool of residents, as well as 2 million jobs, within the next twenty-five years. If current trends continue, the Washington, DC, region will experience a 37 percent increase in daily vehicle miles driven by 2030 and a 16 percent increase in freeway and arterial lane miles by 2030 (National Capital Region Transportation Planning Board 2005).

Phoenix is an excellent example of the efforts of a sprawling metropolis to provide adequate public transportation. During the past twenty years, the Phoenix region has grown by about 1.5 million people to an estimated 2005 population of 3,805,123, and there is every indication that population growth will continue unabated (Valley Metro/Regional Public Transportation Author-ity 2004a). The majority of the population (3,590,804) or 94 percent is located within Maricopa County. Public transportation, as in most metropolitan areas, is funded through a combination of local, state, and regional transportation authority, and federal funding as well as user fees. In 1985, the Arizona leg-islature passed a law enabling citizens in Maricopa County to vote on a sales tax increase to fund freeway improvements and provide for the creation of the Regional Public Transportation Authority (RPTA), which operates under the name Valley Metro. In October of that year, the voters in Maricopa County approved a 0.5 percent sales tax to fund highway improvements and provide $5 million (inflated annually) as seed money for regional transit service expansion through 2005. The RPTA was charged with developing a regional transit plan, finding a dedicated funding source for transit, and developing and operating a regional transit system that includes local and regional bus and dial-a-ride services, bus-rapid services, and light rail. Membership in RPTA is open to all municipalities in Maricopa County and to the county government. As of

2005, eighteen cities were members of RPTA, including the cities of Phoenix, Scottsdale, Mesa, and Tempe. As members of RPTA, each municipality must spend Local Transportation Assistance Funds (revenues from the Arizona lottery) on public transportation.

In response to continued population growth in the region and demand for transportation options from the public, the Maricopa Association of Governments and the RPTA (2004) partnered in the development of a Regional Transportation Plan to address current and future transportation needs. In November 2004, county residents approved an extension of the 0.5 percent countywide sales tax to fund regionally integrated "super-grid" bus service, new buses, more regional park-and-rides, and fifty-seven additional miles of light rail. The light rail system is projected to be the backbone of the regional public transportation system. The tax extension will fund $2.8 billion of transit improvements, or about $100 million each year for regionally significant routes, ensuring consistent service levels across the valley (Valley Metro/Regional Public Transportation Authority 2005). Although RPTA is responsible for regional transit planning, operation of regional bus and dial-a-ride services, the regional ridesharing program, and a regional vanpool program, cities and towns use funding from their own sources on those routes and services that serve their particular needs and that provide connectivity to the regional network. For example, the cities of Glendale, Mesa, Phoenix, and Tempe provide a fixed route service within their jurisdictional boundaries (Valley Metro/Regional Public Transportation Authority 2004a) and have developed intergovernmental agreements among neighboring communities to connect the fixed routes that cross municipal boundaries.

Valley Metro has recently finished the first light rail line to serve the region. Construction on the twenty-mile, twenty-seven-station line began in the summer of 2004. The local funding is provided by a dedicated sales tax of 0.4 percent approved by the voters in Phoenix, Tempe, and Mesa, and a 0.5 percent local sales tax approved by the voters in Maricopa County. Valley Metro projects that the system will initially carry 3,000–5,000 passengers per hour during peak hours, the equivalent of an arterial street. Once the system is in full operation, the system is projected to carry the equivalent number of people as a six-lane freeway—12,000 to 15,000 people per hour (Valley Metro/ Regional Public Transportation Authority 2004b). It is projected that the new light rail system will reduce the pressure to construct more highways, entice commuters out of their automobiles, and thereby reduce traffic congestion.

Will the system entice people to leave their automobiles? Only time will determine how successful the system will be. As indicated previously, a population density greater than that of the Phoenix region is normally required for a fixed-rail system to be viable. Regardless of the rosy ridership projections, it is doubtful that the number of highway users enticed to take public transportation will be sufficient to create a noticeable impact on the congestion and the pressure to build more roads. Additionally, the level of the public subsidy may be more than the taxpayers will tolerate if there are not sufficient riders. One survey of public transit riders in the Phoenix region indicated that ridership would increase if service were offered on a more frequent basis and there were closer bus stop locations (Valley Metro/Regional Public Transportation Authority 2004b). However, given the sprawling nature of the Phoenix region, the cost of more frequent service and more convenient stops might be prohibitively expensive for the few additional riders attracted.

Financing Transportation

State revenue sources account for 50 percent of total revenue for roads, with local sources accounting for 28 percent and federal sources for the remainder. The state gasoline tax is the largest revenue source for highway funding, comprising 40 percent of total highway revenues. However, state gasoline tax receipts are stagnating as America's automobiles become more fuel efficient. There is also a greater movement to generate revenues from toll roads. Almost 5 percent of highway revenue comes from tolls (Puentes and Prince 2005). In addition, local property taxes are needed to help finance roads. Thus, motorists are heavily subsidized from public tax receipts. For example, one study found that Seattle motorists in 1991 received a $792 subsidy from Seattle taxpayers plus $1,920 in free parking. Less than half of the $90 million Minneapolis spends on highways comes from user fees (Nozzi 2003, 6). Because gas tax receipts are mainly restricted to highway use, public transportation systems have turned to sales taxes for a funding source.

Distribution of state and federal shares of transportation dollars is biased in favor of road projects over public transportation projects. The bulk of the federal gas tax is used for highways, with only about 6 percent spent on mass transit systems. Over half the states require that gas tax receipts be used exclusively for funding highway construction and maintenance. The federal-funds match for public-transit New Starts capital projects are capped at 80 percent but depending on congressional appropriations may be only 60 percent. In contrast, highway funding continues to enjoy a federal matching ratio of 90 percent on the interstate highway system and 80 percent for most other projects. In a recent analysis, federal funds provided only 47.2 percent of the capital funds for public transit agencies. Even though the FTA allowable share was up to 80 percent, local sources provided 42 percent, and state sources provided 10.7 percent (Beimborn and Puentes 2005, 264; U.S. Department of Transportation 2006). With the federal match much higher for highways and the bureaucratic approval process much less costly and burdensome, it is much easier to build and maintain roads than it is to build and maintain public transit systems with federal dollars. Moreover, state money is more readily available for highway projects than for public transit. Consequently, public transit is the orphan of the intergovernmental funding system and is heavily dependent on local government for funding and support.

There is also much more federal red tape involved in public transit projects than in road projects. Unlike highway projects, the Federal Transit Administration must approve each public transit project. Moreover, because the amount of transit funding available is so small, there is intense competition for the funds. In the highway act of 2005, only $6.6 billion was earmarked for New Starts funding over the five-year life of the act through fiscal 2009 as compared with $8.2 billion that was authorized in the TEA-21 legislation. This is only 14.5 percent of the total $45.3 billion for all Federal Transit Administration programs through fiscal 2009. Although total FTA funding is $4.3 billion more than the $41 billion for FTA programs in the previous federal transportation spending bill, the proportion of total FTA funding dedicated to capital financing through New Starts is down considerably from the 20 percent level authorized in the TEA-21 legislation. New Starts is specifically designed to support locally planned new fixed guide-way systems or extensions to existing systems.

In addition, the 2005 legislation authorized 330 projects, which competed for the limited funding, compared to the 200 authorized projects in the 1998 legislation. Few of these projects will be built since the available federal funds were far less than required to fund them all. This was also the case in the 1998 legislation. The New Starts funding is discretionary and approved by the federal administrators on a competitive project basis. In contrast, highway funds are not competitive and do not require congressional earmarks although funds are often earmarked for specific projects. The majority of the funds for highways are distributed based on formulas and once distributed can be used by the states as they determine the need within the guidelines of the grants (Beimborn and Puentes 2005; U.S. Department of Transportation 2006).

Distribution of the state and federal share of transportation dollars is often biased against urban areas in favor of rural areas. Distribution formulas for the state gas tax penalize urban areas because they are often based on equal distribution to counties not on need or population, or they are based on historical formulas when the state highway network was being built and major building was being done in rural areas. This holdover from the states' past years of active rural highway construction ensures that built-out urban counties fail to receive a sensible share of funding. Colorado and Ohio provide two examples of state distribution systems that penalize urban areas. The Denver region's share of state transportation dollars declined from 46 percent to 28 percent between 1998 and 2003. The region receives back only sixty-nine cents of every gasoline tax dollar contributed. The Cleveland, Ohio, region, the largest metropolitan area in the state, is the second from the last region in the amount of transportation dollars allocated by the state (Hill et al. 2005).

Moreover, the states own a substantial portion of the roads in rural areas. By contrast, local governments generally own most of the roads and the transit systems located in metropolitan areas. This arrangement saddles local municipalities with sole responsibility for building and maintaining the transportation system in incorporated (more urban) places while states and counties maintain roads in rural and unincorporated urban areas. Transportation funding is also biased in favor of newer communities over existing jurisdictions. A Brookings Institution study found that 58 percent of road and bridge projects in Pennsylvania went to newer communities on the metropolitan fringes that had only 42 percent of the population (Katz and Puentes 2006).

Transportation and Quality of Life

Because of sprawl and decentralization, suburban America is dependent on the automobile. Health problems are exacerbated by the pollution caused by the automobile. In addition, time spent in commuting and traffic jams contributes to stress, and thus, perhaps, to higher blood pressure, heart disease, and back problems. A new term "road rage" has been coined to describe the bizarre, antisocial behavior of people involved in traffic incidents. Studies have found that people living in spread-out suburban communities tend to weigh more than city residents and to suffer more from chronic health problems, including arthritis, asthma, obesity, and headaches (Wheeler 2005). One study reported that a suburbanite living outside Cleveland tends to be 6.3 pounds heavier than if that same person was living in Cleveland. Moreover, the elderly and children under age sixteen, who cannot drive, can be extremely isolated in suburbia. Those who do drive do not have the rich social experiences that one would encounter in a walkable community. Commuters have less time to enjoy family and friends (Dreier, Mollenkopf, and Swanstrom 2004, 84).

Congestion may be the price Americans pay for their quality of life. Congestion, however, erodes quality of life as well. Mobility affords Americans more choices as to where they want to live and expands opportunities for work. If the quality of life includes a house in a reasonable park-like setting in the suburbs with some space and privacy from neighbors and separation from the noise and pollution of the city, an automobile is necessary to connect people from their enjoyment of this lifestyle to their place of work. The result is congestion and sprawl. Many commuters, in fact, do not mind the commute in their private automobile as it gives them private time and time to relax and unwind from the pressures of the workplace.

Many people by their choices and support of government policies separating home from other life activities have increasingly opted for a lifestyle that forces them to commute long distances for work and requires automobile travel for shopping, recreation, school, and church. Their choices indicate that they are willing to trade the inconvenience of some traffic congestion for the benefit that comes from their enjoyment of a suburban lifestyle. Not only are the current suburbanites living their preferred lifestyle but many more are seeking to join them, as attested by the continued population growth of the suburbs. The evidence points to the suburbs as the place where those who can afford it move to enhance their quality of life. Despite the increases in congestion, travel time, and gridlock, as suburban areas continue to sprawl, few are willing to give up the other amenities that constitute their quality of life in the suburbs and move back into a denser, noisier, more confining, polluted, less private, and lower quality of public services environment that the city represents.

Even though the average amount of time spent behind the wheel for peak-hour commuters in one study of seventy-five metropolitan areas was estimated to have increased from sixteen hours in 1982 to sixty-two hours in 2000, the suburbs continue to attract population. Driving during rush hours has increased a normal trip of twenty minutes to twenty-five minutes, an increase of 16 percent over rush-hour travel times in 1982 (Downs 2004, 23). Moreover, the increased time spent in the automobile does not motivate most people already living in the suburbs, who experience the increased traffic congestion and gridlock, to move into the city to reduce their commuting time. Indeed, anecdotal evidence suggests that these suburbanites, rather than moving to the city to escape the traffic congestion and long commute, move farther out to the edge of the suburbs, adding to the length of their commute, to recapture the quiet suburban lifestyle that they had before the additional population and economic growth came to their suburban community.[2]

Policies to Improve Transportation in Metropolitan Areas

There are a number of policies that would improve transportation in metropolitan areas. A region-wide focus and approach are essential to solving transportation-induced problems. The federal government has the right approach with MPOs. However, MPOs should be strengthened and given more decision-making authority over the federal funds allocated for the region. These organizations should also cover the entire commuting area so they can be in a better position to develop plans, set priorities, allocate funds, and coordinate development and implementation of the various transportation systems across the region. The federal government should also increase the resources that flow directly to MPOs. These regional institutions are, after all, in the best position to use transportation funding in tandem with land use, housing, workforce, and economic development policies. Moreover, Congress should expand transportation choices for metropolitan residents by providing a more balanced federal approach to highway and transit projects and by leveraging existing transit investments to promote more compact development. Federal dollars should spur maximum use of the current road and transit network. Metropolitan long-range planning requirements should contain a provision requiring the consideration of alternative regional land use scenarios incorporating policy goals or regional visions rather than simply extrapolating from past trends. In addition, a key criterion for allocating transit funding should be the consistency of local land use plans and zoning codes with transit-supportive land uses (Katz, Puentes, and Bernstein 2003, 12).

In addition, other regional agencies should have more input in transportation planning. Regional environmental agencies with regulatory power can be effective partners in improving transportation. For example, the South Coast Air Management District covering California's Los Angeles area has been charged by the state with preserving air quality. This agency worked with transportation agencies to establish transportation policies to reduce air pollution. As a result, new public transit facilities were built, car-pool lanes were established, and local land use decisions were impacted. This change occurred because of the funding and flexibility provisions of the federal highway laws and the aggressive posturing of the agency (Dreier, Mollenkopf, and Swanstrom 2004, 233). This could also be done in other areas with an empowered, aggressive regional agency.

All regional agencies that impact or are impacted by transportation policy should coordinate with each other. There should be one overall coordinating agency with authority to ensure that transportation decisions are in the best interests of the region. For example, the State of Illinois recently approved the merger of the Northeastern Illinois Planning Commission and the Chicago Area Transportation Study to form the Regional Planning Board (now called the Chicago Metropolitan Agency for Planning), which will make it possible to better coordinate land use and transportation projects and issues, give the region a stronger voice in competing for federal funds, and better unify the region in order to compete with other U.S. regions.

For low-income people who are dependent on public transportation as a means of travel to work, public policies should focus on making suburban job location more accessible. Three strategies should be considered:

- Enhancements to existing fixed-route public transit service in dense urban areas to improve mobility and access in neighborhoods where transit use is highest and residents are underserved. Better access to public transportation for purpose of transporting low-income workers to work is viable only where express bus service can take workers to concentrated job locations;
- Demand-response service in areas where densities are too low to support fixed-route service but high enough to make demand-responsive service viable; and
- Automobile programs to assist low-wage workers whose travel needs cannot easily be accommodated by public transit (Blumenberg and Waller 2003, 7). Automobile programs to improve access to reliable, private automobiles for the working poor can be achieved through establishing car pools, subsidizing the purchase of automobiles by raising or eliminating the vehicle asset limit to qualify for federal work-support programs, and by providing low-interest loans to purchase or lease automobiles. Improved access to reliable automobiles is the most cost-efficient public policy for travel from central city residences to suburban job locations. Policies should make automobile ownership more affordable for low-income families. Studies show that, in fact, poor families tend to pay $500 more on average for similar cars than buyers from higher-income communities. They also pay more in borrowing costs and insurance. For example, the average driver living in Baltimore's inner city pays 60 percent more in insurance than the same driver would pay in the suburban areas of Baltimore County (Waller 2005).

Metropolitan area residents fully understand the importance of transit to their competitive future. Yet, despite earlier reforms, federal policy and practice continue to place transit projects at a disadvantage. The federal government should continue the funding guarantees for transit and ensure that the federal share of transit projects equals the federal share for highways. There should be an increase to an 80/20 match between federal and state/local funds for new fixed-rail transit projects; making it the same as for highway construction. Roadway projects using federal funds should face the same level of scrutiny as new rail projects. Similarly, long-range financial requirements for highway projects should be disclosed as they now are for transit projects. Congress should give incentives to states to remove legal barriers that currently prohibit the use of state gas tax revenues for transit purposes (Katz, Puentes, and Bernstein 2003, 13).

There is a growing recognition that it takes more than transportation solutions to address transportation problems. Whether or not we can build our way out of our transportation problems, it is becoming increasingly clear that solutions that depend solely on increasing or managing transportation capacity are not a sufficient strategy. The best way to address transportation problems must be through land use strategies that establish the growth and development patterns to which transportation issues are inexorably linked. The recognition of this link is even stronger today. The U.S. Department of Transportation has stressed tighter coordination among land use, zoning, and housing authorities in order to address transportation challenges. Without such coordination, transportation improvements often lead to urban sprawl, which, as has been discussed elsewhere in this chapter, increases the amount of developed land and also the demand for transportation. The correct level to address these land use and transportation issues is at the metropolitan level, through the MPO structure (Puentes and Bailey 2003, 11).

Congestion pricing should be instituted where possible. This would reduce congestion, increase revenue, and maximize the use of existing roads. Congestion pricing could be used in conjunction with a toll collection system. With congestion pricing, the government would charge a premium for travel when the roadways are most congested or in downtown areas that are congested most of the time. Although there are political ramifications and higher collection costs from congestion pricing, it has been used in Singapore for twenty-five years and was instituted in London in 2003 (Wachs 2005).

If the costs of transportation were more fully paid by motorists, it might encourage people to rely less on automobiles in favor of public transportation. Car-sharing programs are growing and have spread to fifty-seven cities with more than 100,000 customers. This program makes it possible for people to forego automobile ownership but to access one as needed. With car sharing, the major reliance for transportation is on public transportation instead of private automobiles. Members are charged on a per hour basis for use of the automobiles. Automobiles are housed in various spots around the city to be convenient to the users. This program has been popular in Europe for some time but is relatively recent in the United States and has started to expand only in the past few years (Sector 2006).

Private commuting should be at a premium. High-occupancy-vehicle lanes should be established on major thoroughfares in metropolitan areas. There could also be a greater use of toll roads so that vehicle users would pay a greater share of their transportation costs. Policies should be instituted to make those using private automobiles more completely pay their costs. Motor vehicle user fees cover only about half of the costs that motorists impose on society. The Federal Highway Administration estimated that user fees, such as gas taxes, vehicle registration, and tolls would need to be increased more than 43 percent to cover the direct costs of transportation. If pollution, accidents, and time lost in congestion were factored in, the percentage would be much higher (Nozzi 2003, 6).

With a regional approach and strong and aggressive regional agencies, regional transportation can become more comprehensive and integrated. A regional approach is necessary to develop a comprehensive plan for both public and private transportation to address transportation problems. Land use decisions that are combined with a public transportation plan strengthen both and provide private market benefits through transit-oriented development. A public transportation system that provides mobility between the central city and suburbs and between suburbs at a reasonable cost to low-income residents, and that entices commuters out of their automobiles, will reduce congestion and air pollution and therefore improve public health. The quality of life for all metropolitan residents will be positively impacted by such a comprehensive and integrated regional transportation approach. Until these reforms are instituted, motorists will remain stuck in traffic in our major U.S. metropolitan regions.

Notes

1. However, according to the *Chicago Tribune* (Hilkevitch 2006), the overall ridership in the metropolitan area has increased since 2001. Using figures reported by the transit agencies, Hilkevitch reports 571 million riders in 2001 and 574.5 million riders in 2005. However, between 2001 and 2005, the number of riders declined to a low of 552.5 million in 2003 before increasing to above the 2001 level.

2. Even though some suburbanites are moving into the city and some city neighborhoods are regentrifying, the major population growth is still suburban oriented.

References

American Public Transportation Association (APTA). 2006. "Public Transportation Fact book." Available at www.apta.com/research/stats/factbook/ (accessed November 2006).

Arrington, G.B. 1998. "At Work in the Field of Dreams: Light Rail and Smart Growth in Portland." Available at www.Trimet.org (accessed February 2006).

Atlanta Regional Commission. 2006. "Envision6." Available at www.atlantaregional. com (accessed January 12, 2007).

Beimborn, Edward, and Robert Puentes. 2005. "Highways and Transit: Leveling the Playing Field in Federal Transportation Policy." In *Taking the High Road: A Metropolitan Agenda for Transportation Reform,* ed. Bruce Katz and Robert Puentes, 257–85. Washington, DC: Brookings Institution Press.

Bernstein, Scott; Carrie Makarewicz; and Kevin McCarty. 2005. *Driven to Spend: Pumping Dollars Out of the Economy.* Chicago: Surface Transportation Policy Project and Center for Neighborhood Technology.

Blumenberg, Evelyn, and Margy Waller. 2003. *The Long Journey to Work: A Federal Transportation Policy for Working Families.* Washington, DC: Center on Urban and Metropolitan Policy, Brookings Institution (July).

Corporan, Camisha. 2005. Acting Senior Transit Research Specialist for Metropolitan Atlanta Rapid Transit Authority. E-mail to Curtis Wood, December 8.

Downs, Anthony. 1992. *Stuck in Traffic: Coping with Peak-Hour Traffic Congestion.* Washington, DC and Cambridge, MA: Brookings Institution and Lincoln Institute of Land Policy.

———. 2004. *Still Stuck in Traffic: Coping with Peak-Hour Traffic Congestion.* Washington, DC: Brookings Institution Press.

Dreier, Peter; John Mollenkopf; and Todd Swanstrom. 2004. *Place Matters: Metropolitics for the Twenty-First Century.* 2d ed., rev'd. Lawrence: University Press of Kansas.

Farren, David. 2003. Prepared witness testimony to the House Committee on Energy and Commerce (July): Available at http://energy.commerce.gov (accessed January 2006).

Georgia Department of Transportation. n.d. Georgia Rail Consultants. Available at www.garail.com (accessed January 2006).

Hamilton, David K. 1999. *Governing Metropolitan Areas: Response to Growth and Change.* New York: Garland.

Harrigan, John J. 1993. *Political Change in the Metropolis.* 5th ed. New York: HarperCollins.

Henderson, Harold. 1996. "Light Rail, Heavy Cost." In *Annual Editions: Public Administration,* ed. Howard R. Balanoff, 4th ed., 165–70. Guilford, CT: Dushkin/Brown and Benchmark.

Henry, Lyndon, and Samuel J. Archer. 2001. "Projected Ridership for New Light Rail Starts: Issues of Accuracy and Impact on Congestion." Paper presented at the American Public Transit Association Rail Transit Conference. Boston (June).

Hilkevitch, Jon. 2006. "RTA to Make a Case for Added Funding." *Chicago Tribune,* November 6: 2, 1.

Hill, Edward; Billie Geyer; Robert Puentes; Kevin O'Brien; Claudette Robey; and John Brennen. 2005. "Slanted Pavement: How Ohio's Highway Spending Shortchanges Cities and Suburbs." In *Taking the High Road: A Metropolitan Agenda for Transportation Reform,* ed. Bruce Katz and Robert Puentes, 101–35. Washington, DC: Brookings Institution Press.

Katz, Bruce, and Robert Puentes. 2006. "Remaking Transportation Policy for the New Century." Presentation to the Institute of Transportation Engineers, Washington, DC, January 23.

Katz, Bruce; Robert Puentes; and Scott Bernstein. 2003. "TEA-21 Reauthorization: Getting Transportation Right for Metropolitan America." Washington, DC: Center for Urban and Metropolitan Policy, Brookings Institution (March).

Kotval, Z. 2004. "Presentation and Housing as Catalysts for Economic Growth." *Economic Development Journal* 3, no. 1: 43–49.

Lincoln Institute of Land Policy. 1995. *Alternatives to Sprawl.* Cambridge, MA.

LKC Consulting Services. 2001. "2001 On Board Origin and Destination Survey: Executive Summary." Available at www.Valleymetro.org (accessed December 2005).

National Capital Region Transportation Planning Board. 2005. "The Region: Facing up to Transportation Challenges." *Annual 2004 Report* 44. Available at www.mwcog.org/uploads/pub-documents/8VpbWg20060223153304.pdf (accessed May 2006).

National Safety Council. 1998. "What You Can Do About Car Emissions." Available at www.nsc.org (accessed December 2006).

Nozzi, Dom. 2003. *Road to Ruin: An Introduction to Sprawl and How to Cure It.* Westport, CT: Praeger.

Puentes, Robert. 2000. "Flexible Funding for Transit: Who Uses It?" Washington, DC: Center for Urban and Metropolitan Policy, Brookings Institution.

————. 2004. "Reauthorization of Transportation Equity Act for 21st Century." Testimony given before Congressional Black Caucus Hearing, Washington, DC. (March).

Puentes, Robert, and Linda Bailey. 2003. "Improving Metropolitan Decision Making in Transportation: Greater Funding and Devolution for Greater Accountability." Washington, DC: Center for Urban and Metropolitan Policy, Brookings Institution, October.

Puentes, Robert, and Ryan Prince. 2005. "Fueling Transportation Finance: A Primer on the Gas Tax." In *Taking the High Road: A Metropolitan Agenda for Transportation Reform,* ed. Bruce Katz and Robert Puentes, 45–76. Washington, DC: Brookings Institution Press.

Regional Transportation Authority. 2006. Available at www.rtachicago.com (accessed January 12, 2007).

Regional Transportation District. 2006. "Fastracks." Available at www.rtd-denver.com (accessed January 12, 2007).

Replogle, Michael A. 2002. "Improving the Efficiency of America's Transportation with Better Planning and System Management." Testimony given before the Committee on Transportation and Infrastructure. Available at www.environmentaldefense.org (accessed January 2006).

Sanchez, Thomas. 2006. "An Inherent Bias? Geographic and Racial-Ethnic Patterns of Metropolitan Planning Organization Boards." Washington, DC: Metropolitan Policy Program, Brookings Institution (January).

Sector, Bob. 2006. "All the Car—Without All the Fuss." *Chicago Tribune,* September 1: 1, 1.

Small, Kenneth A., and José Gómez-Ibáñez. 1999. "Urban Transportation." In *Handbook of Regional and Urban Economics: Applied Urban Economics,* ed. Paul Cheshire and Edwin S. Mills, 1937–99. Amsterdam: North-Holland Press.

Tennyson, E.L. 2004. "Light Rail Transit: A Bargain Compared to Toll Roads." Available at www.lighrailnow.org (accessed January 2006).

Texas Transportation Institute. 2005. *Urban Mobility Report.* College Station: Texas A&M University.

TriMet. 2005. "Facts about TriMet." Available at www.trimet.org (accessed December 2005).

U.S. Census Bureau. 1990. "Means of Transportation to Work." Summary File 3, Table PO 49. Available at http://factfinder.census.gov/gttable/ (accessed October 27, 2006).

————. 2000. "Journey to Work." Census Summary File 3, Census Table QT-P23. Available at http://factfinder.census.gov/gttable/ (accessed October 27, 2006).

————. 2005. "American Community Survey." Available at http://factfinder.census.gov (accessed October 27, 2006).

U.S. Department of Transportation, Federal Transit Administration. 2006. "SAFTEA-LU and New Starts." Available at www.fta.dot.gov (accessed October 28, 2006).

U.S. Department of Transportation, Federal Highway Administration, Office of Operation. 2005. "Traffic Congestion and Reliability: Trends and Advanced Strategies for Congestion Mitigation." Available at www.ops.fhwa.dot.gov/congestion_report/index.htm (accessed October 25, 2006).

Valley Metro/Regional Public Transportation Authority. 2004a. "Annual Transit Performance Report." Available at www.valleymetro.org (accessed April 2006).
———. 2004b. "Light Rail Information." Available at www.valleymetro.org (accessed April 2006).
———. 2005. "Annual Transit Performance Report." Available at www.valleymetro.org (accessed April 2006).
Wachs, Martin. 2005. "Improving Efficiency and Equity in Transportation Finance." In *Taking the High Road: A Metropolitan Agenda for Transportation Reform,* ed. Bruce Katz and Robert Puentes, 77–97. Washington, DC: Brookings Institution Press.
Waller, Margy. 2005. *High Cost or High Opportunity Cost? Transportation and Family Economic Success.* Policy Brief. Brookings Institution (December).
Wheeler, Timothy B. 2005. "Is Suburbia Harmful to Your Health?" *Chicago Tribune,* December 4: 16, 10.

10

BEVERLY A. CIGLER

Economic Development in Metropolitan Areas

Most decisions about the economy are made in the private sector by employers, organized labor, and workers. Whether or not those decisions produce economically and socially desirable outcomes for employees, families, local communities and their regions is of interest to government. The primary responsibility for governmental economic development policy lies at the state and local levels where governments play the important role of creating an environment in which economic development can occur. Vibrant regional economies fuel macroeconomic growth so the U.S. economy's ability to compete globally is increasingly determined by how well individual regions of the nation compete (Drabenstott 2006). This places states and communities in the pivotal position to maintain metropolitan workforces that are able to prosper as individuals and family members and to enable and nurture businesses to compete in the new economy.

The role of the states and local governments in sharpening metropolitan economies is the primary focus of this chapter. Context is important, however, because subnational policies are largely driven by the myriad of federal economic development programs that were created at different times and with different goals and ways to implement them. The world has changed, but federal and subnational policies have not kept pace. Globalization of goods, services, capital, labor, and currencies has fundamentally changed the U.S. economic landscape. City, state, and federal government programs were created for a twentieth-century—not twenty-first-century—economy.

This chapter helps to explain how policies are being aligned with the new global economy and why metropolitan regional approaches are gaining in popularity. The framework in which economic development programs operate is presented by reviewing the drivers of regional growth, including competitive processes, regional capacity to innovate, and the ability to grow entrepreneurs. It is argued that several key shifts in subnational economic development are important in helping regions to prosper.

Background and Overview

Traditionally, U.S. economic growth had its foundations in physical resources and the products that the nation's workforce produced. America's first 100 years over the 1750s–1850s were characterized by raw goods produced from agriculture and natural resources. The leading goods in the next 100 years were manufactured in factories, and the ingredients for success were largely tangible. The primary assets of companies were plants and equipment. Growth meant finding the capital to build more manufacturing capacity. The workforce needed to be competent but only modestly educated. The physical transportation infrastructure was essential for shipping the goods produced. This was the era of Great City ascendancy in the United States, built by exuberant capitalism. The next fifty years, 1950–2000, brought us into the era of intrametropolitan economies, where a broad swath of suburbia developed to create, along with its core city, a mutually dependent labor market, industrial cluster, and consumer audience. Today, the United States has its intrametropolitan economies challenged by globalization, that abundant pool of low-skilled labor worldwide, and technological change, which brings less need for labor. American companies are unable to compete effectively in producing mass-manufactured goods; other companies grow leaner through the introduction of technological changes. Both trends result in significant job losses. Government has joined these private-sector trends. Interstate highway toll takers are replaced by E-ZPass automatic wireless toll deductions. Airport check-in is paperless and accomplished by machines and preprogrammed phone support systems.

Today, America excels in services, characterized by mostly intangible ingredients such as intellectual property. Growth depends on innovation and aggressive, effective marketing. A highly educated workforce and rapid and reliable telecommunications infrastructure share information. American companies are the leading drivers in the world of innovation for such fields as financial services, pharmaceutical and biomedical research, information technology, marketing and sales, advanced manufacturing, entertainment, and more. America is becoming a knowledge-based economy.

The United States leads the world in services, with high-skilled office, education, health care, and other service workers outnumbering factory workers by a ratio of seven to one. Most of the growth in services jobs occurs in better-paying office jobs in the knowledge fields of finance and management, computers and information technology, and not in lower-paying retail work. While it is vital to support and nurture the manufacturing sector, new policies have to be crafted to help the services sector workers, individually and with their families. The ultimate goal is to eliminate all barriers to employment mobility. Through all of this economic turbulence, metropolitan regions remain important because of "the importance of timeliness and face-to-face communications for rapid product development" (Saxenian 1999, 5) and for quick access to the venture capital necessary to finance innovation.

U.S. metropolitan areas are the powerhouses of the American economy. Ranking all 363 U.S. metropolitan area economies for 2005 alongside those of 179 of the world's nations makes it bluntly clear that U.S. metropolitan economies are national economic linchpins. There are 43 of the U.S. metro areas represented among the top 100 world economies (see Table 10.1) (U.S. Bureau of Economic Analysis, International Monetary Fund). The New York City metropolitan area ranks tenth, positioning it ahead of 170 countries. Ranked alongside the states, it trails only the state of California's gross product. It is these local metropolitan economies that must continue to compete for economic development within today's global and knowledge marketplaces. The enormity of the wealth in U.S. urban regions as compared with the rest of the world makes economic development a high-stakes global game for these metropolitan areas. Assessing this economic landscape, William Barnes and Larry Ledebur observed, "it becomes clear that the U.S. economy is in reality a common market of local economies, most of them centered in metropolitan areas (1998, 5)." The conceptual framework to describe this reality where jurisdictional boundaries no longer define local economies was honed over several years by Ledebur and Barnes (1992, 1993, 1995).

Regions and Economic Development

Economic activity is defined by the labor market, not political jurisdictional boundaries. In effect, a state is an aggregation of numerous different economic regions and there is not a single statewide economic labor market. Even in the global economy, in which technology, capital, and knowledge disperse internationally, national prosperity is locally and regionally dependent.

It is at the regional level where businesses, workers, universities and other research institutions, and governments interact most directly. Proximity, and whatever assets can be brought to bear to support innovation and productivity, can spawn prosperity. The Internet has had a leveling effect in reducing the reliance on direct personal interactions in the pursuit of local and regional economic activity; however face-to-face interactions and networks remain very important for economic connectivity. Moreover, it is in a region that companies access and influence the development of specialized infrastructure that supports their particular economic cluster.

Table 10.1

Gross Product of Nations and U.S. Metropolitan Areas, Top 100 Places, 2005

Rank	Places	Gross product 2005 (in U.S. current $)	Rank	Places	Gross product 2005 (in U.S. current $)
1	United States	12,452,417,000,000	26	Houston metro	316,332,000,000
2	Japan	4,672,291,000,000	27	Dallas metro	315,544,000,000
3	Germany	2,799,757,000,000	28	Saudi Arabia	314,195,000,000
4	United Kingdom	2,196,837,000,000	29	Austria	306,833,000,000
5	France	2,113,425,000,000	30	Philadelphia metro	295,236,000,000
6	China	1,909,659,000,000	31	Norway	294,572,000,000
7	Italy	1,718,903,000,000	32	Poland	285,712,000,000
8	Spain	1,124,463,000,000	33	Indonesia	270,209,000,000
9	Canada	1,106,213,000,000	34	San Francisco metro	268,300,000,000
10	New York City metro	1,056,381,000,000	35	Boston metro	261,086,000,000
11	Korea	799,747,000,000	36	Denmark	252,465,000,000
12	Brazil	789,315,000,000	37	Atlanta metro	242,382,000,000
13	Russia	772,097,000,000	38	South Africa	234,125,000,000
14	Mexico	758,054,000,000	39	Miami metro	231,806,000,000
15	India	746,120,000,000	40	Greece	219,587,000,000
16	Australia	683,759,000,000	41	Iran	203,310,000,000
17	Los Angeles metro	632,407,000,000	42	Ireland	200,106,000,000
18	Netherlands	622,771,000,000	43	Detroit metro	198,630,000,000
19	Chicago metro	461,374,000,000	44	Finland	190,921,000,000
20	Belgium	364,985,000,000	45	Seattle metro	182,170,000,000
21	Switzerland	364,848,000,000	46	Argentina	177,340,000,000
22	Sweden	354,021,000,000	47	Portugal	173,824,000,000
23	Turkey	353,205,000,000	48	Hong Kong	173,556,000,000
24	Washington, DC metro	347,631,000,000	49	Minneapolis metro	171,361,000,000
25	Taiwan	330,740,000,000	50	Thailand	167,853,000,000

(continued)

Table 10.1 (continued)

Rank	Places	Gross product 2005 (in U.S. current $)	Rank	Places	Gross product 2005 (in U.S. current $)
51	Phoenix metro	160,028,000,000	76	Nigeria	94,326,000,000
52	San Diego metro	146,341,000,000	77	Kansas City metro	91,169,000,000
53	United Arab Emirates	133,757,000,000	78	Cincinnati metro	90,963,000,000
54	Malaysia	132,621,000,000	79	Egypt	90,707,000,000
55	Denver metro	131,551,000,000	80	Orlando metro	89,402,000,000
56	Venezuela	131,000,000,000	81	Indianapolis metro	87,645,000,000
57	Israel	124,072,000,000	82	Sacramento metro	84,828,000,000
58	San Jose metro	123,305,000,000	83	Columbus metro	82,745,000,000
59	Czech Republic	121,799,000,000	84	Ukraine	82,268,000,000
60	Pakistan	119,677,000,000	85	Las Vegas metro	80,486,000,000
61	Baltimore metro	118,063,000,000	86	Romania	79,910,000,000
62	St. Louis metro	116,215,000,000	87	Peru	77,212,000,000
63	Singapore	115,324,000,000	88	Milwaukee metro	73,333,000,000
64	Colombia	112,270,000,000	89	Bridgeport metro	72,725,000,000
65	Hungary	107,935,000,000	90	Nashville metro	68,639,000,000
66	New Zealand	107,099,000,000	91	Kuwait	68,368,000,000
67	Charlotte metro	106,408,000,000	92	Hartford metro	67,038,000,000
68	Algeria	105,014,000,000	93	San Antonio metro	67,006,000,000
69	Pittsburgh metro	102,053,000,000	94	Virginia Beach metro	66,715,000,000
70	Riverside metro	101,561,000,000	95	Austin metro	65,813,000,000
71	Tampa metro	100,952,000,000	96	New Orleans metro	61,911,000,000
72	Chile	100,737,000,000	97	Bangladesh	60,970,000,000
73	Cleveland metro	99,338,000,000	98	Providence metro	59,411,000,000
74	Portland metro	95,573,000,000	99	Memphis metro	56,694,000,000
75	Phiippines	95,382,000,000	100	Richmond metro	55,616,000,000

Sources: U.S. Bureau of Economic Analysis, International Monetary Fund

The United States has nearly 90,000 local governments of various types with varying and overlapping boundaries often competing with each other for development. Businesses have a major challenge because economic boundaries of metropolitan areas do not correspond to political boundaries. We have not yet developed integrated public systems that are aligned with the realities of laborsheds. Too few regions have a shared economic vision or set of priorities. Few states have a single entity with responsibility for bringing the different systems and key stakeholders together to coordinate workforce programs and ascertain needs. When everyone is in charge, no one is in charge, leading to lost opportunities for collaboration, leveraging resources, and coordinating information that could lead to a clearer understanding of industries and workers and their respective needs.

The misalignment between the private and public systems is not only very complicated, it also poses significant obstacles to having the capacity to help the business community and can be a deterrent to businesses seeking public services. The locational choices of companies seeking to move to a region are hindered by this complex regional array. Bartik argues that local economic development policies must be coordinated or organized on a labor market area. Individual jurisdictions acting alone may overinvest in attracting businesses that produce high tax revenues to the jurisdiction but low labor-market and fiscal benefits to the region (Bartik 2003). The key forces that constrain or spur development are regional in nature, including real estate and labor markets, transportation systems, natural resources and other amenities, and access to money markets.

North Carolina is an exemplar among the states for approaching economic development based on a regional approach. Every one of its 100 counties is part of a scheme of seven regional partnerships. These were designed to compete effectively for new investment and to devise strategies for economic development based on regional attributes and opportunities. The regional partnerships offer single points of contact for businesses seeking relocation or wanting to expand in a region. They connect businesses with community officials, the private sector, and state government.

The regional partnerships work with government officials at all levels as well as various other economic development organizations, provide financial assistance to counties, help to market programs, participate in special projects, help diffuse technology and provide training, coordinate strategic development plans, and generally facilitate regional cooperation. The state promoted regional economic development strategies that helped the metropolitan areas of Charlotte, Raleigh, and Durham each to grow by more than 30 percent between 1990 and 2000. During the same period, Winston-Salem and Greensboro grew by more than 20 percent.

The Role of Knowledge

The U.S. Bureau of Labor Statistics (2007) classifies industries into a high-knowledge category when 40 percent of the occupations within the industry are knowledge occupations. These high-knowledge industry occupations accounted for a third of all occupations in the United States in 2000, versus a fourth in 1980.

Knowledge-based U.S. industries paced gross domestic product (GDP) growth from 1991 to 2001, and their importance has accelerated since 1995 (Henderson and Abraham 2004) as high-skilled labor, colleges and universities, dynamic business networks, and infrastructure fuel the economic engine. Today, knowledge drives the economy by generating new ideas and innovations that boost productivity and create new products, businesses, jobs, and wealth. A college degree is more important today than the high school diploma that 90 percent of American workers have. Factory jobs have declined in importance, and most workers have multiple employers during their working lives.

For metropolitan areas to garner high-knowledge industries, states and metropolitan areas must create world-class educational systems and world-class cities. Within a metropolitan area, such factors as college or university choices, labor force skills, local amenities that enhance the quality of life, venture-capital support, and mobility infrastructure are all important to attracting and fostering high-knowledge occupations.

Because of the variety of factors that are critical to the concentration of knowledge-based activity, state and local governments use a variety of strategies to strengthen metropolitan economies. Some tap higher education institutions for innovations. Others leverage scenic and other lifestyle amenities to attract young knowledge workers. Many are building twenty-first-century mobility infrastructure such as high-volume hub airports or wireless downtowns.

The Clustering of the Creative Knowledge Class

The clustering of people and industry by cities has been recognized since at least 1925 when Park, Burgess, and McKenzie explained the role of cities in promoting human creativity. A key legacy of Jane Jacobs's 1961 book, *The Death and Life of Great American Cities,* was her view that cities are for people and that cities function as open systems that can attract talented people from various backgrounds and then stimulate their creative capacities. Building on Jacobs, Thompson (1965) referred to cities as incubators of new ideas and innovation.

The economic strategies to attract and maintain the knowledge class and to maintain all types of cluster development are associated with entrepreneurship. The regional entrepreneurship research initially focused on such factors as tax rates, transportation costs, and scale economies at the plant level (Bartik 1989; Kieschnick 1981). In 1988, Lucas extended the work of Jacobs to offer a basic theory—that cities function as collectors of human capital, which generate new ideas and economic growth. In 2001, Desrochers argued that economic diversity is a key factor in city and regional growth, in that creative people from varied backgrounds come together to generate new and interesting combinations of existing technology and knowledge to create innovation, and, as a result, new firms.

In the mid-1990s, Reynolds, Storey, and Westhead (1994) found unemployment, population density, industrial clustering, and availability of financing important in explaining regional variation in the formation of firms. In 2002, Armington and Acs found industrial intensity, income growth, population growth, and human capital to be closely related to new firm formation, and Kirchhoff and colleagues (2002) found academic research and development expenditure significantly associated with rates of new firm formation across regions. The economic strategies to attract and maintain the creative class and to implement all types of cluster development are associated with entrepreneurship.

In 2001, Florida and Gates found a positive association between diversity and regional high-tech output and growth. Richard Florida's book *The Rise of the Creative Class and How It's Transforming Work, Leisure, Community and Everyday Life* (2002) popularized these ideas into a regional strategy for economic development that relies on policies centered on creativity, calling specifically for the building of communities that attract "creative class workers."

Lifestyle Amenities

It is creativity and innovation spawned by open and diverse and amenity-laden cities that attract talented people to knowledge-industry jobs. Florida correlated a region's economic development with its share of creative talent, tolerance toward diversity, capacity to invent or improve technology, and the richness of its public amenities. Such communities, it was argued, attract young, educated, and creative people who contribute directly to economic growth. The creative class includes engineers, scientists, designers, architects, educators, artists, musicians, entertainers, and others who establish new ideas technology or content to stimulate a region's economy. The creative class includes knowledge workers who solve complex problems using independent judgment.

Florida claims that more than 30 percent of the workforce in the U.S. economy is comprised of the creative sector, which accounts for about 50 percent of all wages and salary income. Such numbers are especially important if a lack of diversity, tolerance, and a knowledge-based regional economy results in the out-migration of creative people, that is, the so-called brain drain to other regions. With creativity as the new economic force, the way cities compete must change, with creative regions using economic development strategies that make their communities attractive to the creative-class workers. Well-known high-tech regions such as California's Silicon Valley, Seattle's Microsoft, and Boston's Route 128, or Charlotte's financial agglomeration are widely recognized examples. The region surrounding Washington, DC, has the nation's largest concentration of knowledge workers with 1.1 million knowledge workers concentrated in such key sectors as research, science, education, health care, and professional services. Large concentrations of knowledge workers are important for metropolitan areas as drivers of innovation. Knowledge-based jobs, in addition, often pay very well, thus bringing prosperity to a region. The median household income for a knowledge worker in 2007 in the greater Washington, DC, areas, for example, is nearly $75,000 (Greater Washington Initiative 2007).

If human creativity is the driving force in contemporary urban development, how can cities, metropolitan areas, or entire regions provide the nurturing and stimulating environments to attract creative talent? How can places ranked high in creativity maintain their base of talented people, who are highly mobile and willing to move to other areas that offer both economic opportunities and lifestyle amenities? To explain the new economic geography of creativity and its impact on economic development, Florida's 2002 book explained the 3Ts of economic development: talent, tolerance, and technology.

Florida combined the three dimensions of talent, tolerance, and technology into a creativity index that ranks the creative potential of metropolitan regions. Ranking regions using his index, the most creative are Austin, Texas; San Francisco, California; San Jose, California; Raleigh-Durham, North Carolina; and Seattle, Washington. Florida posits that cities such as St. Louis and Pittsburgh, which have outstanding technology and world-class universities, fail to grow because they have not been sufficiently tolerant and open to attract and retain top creative talent. Miami has the lifestyle amenities but lacks the necessary technology base.

Acs and Megyesi (2007) added a fourth T, territory, and used it to study a traditionally industrial economy, Baltimore, to explain why it ranks relatively high (seventeenth) on the creativity index for large cities. The territory dimension incorporates the concept of "access"—to the Atlantic Ocean through the Chesapeake Bay, state parks, historic towns, and ethnic neighborhoods, proximity to Washington, DC, as well as affordable housing. Florida's second book (2005) highlighted affordable housing among the amenities provided by creative cities or regions. Metropolitan areas need to address safety, available housing, and amenities in the economic development quest to retain current educated employees or to recruit to the region.

Diversity of Workforce

Researchers besides Florida have found the coexistence of a region's tolerance toward diversity and its capacity to invent or improve technology. Researchers at Duke University (2007) found that 25.3 percent of the U.S. engineering and technology companies established in the past decade were founded by immigrant entrepreneurs, located primarily in metropolitan regions. Together, the pool of immigrant-founded companies generated an estimated $52 billion in 2005 sales and created just under 450,000 jobs as of 2005. While much of the nation's immigration debate focuses solely on unskilled laborers who cross the U.S. border illegally, the Duke research shows the benefits of a region's ability to attract and assimilate the best and brightest from across the world.

Regional rates of firm formation are associated with high levels of immigration (Kirchhoff et al. 2002; Reynolds et al. 1994, Saxenian 1999). Most immigrants are less educated and lack relevant skills for success in the United States, but others are highly educated and equipped with good skills. Both groups may be risk takers. And both may participate in networking activities that provide contacts and financial support. Saxenian (1999) found such extensive networks among Chinese and Indian workers in Silicon Valley; and Stuart and Sorenson (2003) argue that businesses cluster because geographical proximity affords them the opportunity to utilize the social ties important in mobilizing key resources. These findings imply that the social relationships of entrepreneurs are important, if not essential, to firm or other organization formation.

Venture-capital Support

States and communities create bridges to bring together entrepreneurs, academics, labor leaders, company officials, and public sector leaders. By facilitating enhanced interactions and communications, boundaries are broken, partnerships are created, and entrepreneurship is fueled across a region. Highly successful regional partnerships, identified by the Council on Competitiveness (2007), include three categories of best practices: creating entrepreneurial investor networks, leveraging knowledge assets, and catalyzing connectivity.

Metropolitan areas seek to create new sources of financing for start-ups and early stage companies, because entrepreneurial companies drive innovation, a feature historically dominated by large companies with substantial research and development budgets, but now being supplemented by small companies. Small firms make commercializing breakthroughs through discoveries and new technologies. Hewlett-Packard and Google, for example, spun off from university-based research. Small firms create world-changing innovations, such as the integrated circuit and biosynthetic insulin (Baumol 2002). Larger firms often invest in start-ups of small firms, acquire those with promising technologies, and partner with them in product development as ways to cope with the pace of innovation and change.

The payoffs for venture capital investments are enormous. For example, $23 billion was invested in 2005, which represented just 0.2 percent of U.S. GDP. However, the revenue generated by the universe of venture-backed companies in that year corresponded to 16.6 percent of GDP. Venture-capital-financed companies are found in all sectors of the American economy, with innovative venture-capital-backed businesses such as Genentech, Medtronic, Microsoft, Home Depot, and Intel among the companies that received venture capital early in their development and that are now leading employers in their respective metropolitan areas. California, Texas, Pennsylvania, Massachusetts, and Georgia are the top national job creators measured by venture-capital-backed companies headquartered in those states' major metropolitan areas. Five industry sectors lead in employment and revenue: media/entertainment retail; computer and peripherals; industrial/energy; financial services; and software.

Entrepreneurial Education Laws

The realities of twenty-first-century global competitiveness require more citizens to have an entrepreneurial approach to employment. The fluctuating economy necessitates frequent career changes and forces workers to identify and follow opportunities that will result in success. The forces that require workers to be adaptive have been called "creative destruction" by the influential twentieth-century economist Joseph Schumpeter. Creative destruction is the process of transformation and radical innovation as new firms are created and older firms die. This churning of the economy means that, in any given quarter, about one in twenty establishments opens or goes out of business. The United States lead in world productivity growth is explained, in part, by churning as the best-performing companies grow at faster rates than the less-productive ones.

State leaders are beginning to realize that workforces with strong entrepreneurial skills will likely be innovators, bringing new jobs to the region they reside in and helping regions to adapt quickly to an evolving economy and to exploit its emerging opportunities. A fraction of the small, relatively new (less than five years old) companies created most of the new jobs in the United States since 1980, while more mature firms lost jobs.

The Education Commission of the States (Zinth 2007) recently tracked the ways that eighteen states harness and nurture entrepreneurship through their public school and higher education systems. The policies fall into five broad categories, listed here in order of frequency: K–12 education, postsecondary entrepreneurship, public–private cooperation, entrepreneurial education centers, and opportunities for handicapped individuals. Notable examples of the states' entrepreneurial education laws include California, Florida, Iowa, and Virginia, which are among a handful of states that require that entrepreneurship be included in the K–12 curriculum.

Workforce Sector Strategies

Between 1997 and 2003, the number of U.S. jobs lost due to displacement increased significantly. From 1997 to 1999, 3.3 million workers lost jobs and from 2001 to 2003, the number increased to 5.3 million. The rate of displacement (the share of displaced workers relative to the workforce as a whole) went from 2.4 percent in the 1997 to 1999 period to 4.0 percent in the 2001 to 2003 period, the last period for which data are available. Displacement rates increased across all categories of gender, race, age, education, and household type.

One-third of all jobs lost due to displacement in the 2001 to 2003 period were in manufacturing. Forty-two percent of those jobs that were displaced were held by people with a high school education or less. Manufacturing accounted for more than a third of American jobs in 1960 but employs less than 15 percent of Americans today (U.S. Census Bureau 2007). Over the 1997–2003 period, for all workers displaced, the length of time between jobs increased. The percentage of workers who remained out of work longer than forty weeks increased substantially over time. Such statistics suggest a looming crisis, if reliable workforce retraining programs are not implemented within metropolitan areas.

This shortage of skilled workers creates competition to attract and retain employers within metropolitan areas and across regions. Tax breaks alone are no longer adequate as incentives for attracting new businesses that are interested in a region's ability to provide a steady supply of skilled workers. Fragmented governance systems within a metropolitan area and the larger region hamper the public sector's ability to be responsive to industry's skills needed for its workers because public education, economic, and workforce development systems often work at cross-purposes.

A promising regional approach to regional employment and economic development policies is the development of a workforce sector strategy. In this approach, the focus is on the workforce needs of businesses and industries in the regional labor market. Employers, workforce training providers such as community colleges, and other stakeholders develop programs around the specific needs of businesses and industries presently in the region or for businesses and industries being recruited to the region. These partnerships address the workforce needs of employers and the training, employment, and career advancement needs of unemployed, displaced, or underskilled individuals in the region.

Workforce-sector strategies develop customized solutions for a specific industry at the regional level, with a workforce intermediary playing the central role in bringing together the industry partnerships. A workforce intermediary is an organization with in-depth understanding of worker and employer issues in a specific industry. Workforce investment boards, business associations, unions, community colleges, chambers of commerce and trade associations, labor-management partnerships, one-stop agencies, placement firms, and faith- and community-based organizations act as workforce intermediaries. Workforce intermediaries lead efforts to facilitate the individual's transition to work, to improve job quality, and to develop more productive workers. The workforce intermediaries focus both on business and workers, coordinate services to build the capacities of both, integrate funding streams, integrate services and information services, and generate ideas and innovative approaches to respond to the needs of employers and workers (Giloth 2004).

These quasi-governmental workforce intermediaries are increasingly seen as a way to power the regional economy (Fischer 2005). An example is the Annie E. Casey Foundation's Jobs Initiative, which worked with six cities to reform local labor markets and to help connect low-income, low-skilled young people to good jobs. Another example is Central Piedmont Community College in Mecklenburg County in North Carolina, which shifted its focus from being a feeder system to the traditional four-year educational track to a jobs and career feeder system. Inner cities and inner suburbs are especially in need of strong workforce-sector strategies to meet the training, employment, and career advancement needs of unemployed, displaced, or underskilled individuals.

Mobility Infrastructure

The placement of state resources has a significant impact on regional growth patterns. While state and U.S. transportation policies that emphasize suburban highways may increase metropolitan economic growth and thus jobs within a metropolitan area, they can also inflict major damage at the city level. Highways that expedite downtown-to-suburb commutes carve cities into unnatural pieces, divide neighborhoods, and can erode downtown business. Suburban ring roads expedite cross-suburban commutes and low-cost commercialization, a combination with which many cities cannot compete. Jobs and people are drained away, and this dual out-migration deflates residential and commercial prices by creating excess stock. And without an anticipated profit, investors let maintenance slip, further eroding the value of existing property. Those state and national policies that made it easier and cheaper for developers to build throughout the suburbs, without countervailing policies to give other advantages to core cities, drain core city economies.

City residents without automobiles can have difficulty reaching suburban jobs, translating into unemployment for city workers, when reverse commute options are not available. States can boost the employability of city workers by providing convenient public transportation to suburban jobs, and improving the economics of suburban mass transit through suburban transit-oriented density planning rather than dispersed growth.

States can bolster urban economies when they enable cities to get a fair share of the allocation of funding for facilities, such as highways, through the use of state-imposed criteria. Maryland, for example, utilized its infrastructure process, including highway placement and school funding, to reward local land use decisions that favored main streets and urban cores, helping both small towns and cities. Local use of transit-oriented density zoning helps to cluster both people and commerce, and it supports a more economical regional mass transportation network.

Some metropolitan areas promote smart growth in conjunction with economic development by reducing regional sprawl and promoting inner city revitalization (Cigler 2003). This can be achieved in a wide variety of ways, such as tax policy changes, designated growth centers, transit-oriented developments, subsidies to promote public transit, regional tax base or tax revenue sharing, or inclusionary zoning that specifies affordable housing for low- and moderate-income households.

Recent years have seen dramatic transportation reform at the regional (and state) levels. It is increasingly recognized that transportation reforms can help fight poverty, improve public health and public safety, foster smarter growth and more livable communities, and improve environmental quality. Chicago, for example, has located a day care center near an urban rail station. Washington, DC's Metro rail system has child care facilities at some stations. San Jose, California, located a child care center at a light rail stop that also offers dinners to go, dry cleaning, and haircuts. Location-efficient mortgages, which rewards housing near transit-rich, walkable neighborhoods, are being promoted in such places as Seattle, Chicago, and Atlanta.

Metropolitan planning organizations at the regional level and local transit agencies have changed funding priorities and decision-making processes to better serve communities. Transit services for low-wage workers have been increased in such places as Columbus, Ohio, and East St. Louis, Illinois. The Chicago Transit Authority was prevented from closing its Lake Street transit station and, instead, reinvested in it as an anchor for economic development.

Traditional Fragmented Economic Development

Historically, metropolitan economic development systems have focused on single employers and single strategies. Communities focused on recruitment of single firms, frequently offering incentive packages to attract companies and creating fierce competition among and within regions. Metropolitan economic development traditionally practiced tunnel vision.

Traditional business recruitment approaches are tax incentives and subsidies given to individual firms to induce them to relocate to a metropolitan area, a practice commonly called "smokestack chasing" or "buffalo hunting" (Atkinson 2002; Grant, Wallace, and Pitney 1995; Leicht and Jenkins 1994). The array of development subsidies and enhancements has included:

- Tax abatements or credits that reduce or eliminate a company's taxes;
- Industrial revenue bonds that reduce the cost of borrowing money;
- Infrastructure assistance that shifts the costs of roads, sewers, water lines, and other utilities to local governments;
- Grants given as cash to companies;
- Land price write-downs that reduce the cost of purchasing land;
- Tax increment financing, which uses the property tax collected on the increased property value of a new development to pay for infrastructure, land acquisition, or other development costs; and
- Enterprise or empowerment zones that designate economically depressed areas for which companies get multiple subsidies.

Subsidy policies, however, lack transparency and public participation, and traditionally have lacked any binding requirements regarding the benefits a company must produce for workers or the community. Furthermore, it is difficult for local governments to assess the hidden costs of subsidies in terms of uncollected income, sales, and property taxes.

Even though these incentive packages to attract companies can create fierce competition among and within regions, they generally have little effect on the location decisions of firms (Wolman 1988) and are rarely a cost-effective use of public resources (Brace 1994; Lowery and Gray 1992, 1995; Lynch

1995). On the other hand, elected officials receive praise for visible smoke-stack-chasing policies (Eisinger 1988) so they may be good political, if not economic development, strategies (Dewar 1998).

Other economic development approaches traditionally used at the state and local levels have their roots in national policies and are piecemeal in nature. Drabenstott (2006) estimates that federal economic development programs include 180 programs and spend more than $180 billion. The current lack of integration of the education, workforce, and economic development systems within states and regions is a product of the federal funding stream, along with a number of other longstanding issues.

Thus, narrow funding streams lead organizations to focus on specific categories of individuals (e.g., welfare recipients, unemployed workers) or single firms, making it difficult to focus on the larger challenges confronting regional economies because of worker displacement. There are cultural differences among and between organizations that use different terminology, different definitions of customers, and different performance measures, all of which hamper collaborative efforts.

Emerging Holistic Economic Development

Metropolitan economic development now includes a broader, more holistic range of activities that relate to business creation, retention, expansion, and attraction, increasingly focused on entrepreneurship and innovation. The role of state and local governments has expanded to include the facilitation of strategic planning; assistance in promoting products and services; business creation, attraction, and retention; workforce development; support services and technical assistance; and promotion of a better business climate through tax policies, infrastructure investments, regulations, workforce training, and public education. Local jurisdictions have reorganized their economic and workforce development organizations and governance structures to help bring resources together under one umbrella, or to create a unified economic development plan across a variety of departments.

State and local governments' role in the broadened definition of economic development embraces the promotion of an array of quality-of-life issues, including worker housing, public transportation, downtown redevelopment, clean and safe initiatives, sports and entertainment. Similarly, there have been structural realignments of agencies and organizations. Examples of policies to create more holistic economic development include broadened opportunities for continuing education and lifelong learning, transitional assistance to those who lose jobs in manufacturing and who need to transition to new careers, and training and education for those in manufacturing and low-skilled service jobs who seek new skills and opportunities. For workers in transition, traditional government policies that were created in an era of static and permanent employment with one company are inadequate.

Montgomery County, Maryland, moved the workforce function from an outside organization to the county economic development agency. In California, Stanislaus County created a new entity to house both workforce and economic development functions. Denver combined workforce, housing and neighborhood development, business development, and small business services under the city's Office of Economic Development.

Civic Involvement

As the definition of economic development shifts, a more connected, systems view of economic development emerges. Nongovernmental organizations are starting to become more involved, in many instances taking the lead, in regional economic development and in developing partnerships with the governmental sector. One example is Tucson, Arizona's recent economic development public/private partnership. The partnership revolved around Tucson Regional Economic Opportunities Inc. (TREO), which conducted surveys and planning that involved 6,000 community residents and set forth what TREO called "the power of five" interlocking wheels for progress: high-wage jobs, educational excellence, urban renaissance, livable communities, and collaborative governance and stewardship. The strategy recognizes that economic development includes initiatives on both workforce and community development.

TREO is implementing the features of its "power of five" with these foci. The jobs focus is to improve job quality, not quantity, by targeting high-growth industries and attracting and keeping the best workers. An "education first" culture is promoted by increasing funding and revamping curriculum. Public/ private downtown development is promoted through targeting "quality growth zones" in the downtown and surrounding areas. The "Livable Communities" concept is focused on improving transportation and infrastructure, including dealing with water, housing, and crime issues. Collaborative governance is a goal because regional collaborative is needed in the "Sun Corridor" that spans Prescott through Phoenix and Tucson to Nogales to improve government efficiency in areas such as permitting and encouraging private-sector leadership to face community challenges.

Cluster Development

Another holistic approach is to target entire industries through cluster development strategies. Clusters are groups of companies and institutions located in a specific geographic region, linked by interdependencies in providing a group of products and/or services. Public policies that focus less on single employers and more on industries that have similar skill needs and draw on the same labor pool all receive benefits.

Cluster-based development helps all to achieve greater efficiencies in the costs of new program development across multiple firms. Companies operate with high levels of efficiency as they draw on specialized assets, human resources, and suppliers in an accessible area. They enjoy knowledge spillovers, organizational learning, and close interaction in networks that spur high levels of innovation and trigger new business start-ups in external suppliers and partners in the cluster. There is pressure for higher performance due to direct competition (Doeringer, Terkla, and Topakianh 1987; Ketels 2003). Clusters can reduce the transaction costs of failure since entrepreneurs can move to other opportunities in the same field.

There are many different types of clusters, which are usually classified by products and services provided, such as financial services, nanotechnology, life sciences, financial services, port-dependent industries and businesses, and pharmaceuticals. Clusters develop over time and can do so because of the proximity to resources, such as coal deposits close to Pittsburgh for developing the steel industry and universities near North Carolina's Research Triangle Park. Early state adopters of cluster strategies include Arizona (Waits 2000), Florida, Massachusetts, and Illinois.

Leading regional cluster approaches are California's Silicon Valley and such cities as Austin, Minneapolis, Charlotte, and Tampa. Worcester, Massachusetts, was successful in building a biotech cluster in the 1980s in this way. Albany, New York, more recently focused on expanding its semiconductor cluster by recruiting semiconductor-related firms to the region. Yakima, Washington's Lean Manufacturing training initiative works with more than fifty companies to help them understand and implement lean manufacturing practices.

The articles and books of Harvard Business School's Michael Porter (1990, 1998, 2003) over the past two decades on the importance of cluster-based development approaches took the theory of agglomeration to a new level by examining the individual firm to explain the microeconomic foundation of U.S. prosperity and growth. Porter turned regional specialization, which he called industry clusters, into a national and regional competitiveness strategy. Attention has shifted from decades of concern with macroeconomics to a changed mindset at the state and local levels focused on the value of associative behavior, networking, and learning found with clusters. Rather than a single focus on individual employers, cluster thinking aggregates demand and addresses the collective needs of the regional economy.

Porter's demand-driven model to describe competitiveness is called the "diamond." Its four corners are: (1) factor conditions, such as physical infrastructure and skills; (2) related and supporting industry, that is, the breadth and depth of the cluster; (3) demand conditions, such as customer sophistication and product and consumer regulation; and (4) the context for firm strategy, structure, and rivalry, which is influenced by taxation, competition law, and other companies' strategies (Porter 1990). All of the elements outlined by Porter interact, and clusters do not have political geographic boundaries. Instead, boundaries are defined loosely by the distance and time that people are willing to travel for employment and that employees and companies consider reasonable for meeting and networking.

Building research parks appears to be a major cluster development. Thirty miles northeast of Charlotte, North Carolina, the University of North Carolina, North Carolina State University, and Duke University are partnering with the owner of Dole Foods Company, which formerly owned a textile factory there, to transform the mill site into a 350-acre campus for university and corporate researchers and for start-up businesses based on the technologies developed there. Plans are for $1 billion worth of investment and the creation of 35,000 jobs with 100 companies. This is a new type of cluster formation support, with entities from across a state working together in one region, the North Carolina Research Campus in Kannapolis.

Research Triangle Park (RTP), an industrial and commercial park also in North Carolina, was the first and most successful, established in 1959 as a public/private, planned research park, created by leaders from business, higher education, and industry. With boundaries adjacent to the campuses of the University of North Carolina-Chapel Hill, Duke University, and North Carolina State University, hence the triangle, Research Triangle Park, benefiting from the state's educational investment, has nurtured both the Durham and Raleigh metropolitan economies. RTP includes nearly 160, mostly research and development-related, organizations. More than 80 percent of the 39,000 full-time employees in the park work for multinational corporations and the average salary of an RTP employee is $56,000 (Research Triangle Park 2007).

Research parks do not require huge acreage to be successful. Boston and Cambridge were successful with twenty-seven acres at the University Park at Massachusetts Institute of Technology. Seattle is creating a fifty-acre waterfront research park at South Lake Union. In Portland, the Oregon Health & Science University is running out of room to expand, so it plans to develop a new waterfront campus in a former industrial district along the Willamette River. Denver, New York, Chicago, Baltimore, San Francisco, and other regions have developed or are developing special campuses to house research and development facilities.

Regional Branding

Clusters are a key to creating regional brand identities that help to establish a unique experience in the consumer's mind and also help attract yet more businesses to a cluster. Examples are wine-tasting events in wine country that also promote wine tours, artistic photography, and music groups. Here, an "experience" is created for "baby boomers" around what otherwise would be a mere commodity. Local governments working together can play a key role in achieving brand awareness by identifying functioning and latent clusters, including the basic commodity produced, their location, and regional scope.

In June 2007, Cleveland, Ohio, created a chief of Regional Development, who will work with the city's suburbs to identify and promote clusters, in part. The Cleveland region recently chose a "brand" for the region: Cleveland +. Greater Cleveland and Metro Cleveland seemed too small in scope and the North Coast meant little to those from out of town. Northeast Ohio was too big and confusing to those who did not understand the area's geography. Because most people already recognize the name Cleveland by virtue of its size and attractions, such as the Rock and Roll Hall of Fame and Museum, the Cleveland Clinic, the Indians, and the Cleveland Orchestra, making it the anchor for the brand made sense. The plus sign conveys the regional geography to denote Cleveland+Akron+Canton+Youngstown, as well as a positive attitude. Cleveland+ will appear on everything from out-of-state newspapers, magazines, and radio advertisements to area billboards and public service announcements.

Business leaders from Louisville, Kentucky, and southern Indiana worked together in 2007 to sign a twelve-point cooperative agreement to brand and market initiatives and promote environmentally friendly business practices and higher educational attainment across that region. The two largest chambers of commerce in the areas, for example, will tell each other about local companies looking to move from one side of the river to the other but will recommend using tax incentives for such moves only for new jobs, not existing ones. That will discourage companies from moving short distances within the metro area simply to capture economic incentives from a different state government. The agreement includes that the two groups will work together to lure new companies to a twenty-five-county region, share data on wage surveys and market research for the region, work together on grants and other funding to improve educational attainment and workforce skills, and encourage businesses to stay in the region. With the agreement in place, efforts to name the brand are under way.

Creating regional brand identities around clusters can also link urban and rural businesses. Examples are the promotion of the Brandywine Region

Mushrooms in the Philadelphia, Pennsylvania, region and the raisins of Fresno, California. Tupelo, Mississippi's furniture cluster benefits the entire region as does the jewelry cluster in Rhode Island and southern Massachusetts. Biotech clusters are far reaching in Boston, Philadelphia, and San Diego, as are automobile-related clusters in southeastern Michigan. While northern California's Silicon Valley high-tech firms, research universities, technical colleges, venture capitalists, and other supporting institutions probably form the best-known cluster brand, clusters are in many service sectors. This includes financial services in New York, media with movies and music in Hollywood, Seattle's software, and tourism, such as Las Vegas and the gaming industry (Atkinson and Correa 2007).

Regional Variations

As knowledge-based activity paces U.S. economic growth, U.S. regions do not share equally in the wealth. Metropolitan areas tend to fare better than rural areas, and the concentration overall is more varied (Henderson and Abraham 2004). Between 1980 and 2000, high-knowledge occupations increased in every state, but growth was strong in only a few geographic quadrants of the United States.

The Mid-Atlantic and New England states led all states in knowledge-based jobs growth, with the Far West and Rocky Mountain regions close behind. A lower concentration of knowledge industries occurred in the Southeast and Southwest regions but those same regions experienced some of the fastest growth, trailing only the Rocky Mountain region in growth rate. Within a region, the concentration of knowledge occupations is uneven. Nonmetropolitan or rural areas trail metropolitan areas in the concentration of high-knowledge occupations.

Among the nation's 361 metro areas, the 50 fastest-growing are almost evenly distributed between only two regions—23 in the West and 25 in the South. One interstate metro area, Fayetteville-Springdale-Rogers, straddles both the south and midwest regions but Sioux Falls, South Dakota, is the lone metro area among the 50 fastest-growing that is located completely in the Midwest. None of the 50 is in the Northeast. The fastest-growing metro areas between April 1, 2000, and July 1, 2000, are Atlanta-Sandy-Springs-Marietta in Georgia, Dallas-Fort Worth-Arlington, Houston-Sugar Land-Baytown, Phoenix-Mesa-Scottsdale, and Riverside-San Bernardino-Ontario (U.S. Census Bureau, 2007).

Regional Resilience

Who benefits, where, and how from regional economic development? Rather than a comparative study or one that attempts to decipher patterns across regions, Chapple and Lester (2007) examined why, when confronted with a similar challenge, some regions rebound and others falter over time. The research examined population and employment levels and growth, industry diversity, innovation, education attainment of the workforce, and demographic trends. Their sample of 192 regions classified most as stagnant, based on slow wage growth. Just 11 regions were "transformative" on average earnings per worker. These are most closely associated with high-technology: Austin, Raleigh-Durham, and Boulder, or medium sized, industrial regions such as Milwaukee, Wisconsin, and Trenton, New Jersey.

Chapple and Lester found that participation in the knowledge-based economy is strongly associated with resilience, in terms of maintaining high wages or reversing a downward trend. Regions that attract highly skilled workers and are engaged in innovation create enough regional income to increase the average earnings per worker over time. Their exploratory study suggests, however, that rising average wages may likely be associated with rising inequality.

In the face of suburban poverty, relatively mature regions were best able to turn themselves around, for example, large cities such as New York and Los Angeles, as well as smaller deindustrializing metros in New York and New England. Regions with a resilient middle class tended to be low growth, with fewer Latinos and/or immigrants. Large, mature metros with established concentrations of minorities and immigrants, as well as high civic capacity in suburban poverty-related intermediary organizations were able to avoid the trend of growing suburban poverty. The most resilient regions in terms of capacity in labor-related intermediaries were large, segregated cities that are restructuring into the New Economy.

World-Class Regions

Were the typical person to be asked for an opinion on world-class regions, the responses would be varied, yet all would agree that they know a world-class region when they see one. High on anyone's list, and, as noted above, of particular importance to the creative class, are safety, available housing, and amenities in the economic development quest to retain current educated employees or to recruit to the region.

Local governments can establish programs to reduce crime that can stifle private investment through programs such as Washington, DC's effort that places highly visible city docents every few blocks in major pedestrian traffic sectors, or Baltimore's deployment of security cameras at major or high-crime intersections to provide quick visibility. States can establish programs in metropolitan areas such as housing trust funds to provide money for workforce housing. They can also build facilities to anchor developing areas and attract private investment, such as state office buildings and convention centers in downtown central cities. State capitals usually do better than comparably sized cities in the same state, reflecting the benefits of this policy. The shortcoming of placing state government buildings in the city is the revenue lost due to government ownership of property, but the state can help offset this by allowing the levying of a wage tax. In smaller cities, state prisons in particular can improve urban government fortunes.

Regional Collaboration Across Policy and Service Delivery

Although competition among communities and regions is still the norm (Peterson 1981; Schneider, Teske and Mintrom 1995; Steinacker 2004), collaborative interactions are becoming more common across a range of service and policy areas (Cigler 1992, 1999; Feiock and Carr 2001; Parks and Oakerson 1989; Thurmaier and Wood 2004). This includes economic development (Agranoff and McGuire 2003; Johnson and Neiman 2004).

Increasingly, cities and their regions are recognizing the interdependencies of their economies and are beginning to work together (Barnes and Ledebur 1995; Weissbourd 2001). When cities do well, so do suburbs and vice versa. Economic distinctions within a region are disappearing as global trade becomes the definer of regions as economic units (Hill, Wolman, and Ford 1995; Ledebur and Barnes 1992, 1993; Savitch et al. 1993).

Olberding (2002a, 2002b) identified 191 regional partnerships for economic development in 244 metropolitan areas that coordinate and support marketing and recruitment efforts, and, in some cases, impose constraints on member governments. Interlocal cooperation among local governments is linked to "new regionalism" (Agranoff and McGuire 2003; Cigler 1999, 2003; Norris 2001).

Attention is less focused on attempts to consolidate or merge governments; instead, targeted regional actions through interlocal agreements, the creation of special districts, and informal and formal partnerships predominate. Jaffe, Perry, and Fitzgerald (2004) developed a typology of six broad categories to examine regional structures, comprising fiscal, economic, jurisdictional, functional, planning, and civic alliances. Their survey research generated a national database of 124 examples of regional collaboration within the 30 largest U.S. metropolitan areas. They found that economic and civic/political alliances represent the types of intergovernmental collaboration that most directly influence regional economic development policy.

Economic alliances include economic development commissions, regional training partnership, and other sectoral strategies. These are usually public–

private partnerships that focus on the comprehensive needs of firms in a particular sector, such as manufacturing or biotechnology, and include workforce development, regulations, and physical plant. Economic alliances also include regional marketing collaboratives and chambers of commerce that design and disseminate regional advertising. Civic and political alliances include civic organizations and political coalitions that organize forums, conduct research, create policy coalitions, and support and fund regional action.

Researchers have found that government plays a lesser role in many alliances than do other regional actors, and interactions vary by region (Henton, Melville, and Walesh 1997; Jaffe, Perry, and Fitzgerald 2004). In Chicago, for example, a predominant player is the Chicago Metropolitan Mayors Caucus. Oakland, San Francisco, and San Jose have a Bay Area Council led by chief executive officers from nonprofit organizations.

Ten megaregions—areas geographically larger than metropolitan areas—overlap their commutersheds, freight corridors, and economic systems. These megaregions are where 70 percent of America's projected population growth will take place. The northeast megaregion, which stretches from Boston to Washington, DC, and includes major cities, their suburbs, second tier cities, and protected open spaces, is expected to add 18–20 million new inhabitants by 2050.

Newer megaregions such as the Piedmont Atlantic Megaregion (Birmingham-Atlanta-Charlotte-Raleigh-Durham), the Texas Triangle (Dallas-Fort Worth-Houston-San Antonio-Austin), Southern California (San Diego-Los Angeles-Tijuana), and the Arizona Sun Corridor (Flagstaff-Phoenix-Scottsdale-Tucson) are fast growing and struggling to maintain quality of life while facing tremendous population growth and the resulting traffic congestion, school crowding, and air pollution. Transportation, housing, environmental, water, and energy policies must increasingly be addressed at these levels: states, regions, and metropolitan areas (America2050 2007).

Because of the difficulties in getting cooperation across regions, a number of states have become proactive in devising strategies to encourage regional cooperation, especially for technology-based economic development. The John Adams Innovation Institute in Massachusetts promotes partnerships among municipalities, economic development agencies, industry associations, educational institutions, and other nonprofit organizations to receive funding for the development, retention, and growth of local cluster employment. Indiana takes a similar approach with a grant program that provides matching funds to organizations that create and implement initiatives that increase regional competitiveness through its Indiana Economic Development Corporation. Mississippi awards regional strategies through its Mississippi Technology Alliance, which established regional tech councils. Virginia has a Regional Competitiveness Program that funds projects that promote regional cooperation and address economic competitiveness, such as the Hampton Roads Partnership and Hampton Roads Technology Council. Ohio voters approved a bond issue to fund the state's entrepreneurial Signature Program to increase tech-based entrepreneurial commercialization in six geographic regions.

Conclusion

The realities of both the changing national demographics and a globalizing economy, coupled with an unrelenting competition for knowledge, continue to require that economic success be tied to place. It is in America's regions that the most innovative work occurs through face-to-face interaction. As a result, economic development policies have shifted toward ways to build the knowledge economy yet maintain quality jobs and quality of life in communities. Regions have many natural assets: geography, climate, resources, or population. The great leveler is that they can also create economic assets: world-class universities, cluster-based research centers, entrepreneurial culture, networks of information, or knowledge-rich workforces that foster vibrant places to live, work, and relax.

References

Acs, Z.J., and M.I. Megyesi. 2007. "Creativity and Industrial Cities: A Case Study of Baltimore." Discussion Papers on Entrepreneurship, Growth and Public Policy no. 0807 (January). Jena, Germany: Max Planck Institute of Economics.
Agranoff, R., and M. McGuire. 2003. *Collaborative Public Management.* Washington, DC: Georgetown University Press.
America2050. 2007. Available at www.america2050.org (accessed April 2007).
Armington, C., and Z. Acs. 2002. "The Determinants of Regional Variation in New Firm Formation." *Regional Studies* 36, no. 1: 33–45.
Atkinson, R.D. 2002. *The 2002 State New Economy Index: Benchmarking Economic Transformation in the States.* Washington, DC: Progressive Policy Institute.
Atkinson, R. D., and Correa, D. K. 2007. "2007 State New Economy Index." February 27. Available at ssrn.com/abstract=965869 (accessed March 2007).
Barnes, W.R., and L. Ledebur. 1995. "Local Economies: The U.S. Common Market of Local Economic Regions." *Regionalist* 1, no. 2: 7–32.
———. 1998. *The New Regional Economies: The U.S. Common Market and the Global Economy.* Thousand Oaks, CA: Sage Publications.
Bartik, T. 1989. "Small Business Start-Ups in the United States: Estimates of the Effects of Characteristics of States." *Southern Economic Journal* 55, no. 4: 1004–1018.
———. 2003. "Local Economic Development Policies." Staff Working Paper no. 03–91 (January). Kalamazoo, MI: Upjohn Institute for Employment Research.
Baumol, W.J. 2002. *The Free-Market Innovation Machine: Analyzing the Growth Miracle of Capitalism.* Princeton, NJ: Princeton University Press.
Brace, P. 1994. *The Political Economies of the American States.* Washington, DC: Congressional Quarterly Press.

Chapple, K., and B. Lester. 2007. "Emerging Patterns of Regional Resilience." Working paper for the Building Resilient Regions Network, January 10. Berkeley, CA: Institute of Urban and Regional Development.

Cigler, B.A. 1992. "From Networking to Collaboration: Intercommunity Relations." In *Proceedings of the National Public Management Research Conference,* ed. B. Bozeman, 204–11. Syracuse, NY: Syracuse University Press.

———. 1999. "Pre-Conditions for the Emergence of Multi-community Collaborative Projects." *Policy Studies Review* 16, no. 1: 86–102.

———. 2003. "A Case of the Smarties." *Public Manager* 32, no. 3: 18–22.

Council on Competitiveness. 2007. *Where America Stands: Entrepreneurship Competitiveness Index.* Washington, DC (February).

Desrochers, P. 2001. "Local Diversity, Human Creativity, and Technological Innovation." *Growth and Change* 32 (Summer): 369–94.

Dewar, M.E. 1998. "Why Do State and Local Economic Development Programs Cause So Little Economic Development?" *Economic Development Quarterly* 12, no. 1: 68–87.

Doerginer, P.B., Terkla, D.G. and Topakianh, G.C. 1987. *Invisible Factors in Local Economic Development.* New York, NY: Oxford University Press.

Drabenstott, M. 2006. "Rethinking Federal Policy for Regional Economic Development." *Economic Review* (Fourth Quarter): 115–42. Federal Reserve Bank of Kansas City.

Duke University. 2007. "America's New Immigrant Entrepreneurs." Durham, NC: Center for Globalization, Governance & Competitiveness, Duke University.

Eisinger, P. 1988. *The Rise of the Entrepreneurial State.* Madison: University of Wisconsin Press.

Feiock, R.C., and J.B. Carr. 2001. "Incentives, Entrepreneurs, and Boundary Change: A Collective Action Framework." *Urban Affairs Review* 36 (January): 382–405.

Fischer, D.J. 2005. *Workforce Intermediaries: Powering Regional Economies in the New Century.* Baltimore, MD: Annie C. Casey Foundation (May).

Florida, R. 2002. *The Rise of the Creative Class and How It's Transforming Work, Leisure, Community and Everyday Lif*e. New York: Basic Books.

———. 2005. *The Flight of the Creative Class: The New Global Competition for Talent.* New York: HarperCollins.

Florida, R., and G. Gates. 2001. *Technology and Tolerance: The Importance of Diversity to High-Technology Growth.* Washington, DC: Brookings Institution.

Giloth, R.P., ed. 2004. *Workforce Development Politics: Civic Capacity and Performance.* Philadelphia: Temple University Press.

Grant, D.; M. Wallace; and W. Pitney. 1995. "Measuring State-Level Economic Development Programs, 1970–1992." *Economic Development Quarterly* 9, no. 2: 134–45.

Greater Washington Initiative. 2007. *Human Capital: Greater Washington's Knowledge Workers.* Washington, DC.

Henderson, J., and B. Abraham. 2004. "Can Rural America Support a Knowledge Economy?" *Economic Review* (Third Quarter): 71–95. Federal Reserve Bank of Kansas City.

Henton, D.; J. Melville; and K. Walesh. 1997. *Grassroots Leaders for a New Economy: How Civic Entrepreneurs Are Building Prosperous Communities.* San Francisco: Jossey-Bass.

Hill, E.W.; H.L. Wolman; and C.C. Ford III. 1995. "Can Suburbs Survive Without

Their Central Cities? Examining the Suburban Dependence Hypothesis." *Urban Affairs Review* 31, no. 2: 147–74.

International Monetary Fund. 2005. "World Economic Outlook Database, September 2005, All countries, Gross domestic product, current prices US dollars, billions." Available at www.imf.org/external/pubs/ft/weo/2005/02/data/index.htm (accessed October 2007).

Jacobs, J. 1961. *The Death and Life of Great American Cities.* New York: Random House.

Jaffe, M.; D.C. Perry; and J. Fitzgerald. 2004. "The Politics of Promise: The Rhetoric and Practice of 'Non-governmental Regionalism.'" Paper presented at the City Futures Conference. Chicago, July 8–10.

Johnson, M., and M. Neiman 2004. "Courting Business: Competition for Economic Development Among Cities." In *Metropolitan Governance: Conflict, Competition, and Cooperation,* ed. Richard Feiock, 124–46. Washington, DC: Georgetown University Press.

Ketels, C.H.M. 2003. "The Development of the Cluster Concept—Present Experiences and Further Developments." Paper presented at the NRW Conference on Clusters. Duisburg, Germany, December 5.

Kieschnick, M. 1981. *Taxes and Growth: Business Incentives and Economic Development.* Washington, DC: Council of State Planning Agencies.

Kirchhoff, B.; D. Armington; I. Hasan; and S. Newbert. 2002. *The Influence of R&D Expenditures on New Firm Formation and Economic Growth.* Washington, DC: U.S. Small Business Administration.

Ledebur, L., and W. Barnes. 1992. *City Distress, Metropolitan Disparities and Economic Growth.* Washington, DC: National League of Cities.

———. 1993. *All in It Together.* Washington, DC: National League of Cities.

Leicht, K., and J.C. Jenkins, 1994. "Three Strategies of State Economic Development: Entrepreneurial, Industrial Recruitment, and Deregulation Policies in the American States." *Economic Development Quarterly* 8, no. 3: 256–69.

Lowery, D., and V. Gray. 1992. "Holding Back the Tide of Bad Economic Times." *Social Science Quarterly* 73, no. 3: 483–95.

———. 1995. "The Compensatory Impact of State Industrial Policy: An Empirical Assessment of Midterm Effects." *Social Science Quarterly* 76, no. 2: 438–46.

Lucas, R.E. 1988. "On the Mechanics of Economic Development." *Journal of Monetary Economics* 22, no. 1: 3–42.

Lynch, R.G. 1995. *Do State and Local Tax Incentives Work?* Washington, DC: Economic Policy Institute.

Norris, D.F. 2001. "Prospects for Regional Governance Under the New Regionalism: Economic Imperatives Versus Political Impediments." *Journal of Urban Affairs* 23, no. 5: 557–71.

Olberding, J.C. 2002a. "Does Regionalism Beget Regionalism? The Relationship Between Norms and Regional Partnerships for Economic Development." *Public Administration Review* 62, no. 4: 480–91.

———. 2002b. "Diving into the 'Third Waves' of Regional Governance Strategies: A Study of Regional Partnerships for Economic Development in U.S. Metropolitan Areas." *Economic Development Quarterly* 16 (August): 251–72.

Park, R.; E. Burgess; and R. McKenzie. 1925. *The City.* Chicago: University of Chicago Press.

Parks, R. B., and R. J. Oakerson, 1989. "Metropolitan organization and governance: A local public economy approach." *Urban Affairs Quarterly* 25, no. 1: 18–29.

Peterson, P.E. 1981. *City Limits.* Chicago: University of Chicago Press.

Porter, M.E. 1990. *The Competitive Advantage of Nations.* New York: Free Press.

———. 1998. "Clusters and the New Economics of Competition." *Harvard Business Review* 76, no. 6: 77–90.

———. 2003. "The Economic Performance of Regions." *Regional Studies* 37, nos. 6–7: 549–678.

Research Triangle Park. 2007. Available at www.rtp.org (accessed March 2007).

Reynolds, P.; D.J. Storey; and P. Westhead. 1994. "Cross-National Comparison of the Variation in New Firm Formation Rates." *Regional Studies* 28, no. 4: 443–56.

Savitch, H.V.; D. Collins; D. Sanders; and J.P. Markham. 1993. "Ties That Bind: Central Cities, Suburbs and the New Metropolitan Region." *Economic Development Quarterly* 7, no. 4: 341–57.

Saxenian, A. 1999. *Silicon Valley's New Immigrant Entrepreneurs.* San Francisco: Public Policy Institute of California (June).

Schneider, M.; P. Teske; with M. Mintrom. 1995. *Public Entrepreneurs: Agents for Change in American Government.* Princeton, NJ: Princeton University Press.

Schumpeter, J.A. *The Concise Encyclopedia of Economics.* Available at www.econlib. org/library/Enc/bios/Schumpeter.htm (accessed February 2007).

Steinacker, A. 2004. "Game Theoretic Models of Metropolitan Cooperation." In *Metropolitan Governance: Conflict, Competition and Cooperation,* ed. R.C. Feiock, 46–66. Washington, DC: Georgetown University Press.

Stuart, T., and O. Sorenson. 2003. "The Geography of Opportunity: Spatial Heterogeneity in Founding Rates and the Performance of Biotechnology Firms." *Research Policy* 32: 229–53.

Thompson, W. 1965. *A Preface to Urban Economics.* Baltimore: Johns Hopkins University Press.

Thurmaier, K., and C. Wood. 2004. "Interlocal Agreements as an Alternative to Consolidation." In *Reshaping the Local Landscape: Perspective on City County Consolidation and Its Alternatives,* ed. J. Carr and R.C. Feiock, 113–30. Armonk, NY: M.E. Sharpe.

U.S. Bureau of Economic Analysis. 2005. "Gross Domestic Product by Metropolitan Area." Available at http://www.bea.gov/regional/gdpmetro/ (accessed October 2007).

U.S. Bureau of Labor Statistics. 2007. Available at www.bls.gov/ (accessed April 2007).

U.S. Census Bureau. 2007. Available at www.census.gov (accessed February 2007).

Waits, M. 2000. "The Added Value of the Industry Cluster Approach to Economic Analysis, Strategy Development, and Service Delivery." *Economic Development Quarterly* 14, no. 1: 35–50.

Weissbourd, R. 2001. *Cities and Economic Prosperity: A Data Scan on the Role of Cities in Regional and National Economies.* Boston: CEOs for Cities.

Wolman, H. 1988. "Local Economic Development Policy: What Explains the Divergence Between Policy Analysis and Political Behavior?" *Journal of Urban Affairs* 10, no. 1: 19–28.

Zinth, K. 2007. *Entrepreneurial Education Laws in the States. State Notes: Economic/ Workforce Development.* Denver: Education Commission of the States (February 8).

11

DAVID K. HAMILTON AND CHRISTOPHER STREAM

Regional Environmental Policy

Six and a half billion of us live together on one planet, our futures connected by how we individually manage our impact on our earth. No other policy issue that we live with is simultaneously so personal and so universal. We are able to speak of the environmental movement because of the grassroots mobilization that has fueled much of the environmental progress in the United States. The practice of governance had some of its earliest successes in the environmental movement, when many different groups and individuals joined together. They formed an environmental coalition and achieved much more through cooperative lobbying than they would have separately.

Americans, until the 1970s, were not overly concerned with pollution and the environment. Americans saw environmental protection as primarily a state and local responsibility. The land and the quality of air and water, were traditionally viewed as economic resources for states and cities to exploit. For the most part, state and local governments paid little attention to environmental protection and pollution.

This changed on April 22, 1970, the first Earth Day. Beginning in the early 1970s, increased public concern about the environment pressured the government to assume a greater role in its protection. The focus of early environmental activists was for the federal government to assume a major policy leadership role. Many environmental groups argued that state and local governments could not be trusted to protect their own environmental resources because they were too focused on promoting local development.

During the 1980s and 1990s, the role of the federal government decreased as regulation devolved to the states. Devolution meant that states and local governments needed to become more involved in addressing pollution issues such as clean air, clean water, sustainability, and environmental justice. As metropolitan areas continued to expand and consume more land, the public became increasingly concerned with environmental issues that affected the quality of life. Public pressure to preserve the environment escalates as the quality of life in urban areas deteriorates. Public officials are becoming more environmentally conscious as the public becomes more concerned. One survey of public officials in the Chicago region found environmental concerns near the top of the list of the major problems facing the metropolitan area (O'Keefe 1991). Since most environmental issues transcend municipal boundaries, there is increasing awareness that protecting the environment requires a regional, coordinated approach. In addition, preservation of open space is becoming a much more critical issue in metropolitan areas due to the sprawl and development patterns. Large tracts of open space can only be preserved through a region-wide effort.

Pollution and Land Use Controls

The problem of pollution is not something that can be successfully addressed through the actions of one body of government, even those of the national government. These are problems that are too large for any single unit of government. With a problem this large, no top-down solution will suffice. The federal government can create an agency and propose regulations, but to be truly victorious in the battle against pollution, there must be a coordinated and cooperative effort at the local level. Yet most municipal governments do not have legal jurisdiction over the full range of their water resources or over the facilities in their jurisdictions producing air pollution. Much of the work of pollution control and environmental regulation has to be accomplished through the complex intergovernmental network in the United States. Managing environmental problems is a challenge for metropolitan areas. Most problems require a multijurisdictional, collaborative approach.

A successful movement toward protecting the urban environment should have a regional focus. This chapter provides a regional perspective on environmental problems in metropolitan areas. The chapter also describes how the federal, state, and city governments deal with negative externalities and internal pressures that affect urban land, air, and water pollution issues.

Federal Policy

Beginning in the late 1960s and early 1970s, increased public concern about the environment caused the federal government to assume a policy leadership role. In 1969, President Richard Nixon created the Environmental Protection Agency (EPA). During the 1970s, the Clean Air Act and the Clean Water Act, major environmental protection laws, were adopted by the federal government. This legislation, however, relied on the states to implement and enforce the federal laws and regulations.

Congress passed other environmental laws in the 1970s, including coastal zone management resources planning in 1972, noise pollution control in 1972, disaster assistance planning in 1974, endangered species protection in 1973, environmental review in 1969 (though signed into law in 1970), and solid waste management planning in 1976. At the time, these programs required a regional plan or a regional planning organization as a condition of funding, or gave preference to regional councils within a pool of eligible recipients.

During the 1970s and 1980s, the federal government did more than just pass environmental legislation. The federal government also provided money and funding to help newly created state environmental protection agencies carry out the national mandates. In this way, federal government officials were responding to the demands of environmental interest groups and the national public mood regarding environmental policy.

The federal government was also concerned with environmental policy fragmentation. That is, while the federal government had set "minimum" standards that each state had to meet in terms of clean air and water, there was, in fact, great variation among the states in terms of their ability and/or willingness to enforce national environmental laws. Thus, during the 1970s and 1980s, one federal goal in terms of environmental protection was to ensure that each state complied equally with national environmental standards. However, as Rabe (1986) argued at the time, these federal efforts in funding or attempts to overcome state fragmentation efforts were only sporadic and often ineffective. In hindsight, critics can find fault with many of those early federal efforts to achieve their lofty environmental goals. Those critics, however, cannot take away the watershed it represents for the development of major environmental policies over a very brief time span.

Public Opinion and the Environment

Figure 11.1 gives an indication of Americans' concern for the environment. The figure shows a relationship between environmentally friendly presidents and concern for the amount of money the federal government was giving for environmental issues. Soon after Earth Day in 1970, Americans who believed there was too little government spending on the environment dramatically decreased through the 1970s and early 1980s. During Ronald Reagan's presidency (1981–89), the percentage of Americans who felt the government was spending too little on the environment increased considerably.

Support for more government spending on the environment remained strong during the presidency of George H. Bush (1989–93) and then dropped again to mid-1980s levels. During the presidency of Bill Clinton (1993–2001), those who felt that there was too little government spending on the environment steadily increased but never reached the highs of the early 1990s. During the

Figure 11.1   **Percentage of Americans Who Believe the Federal Government Is Spending Too Little on the Environment, 1973–2002**

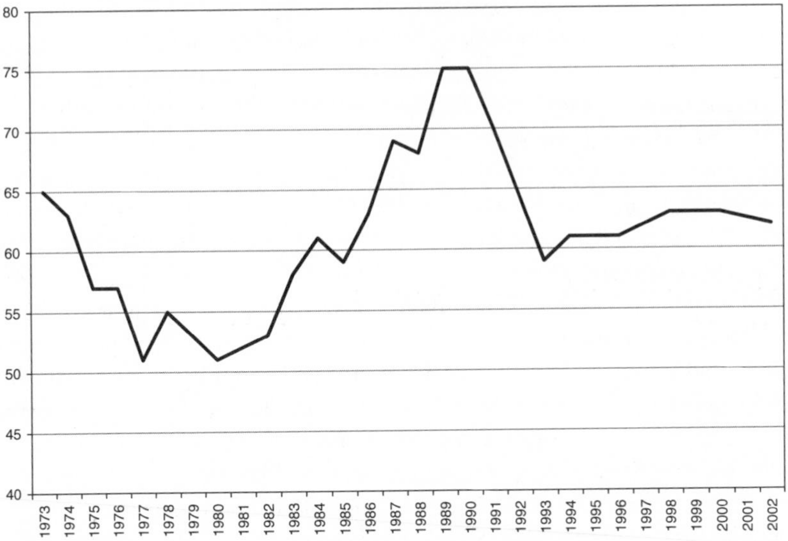

Source: General Social Survey. Figure created by authors.

Clinton presidency, Congress, controlled by Republicans, took steps to create state variation of environmental regulation by devolving environmental enforcement to states and localities. The main theory behind the devolution of environmental control was the notion that the one-size-fits-all federal rules regarding environmental policies should not apply to all states and localities with their different problems. For example, clean air standards that may have been easily met by South Dakota could be difficult to achieve in California.

Urbanization and Pollution

Urbanization has had a major impact upon the environment within our urban areas and upon life far beyond the boundaries of those urban areas. The internal environment of rapidly growing metropolitan areas is often characterized by density, overcrowding and overburdened infrastructure, and a variety of environmental problems, such as air pollution, which substantially deteriorate the quality of urban life.

The external environment is also negatively affected by urbanization. The release of solid wastes into the water and toxins into the air has an obvious impact on natural resources. In addition, metropolitan areas are consumers of resources, depleting foodstuffs, water, wood, petroleum, and other materials (Wolman and

Goldsmith 1992). Through these processes, metropolitan areas influence their external environments far beyond their concentrated populations.

Industrial and economic development has had profound impacts on metropolitan areas. During the nineteenth century, industrialization and population growth combined to have serious environmental consequences for cities. In 1850, the total population of the United States was approximately 23 million; by 1920, it was 106 million. As the population continued to grow, it concentrated increasingly in the cities. The population of several metropolitan areas such as New York, Chicago, San Francisco, and Los Angeles doubled during the last three decades of the nineteenth century (U.S. Census Bureau 1975).

In 1790, less than 5 percent of U.S. residents lived in an urban area. By 1990, nearly 80 percent of the U.S. population lived in a metropolitan or urbanized area. Today, over one-third of the states have more than half of their populations living in metropolitan areas. With the urban population rising steadily and the majority of the labor force attracted to industrial jobs, city governments were hard-pressed to maintain, let alone expand, existing infrastructure. The result was any number of growing environmental problems.

Those suffering the greatest repercussions of the new urban environmental crisis were the working class. Among the most obvious problems in the growing cities were those associated with overcrowding. Forced to live near their places of employment, many urban workers found themselves crammed into the escalating slums in the central city. Housing was at a premium, and few Americans could afford to buy single-unit dwellings (Cochran and Miller 1961). Further, the proximity of living close to the workplace and its hazards meant urban workers and their families were constantly exposed to a wide range of direct and indirect industrial pollutants.

Not only were individual living quarters overcrowded, but neighborhood densities were overwhelming. The average city block density in lower Manhattan increased from 157.5 persons in 1820 to 272.5 persons in 1850. New York City's Sanitary District "A" averaged 986.4 people to the acre for thirty-two acres in 1894—or approximately 30,000 people in a space of five or six blocks (Cochran and Miller 1961). The crowded conditions and limited services provided by cities created health and sanitation problems. The 1873 yellow fever epidemic in Memphis, which was one of the most publicized medical calamities of its time, was alleged to have started in overcrowded slums and took the lives of almost 10 percent of the city's population. In another example, residents of New Orleans were exposed to typhus through sewage flowing on the unpaved streets. Moreover, day-to-day living created a host of interrelated problems in many cities, with common problems being smoke from wood-burning and coal-burning stoves and fireplaces that fouled the air, and noise levels that were deafening (Melosi 1993).

As the industrial city rose skyward and outward, two distinct processes of growth contributed to urban environmental problems. First, population growth overwhelmed city services and local governments were not prepared to provide the necessary pollution control services. Garbage accumulated faster than it could be collected, and the system for removal of wastewater was relatively primitive. Sanitation systems often served only the business districts of the city and the "better," wealthier residential areas. Even in those instances, most sewage systems merely transferred the waste into nearby rivers and lakes thereby shifting the problem downstream.

Second, advances in technology critical to the development of a city's central business district also contributed to pollution. The balloon frame, the steel girder, and the elevator, which made high-density building possible, further strained limited public services and added to the congestion problems. Also, transportation advances, such as the horse-drawn or electric streetcar, increased congestion, and, in the case of horses, contributed directly to street-level pollution.

As urban areas expanded, the uprooting of plants and trees, the surfacing of new roads, and the construction of new buildings reduced oxygen generation and transformed cities into "heat islands" where temperatures were hotter at the urban core than in the nearby suburbs. Outward expansion also produced a variant to the environmental problems of inner cities. Early suburbs suffered because they were often too far removed from much-needed public services to deal with pollution and other environmental concerns, and later the suburbs suffered because they were too close to core-city pollution (Melosi 1993).

Thomas R. Detwyler and Melvin G. Marcus (1972) noted that the city—population together with environment—is a relatively new kind of ecosystem on the face of the earth. It is an ecosystem whose management presents city and county officials in large metropolitan areas with many of the same challenges (clean air, clean water, sustainability, and environmental justice) that confront federal and state officials. On the broadest level, urban environmental concerns need to be understood in terms of their physical effects on the city and on urbanites themselves.

These concerns have led governments to adopt laws and regulations designed to make city planning more environmentally friendly. Greater emphasis has been placed on government land use planning and the imposition of controls over the rights of individuals and businesses to use their land as they wish. These land control policies (e.g., planning and zoning) are designed to protect the environment through specific actions, such as preserving green space, scenic areas, and natural resources, often with the stated purpose of controlling the growth and sprawl pattern of development of urban regions.

Comprehensive planning (or master planning, often used interchangeably) became the solution for many urban areas. Comprehensive municipal zoning ordinances, which can be traced back to nineteenth-century France, were first adopted in the United States by New York City in 1916 (New York City Department of Planning 2006). The New York City model became the basis for many state and city comprehensive planning programs around the country. The basic premise of comprehensive planning remained largely unchanged through the 1960s. Comprehensive planning through this period was an instrument that established long-range, general policies for the physical development of the community in a coordinated, unified manner (Morgan, England, and Pelissero 2007).

Environmentalism and Development

The environmental movement has increasing support. However, developers also have substantial clout. Environmentalists advocate area-wide government or a regional approach to addressing environmental issues because pollution cannot be isolated within political boundaries. Area-wide government with land use authority can regulate and control development for orderly development that is sensitive to environmental impact. Developers are opposed to regional land use controls because it would constrain development. In most instances in the clash between developers and environmentalists, developers and the promise of providing jobs and increased tax base win out.

Weir (2000) studied regionalism in Oregon and California, two states with strong environmental movements. Oregon has adopted strong regional land use controls, whereas California has not. Weir concluded that the environmental movement, without additional support and facing strong opposition from developers and government leaders fearing the loss of local land use controls, did not have the political power to move land use authority to a regional level. In Oregon, environmentalists had the support of a popular and environmentally friendly governor and of farmers, who feared that they would lose their land to development. The development community was also weak, and disorganized. Weir attributes the environmental movement's ability to push through regional land use laws to the support of the other groups and to the lack of organized opposition from the development community.

As our metropolitan areas develop and add population, farmland and natural areas shrink. An example of the shrinkage is the Chicago metropolitan area. In 1972, urbanization covered just 19 percent of the land, or approximately 880 square miles, in the metropolitan-designated area. In 1997, urban development and associated growth covered 28 percent of the area or about 1,270 square miles. Moreover, agricultural land declined from 52 percent of the region to 33 percent (Chicago Metropolis 2020 2001). Some of the most productive agricultural land in the nation is located near metropolitan areas.

Land Use and Smart Growth

In the 1960s, the issue of land use controls gradually moved from plans just for physical development to plans that considered social and environment issues. The rise of the environmental movement was the catalyst for countless studies, academic articles, government committee reports, and newspaper stories on the link between land use and environmental issues in states and cities. The issues have, over the years, gone under different, appealing but vague, names: land use and "carrying capacity" in the 1970s, "growth management" in the 1980s, "sustainable development" in the early 1990s, and today it is most often referred to as "smart growth."

While growth measures may be effective within a local government jurisdiction, they have no cumulative effect on reducing either the residential or nonresidential construction in the region for at least two reasons. First, most of the issues local governments attempt to regulate through growth control measures are regional in scope. However, local growth control measures have no authority outside the community boundaries. Thus, residents living in a growth control community will continue to experience traffic congestion, environmental decay, and other effects of sprawl outside their community. Second, sprawl and higher-density land use will continue in the region despite growth control measures because developers will simply move to adjacent communities (Glickfeld and Levine 1992). Economist Anthony Downs argues that growth-related problems in metropolitan areas, such as traffic congestion, affordable housing, air pollution, solid-waste disposal, retention of open space, and siting locally undesirable land uses, must be addressed on a regional basis if the region hopes to solve these problems (Downs 1994, 27–30).

Despite the regional nature of environmental problems and the interrelationship with land use, most state legislatures have been slow to require regional land use plans. While some states have attempted to take control of zoning issues by adopting state-level zoning reforms, the majority of state legislatures have refused to modify or reconsider the long tradition of delegating planning and zoning authority to municipal governments. As a result, with the possible exception of Oregon, America remains zoned for sprawl.

Sprawl, then, is blamed for the majority of environmental metropolitan problems, including traffic congestion, social decay, pollution, and loss of irreplaceable open space. Sprawl is the result of actions by developers, individual buyers, businesses, and governments. Under the decentralized land use regulation system that presently exists in most areas of the country, each community establishes zoning and building codes and issues building and subdivision permits independently and without regard to the impact of their decisions on neighboring communities or the region as a whole.

Indeed, due to the fact that development enhances a community's tax base, development is encouraged by most local governments on the fringes of metropolitan areas. Municipalities, seeking growth to expand their tax base, have often made hasty decisions in granting permits that have resulted in poorly constructed housing, congestion, pollution, and health risks from inadequate sewer and water provision. Governments are often forced to upgrade infrastructure or to clean up environmental pollution at substantial cost from ill-conceived decisions encouraging rapid development.

A Rutgers University study estimated the capital costs of sprawl in New Jersey over a twenty-year period for new roads, schools, and water and sewage systems at $1.38 billion, with $400 million in additional annual operating costs. The authors also estimated that sprawl patterns of development will use an additional 30,000 acres of farmland and 29,000 acres of forests, steep slopes, and watersheds. Moreover, due to sprawl, it was projected that the state would consume an additional 2.5 million gallons of water and create an additional 800,000 gallons of sewage per day (Kasowski 1993, 4).

Despite the local nature of land use controls, some smart growth municipalities are taking action beyond their borders to limit sprawl through intergovernmental agreements, metropolitan organizations, or the purchase of land. For example, voters in Boulder, Colorado, approved sales tax increases to be used for open space acquisition. The proceeds have been used to purchase land both within Boulder and in the unincorporated area to preserve open space. Its purchases cover an area twice the size of the city itself.

A major problem with smart growth is that it is generally supported by central cities and mature suburbs with little or no land to develop, but it is usually resisted by suburban communities that are rapidly developing and have plenty of vacant land that is or could be attractive to developers. Thus, Austin, Texas, has embraced smart growth and has set aside proceeds from bond issues to purchase land to preserve open space in the city. However, the city is ringed by suburbs that are more interested in development than smart growth controls (Lorentz and Shaw 2000).

State Action to Protect the Environment

The first set of state reforms, driven by the environmental movement, focused on the protection of "critical areas" and the creation of permit systems for development actions that had a regional impact. Among the most successful of these reforms were efforts to limit development along the California coast and in the pinelands of New Jersey. However, many environmental nonprofit nongovernmental organizations (NGOs) contend that these initial statewide reforms were a failure largely because state legislatures weakened these laws with procedural and administrative changes, while others budgeted them out of existence.

With the exception of reforms in Oregon and Hawaii, these early reforms had no significant effect on the state, regional, or local areas they were intended to protect. In the mid-1980s and early 1990s, seven states (Vermont, Florida, New Jersey, Rhode Island, Georgia, Maine, and Washington) adopted programs featuring state goals and local plans. There was an expectation among environmental activists that this second generation effort, focused on the idea of "comprehensive plans," would bring about a national rebirth in land use planning reforms. After this initial flurry, however, few states followed and many of these early programs were scaled back or eliminated. In Vermont and Maine, for example, program funding was drastically reduced, while in Rhode Island, Georgia, and New Jersey, where plans were voluntary on the part of development interests, the conclusion is that comprehensive planning programs had little long-term effect.

Air Pollution

A major environmental concern with the sprawl pattern of development is air pollution. Emissions from the nation's nearly 200 million cars and trucks account for about half of all air pollution in the United States and more than 80 percent of air pollution in cities. The American Lung Association estimates that America spends more than $60 billion each year on health care as a direct result of air pollution (Ohio EPA 2007). However, since the passage of the Clean Air Act of 1970 and subsequent amendments, Americans have cut releases of air pollutants by more than 50 million tons. It would take twenty of today's new cars to generate the same amount of air pollution as one mid-1960s model car (Foundation for Clean Air Progress 2005). Although America's cars are more efficient than ever, our rate of fuel use continues to grow. Since 1980, the miles-per-gallon rating of passenger cars has improved 39 percent, yet fuel consumption is up 19 percent because Americans are driving 50 percent more miles (Ohio EPA 2007). Typical vehicle emissions have been reduced substantially, but suburban sprawl and the increased use of the automobile have negated the improvement in air quality sought by the legislation. The number of miles and the increasing number of automobiles have offset much of the emission control progress. The net result is a modest reduction in each automotive pollutant except lead, for which aggregate emissions have dropped by more than 95 percent (U.S. EPA 2005).

Table 11.1 shows the number of days that jurisdictions in a state exceeded federal ozone health standards. California, a highly urbanized state, is easily the state with the most clean air violations—more than five times the num-

Table 11.1

Unhealthy Levels of Ozone, 2003

Cumulative number of days each states' urban areas exceeded federal
health ozone standards

California	2,298	Alaska	0
Texas	449	Hawaii	0
Ohio	205	Montana	0
Pennsylvania	156	Nebraska	0
Michigan	122	North Dakota	0
North Carolina	110	South Dakota	0
New York	103	Wyoming	0
Indiana	93	Vermont	0
Louisiana	89	Oregon	0
Wisconsin	80	Idaho	0

Source: U.S. Environmental Protection Agency.

ber of days as second place Texas. In 2003, California had 2,298 days that
exceeded ozone standards. Texas was a distant second at 449 days. At the
other extreme, we see from this chart that several more rural states did not
exceed ozone levels by a single day. The key difference between the states
with many high ozone days and those with few or none lies with the extent of
urbanization of people in the state. Metropolitan areas have taken a variety of
actions to clean up their environmental contamination. Some areas, however,
have been more successful than others.

Table 11.2 shows the metropolitan areas with worst ozone pollution in
2005. The top five metropolitan areas with the worst ozone air pollution
problems come from the state of California. The major polluter in California
is the automobile. The Houston metropolitan area (ranked sixth on the list) is
an area dominated by the oil industry. The ninth and tenth metropolitan areas
on this list, the New York and Philadelphia metro areas, give an indication
of the complexity of the jurisdictional problems faced by metropolitan areas
in addressing pollution problems. Indeed, in order to deal with the negative
externalities of air pollution, metropolitan areas need the involvement of
higher-level governments.

A few metropolitan areas have programs to educate the public on the dan-
gers of air pollution. One program, called "Sustainable Seattle," focuses on
the number of good air quality days per year, with a "good day" defined as one
where none of four designated pollutants (carbon monoxide, sulfur dioxide,
ozone, and suspended particulate matter) goes beyond a "good" standard. The
program seeks reduction from all sources. Boulder has two programs in regard
to air pollution. One is a public education and awareness program sponsored

Table 11.2

Metropolitan Areas with the Worst Ozone Air Pollution, 2005

Rank	Metropolitan area
1	Los Angeles-Long Beach-Riverside, CA
2	Bakersfield, CA
3	Fresno-Madera, CA
4	Visalia-Porterville, CA
5	Merced, CA
6	Houston-Baytown-Huntsville, TX
7	Sacramento-Arden-Arcade-Truckee, CA-NV
8	Dallas-Fort Worth, TX
9	New York-Newark-Bridgeport, NY-NJ-CT-PA
10	Philadelphia-Camden-Vineland, PA-NJ-DE-MD

Source: American Lung Association.

by the Boulder County Clean Air Consortium, and the other seeks to help small businesses to reduce emissions. Chattanooga has instituted a program of alternatively-fueled public transit vehicles (Portney 2003, 81).

The Atlanta metropolitan area, one of the fastest growing areas in the nation, is especially vulnerable to the problems of air pollution. Topographical conditions often cause air to stagnate over the section of the southeastern United States where Atlanta is located. Atlanta is not able to meet the federal clean air standards. Almost half of the ozone in Atlanta is caused by automobile emissions. If automobile emissions were reduced, the ozone levels would also be reduced (Brookings Institution 2000).

Municipalities often do not have direct control over nonpoint pollution control, such as car exhaust, because such regulation often falls within the purview of state or county governments. Moreover, because air pollution does not respect borders, it requires, at a minimum, a regional approach to air pollution control programs. Municipalities can certainly encourage alternative forms of transportation, such as mass transit and carpooling, but the tools necessary to regulate an externality like air pollution comes from governments covering larger geographical areas. Without senior-level pollution control programs, urban areas suffer the ill effects of air pollution from neighboring jurisdictions.

Environmental Justice

Support for environmental issues is generally stronger from those who are relatively well educated and relatively wealthy. The poor and nonwhite have been less supportive. However, more recently, groups representing the poor and minority communities have become more vocal over environmental racism, because of the preponderance of waste dumps and other environmental hazards in poor minority communities and neighborhoods. Minorities suffer disproportionately from toxic contamination in their communities.

There is general agreement that the environmental justice movement began in 1982 with community reaction in Warren County, North Carolina, a 65 percent African-American community, against the proposed siting of a large hazardous waste landfill. National organizations and the local community demonstrated, resulting in the arrest of more than 5,000 people. In many urban areas, a coalition of civil rights and environmental groups has formed to focus on the disproportionate and adverse exposure to environmental hazards in low-income communities. For a variety of reasons, businesses that often cause air, water, and land pollution will locate in or near poor communities, often populated by minorities. One reason is that land is cheaper in these communities, and poorer areas may be willing to accept the environmental risks in return for jobs and economic development. Yet there is a good deal of controversy over whether differential exposure is the result of racism or other factors (Ringquist 2005).

An environmental injustice exists when members of disadvantaged, ethnic, minority, or other groups suffer disproportionately at the local, regional, or national levels from environmental risks or hazards. Environmental injustice occurs when identifiable minority groups suffer disproportionately from violations of fundamental human rights as a result of environmental factors or are denied access to the same environmental benefits enjoyed by the majority of society. Minority groups should be able to enjoy the same environmental investments, natural resources, access to information, and justice in environment-related matters as other members of society.

A study of brownfields in Chicago indicated that the majority of brownfield sites are located on the south and west sides of the city, areas that are heavily dominated by minority and poor residents. Sixty-two percent of the brownfields are located in neighborhoods with between 80 percent and 100 percent minority population. Eighty-one percent are located in neighborhoods with a minority population between 60 percent and 100 percent.

Further evidence of environmental injustice is within a study by the U.S. General Accounting Office, now U.S. General Accountability Office, that concluded that minorities make up the majority of the population in three out of four communities where landfills are located (U.S. General Accounting Office 1983). The United Church of Christ Commission for Racial Justice "Toxic Wastes and Race" (1987), extended the GAO study. It was based on a national study that mapped the location of toxic waste sites and the racial composition of the community. They found that people of color were twice as likely as white people to live in a community with a commercial hazardous waste management facility and three times as likely to live in a community with multiple facilities. Further analysis and studies by others proved that race is the number one predictor of where toxic sites are located.

Waste Disposal and the Metropolitan Environment

One of the major environmental problems plaguing metropolitan areas is waste disposal. Indeed, the issue transcends political borders, and what one community in a metropolitan does or does not do affects other communities in the metropolitan area. Regional approaches have often resulted from environmental health issues. For example, one of the major reasons for the establishment of the Metropolitan Council in the Twin Cities in 1967 was to tackle the issue of inadequate sewage disposal in the region that was contaminating the water supply. Pollution of the lakes and waterways from municipal dumping of raw sewage in the Seattle region resulted in the closing of beaches. This led to the establishment of efforts to obtain voter approval for a multipurpose metropolitan-wide district with authority over sewage and solid waste disposal as well as a number of other regional functions. The voters ultimately approved a countywide agency with authority only over sewage disposal. One of the major reasons metropolitan government was established in the Toronto metropolitan area was to provide for sewage disposal in the suburbs.

Solid waste disposal has become a major issue for regions as landfills are closing and the expense of disposal becomes prohibitive for individual municipalities. Garbage disposal has traditionally been a local government function, with each local government establishing its own arrangements for disposal. However, as metropolitan areas grew, the pollution and health issues involved required different approaches. States started mandating recycling, and other approaches to disposal. Regional approaches in the disposal of garbage are becoming more common. Suburban municipalities in some metropolitan areas have formed authorities to handle solid waste disposal. In other areas, states have mandated a regional approach to solid waste disposal.

New Jersey is an example of the state establishing the county as the government to be responsible for the solid waste function. The state had originally considered establishing "wastesheds" but opted for county provision. Connecticut established "wastesheds" and a system of burn facilities to produce energy from the garbage. By 1994, over 60 percent of its solid waste was being burned—almost four times the national average. New York had regionalized the solid waste function to the county level except on Long Island (Benjamin and Nathan 2001, 230, 248).

Environment Versus Development

One of the major issues in the environmental debate is the question of whether we can protect the environment and have development. There is no doubt that environmental regulations increase the costs of production. Air pollution controls on automobiles have added several hundred dollars to the cost. The question of global competitiveness with pollution costs is a major consideration. Can industry compete with industry in other countries that do not have pollution control equipment?

However, there are also societal costs from environmental degradation. For example, if air quality were to revert to the level of 1970, it is estimated that the health bill for increased illnesses would total $40 billion per year. By contrast, the cost of implementing the Clean Air Act amendments of 1990 has been estimated at $20 billion per year (Harrigan and Nice 1997). If these figures are anywhere close to being accurate, the benefits of clean air outweigh the costs of pollution. At issue, however, is who bears the costs. If society bears the costs of health and industry bears the costs of pollution control, the industry becomes less competitive in the marketplace vis-à-vis industry in other places that do not have to pay for pollution control equipment.

Although the public is more environmentally conscious and aware of the health issues from pollution, when it comes to environmental protection programs and job growth, there is substantial pressure to relax environmental standards to foster job growth. This is especially so in an economic decline. Businesses naturally resist pollution controls that increase the cost of doing business, particularly if they perceive that their competitors in other countries are not subject to the same pollution controls.

Solutions to the Urban Environmental Problems

Government structures and intergovernmental relationships within and outside metropolitan areas may facilitate or possibly hinder the implementation of policies that impact the environment. For example, national and state governments do not exercise meaningful oversight over metropolitan land use policies. Municipal governments use zoning controls for their own parochial purposes (Judd and Swanstrom 1994). This fragmentation of interests often hinders comprehensive regional planning and results in uncoordinated development in metropolitan areas. This sprawl development pattern in U.S. cities reflects the high degree of autonomy granted to municipalities in our intergovernmental system (Judd 1995).

While regional environmental policy planning within urban areas is difficult and often impossible to achieve, nonprofit organizations concerned with environmental degradation have collaborated with governments to develop policies and programs to improve the environment and our quality of life. The following case studies are illustrative of positive developments of collaborations with NGOs and cooperation among governments to address environmental problems in metropolitan areas.

Baltimore Metropolitan Council

The nineteenth largest market in the nation is Baltimore. The Baltimore region is home to over 2.5 million people (Baltimore Metropolitan Council 2006a). Throughout the years, there have been attempts to address environmental problems in the region to try to improve the quality of life. The first effort was the founding of the Regional Planning Council, which was within the State Planning Department in 1956. In 1984, it separated from the State Planning Department, and in 1992, the council adopted its present name, Baltimore Metropolitan Council (Maryland State Archives 2006).

The Baltimore Metropolitan Council (BMC) is composed of the county executives of Anne Arundel, Baltimore, Carroll, Harford, and Howard counties, along with the mayor of Baltimore City. The BMC is committed to identifying regional interests and developing collaborative initiatives to improve the region's quality of life and economic vitality (Greater Baltimore Committee 2005, 2). Among the issues the council deals with are air pollution, water pollution, transportation planning, and emergency planning.

The council's mission statement is to facilitate the development of a region with clean air and water, well designed public transit system, clearly defined borders between developed areas and open spaces, and parks accessible to all citizens; with a culture that protects natural resources, enforces environmental laws, promotes energy efficiency, provides incentives for environmental stewardship, and offers environmental education for all students (Baltimore Metropolitan Council 2007).

A recent council initiative was the creation of Vision 2030, a blueprint, or roadmap for action with a regional conscience. Starting in the summer of 2001, BMC held focus groups and stakeholder interviews to identify "hot button" issues for the residents (ibid.). Through extensive public involvement utilizing forums, displays, and questionnaires, Vision 2030 was created. Vision 2030 focuses on spatial planning, the issues of growth and fragmentation, public transportation, economic planning, environmental planning, and transportation planning.

One way to assess the impact of Vision 2030 is the manner in which the BMC has influenced change in policy. For example, in 2005, the state of Maryland announced the "Greater Baltimore Bus Initiative," which proposed a restructuring of the region's bus system. The Maryland Transportation Authority asked the BMC to conduct an independent review of its proposal. BMC held open forums and presented its report, which made a number of recommendations. After consideration of the study, the state altered its proposal and agreed not to cut service to a number of regional employment centers, and it also did not cut existing peak commuter express services (Baltimore Metropolitan Council 2006b).

Through action and cooperation, the BMC and the region are attempting to improve the quality of life in the region through strategies that deal with increasing the enforcement of air and water pollution controls, coordinating land use and transportation planning, and providing sound developmental incentives. In addition, BMC is working on protecting rural land from development through better zoning of open space and agricultural lands, establishing energy efficiency as a fundamental principle for projects in local government, and creating public awareness programs to inform and assist individuals, families, and property owners in making environmentally friendly choices and practices for their homes and business (Baltimore Metropolitan Council 2007).

Chicago Metropolitan Mayors Caucus

The Chicago Metropolitan Mayors Caucus was created in 1997 as a way for elected municipal officials to be able to come together and work toward a better future, not just for their own municipality, but for the region as a whole. The caucus is comprised of 272 mayors. It addresses major issues that impact the region such as crime, education, housing, transportation, economics, and the environment (Metropolitan Mayors Caucus 2007).

One environmental program in which the caucus is involved is the Clean Air Counts program. This program is aimed at reducing smog-forming pollutants as well as reducing the consumption of energy in the Chicago metropolitan area (Clean Air Counts 2005). This program is a partnership of the Metropolitan Mayors Caucus, the Illinois Environmental Protection Agency, the U.S. Environmental Protection Agency Region 5, and the Delta Institute. The goal of the program is to educate and motivate businesses, organizations, and citizens to voluntarily reduce their emissions of pollutants that are not regulated. The program was awarded the Clean Air Excellence Award sponsored by the Environmental Protection Agency's Office of Air and Radiation on April 7, 2005 (Metropolitan Mayors Caucus 2006).

The Clean Air Counts program utilizes multiple programs to combat air pollution. First, the program is aimed at informing individuals that there are alternatives to the status quo. Status quo in this case means the way that individuals go about their lives, without thinking about the regional consequences. The program raises awareness of issues that affect the quality of air in the Chicago metropolitan region. Raising awareness is the first step to improving the quality of life in the region, but there are other parts of the program that take concrete steps to improve the air quality. The educational aspects of the program are directed at informing people on ways to improve the efficiency of their business, home, and automobiles.

Second, working through the municipalities, the program offers opportunities that can create positive changes. The program offers a lawn-care buyback program, gas-can trade in, and a diesel retrofitting program. Each one of these programs has a positive effect on air pollution every time an individual takes advantage of the program. The lawn-care buyback program gives people a $100 coupon toward the purchase of a new energy-efficient lawn mower when they turn in their old gas mower.

Ohio-Kentucky-Indiana

The Ohio, Kentucky, Indiana Regional Council of Governments (OKI) consists of business organizations, community groups, and local governments that are committed to developing collaborative strategies to improve the quality of life in the region. The presence of such a collaboration of interest is evidence that there is a multistate regional concern. These three states have decided that the best way to combat collective problems is to deal with them cooperatively and collaboratively (Ohio, Kentucky, Indiana Regional Council of Governments 2006).

This partnership was formed in 1964. Since then, the OKI has been fostering relationships and building alliances with local government councils, businesses, and the federal government. OKI currently represents 103 governmental, social, and civic groups from 198 different communities in a region that spans three states, and encompasses eight counties (ibid.). OKI has made air quality a key element of its plans and projects. With a commitment to cleaner air for the region, OKI has pursued projects to reduce the number of trips that individuals take in a car by themselves through the promotion of rideshare programs. It has also supported pedestrian and bicycle paths, smart growth, and high-occupancy-vehicle lanes as an alternative to expansion of the highways. OKI also promotes expansion of public transportation, through light rail, buses, and the development of park-and-ride lots (Ohio, Kentucky, Indiana Regional Council of Governments 2007).

OKI has a Regional Bicycle Plan with the goal of making the roadway network more accommodating to bikers. It has offered communities technical assistance as well as funding through its Transportation Improvement Program to develop a regional network of bicycle trails. In 2005, Congress approved funding for sections of the Ohio River Trail in Cincinnati and Anderson Township. There is also a regional pedestrian program, which encourages development of a more walkable region. At present, there are Safe Routes to School programs that are being developed in the region (ibid.).

The goal of reducing the volume of individuals who drive places by themselves is being combatted through a program called Ride Share in the tristate region. OKI's Ride Share program provides a database that has over 1,200 commuters who commute using its vanpools. One very interesting part of this rideshare plan is called the "Guaranteed Ride Home" section. The program will reimburse the individual 80 percent of the cost of their cab fare or transit cost home. This "Guaranteed Ride Home" portion of the program can be utilized up to four times a year. The employees who take advantage do not have to worry about the stress of driving to work everyday. The advantage of the program is fewer cars on the road and smaller parking lots at business establishments (ibid.).

OKI's Regional Ozone Coalition is similar to Chicago's Clean Air Counts program. The Regional Ozone Coalition is a collaboration of local governments and businesses that volunteer to help reduce smog in the region through action, education, and outreach services. A major objective of this voluntary coalition is to raise public awareness. Since 1996, the Regional Ozone Coalition, in conjunction with the Southwest Ohio Regional Transit Authority, and the Transit Authority of Northern Kentucky has offered fifty-cent bus fares during the summer months. This is a great example of the coalition teaming with the public sector to improve the quality of life in the region (Clean Air Counts 2006).

The coalition has also teamed with the private sector. In 1998, in conjunction with BP Oil Company, the coalition offered the nation's first gas-cap testing replacement program. The program was aimed at testing and replacing gas caps that were leaking fumes into the air through evaporation. An estimated 23,000 leaking caps were replaced, which saved nearly four tons of emissions from being released daily (Clean Air Counts 2006).

Lessons and Conclusions

These regional coalitions have been able to make a difference. Public–private partnerships have made advancements not only in furthering regional governance but also in benefiting the environment. It is important to remember that issues are unique to their own region. What works in Utah may not work in Michigan. These case studies show tangible examples of regional coalitions that have made a positive impact on the environment.

These organizations have, through the engagement of the public—whether it is a traffic study in Baltimore, a Clean Air Counts billboard in Chicago, or advertising a rideshare program in Cincinnati—encouraged the public to think regionally and environmentally. Quality of life and quality of one's environment are linked. It is to the benefit of those who live in the region to have clean air and viable transportation. Through action and planning, these regional coalitions are working together in an attempt to combat the negative effects of pollution. The fact that all of these different regional coalitions have deemed air pollution a regional problem gives credence to the fact that environmental issues can be dealt with in a regional manner. The fact that these regional coalitions are attacking the problem of air pollution voluntarily shows that the action taken at the federal and state levels is just a start and that programs at the regional level are essential.

Improving urban environments requires strengthening the governance of metropolitan areas. In this chapter, we have examined several approaches to alleviating environmental problems at the metropolitan level. Protecting the environment requires cooperation among local governments and collaboration with NGOs. Effective governmental policies require not only strengthened governments but also the involvement of many other actors from both the public and private sectors. In order to better control the impact of externalities and internal pressures it is essential for local governments to develop more regional and community-based approaches.

These concerns have led governments in metropolitan areas to adopt laws and regulations designed to allow city planning to be more environmentally friendly. In recent years, greater emphasis has been placed on government land use planning and the imposition of controls over the rights of individuals and businesses in specific instances to use their land as they wish. These land management policies are designed to preserve green space, scenic areas, and natural resources; to manage the growth of cities and suburbs; and to combat environmental problems.

In the complex policymaking milieu that produces environmental policy, the role, the priorities, and the institutional capacity at the local level are often overlooked. Given our environmental protection challenges, and the historic reliance on single-agency solutions, we are accustomed to seeing federal and state governments as the primary policymaking actors. While the federal government tends to dominate the establishment of national environmental goals, and while state governments direct the design and implementation of environmental protection policies, it is the cities and suburbs that have become more actively involved in recent years in the monitoring and enforcement of environmental regulations in the intergovernmental system. Pressure at the grassroots level and a national government absent in its commitment to the environment during the first years of the twenty-first century are the two trends that will accelerate our urban governments' environmental protection support.

References

Baltimore Metropolitan Council. 2006a. "Metropolitan Report, Impacts on the Region." Available at www.baltometro.org/content/view/34/190/ (accessed June 2006).
———. 2006b. "Partners in Progress Report." Available at www.baltometro.org/content/view/34/190/ (accessed June 2006).
———. 2007. "Vision 2030." Available at www.baltometro.org/vision2030.html (accessed January 2007).
Benjamin, Gerald, and Richard Nathan. 2001. *Regionalism and Realism: A Study of Governments in the New York Metropolitan Area.* Washington, DC: Brookings Institution.
Brookings Institution. 2000. *Moving Beyond Sprawl: The Challenge for Metropolitan Atlanta.* Washington, DC.
Chicago Metropolis 2020. 2001. *Regional Realities: Measuring Progress Toward Shared Regional Goals.* Chicago.
Clean Air Counts. 2005. "Diesel Retrofit." Available at http://cleanaircounts.org/dieselretrofit.shtml (accessed September 2005).
———. 2006. "Air Quality in Greater Cincinnati." Available at www.oki.org/cleanair/airquality/airqualiy.html (accessed June 2006).
Cochran, Thomas C., and William Miller. 1961. *Age of Enterprise: A Social History of Industrial America.* New York: Harper.
Detwyler, Thomas R., and Melvin G. Marcus. 1972. *Urbanization and Environment: The Physical Geography of the City.* Belmont, CA: Duxbury Press.
Downs, Anthony. 1994. *New Visions for Metropolitan America.* Washington, DC: Brookings Institution.
Foundation for Clean Air Progress. 2005. "Air Pollution Facts." Available at www.cleanairprogress.org (accessed May 2005).
Glickfeld, Madelyn, and Ned Levine. 1992. *Regional Growth . . . Local Reaction: The Enactment and Effects of Local Growth Control and Management Measures in California.* Cambridge, MA: Lincoln Institute of Land Policy.
Greater Baltimore Committee, Economic Alliance of Greater Baltimore, and Baltimore Metropolitan Council. 2005. *Greater Baltimore State of the Region Report.* Baltimore.
Harrigan, John, and David C. Nice. 1997. *Politics and Policy in States and Communities.* 7th edition. New York: Addison Wesley Longman.
Judd, Dennis, R. 1995. "Cities, Political Representation, and the Dynamics of American Federalism." In *The New American Politics: Reflections on Political Change and the Clinton Administration,* ed. Bryan D. Jones, 212–31. Boulder: Westview Press.
Judd, Dennis R., and Todd Swanstrom. 1994. *City Politics: Private Power and Public Policy.* New York: HarperCollins.
Kasowski, Kevin. 1993. "The Costs of Sprawl, Revisited." *PAS Memo,* February. Chicago: American Planning Association.

Lorentz, Amalia, and Kirsten Shaw. 2000. "Are You Ready to Bet on Smart Growth?" *Planning* (January): 4.

Maryland State Archives. 2006. "Baltimore Metropolitan Council, Origin & Functions." Available at www.msa.md.gov/msa/mdmanual/35interc/01baltf.html (accessed June 2006).

Melosi, Martin V. 1993. "Down in the Dumps: Is There a Garbage Crisis in America?" In *Urban Public Policy*, ed. Melosi, 100–128. State College: Pennsylvania State University.

Metropolitan Mayors Caucus. 2006. "Clean Air Counts." Available at www.mayorcaucus.org/pages/Home/Clean_Air_Counts/ (accessed January 2006).

———. 2007. "About the Caucus." Available at www.mayorcaucus.org/pages/Home/About_the_Caucus/ (accessed January 2007).

Morgan, David R.; Robert E. England; and John P. Pelissero. 2007. *Managing Urban America*. 6th ed. Washington, DC: Congressional Quarterly Press.

New York City Department of Planning. 2006. "Zoning History." Available at www.nyc.gov/html/dcp/html/zone/zonehis.shtml (accessed May 2006).

Ohio EPA. 2007. "Energy and Pollution Prevention." Available at www.epa.state.oh.us/opp/consumer/carp2.html# (accessed February 27, 2007).

Ohio, Kentucky, Indiana Regional Council of Governments. 2006. "At a Glance." Available at www.oki.org/overview/overview.html (accessed June 2006).

———. 2007. "Home Page." Available at www.oki.org (accessed January 2007).

O'Keefe, Joyce. 1991. *Regional Issues in the Chicago Metropolitan Area*. Chicago: Metropolitan Planning Council.

Portney, Kent E. 2003. *Taking Sustainable Cities Seriously*. Cambridge, MA: MIT Press.

Rabe, Barry. 1986. *Fragmentation and Integration in State Environmental Management*. Washington, DC: Conservation Foundation.

Ringquist, Evan. 2005. "Environmental Justice: Normative Concerns, Empirical Evidence and Governmental Action." In *Environmental Policy*. 5th ed. eds. Norman J. Vig and Michael E. Kraft, 239–64. Washington DC: CQ Press.

United Church of Christ. 1987. *Toxic Wastes and Race*. Commission for Racial Justice. Seattle.

U.S. Census Bureau. 1975. *Historical Statistics of the United States: Colonial Times to 1970, Part 1*. Washington, DC: Government Printing Office.

U.S. General Accounting Office. 1983. *Siting of Hazardous Waste Landfills and Their Correlation with Racial and Economic Status of Surrounding Communities*. Pub. No. B-211461. Washington, DC: Government Printing Office.

U.S. Environmental Protection Agency (EPA). 2005. "Automobile Emissions: An Overview." Available at www.epa.gov/otaq/consumer/05-autos.pdf (accessed May 13, 2007).

Weir, Margaret. 2000. "Coalition Building for Regionalism." In *Reflections on Regionalism*, ed. Bruce Katz, 127–54. Washington, DC: Brookings Institution.

Wolman, Harold, and Michael Goldsmith. 1992. *Urban Politics and Policy: A Comparative Approach*. Cambridge, MA: Blackwell.

12

PATRICIA S. ATKINS

Epilogue
Toward Metropolitan Livability for the Twenty-First Century

The metropolitan scale is the elemental scale for working on the nation's major urban challenges of the twenty-first century. If we move down to the municipal level to handle major challenges, we lose metropolitan area inter-connections. For example, we lose the ability to connect the land use actions of one community to the land use actions of another community and thence to the transportation network that will best connect those different land uses. If we move up to the state level, we lose the sense of place that provides the motivation and connection for community betterment. Someday, sooner than we may think, the cooperative level for working on the nation's major urban challenges will migrate to the global arena. For now, we are stuck at the met-ropolitan level. Sometimes, as David Hamilton, Laurie Hokkanen, and Curtis Wood explained earlier in the book, we are also stuck in traffic.

Up until about 100 years ago, most of America's great cities were able to bring their hinterland populations within the city borders through annexation or consolidation, thereby extending their reach to the metropolitan area's en-tire population. Edmund James observed back in 1899 that, while sometimes there was a lag in the process of bringing together everyone in the urbanized territory through annexation or consolidation into one government, the gap ultimately would be closed. He explained,

> Thus it is plain that if a given suburban region is to be settled up rapidly, it lies in the interests of the city, and, in the long run, of the suburban region itself, that the area shall be added to the city soon enough in the history of its development that the general scheme of streets, of sewers and drainage, of water supply, the general school system, etc., can be easily harmonized and integrated with the existing system of the city. . . . So difficult is this problem of adjustment between the interests of the suburban regions and the cities that long periods have elapsed in the history of many of our great

cities after the time when suburban regions should have been annexed before it was possible to overcome the opposition of conflicting interests and bring about the adjustments that lay in the wider and larger interests of all. (James 1899, 13, 14–15)

Community acceptance in the nineteenth century of the monolithic city happened because the lands surrounding cities were unincorporated places prone to habitation by those in the practice of, as those of James's time would describe, certain vices such as banditry, bootlegging, or prostitution. Cities were the safe places. Slowly, public perception shifted, when cities' livability for the well-to-do diminished because of overcrowding, putrid air, industrial wastes, and disastrous fires, among other unhealthy aspects. Unincorporated land adjacent to cities was kept green, made safe, and made habitable through large-scale corporate-led residential developments using some of the practices invented in company towns' creation. Those developers laid down private roads or trolleys to complete the transportation route to their residential communities, extending that route from the public terminus of roads and trolleys at the cities' edges.

Well-to-do Americans began to see they could not obtain within central cities the quality of life they envisioned for themselves and their families. Emigration outward from the cities had begun, but America's Open Door immigration policy of the 1890s provided a flood of newcomers to cities whose presence would offset the outbound trend for decades; then national traumas of World War I and World War II, and the Great Depression episodically dampened the suburbanization trend. Finally, though, the thriving postwar economy in mid-century would give Americans the financial means to purchase the moderately priced houses being built out in the suburbs where land was cheap and autos available for mobility.

In this way, over the past 100 years, our city governments ceased to be our metropolitan governments, and responsibility for metropolitan quality of life ceased to have a champion with authority to match the metropolitan territory.

Metropolitan livability, as compared with municipal livability, has been the output of local government only when the boundary of a single government matched the space all people in the metropolitan area occupied. Beginning in the 1960s, when worrisome features of suburbanization's impact upon cities began to fully emerge, some urban reformers began to advocate that the two—metropolitan government and metropolitan occupants—again be coterminous through the adoption of structural reforms such as city–county consolidation. A few partial metropolitan government efforts were successful, but true metropolitan-wide government requires multicounty consolidation, both structurally and functionally. In the United States, the Portland, Oregon, area's Metro is multicounty in geographic scope, the closest to this form in the United States, but it does not functionally or structurally provide complete consolidation of government.

This quest to structurally connect metropolitan community and metropolitan government has largely failed in the second half of the twentieth century. David Miller explains that the failure is no surprise. To succeed, he observes, metropolitan government requires the simultaneous existence of two mutually exclusive situations. These are subjugation of local governments through imposition of metropolitan government (either imposed by the state or selected by residents), and local sovereignty on freedom of association to act politically and societally for the local government's self-interests. When metropolitan government's trendier cousin, metropolitan governance, fails, it does so for a similar reason. Try as they might, Miller remarks, few metropolitan strategies are able to circumvent this fundamental tension.

Without metropolitan-wide government, metropolitan livability is a composite accumulation of outputs produced independently by many different local government policies and many different private decisions by the other sectors within the metropolitan area, as Nelson Wikstrom explains. He recounts the many attributes of a good metropolitan quality of life, touching upon personal safety, purity and availability of elements essential to human life, infrastructures for life-long learning and artistic expression, multiple mobility choices, plentiful employment opportunities at least at living wages, a people-scaled and lively built environment, political efficacy, and a sense of community. These attributes are approached in piecemeal fashion by many different stakeholders and governments in metropolitan areas, and the result is a livability patchwork. Some communities reach a very desirable living status; others do not.

Without the ability to row in the same direction that a metropolitan-wide government potentially provides, polycentric metropolitan communities have to find other mechanisms for assuring a good life in their metropolitan areas. What will allow them to achieve a compromise upon the different preferences of households, and then to initiate that compromise into reality through policies, enforce it through legal means, and sustain and amend it over time? Traditionally, at the national and state levels, such compromise is effectuated through constitutions; and, at the local level, granted by states through charters. States, because of the tension described by David Miller, have not granted general charters to metropolitan areas, and the metropolitan level therefore has lacked such a mechanism.

The fallacy of a significant part of twentieth-century thought was to assume that from each metropolitan area, lacking a constitution or charter, some sort of voluntary mechanism would emerge to carry the metropolitan cause because the benefits of cooperation or consolidation would be so transparent that local governments would surrender all or even a segment of local autonomy. What such thinking has failed to recognize and accommodate are those parochial local interests that necessitate usage of regional compromise mechanisms.

Late twentieth-century thought on metropolitan reform became more sophisticated, nimble, compromising, and inclusive. With the many local political laboratories of democracy that the United States enjoys through its nearly 90,000 local governments, some communities, in the face of pressing needs for regional cooperation, relaxed their thinking and the rules, and a new regional governmental process began to emerge. This was the beginning of the formation of the fifth wave of regionalism: a regional civic infrastructure with a shared sense of values and a common vision of the desired quality of life, as described in the chapter by Allan Wallis. David Miller provides a theoretical underpinning, explaining how we are moving from a paradigm centered on government to one centered on governing that is no longer the exclusive domain of governments. A variety of forces described by Patricia Atkins have driven this paradigm, including usage of private companies and nonprofit organizations to deliver public goods, multiple partnerships to deliver those goods, the ability of an organization to collaborate externally and instantaneously, increased citizenry sophistication in demands for more control over and choice in their governmental goods, globalization of information, globalization of the economy, new influences on public policies from postings on blogs and Web sites, worldwide environmentalism, and a national government preoccupied overseas and less able to assist its domestic partners. She has suggested a new term called "synercentrism" to capture this concept of partnership governance.

Synercentrism is a voluntarily entered, though possibly legally binding, networked system of cooperation that uses the self-interests of its partners from governments, firms, nonprofits, charities, citizens, faith-based associations, or locally unique sectors to provide public goods while moving toward a multiple bottom line for metropolitan regions.

Many activities occur under the guise of synercentrism. Private firms have been contracted by governments to provide public goods in imaginative settings, including management of major airport hubs and supermax prisons. Governments have entangled themselves in complicated private–public sector employee or services delivery contracts. Nonprofits cooperate with governments in many metropolitan regions to provide shelter and food to those who are underserved by government. Traditional public policies have begun to combine market forces and political forces to boost the effectiveness of public policy efforts. Public policymakers realize that government is only one participant in an enormous set of public policy participants who join into coalitions and networks within metropolitan regions to accomplish their objectives.

Synercentric advocates assume that there is some wedge of common ground between local interests and metropolitan interests, and that there should be a trade made between local interests and the larger regional interests. Further, the tradeoff does not have to happen through governmental policies, but can include market-based policies. The smoothness of the tradeoff between one jurisdiction's interests and another's is going to depend on the ease of resolving transaction costs that accrue to each jurisdiction as they achieve regional interests that benefit the metropolitan area. The agreements or contracts that codify these transaction costs can run into hundreds of pages and provide terminology that is excruciatingly detailed. In the absence of a regional charter or constitution, these regional agreements specify common expectations and manipulate the transaction costs into a price range where the benefits of cooperation exceed the costs.

Synercentrism posits that through such agreements or contracts local governments and other sectors that are more advantaged regarding a particular public commodity will deed some of their advantage to less-advantaged governments and sectors, so that the status quo, their own self-interest, is minimally disturbed or is improved. The better-off government or sector has determined that, by not providing a satisfactory inducement to the less advantaged government or sector, there will be a change in the commodity that will be detrimental to their parochial interests.

An example comes from land use policy, a policy that Miller notes is a near-monopoly local power under the associational rights of a community to define and shape the purpose and nature of the community it wants to be. A local government exercises this land use right independent of the impact its actions will have on neighboring jurisdictions or on the larger.

Allan Wallis provides ample verification of how freedom of association, coupled with market-based development, has supported a less-dense land use that requires longer commutes, requires new development that lacks funds for infrastructure, has problems locating objectionable land uses, and involves difficulty coordinating infrastructure construction. Despite these concerns, concerns that might ignite efforts at amelioration through regional land use planning, Wallis observes that decades of attempts to achieve such planning have fallen short and that land use challenges seem to be mounting faster than the development and adoption of effective solutions. Based on the local associational rights preventing state action, Miller's fundamental tension the joint legitimacy of competing notions—predicts such an outcome.

The practice of synercentrism led local governments, concerned by the impact of the earlier-mentioned trends of lower density, infrastructure short-falls, and noncoordination on their current high quality of life within their metropolitan area, to cede some local authority to regional land use agree-ments that they believed would safeguard their own quality of life; while local governments in other metropolitan areas, facing their own similar concerns, turned to a different, market-based approach to create regional land use coor-dination. The former appeared in the Denver region as the Mile High Compact described by Allan Wallis and the latter was an early planning feature of the Regional Districts in British Columbia covered by Patricia Atkins.

The Mile High Compact is an arrangement where collaboration has been based upon the premise that local jurisdictions continue to have strong incentives to compete with one another, thus direct inducements must be specified and provided to elicit cooperation. It is an exercise in inducing the Denver region's municipalities to voluntarily adopt urban growth boundaries. Approximately two-thirds of the region's municipalities and counties have adopted the boundaries. As a cooperative inducement, the regional council has a policy of allocating federal transportation infrastructure funding based partly on a community's adoption of the Mile High Compact. The purpose of the compact is to steer growth into selected areas so that more land is left to nature and other low-impact purposes.

Most antisprawl individuals are critical of the impacts of sprawl rather than the low density itself. What is alarming to most is the disappearance of green space. Absent any local government influences, population dispersing incrementally outward from the central core will become less dense at fur-ther distances, a situation to which we should ascribe neither evil nor good intentions, but many people prefer to do exactly that. It is simply a geometric phenomenon that the further an individual moves outward from the core, the more land there is to spread onto. Ten thousand individuals moving to unsettled land that lies in the band 5 to 10 miles out from the city center will create a density of 42 persons per square mile, while those same 10,000 individuals moving into a band of land 45 to 50 miles out will create a much less dense presence of 6.7 persons per square mile, and those 10,000 moving to a band spanning the 95 to 100 mile circumference will create a density of 3.3 persons per square mile. The debate thus should not be an argument about exurbia being so much less dense than suburbia or than the urban core, because geometry puts it behind before the argument begins.

The debate over land use must first focus upon a region determining what is an adequate green reserve for the future of its biodiversity, humans and otherwise, and then working to preserve that degree of green space. If a region determines its green-space requirements for an appropriate time horizon, whether ten or fifty years hence, and successfully locks in that green space in perpetuity, then some of the concerns about exurban settlement are mitigated. Once we move to the fact that what we term sprawl is a geometric-based phenomenon, albeit bound into place by policies such as subdivision zoning and local road design, we can discuss how to handle it.

An example of a region that has initiated such a land inventory process is Southeastern Pennsylvania's GreenSpace Alliance. This five-county organization has inventoried nature preserves, wildlife preserves, county parks, state parks, historic and cultural heritage sites, national parks, state gamelands and forests, historic homes and gardens, private arboreta, and battlefield parks. They excluded for-profit greenspaces and small local parks (National Association of Regional Councils 2000, 44).

They discovered that more than half their region's 2.5 million acreage remained as open space. They then determined their green-space needs for thirty years hence, and learned that only 10 to 15 percent of what they would need—needs that would have to come out of the existing open space—currently wore a protective mantle. This fact-based approach provides a neutral lens to initiate discussion among the many parties that will have to cooperate to provide an adequate green-space land bank. Even so, many individuals in the United States believe that decisions regarding land usage should be left to market forces.

A greenshed moves a region partly toward a better quality of life. A protective mantle wrapped around a region's green-space requirements will obviate one of the concerns associated with sprawl, the loss of open space. With green space protected, the debate over having more or less density could be retired and current residents in exurbia could continue to practice unencumbered the associational rights that Miller mentions, but for one significant issue—mobility. Resolving greenspace needs would not remove density questions from the table of debate because our present system of transportation creates a series of corollary challenges that are impacted by density.

The majority of Americans use automobiles as a primary means of transportation. Given that our present automotive fuel emits significant carbon emissions into the air, and, given that many of us are frequently in our automobiles, we generate a problem with both air pollution and a warming atmosphere. We presently have four options. We need either collectively to drive more environmentally friendly automobiles, to double and triple up per car for our commutes, to get out of our automobiles and into some other means for our commute between jobs and homes, or to situate ourselves closer to our most frequent auto-dependent activities.

This transportation issue is what takes us back around to the density issue. Multiple-rider transportation systems need a minimum population density in order to avoid either deep public subsidies or else fees that would price many out of participation in public transportation. For example, as Hamilton, Hok-kanen, and Wood observe, in order for a fixed-rail system of transportation to be viable, a population density greater than that of the Phoenix region is necessary. They suggest both competitive market and monopoly government mechanisms to address the conundrum of managing the housing, transportation, and employment triad that twenty-first-century human behavior propels us into.

One government-based solution that they advocate includes binding more closely together the policies generated in the policy silos of transportation, land use, zoning, and housing. An example is the San Joaquin Valley Blueprint Planning Process that involves eight counties, an air pollution control district, and the area's nonprofit organization that facilitates regional-level projects.

A market-based approach is congestion pricing, where vehicles are charged a fee that permits them to travel on the most congested roads or during the most congested times. London instituted this in 2003, the co-authors report. This approach is proposed in the just-released 2007 NYCPlan 2030.

The housing–transportation–employment triad happens because of the migration of individuals from one community to another community within the region. Migration is the story of America, and migration continues to have monumental impacts upon metropolitan society. Migration occurs as people follow jobs to new locations, either within metropolitan areas or to new geographic locations within the nation. Because this book's subject is metropolitan areas, it focuses upon metropolitan area movements and the trends that cause such movements. One dramatic jobs trend within metropolitan areas that Beverly Cigler analyzes is the drop in manufacturing jobs within the United States.

Traditionally, manufacturing jobs have resided in the core cities of metropolitan areas, but the precipitous drop in such jobs has impacted core cities in many ways. As cities have lost manufacturing jobs, individuals newly unemployed as a result of this trend have been forced to seek work outside of the manufacturing sector or else have been forced into long periods of unemployment. If they choose to seek work outside of the manufacturing sector, they may require job-retraining programs or additional general education to qualify for the more knowledge-based economy that Beverly Cigler mentions is increasingly emerging in the United States. They may be forced to follow service sector jobs into the suburban parts of metropolitan areas, jobs that do not pay as well as manufacturing jobs, and thus will force a family to compromise their quality of living. Metropolitan-area and state leadership has taken note of these employment trends and responded with new workforce retraining programs within state community college systems or with consolidation of their economic and workforce development programs under one umbrella to improve coordination. Stanislaus County in California created a new entity to house both workforce and economic development functions. Mecklenburg County in North Carolina shifted its focus from being a feeder system to the traditional four-year educational track into a jobs feeder system through workforce development courses.

In the United States, macro employment trends are going to affect metropolitan areas. Migration is unavoidable in our free and open society. Migration into neighborhoods within a region and between regions can bring wealth and create wealth, but it can also segregate wealth. Migration can deplete both the rural and the urban neighborhoods left behind, and create concentrated underserved poverty populations, a theme sounded by James Lewis and David Hamilton in their discussion of poverty. It can deplete entire regions. It can perpetuate poverty.

James Lewis discusses how the wealth of and the very size of metropolitan regions permit upper- and middle-class individuals and families to act upon their personal preferences in ways that can privilege them. The larger a region, the more individuals in one part of a region live independently from those in other parts, he finds. He also finds that the wealthier an urban region, location and size accounted for, the more likely it is that poor individuals are to be located in the central city rather than the suburbs, and that those living in the central city's poorest neighborhoods will likely be the last to benefit from the economic growth in these wealth-growing regions.

Furthermore, he continues, the operation of private-sector housing markets results in the further separation of people by race and that diminishes opportunity for some. The marketplace has been a tool, despite laws in place, to perpetuate both racism and classism. He noted the trend toward gated communities, which create visible upper-income segregation. More than 10 percent of new housing units constructed across the nation, particularly in the Southwest and West, are in the form of gated communities.

The barriers of race and class impact government policies as well. David Rusk presents statistics showing that disadvantaged children do best when placed within middle-class schools. He suggests inclusionary zoning as one governmental tool that can accomplish the mixing of income classes. He remarks that the success of this approach has been consistently and deliberately ignored by most politicians and many educators, who will not challenge the racial and class structure of American society. Both David Rusk and David Hamilton reference a well-known example of inclusionary zoning in Montgomery County, Maryland. Since its enactment in 1973, private developers have produced through the program approximately 12,000 moderately priced dwelling units. Developers of housing developments above a minimum size must make at least 12.5 percent of the units affordable to low-income households, with density bonuses given for percentages that go higher.

These intraregional migrations have impacts that challenge us. The barriers of race and class in America that initiate these enclaves of poor are resistant to the mechanisms we have discussed for addressing other metropolitan issues. We could not find evidence of as frequent use of techniques within regions for abating poverty and race issues as for other issues. James Lewis and David Hamilton found it was rare for regional initiatives to embrace poverty reduction as an explicit mission. Regional governance systems were partly motivated by economic considerations, but not expressly to reduce poverty.

Completing his research on this topic, James Lewis concludes that there are no examples nationally of sweeping improvements in the racial equity of an urban region. Any improvements that he observed happened incrementally around specific issues such as litigation that triggered affordable housing or more equitable school funding. Regional planning organizations may manage growth, preserve green space, attract new industry, build more public transportation, or encourage affordable housing, but they prefer not to bluntly address problems of race—problems that may be uncomfortably contentious. With a few exceptions, individuals and groups remain unwilling to address race and racial equity.

It is Lewis's contention that regions work best where people of different backgrounds mingle and they fail in part to the extent to which they facilitate their separation. When people of different backgrounds mingle, he concludes that all residents of a region are more likely to share equally in economic opportunity, to share equally the benefits of schools and city services, and to bear more equally the burdens of environmental hazards.

This situation gets perpetuated in part because the full accounting of the costs of human migratory behavior has been ignored for most of history. That has begun to change, due partly to research such as that done by James Lewis. Totaling up the true full costs of housing locational decisions, some of those costs being less time with family because of long commutes or higher grocery bills because of lack of full-service food stores, helps policymakers and the public see the full scope of choices that are made.

Some change-agent groups have begun to do this multiple bottom line calculus. This effort to more fully account for the costs of human behaviors, attempting to fiscalize more of the hidden costs, was part of a discussion by Patricia Atkins on this expanded cost–benefits ledger, under the concepts of double and triple bottom lines. Many metropolitan policies try to fix the various impacts of human migratory behavior, but, until recently, without the intent of looking more completely at all the costs versus the benefits—thus, an incomplete picture is obtained of how much our human urban activity truly costs. The true cost of human urban behavior includes not just balancing the fiscal checkbook, but also balancing other costs such as environmental and social costs. This multiple ledger brings in the concept of the human footprint on the space we occupy. Are we in our urban environment a net drain on our earth's resources or do we restock what we deplete? Changing a parking lot back into a park is a rare thing in metropolitan America. What is done is usually not undone. The permanent aspect of human environmental impacts has led some governments to adopt laws and regulations designed to make city planning more environmentally friendly in the first place.

As David Hamilton and Christopher Stream explained, the city—its population together with its environment—is a new kind of ecosystem on the face of the earth compared with the eons of ecosystems that have come before it. Cities are ecosystems that represent a built environment that will not readily revert to a natural environment, and thus it disrupts the natural environment. For example, if another ten square miles of asphalt accompanies the development of a new housing subdivision and depletes the tree canopy, thereby creating a rise in the heat index in the metropolitan area, what does the ripple effect of that housing development actually cost? How much more intensely do air conditioners have to run to offset a heat index that has been elevated—and what does that translate into as far as greater expenses for electrical output and for raising the heat index even further? Totaling up the true full costs of housing locational decisions helps policymakers and the public see the full scope of migration choices that are made.

An example of this effort to total the complete costs of housing locational decisions is in a report by the Center for Housing Policy reviewed by David Hamilton, a report that included a more complete accounting of the costs that result from families seeking affordable housing. Looking at twenty-eight metropolitan areas, the research found that families who were spending 50 percent and up of their income on housing conversely spent about 8 percent on transportation for 58 percent of their income, while those who spent 30 percent or less on housing spent 25 percent on transportation for a total of 55 percent of income (Center for Housing Policy 2006, 1). This report aimed to show that any savings gained on housing expenses by living farther in the countryside will be lost in higher transportation costs. Yet, a further calculation would have more starkly presented the cost choice forced by longer commutes, if it had placed a cost on time lost with family. Perhaps that is priceless.

Because these locational costs are hidden, it is not easy for individual families to total up all the individual costs of movement. Affordable housing is readily visible as a cost problem for the working poor who are being priced out of gentrifying neighborhoods, and it is a social problem for those in core city poor neighborhoods who lose job and educational opportunities, but who cannot leave because they lack the mobility of automobile ownership or who do not wish to leave the family networks they depend upon or who cannot afford to move. Some families in poor central city neighborhoods are unable to accumulate a level of equity sufficient to buy even the inexpensive housing available in their neighborhoods. They cannot take advantage of the capacity of home ownership to create monthly housing costs that are cheaper than what is paid in rent. Others in poor core city neighborhoods bought their homes decades ago, but have not seen their house value appreciate, and cannot therefore trade up to a better neighborhood. Some families are trapped by limited capital and mobility in core city, poor neighborhoods while other families must drive far out into exurban neighborhoods to reach the cheaper mortgages affordable with their limited capital. The housing market erodes the quality of life for both groups of families.

For those in core city poor neighborhoods, inability to accumulate equity inhibits migration to a better quality of life. For some of the exurbanites who have moved to exurbia because they could not find affordable housing close to work and for some of the "nuclearbanites" who have remained in the core city (the nucleus), the quest to achieve affordable housing has a dramatic impact on their lifestyles. One group is priced out past suburbia; the other is pushed into poor enclaves. For the former, their solution usually utilizes the marketplace. The nuclearbanites who remain in concentrated poverty enclaves in the city have more governmental housing policy options.

A few local governments have begun to enact housing policies in awareness of these workforce housing difficulties. The most typical type of program that governments employ to assist with workforce housing involves setting aside a percentage of a government-initiated housing development for moderately low-income families, that is, the working poor, to create a mixed-income development. Typical of this approach is the housing being constructed in conjunction with the Biotech Park rising in East Baltimore. Officials have targeted one-third for low-income housing, one-third for workforce housing, and one-third for market-level housing.

Efforts to provide decent housing to individuals and families in concentrated poverty neighborhoods traditionally have been undertaken by the federal government, approaches reviewed within David Hamilton's housing chapter. One ongoing component of current federal policy has been to demolish the massive public-housing projects built as a part of its first housing initiatives, replacing them with much lower density low-rise developments. The federal government also encourages production of low-income housing through tax credits and selective subsidies. Its other major tool is to provide Housing Choice Vouchers, originally called Section 8 Vouchers, to low-income families to find housing on the private market. About 1 million households presently live in public housing authority-managed units, another 1.5 million households live in privately owned projects that are HUD-subsidized, and another 2 million households participate in the Housing Choice Voucher program. This rounds out to approximately 4.5 million households, about 4 percent of U.S. households.

Federal government efforts are unable to provide affordable housing for everyone who needs it, and David Rusk advocates within his chapter for metropolitan-wide inclusionary zoning laws. He observes that, if such laws had been in place over the prior twenty years in the 100 largest metropolitan areas, they would have produced 3.6 million affordable housing units, federal housing programs produced over a longer time period, housing assistance would have reached 8.1 million families. Under such a scenario, inclusionary zoning does more than extend housing to those who need it. Rusk explains that inclusionary zoning will create mixed-income neighborhoods, the most effective educational reform available.

Government has been the most significant source of housing for those with low incomes, but some nonprofits are well known for their efforts to create housing for those underserved by the private housing market. Some nonprofit efforts, notably Habitat for Humanity, ask low-income individuals to replace financial equity with an equity that they do have, often called "sweat equity." Contributing their own labor to Habitat for Humanity housing renovations enables individuals otherwise unable to achieve home ownership to realize their dream of a better life. The dream of a better life is what brought, and brings, so many individuals to the United States. In this book, we have sought to identify the characteristics of that better life and the cases where it has succeeded and failed.

One tenet of the accumulated information from the chapters in this book is that there are a multitude of public policies in metropolitan areas with an inclusiveness and flexibility unknown twenty years ago. This is a new approach to government. It is governance—a process of achieving collective agreement or collective action, one that emphasizes inclusiveness and flexibility. Taking account of all potential participants enables the governance process to better mediate the many interests at the regional table and to more efficiently work toward regional compromise.

A second tenet is the recognition and incorporation of local autonomy rights into the calculation of regional policies to improve regional livability. Conciliation of expectations, agreement on procedures, and cooperation on regional action is assisted with open discussion of parochial self-interests.

We all have the capacity to be metropolitan policy entrepreneurs, to invest our time, our resources, our interests, and our talents, in the hopes of a better return on regional livability. Regional governance makes this role more possible than ever before. No audition is needed. Let your head and your heart take you into the fray.

References

Center for Housing Policy. 2006. *A Heavy Load: The Combined Housing and Trans-portation Burdens of Working Families*. Washington, DC: Center for Housing Policy (October).

James, Edmund J. 1899. "The Growth of Great Cities in Area and Population." *Annals of the American Academy of Political and Social Science* 13 (January): 1–30.

National Association of Regional Councils. 2000. *State of the Regions 2000: A Baseline for the Century of the Region*. Comp. Patricia S. Atkins and William R. Dodge. Washington, DC: National Association of Regional Councils.

About the Editors and Contributors

David K. Hamilton is chair of the Department of Political Science and Public Administration and professor of public administration at Roosevelt University. Current research interests include regional governance, county government reform, and local government service delivery. He is author of *Governing Metropolitan Areas: Response to Growth and Change* (New York: Garland Publishing, 1999). He has published articles in a number of journals including *Public Administration Review, Urban Affairs Review, Journal of Urban Affairs, State and Local Government Review, Public Personnel Management,* and *National Civic Review.* He holds a Ph.D. from the University of Pittsburgh.

Patricia S. Atkins, associate research professor at the George Washington Institute of Public Policy, has a career as an adviser to and scholar of metropolitan regional governance systems. Previously she was with the Institute for the Regional Community at the National Association of Regional Councils (NARC), the Schaefer Center for Public Policy at the University of Baltimore, the Prince George's County Budget Office, and the Metropolitan Fund, a regional think tank. While at NARC, she was co-editor of the quarterly journal, the *Regionalist,* and she co-wrote and researched the first-ever national state of the regions report. She received her M.A. and Ph.D. from the University of Maryland, and B.A. from the University of Michigan.

Beverly A. Cigler is a professor of public policy and administration, Penn State Harrisburg. Her key professional interests are intergovernmental relations, especially state–local relations and intermunicipal relations; governance; public finance; growth management; and emergency management. She has published 150 peer-reviewed articles and book chapters, co-edited/written 9 books, and given more than 140 invited speeches and testimony to national, state, and local organizations. Cigler is the recipient of national and state awards for her research and professional contributions and is an elected Fellow of the National Academy of Public Administration.

Laurie Hokkanen is currently assistant city manager in Chanhassen, Minnesota. She holds a B.A. in public administration from St. Cloud State University in Minnesota and a master's of public administration from Northern Illinois University. She has also worked with the cities of Becker, Minnesota, and DeKalb, Illinois. Previous experience includes work with federal grant programs, social and neighborhood services planning, and transportation planning and administration.

James H. Lewis is a senior program officer at the Chicago Community Trust. His interests include projects addressing problems of race, poverty, and related social and governmental infrastructure. He is former director of the Institute for Metropolitan Affairs at Roosevelt University, where he taught in the Department of Sociology, and was vice president for research and planning at the Chicago Urban League. He earned his Ph.D. in American history at Northwestern University.

David Y. Miller is the interim dean of the Graduate School of Public and International Affairs at the University of Pittsburgh. He was previously associate dean and associate professor. Previous positions include director of the Office of Management and Budget for the city of Pittsburgh and managing director of the Pennsylvania Economy League. He has served as co-director of the Graduate Center for Public Policy and Management in Skopje, Macedonia, and the 1+1 postgraduate program in conjunction with the South Korean government and the Seoul Metropolitan Government. He received his Ph.D. in public policy from the University of Pittsburgh. He is the author of numerous papers and articles focusing on regional governance and of the book *The Regional Governing of Metropolitan America* (Boulder: Westview Press, 2002).

David Rusk is a noted author and consultant. He has published ground-breaking books and articles on regionalism including *Baltimore Unbound, Cities without Suburbs,* and *Inside Game/Outside Game.* He is a former federal Labor Department official, New Mexico legislator, and mayor of Albuquerque, the thirty-fifth largest U.S. city. As a consultant on urban policy, he has worked in over 120 U.S. communities. Abroad, he has lectured on urban problems in Canada, England, Germany, South Africa, and the Netherlands.

Christopher Stream is associate professor in the Department of Public Administration at the University of Nevada, Las Vegas. He received his Ph.D. in public administration and policy from Florida State University. He has served as a policy consultant for a variety of government and private organizations. His research focuses on state health care reform, environmental policy, local delivery services, gaming policy, institutional capacity, and city management. His research has appeared in a variety of journals, including *Public Administration Review, Journal of Public Administration Research and Theory, Political Research Quarterly, International Journal of Economic Development,* and *State and Local Government Review.* His latest book is *State and Local Government* (Belmont, CA: Wadsworth/Thomson Learning, 2005).

Allan Wallis is associate professor of public policy at the Graduate School of Public Affairs, University of Colorado, Denver, where he directs the program in local government. He is former director of research for the National Civic League during which time he authored the series of articles—*Reinventing Regionalism*—for the *National Civic Review.* He is co-author, with Doug Porter, of *Ad Hoc Regionalism*—published by the Lincoln Institute of Land Policy. He is also a co-principal investigator on a comparative study of state growth management practices, also for the Lincoln Institute of Land Policy. He holds a Ph.D. in environmental psychology from the City University of New York.

Nelson Wikstrom is a professor of political science and public administration at Virginia Commonwealth University. He is the author of *Councils of Governments: A Study of Political Incrementalism* (Chicago: Nelson-Hall, 1977) and *The Political World of a Small Town: A Mirror Image of American Politics* (Westport, CT: Greenwood, 1993). In addition, he is the co-author, along with G. Ross Stephens, of *Metropolitan Government and Governance: Theoretical Perspectives, Empirical Analysis, and the Future* (New York: Oxford University Press, 2000), and *American Intergovernmental Relations: A Fragmented Federal Polity* (New York: Oxford University Press, 2007). His research interests include federalism and intergovernmental relations, and the governance of metropolitan areas.

Curtis Wood, assistant professor in the Master of Public Administration Program at Northern Illinois University, teaches courses in public management, regional governance, and ethics. He is a co-author, with H. George Frederickson and Gary Alan Johnson, of *The Adapted City: Institutional Dynamics and Structural Change* (Armonk, NY: M.E. Sharpe, 2003). He has twenty years of municipal government experience.

Index

Annexation, 14, 95, 97
Armington, C., 303
Arrington, G.B., 281, 283
Asians
  income equity of, 148, 152
  in inner suburbs, 28
  job opportunities for, 128
  poverty rate for, 130, 130(tab.)
  quality of life for, 127
  residential patterns of, 134, 135–139,
    136(tab.), 138(tab.), 155
  school integration for, 213–216, 216(tab.)
  –white integration, 139, 145–146,
    147(tab.)
  See also Racial minorities
Atkins, Patricia S., 53–91, 102, 346–359,
  349, 351, 355
Atkinson, R.D., 310, 316
Atlanta (Georgia)
  air pollution in, 280–281, 335
  crime rate for, 250(tab.)
  job opportunities in, 128
  population growth in, 283
  public transportation in, 277, 282
  quality of life in, 40, 41(tab.)
  and regional governance, 158
  regional planning in, 100
Authoritative regions, 12
Automobiles
  commute time, 267–268, 281, 288
  cost of owning, 279, 280(tab.)
  multiple–rider transportation, 291, 342,
    352–353
  number of commuters, 274
  pollution, 267, 280–281, 333, 352
  traffic congestion problems, 266, 268, 281,
    282(tab.), 287–288
  for working poor, 41, 290, 357
  See also Highways
Ayres, Ian, 127

B

Bailey, Linda, 269, 270, 272, 273, 291
Baltimore (Maryland)
  affordable housing in, 177
  crime rate for, 250(tab.)
  economic school integration in, 222–223
  environmental policy in, 339–340
  fiscal disparity in, 74–77, 75(tab.), 76(tab.)
  knowledge–industry jobs in, 304
  residential segregation in, 47, 226–227
Baltimore Metropolitan Council (BMC), 339
Bane, Mary Jo, 235
Banfield, Edward C., 25, 26, 27

Bank of America, 196
Barnes, William R., 61, 64–65, 244, 298,
  318
Barreto, Matt A., 147
Bartik, T., 301
Baumol, W.J., 306
Bay Area Alliance for Sustainable
  Communities, 83
Bay Area Council, 108, 109
Bay Vision 2020, 109
Bebow, J., 192
Been, Vicki, 133, 159
Beimborn, Edward, 285
Bell, Michael E., 54, 74
Bellair, Paul E., 249
Benjamin, Gerald, 337
Benjamin, L., 17
Benner, Chris, 62, 107
Bernstein, Scott, 270, 272, 277, 289, 290
Berry, M., 188
Bicycle trails, 341–342
Bier, Tom, 32
Binford, Henry, 133
Bish, Robert L., 55, 67–68, 69, 70, 73, 74,
  79
Bitterman, Brooks, 142
Black Males Left Behind (Mincy), 42
Blacks. *See* African–Americans; Racial
  minorities
Blackwell, Angela Glover, 62, 181, 185,
  191
Blakey, Edward J., 249
Blau, Judith R., 252
Blau, Peter M., 252
Bledsoe, Timothy, 146
Bluestone, Barry, 234
Blumenberg, Evelyn, 278, 279, 290
*Board of Education of Oklahoma City v.
  Dowell*, 159
Bobo, Lawrence, 146
Bodovitz, Joe, 109
Bollens, Scott A., 11, 15, 16, 18, 61, 64, 65,
  77, 156
Borjas, George J., 245
Boschken, Herman L., 79
Boston (Massachusetts), job opportunities
  in, 128
Bottom line, 55–56, 355
Boulder (Colorado), air pollution in,
  334–335
Bound, J., 235
Boyne, George A., 66, 72
Bozorgmeihr, Mehdim, 128, 145
BP Oil Company, 342
Brace, P., 310

Local government
  absence of theory, 17
  authority of, 6
  in "complex network" regions, 11–12
  and foundational principles, 17–18, 21–22
  intergovernmental authority in, 7
  interlocal cooperation among, 318–319
  in multitiered regions, 10
  two–tiered model, 18–19
  See also Metropolitan governance
Logan, John R., 132, 140, 159, 249
Lorentz, Amalia, 332
Los Angeles (California)
  crime rate for, 251(tab.)
  Hispanic/white integration, 145
  job opportunities in, 128
  poverty in, 245
  public transit in, 279
  quality of life in, 40, 41(tab.)
  residential enclaves in, 135
Lou, Yadong, 112
Lowery, D., 310
Luberoff, David, 257
Luccarelli, Mark, 99
Lucy, William, 259
Lynch, Kevin, 42, 69
Lynch, R.G., 310
Lyons, A., 170

M

MacDonald, Chris, 71
MacKaye, Benton, 109
MacKenzie, W.J., 17
Maine, growth management in, 105
Maney, B., 180
Mansfield, Edward D., 63
Manufacturing jobs, loss of, 234–236, 307, 353
Marando, V.L., 18
Marcus, Melvin G., 329
Marks, Laurence R., 54
Marsh, D.S., 189
Marshall, Harvey, 134
Martin, John, 38
Massachusetts
  affordable housing in, 188–190
  growth management in, 114–117
Massachusetts Bay Transportation Authority, 279
Massey, Douglas S., 133, 134, 135, 139, 142, 237, 238, 245, 246, 255
Mass transit, 26, 273–285, 289–290
Matheson, Alan, 118
Mathur, S., 186

McArdle, Nancy, 129
McCall, Tom, 106
McCarthy, G., 169
McCarville, Sean, 79
McGinnis, Michael D., 4
McGuire, M., 318
McKenzie, R., 302
McNeal, Bill, 218
Meaden, P.M., 175
Meek, S., 188, 189
Megaregions, 319
Megyesi, M.I., 304
Melosi, Martin V., 328, 329
Melville, J., 9, 319
Mendelberg, Tali, 140, 146–147
Mergers/consolidations, 14
Metropolitan Council of the Twin Cities, 12, 36, 46, 103
Metropolitan governance
  cataloging approaches to, 10–16, 11(tab.)
  comparison of forms, 62–63, 63(tab.)
  consolidation approach to, 157
  dimensional framework, 4–5, 5(fig.), 21
  failure of, 346–348
  and fiscal disparity, 53–55
  local/regional balance in, 17–21, 67
  models for. See Monocentrism; Polycentrism; Synercentrism
  and poverty strategies, 258–259
  and racial equity, 156–159
  stakeholders in, 62, 63(tab.)
  structure of, 5–9
  See also Land use; Public goods; Regional planning
Metropolitan Planning Council, 178, 193
Metropolitan planning organizations (MPOs), 35, 269, 270, 271, 272, 288–289, 291
Metropolitan Power Diffusion Index (MPDI), 7(tab.), 7–9, 8(tab.)
Metropolitan regions
  collaboration among, 318–320
  concentric circle theory of, 232–233, 246
  defined, 3–4
  demography of, 25, 29(tab.)
  differences among, 8–9
  fastest–growing, 316
  and federal policy, 34–35
  fiscal disparity in, 53–55, 74–77, 258
  high–tech, 304–305
  integrated and segregated, 139–140, 141(tab.), 142
  megaregions, 319
  and nongovernmental organizations, 36–37
  poverty concentrations in, 40–42, 232–233, 244–245